HARVARD STUDIES
IN COMPARATIVE LITERATURE

Harvard Studies in Comparative Literature
Founded by William Henry Schofield
2 5

PRAISERS OF FOLLY

PRAISERS OF FOLLY

ERASMUS · RABELAIS · SHAKESPEARE

❧❧❧❧❧❧❧❧❧❧❧❧❧❧❧❧❧❧❧❧❧❧❧❧

Walter Kaiser

HARVARD UNIVERSITY PRESS

CAMBRIDGE · MASSACHUSETTS

1963

Library of Congress Catalog Card Number: 63-17202

Printed in the United States of America

CBS
6.20
1-8-64 mw
1-29-64 ev

FOR MY MOTHER AND FATHER

ACKNOWLEDGMENTS

In the course of writing this book, I was often made conscious of how much it owes to others, and it is accordingly a particular pleasure to be able to acknowledge at least some of these debts here.

I am grateful for many courtesies to the staffs of the Widener and Houghton Libraries of Harvard University, the Newberry Library of Chicago, the London Library, the Bibliothèque Nationale and the Bibliothèque de l'École Normale Supérieure of Paris, and the Biblioteca Nazionale, the Biblioteca Laurentiana, and the Biblioteca Berenson of Florence. I should like to express my thanks as well to the Samuel F. Fels Foundation for a grant which relieved me of my teaching duties during the winter of 1959–60, when this study was written, and to the Henry P. Kendall Foundation for help in meeting the costs of preparing a typescript. Clarence H. Miller has kindly permitted me to quote from his definitive edition of Chaloner's translation of the *Moriae encomium*, which is a forthcoming publication of the Early English Text Society.

My thanks are due to Miss Bette Anne Farmer, most gifted of secretaries, for many services on behalf of this book, and to Mrs. Alan Lebowitz of Harvard University Press for her careful and sympathetic editing of a difficult manuscript.

So many friends, teachers, and colleagues have substantially contributed to these pages that, as Petrarch says in an earlier treatise on folly, "were I to enumerate them all, though the memory would be sweet, the list would certainly not be brief." I cannot refrain, however, from registering my indebtedness to three early teachers, Dudley Fitts, J. M. Street, and, above all, Wilfred Freeman. Among those to whom I am grateful for help given in more recent years, whether in the classroom or in informal conversations, by answering specific queries or simply by providing friendly encouragement, are: Herschel Baker, John Bullitt, Douglas Bush, Robert Chapman, Marshall Cohen, John Conway, Herbert Dieckmann, Monroe Engel, Myron Gilmore, Stephen Graubard, Alfred Harbage, Alan Heimert, Phyllis LaFarge Johnson, Sheila LaFarge, Archibald MacLeish, Harold Martin, Perry Miller, Maud Morgan, the late Arthur Darby Nock, Elisabeth Niebuhr Sifton, Charles Singleton, William Slottman, and Daniel Steiner. To Renato Poggioli I am especially obliged for many contributions to this work, including the meticulous reading he gave an early version.

During the past summer, when I was preparing the final draft of this manuscript for the publisher, that task was rendered agreeable by the affectionate kindness of Peter and Mimi Dow, who welcomed me to a house by the sea; my debt to them for exceptional friendship is, however, of much broader scope and longer standing.

To three friends at Harvard I must acknowledge obligations of unusual magnitude. John H. Finley, Master of Eliot House, has allowed me to participate for over a decade in that congenial ambiance of learning and has significantly contributed to my intellectual and personal development at every stage. Walter Jackson Bate not only has given me generous encouragement and wise counsel over a long period but also has taught me most of what I know about the relation of literature to human experience. And Harry Levin, who was my first tutor in college, has continued ever since to guide and support my studies with learning, patience, and extraordinary kindness; he has steadily increased my knowledge and deepened my appreciation of humane letters; and he has assisted the present study from its inception. Without the friendship and inspiration of these men, the past years would have been immeasurably poorer.

Finally, my most continuous and greatest debt, apart from that acknowledged in the dedication, is to four of my oldest friends. For many years now, Edward and Meta Malins and Howard and Eleanor Sachs have sustained my endeavors, offered me homes away from home, provided me with the experience of Europe, and given me their unfailing love. My obligations to them are vaster than I can ever hope to discharge.

W.K.

Eliot House
Cambridge, Massachusetts
January 1963

CONTENTS

NOTE ON TEXTS

In quoting from those authors with whom this book is most concerned, I have in all cases used the definitive editions, which are listed in the bibliography. Generally, such texts are identified in abbreviated form, and these abbreviations are explained below. In the cases of Cervantes, Montaigne, and Rabelais, where the reader may wish to refer to any standard edition or translation rather than to the definitive edition, citations refer not only to the volume and page number of the definitive edition but also to the book and chapter number of the work. Thus, "R V.270/III.xxxvi" would refer to: R[abelais], Lefranc edition, vol. V, p. 270/*Tiers Livre*, ch. xxxvi.

Whenever possible, I have supplied an English translation for quotations in other languages and have assigned the original text to the footnotes. We are fortunate in possessing great contemporary or near-contemporary translations for Erasmus' *Praise of Folly*, Rabelais' *Gargantua and Pantagruel*, Cervantes' *Don Quixote*, and Montaigne's *Essays*. These translations are classics in their own right, and, despite occasional problems of mistranslation, they seem to me to reproduce more accurately the tone and spirit of the original works than any modern translations I know or might have attempted myself. In supplying translations from Chaloner, Urquhart, Shelton, and Florio, I have used the best texts available, and these are also indicated in the bibliography. Though these texts vary in the extent to which the spelling has been modernized, I have regularly reproduced the text at hand without attempting to establish consistency in spelling among them; the one exception to this is the text of Chaloner, where I have silently changed *u, v, i,* and *j* to follow modern usage and have used italics for those words which are set in gothic type in the original. Mistranslations have been corrected only where they falsify in a significant way the original text, and such corrections are always indicated; whenever possible, however, I have let the translations stand as they are, and, since the original texts are always given at the bottom of the page, the reader can easily perceive what the translator has misunderstood, omitted, or added. To have supplied page references to these translations as well as to the original texts would have further encumbered a text already heavy with references.

I am responsible for all other translations.

On the following page are the editions (fuller references for which may be found in the bibliography) and abbreviations used for these texts; also listed are the abbreviations used in both notes and bibliography in the citing of some current periodicals.

TEXTS

C	Cervantes, *Don Quijote*, ed. F. R. Marín.
E	Erasmus, *Ausgewählte Werke*, ed. H. and A. Holborn.
EE	Erasmus, *Opus epistolarum*, ed. P. S. and H. M. Allen.
LB	Erasmus, *Opera omnia*, ed. J. LeClerc.
M	Montaigne, *Essais*, ed. F. Strowski and F. Gebelin.
ME	Erasmus, *Moriae encomium*, ed. J. B. Kan.
R	Rabelais, *Oeuvres*, ed. A. Lefranc et al.

PERIODICALS

BHR	*Bibliothèque d'Humanisme et Renaissance*
BVGO	*Bijdragen voor Vaderlandsche Geschiedenis en Oudheidkunde*
JEGP	*Journal of English and Germanic Philology*
JHI	*Journal of the History of Ideas*
MP	*Modern Philology*
PMLA	*Publications of the Modern Language Association of America*
PQ	*Philological Quarterly*
RER	*Revue des Études Rabelaisiennes*
RR	*Romanic Review*
SAB	*Shakespeare Association Bulletin*
SP	*Studies in Philology*

PRAISERS OF FOLLY

PROLOGUE: THE FOOL

THE traditional motto of the Globe Theatre, *totus mundus agit histrionem*, reiterated an observation that men have made about their lives since classical antiquity. As Caesar Augustus lay dying, he is said to have asked if he had acted the play of life properly; and the last Greek poet worthy of the name, Palladas of Alexandria, as he beheld the ruins of his Hellenistic world, philosophized that all life was a stage and that a man must either learn to put aside his seriousness and play or else endure the pains of existence. Throughout the Middle Ages and the Renaissance, the simile, with its somber attitude toward illusion and reality, continued to capture men's imaginations; and when, as late as the seventeenth century, Don Quixote borrows it from Erasmus to expound it to his simple squire as though it were original with him, Sancho, who is something of an authority on proverbs, caustically replies, "A brave comparison, but not so strange to me, that have heard it often."

Even as he has sat in the theater watching the actors, man has felt the presence of the gods in their theater, watching him enact his part:

> Icy la Comedie apparoist un exemple
> Où chacun de son fait les actions contemple:
> Le monde est le Theatre, & les hommes, acteurs.
> La fortune qui est maitresse de la Scene
> Apreste les habitz, & de la vie humaine
> Les cieux & les destins sont les grands spectateurs.

The metaphor, in pondering the insubstantial pageantry of life, suggests that the life enacted on the great globe itself is no more lasting or significant than that enacted on the stage and concludes that what we live is merely a play or an illusion or a dream. Turning upon the metaphor, men have gone on to make other plays in order to show that we are such stuff as dreams are made on, that *la vida es sueño, der Traum ein Leben*. The implication may or may not be that we shall wake in another, more lasting life, but the emphasis of an imagery that sees life as a play is upon the brevity of this life, upon its lusory or illusory character, and upon the fact that the curtain will finally fall and the play end — that we only live, in Walter Raleigh's words, "a play of passion," and

> Thus march we playing to our latest rest,
> Onely we dye in earnest, that's no Iest.[1]

Yet if life is short, art is long; and the metaphor, though it stresses the mortality of life, manages at the same time to confer the immortality of art. For to say that everyone plays a role in the drama of life is to explain life with the imagery of art and to preserve life's transitory moment in the amber of art's eternity. As such, the metaphor also implicitly contains the basic assumption of all art, that it is an imitation of life. Now in that art which is literature, man has tried to describe the role he plays in the drama of life, and in doing so he has thereby left, whether intentionally or unintentionally, a mimetic chronicle of his existence. If all the world is indeed a stage, one way of looking at this chronicle is to see it as a succession of personae, of literary protagonists who pass across the stage. Though the number of roles that men and women play is infinite and though all of them are being enacted all the time, man, in his literary imitations of life's drama, has given the part of the protagonist now to one and now to another of the actors. Certain figures, that is, have at certain times been chosen from among the infinite variety of roles for positions of predominance on the stage of literary history, because they have somehow seemed to represent symbolically the assumptions and arguments, the aspirations and nostalgias of their age:

---

[1] *The Poems of Sir Walter Raleigh*, ed. A. M. C. Latham (London, 1929), p. 48. For the deathbed query of Augustus Caesar, see Suetonius, *De vita Caesarum*, II.99; for Palladas of Alexandria's epigram, see *Anthologia Graeca*, X.72; for Sancho Panza's remark, see C V.217/II.xii; for Ronsard's poem, see *Oeuvres complètes*, ed. Paul Laumonier (Paris, 1931 —), XIII, 212. A convenient catalogue of classical expressions of this topos is provided in Rudolph Heim, *Lucian und Menipp* (Leipzig and Berlin, 1906), pp. 44ff. For later occurrences, see Jean Jacquot, " 'Le Théâtre du Monde' de Shakespeare à Calderón," *Revue de la littérature comparée*, XXXI (1957), 341–72, and Antonio Vilanova, "El Tema del Gran Teatro del Mundo," *Boletín de la Real Academia de Buenas Letras de Barcelona*, XXIII (1950), 153–8.

En gestes differens, en differens langages,
Roys, Princes & Bergers jouënt leurs personnages.[2]

And the king, the paladin, the shepherd, the savage, the artist, the servant, the merchant, each with his characteristic scenery, gestures, and language, has had his particular moment on the stage when he seemed better able to articulate the thoughts of his time than any of the other dramatis personae.

At one moment, for example, the curtains part to reveal a pilgrim moving along a road. He is middle-aged, and the season is spring; and whether he descends the winding path to earth's infernal core or climbs the craggy Mountain of Virtue or rides the fabled roads eastward to Canterbury or south to Compostela, it is the same man, from the same time, on his way to God. He is Everyman, the symbolic protagonist for his age. Many scenes later, the curtains part again to reveal a man moving along a road, but it is neither the same man nor the same road. This time he is young, and the season is late summer. His step is firm; his pockets are empty; his mind is filled with thoughts of Napoleon, or with Wertherian dreams of love and poetry, or with great expectations. Behind him he leaves the blacksmith's forge or the printer's shop in the provincial town, a devoted friend, a tearful mistress, a loving family; and the road is the coach road to London or Paris. As spectators, we are able to determine many things about his time from the particular figure who is chosen, the landscape against which he moves, and the way in which he behaves. For each of them tells us not only his own personal story, but something about his world as well. He is, as Taine called him, the *personnage régnant* of his epoch; "his sentiments and his ideas are those of an entire generation." [3]

It is with another such symbolic actor, the fool, that this study is concerned. Like all the others, the fool also has his moment as *personnage régnant*, and when he does we may see in him too the embodiment of one aspect of an age and the articulation of a pattern of thought characteristic of that age. Yet there is undoubtedly something surprising about the fact that this should be so, and of all such personae perhaps none comes to the front of the stage quite so un-

[2] Ronsard, *Oeuvres*, XIII, 212.
[3] The theory of the *personnage régnant* is developed in Hippolyte Taine, *De l'idéal dans l'art* (Paris, 1867); see esp. p. 37.

expectedly. We are generally prepared to accept almost any literary hero as spokesman for his age, and as we look back over the centuries it seems understandable that such figures as the shepherd and the knight should have had, at particular times, such predominant roles conferred upon them. But for the fool it seems an unlikely assignment. Not only would his folly seem to make him unworthy of such a part, but also his role would seem, by its very nature, to be subservient to those roles given to figures of greater dignity. Consequently, when he finally does begin to play the protagonist, he denies certain of our assumptions about him and to some degree violates our sense of decorum: we are aware that something extraordinary has happened. Yet move to the center of the stage is precisely what he does. And just as the medieval pilgrim as protagonist would claim that to go through life was to be a pilgrim, so the fool as protagonist has the audacity to invoke the classical image of the world as a stage and claim that to be a fool is to act the play of life.

It was the Renaissance that brought the fool into the limelight on the stage of literature; and though he has antecedents as far back as the world of classical antiquity, the figure evoked by the word *fool* is really a creation of the late Middle Ages. When we hear the word, we think of a small, dwarfish man, often hunchbacked, who wears a coat of motley with its asinine hood and bells and carries a bauble or marotte. Of course, there is also a less specific connotation to the word *fool*: proverbially, it refers simply to any human being who is deprived of reason — the stupid, the ignorant, the mad, the fool-ish. The Rigoletto-type fool evoked by the word — the court jester of the fifteenth century — is in fact only the formal, artificial imitation of the actual fools, the madmen and idiots, who wandered loose through the medieval world. Between the two extremes of the village idiot and the court jester, the natural and the artificial fool, there are as many degrees of fooldom and foolery as there are degrees of madness; but whoever is called foolish, whether the lover, the dupe, the sinner, or the theatrical clown, is called so because he acts like a man deprived of his wits — like the natural fool. Upon this "bell without a clapper," as he was sometimes called, the Middle Ages rang many changes, and when the first major fool of the Renaissance exclaims, "Good lorde, what a *Theatre* is this worlde? how many, and divers are the pageants that fooles plaie therin?" [4] she calls to mind all of the many fools that the Middle Ages had developed. These types and their social, literary, and theatrical histories have been carefully traced and catalogued, notably by Olive Busby, Barbara Swain, and Enid Welsford, and their studies are an essential introduction to any examination of the Renaissance fool. To reiterate all that has been written on this would require a lengthy digression from our subject, and there is little need to repeat what has been so adequately set forth elsewhere. It may be useful, however, to summarize briefly what the Middle Ages thought a fool was, especially since the Renaissance authors whom we shall be considering assumed that their readers had a certain image of the fool in mind.

Since it is upon the prototype of the natural fool that all the more sophisticated and artificial fools are based, we may see these attitudes most clearly and in their most pristine form if we consider what the Middle Ages thought of the simple idiot. The first point to be made is that they knew him well. Indeed, it is hard for us to imagine how common the spectacle of idiocy or insanity must have been in a world that knew neither the techniques of modern medicine nor those of the psychological clinic. Generally such creatures could be seen almost everywhere. Violent madmen, of course, who were thought to be possessed by devils, were tortured and incarcerated, first in the monasteries and later in such institutions as that celebrated etymological source, the Hospital of St. Mary of Bethlehem in London.[5] On the other hand, the feeble-minded were simply allowed to roam free, for they were harmless. Their heads seemed as empty as a pair of bellows, and accordingly from the Latin word for bellows the name *fool* or *fou* was coined for them. Set apart from normal human beings by his empty-headed irrationality, the innocent fool was to the Middle Ages more of a thing than a being, and he became to them simply an object of fun or pity or veneration. For the stupidity of his words and deeds he was often derided; for his inability to behave and understand

---

[4] ME 97: "Deum immortalem, quod theatrum est illud, quam varius stultorum tumultus?"

[5] For a convenient brief discussion of madness in the Middle Ages, see R. R. Read, *Bedlam on the Jacobean Stage* (Cambridge, Mass., 1952), pp. 1–39. For the history of St. Mary of Bethlehem, see E. G. O'Donoghue, *The Story of the Bethlehem Hospital from its Foundation in 1247* (London, 1914).

like other people he was sometimes pitied; and occasionally, because he was thought to be under the special protection of God, he was venerated. For all three reasons he was tolerated.

That such a fool was called "natural" is particularly significant and was to have, especially in the sixteenth century, vast implications. He was, of course, seen as a natural fool because he was thought to have been created foolish by nature. Yet the fact that such an adjective was considered necessary implies that artificial fools, from whom natural fools had to be distinguished, had come into existence. Accordingly, it is not until the fifteenth century, after dramatic and court fools have been developed, that the adjective "natural" is applied in this connection. Later, in the sixteenth century, the phrase had become sufficiently common to be abbreviated; and it is, appropriately enough, from the pen of Sir Thomas More (whose name in Greek means "fool," who kept a famous fool as a member of his household, and whom Erasmus considered the fool par excellence) that we have the first recorded reference to a natural fool as simply "a natural." But the adjective is fitting for the fool in other ways as well. As the child of nature, for example, his appetites and desires are wholly natural. The idiot performs his natural functions naturally, without sophistication or the usage of custom: when he is sad, he cries; when he is happy, he laughs; when he is hungry, he eats. Unconscious of the rules of propriety, he says and does whatever is natural for him to say or do at any given moment. He lives in the fullness of that moment, for he is not intelligent enough to remember the past or to anticipate the future; though he may be frightened by palpable physical threats, the cares and fears of the intellect are obviously unknown to him. For this reason, he was often deemed happier in his simplicity than other men in their wisdom, and Robert Burton was simply expanding into a sophisticated skepticism an attitude that had been prevalent for centuries when he wrote:

Some think fools and disards live the merriest lives, as Ajax in Sophocles; *nihil scire vita jucundissima;* 'tis the pleasantest life to know nothing; *iners malorum remedium ignorantia;* ignorance is a down-right remedy of evils. These curious and laborious sciences, Galens, Tullies, Aristotles, Justinians, do but trouble the world, some think; we might live better with that illiterate Virginian simplicity, and gross ignorance; entire ideots do best; they are not macerated with cares, tormented with fear and anxieties as other men are: for, as he said, if folly were a pain, you should hear them houl, roar, and cry out in every house, as you go by in the street; but they are most free, jocund, and merry, and, in some countries, as amongst the Turks, honoured for saints, and abundantly maintained out of the common stock.[6]

Since he does not comprehend the conventions of society, the natural fool is invariably irreverent of those conventions, not out of any motives of iconoclasm but simply because he does not know any better. This fact, of course, poses a problem for society, because the fool is a potentially subversive element in its midst. For the most part, however, the Middle Ages tended to tolerate the fool's nonconformity; and, though he might appear to mock the laws of society and religion, men tended to understand that the mockery was not intentional, that the natural was simply being his natural self. He was therefore not expected to obey any code, and in this respect medieval tolerance gave the idiot considerable freedom to speak and act in ways for which others would have been summarily punished. To be sure, there were often severe Gonerils who found the fool's behavior too trying to be borne; but for the most part he was "all-licensed," and a comparatively complete freedom was always associated with the natural fool. What he said was either an hilarious joke or, at the very worst, a foolish impertinence which merited him little more than a box on the ears or bed without supper. He was treated, in short, like a child because he had only the intelligence of a child.

It is not hard to see how the combination of the humor he provided and the impunity he enjoyed made him irresistible to the literary imagination. His beguiling, childlike appeal guaranteed him the sympathy of the audience, and at the same time his traditional freedom from punishment made it possible for the author to have him speak out boldly. If anyone should object to what the fool said, it was easy to point out that it was, after all, only a fool who said it. Thus the license of the natural fool was appropriated for the artificial fool; his nonconformity was turned into iconoclasm, his naturalism into anarchy, and his frankness into satire. Whether in the court or on the stage, he was able to criticize the accepted order of things and to voice daring indictments of the church or the throne or the law or society in general. When a normal, reasonable man's natural desires

[6] Robert Burton, *The Anatomy of Melancholy* (London, 1837; 2 vols.), part. 2, sec. 3, mem. 8; vol. II, pp. 84-5.

urge him to rebel against some such order, he is expected to "know better." But because the fool is not expected to *know* anything, he readily became an expression of all the mischievous and rebellious desires in man which society attempts to control or frustrate. In the eternal polemic between law and nature, the head and the heart, the artificially imitated natural fool, whose head was only an empty bellows, was brought forth as the champion of the lawless heart. He was a difficult adversary to combat, precisely because he was only a fool.

If the medieval idiot was countenanced by the society toward which he was subversive, he was also countenanced by the religion of which he was irreverent; and it is from the theological justifications of the fool that the profoundest aspects of his symbolic role were developed. As I have already noted, the feeble-minded were considered by the Middle Ages to be under the special protection of God, and they were tolerated (if not always envied) for this reason above all else. Christ himself had, of course, given the example by favoring fools and idiots and children and by exalting, in such utterances as the Sermon on the Mount, the simple in heart. In the fool God had seemed to create those simple idiots of whom Christ had spoken, and the fool's affinities to the natural order often appeared to indicate a special affinity with God. This seemed especially so of the fool's speech which, for all its ignorance, at times managed to pierce through the veils of convention and propriety to the profound simplicity of a Christlike truth. At such times it was assumed that God had entered into the fool and spoke through his mouth, and this was perhaps the most important reason for granting fools great freedom of speech; it was always possible that when the fool's babbling was not idiotic it was theopneustic. Theologically, such an attitude toward the fool was authorized by St. Paul, who had often explained (especially in his epistles to the Corinthians) that men must become fools for Christ's sake and commanded that those who are considered wise by the world should become fools in order that they may be truly wise. Such Pauline paradoxes were received with particular favor, as one might expect, by the medieval mystics, and all through the Middle Ages the tradition of the Fool in Christ, whether articulated precisely as such or not, was preserved by such figures as Gregory the Great,

Scotus Erigena, Francis of Assisi, Jacopone da Todi, and Raimond Lull.

It was quite late in the Middle Ages, however, and from that northern mysticism which we associate with the names of Eckhart, Tauler, Ruysbroek, and Groot and the movement known as the *devotio moderna* that the humble, analphabetic fool received his most articulate theological justification. Two men in particular, Thomas à Kempis and Nicholas of Cusa, gave the medieval world its final theological apologies for the fool, the one in his manual, *Imitatio Christi*, and the other in his treatise, *De docta ignorantia*.[7] Coincidentally, Kempis finished the last of many versions of his book in 1441, and Cusanus' book first appeared in 1440. It is more than coincidence, however, that in their youth they both attended that school at Deventer which Erasmus was later to attend: the "holy simplicity" of Kempis, the "learned ignorance" of Cusanus, and the "wise fool" of Erasmus are all ideologically derived (at least in part) from the Philosophy of Christ taught at Deventer. This philosophy, in opposing the prevalent scholastic learning, exalted a simple Christianity and a way of life that imitated the foolishness of Christ. Accordingly, Kempis' book prescribed for man a life which, in its pietistic simplicity and humility, resembled that of the fool, and Cusanus in his works laid the philosophical foundations for the concept of the wisdom of folly.

Of the two men, Kempis had the greater practical influence upon later generations, and his book was the more widely read. Cusanus' cryptic, elusive, paradoxical expositions of his philosophy have never achieved the same popularity, and it is only recently that they have even been properly evaluated. But in the history of the figure of the fool (not to mention that of the philosophy of knowledge), Cusanus' work is by far the more important; for, with its fusion of Pauline theology and the Neoplatonism of the pseudo-Dionysius, it established a philosophical schema out of which the first of the great sixteenth-century fools was created. In the two paradoxical keystones of Cusanus' philosophy, *docta ignorantia* and *coincidentia oppositorum*,[8] both the philosophical and stylistic characteristics of Erasmus'

---

[7] Cusanus' theory of *docta ignorantia* is, of course, also developed in his other writings as well (see next note).

[8] On Cusanus a number of studies and editions of texts have been published by E. Hoffman, R. Klibansky, L. Bauer, et al., from 1929-44 in the *Sitzungsberichte der*

Stultitia find their first extensive exposition. The questions that Cusanus poses about the possibility of knowledge, the wisdom he derives from the antithesis between the irrational absolute and logical reason, and the rejection of rational theology to which these lead him help to form the philosophical assumptions upon which Erasmus' concept of the fool is based. Similarly, that irony which, as we shall see, is the essential mode of expression for Erasmus' fool is the result of what Cusanus called the "coincidentia scientiae et ignorantiae, seu doctae ignorantiae." [9] That ability of reason to question itself and yet emerge with wisdom, which Erwin Panofsky has seen as a characteristic of Renaissance thought and which he finds perfectly exemplified in Erasmus' *Moriae encomium*,[10] is the informative characteristic of all Cusanus' antithetical, paradoxical philosophy, and Ernst Cassirer has claimed that "every study that is directed towards comprehending the philosophy of the Renaissance as a systematic unity must take as its point of departure the doctrine of Nicholas Cusanus." [11]

"Everything is folly in this world," commented Leopardi one December day in 1823 in his encyclopedic *Zibaldone*, "except to play the fool." [12] His formulation may be said to describe the point at which the concept of the fool had arrived by the end of the fifteenth

---

Heidelberger Akademie der Wissenschaften. Philosophisch-historische Klasse. A definitive edition of the texts has been published by the same scholars under the title *Nicolai de Cusa Opera Omnia iussu et auctoritate Academiae Litterarum Heidelbergensis fidem edita* (Leipzig, 1932 sq.). For a modern English translation of the *De docta ignorantia*, see Nicolas of Cusa, *Of Learned Ignorance*, tr. Germain Heron (New Haven, 1954). Other particularly useful studies are: Ernst Cassirer, *Individuum und Kosmos in der Philosophie der Renaissance* (Leipzig, 1927); Maurice de Gandillac, *La Philosophie de Nicolas de Cues* (Paris, 1941); Eugene F. Rice, Jr., "Nicholas of Cusa's Idea of Wisdom," *Traditio* XIII (1957), 345–68; R. Stadelmann, *Vom Geist des ausgehenden Mittelalters. Studien zur Geschichte der Weltanschauung von Nicolaus Cusanus bis Sebastian Brant* (Halle, 1929); E. Vansteenberghe, *Autour de la docte ignorance. Une controverse sur la théologie mystique au XVe siècle* (Munster, 1914), and *Le Cardinal Nicolas de Cues* (Paris, 1920); Paul Wilpert, "Das Problem der coincidentia oppositorum in der Philosophie des Nikolaus von Cues," *Humanismus, Mystik, und Kunst*, ed. J. Koch (Leiden, 1953), 39–55.

[9] Letter to Gaspard Aindorffer, 22 September 1452; cited in Cassirer, *Individuum*, p. 14n.

[10] Erwin Panofsky, "Renaissance and Renascences," *Kenyon Review* VI (Spring 1944), 201–36, esp. 234–5.

[11] Cassirer, *Individuum*, p. 7.

[12] Giacomo Leopardi, *Zibaldone*, ed. F. Flora (Milan, 1938; 2 vols.), II, 820: "Tutto è follia in questo mondo fuorchè il folleggiare."

century. Most of the world seemed to be made up of fools, as Brandt showed in 1494 in the passenger list of his *Narrenschiff*. The exception, as Cusanus had philosophized and as Erasmus was to demonstrate in fifteen years, was the fool himself, and this paradox was, by the end of the century, contained within the very word *fool*. For while, on the one hand, it remained a term of opprobrium or condescension (with a mercilessly enlarged application), on the other hand, it had become a term of praise and aspiration. One could say of an idiot that he was only a fool because he was not wise; but one could also say of a wise man that he would be wiser if he were a fool. Such universality gave the fool a predominance that enabled him symbolically to dominate a major aspect of the thought of the following century when, after playing a minor role on the stage throughout the late Middle Ages, he steps forward at the height of the Renaissance to assume one of the main roles in life's drama. As he enacts the part of the protagonist down the length of the sixteenth century, he gives articulation to the doubts and uncertainties of one of the great ideological upheavals in human history; "for the development of the idea of the fool," as Enid Welsford has said, "is one of the products of that uneasy time of transition when the great medieval synthesis was shattered and the new order (if order it was) had not yet been established." [13] As the sober figures of the monk, the pilgrim, the knight, and the scholar begin their long exits, the irreverent, irrational, laughing figure of the fool comes capering forward to take over the play. "Across Europe," in Harry Levin's description, "along the drift from Renaissance to Reformation, from Italy to Germany, stride two gigantic protagonists, the rogue and the fool. In the conflicts of humanistic learning and empirical experience, the war between theology and science, a literature is evolved which has the expansiveness of the picaresque and the inclusiveness of satire. It is the age of Erasmus, Brandt, Rabelais, and Cervantes. It is a time to cry 'Ducdame' and call all fools into a circle." [14]

That circle is the magic circle of comedy, and the fool is the comic character par excellence. To be foolish is, above all, to be risible; and if, as Aristotle said, laughter is the exclusive property of man, the fool is the most human of us all. Indeed, that is precisely what he will

[13] Welsford, *The Fool: His Social and Literary History* (London, 1935), p. 221.
[14] Harry Levin, ed., *Selected Works of Ben Jonson* (New York, 1938), p. 12.

claim when he addresses the sixteenth-century world. His boast is
Falstaff's:

The brain of this foolish, compounded clay, man, is not able to invent
anything that tends to laughter more than I invent or is invented on me:
I am not only witty in myself, but the cause that wit is in other men.

2 Henry IV, I.ii.8–12

Witty and *wit*, however, are equivocal terms; they may refer either
to laughter or to wisdom, to the fool or to the wise. The function of
the professional fool, in imitation of the natural fool, is to create
laughter — a role that Falstaff sees himself in when he calculates how
he will be able to "devise enough matter out of this Shallow to keep
Prince Harry in continual laughter." The function of the wise man,
on the other hand, is to teach the truth. Out of the paradoxical concepts of Kempis and Cusanus, the Renaissance developed the oxymoronic concept of the wise fool, who embodies these paradoxes and
capitalizes upon the equivocation in the word *wit*. He manages, that
is, to present truth by means of comedy, claiming to be wise when
he laughs and to teach us wisdom when he causes laughter in us. The
Renaissance cult of the fool is humanism on a holiday, much as the
medieval *fête des fous* was religion on a holiday; but the praisers of
folly saw that there was in the holiday world as much truth as there
was in the working-day world. James Joyce is said once to have
emended *in vino veritas* to *in risu veritas*,[15] and, though the fool of
the humanists would hate to see anything substituted for wine, he
would agree that laughter is also a source of truth. The fool laughs
because he is human, because he takes a profound delight in life, and
because, like one of Meredith's "very penetrative, very wicked imps,"
he can see the folly of the wise. For a world that was prepared to
consider his laughter irresponsible, the fool of the Renaissance reiterated Horace's rhetorical question: "ridentem dicere verum quid
vetat?" [16]

That he teaches by laughing is also significant of his epoch; for
though the didactic potentialities of comedy and laughter, demonstrated at least as early as Aristophanes, were accepted by classical
antiquity, the Middle Ages seem to have been less certain of them.
At times they did assign a moral or didactic role to comedy — as, for

[15] Richard Ellmann, *James Joyce* (New York, 1959), p. 716.
[16] Horace, *Sermones*, I.i.24–5.

example, in the dramas of Hrotsvitha — but comedy does not here so much indicate humor as describe a genre. There are, of course, certain passages in the plays of the Abbess of Gandersheim that are intended to provoke laughter, but it is doubtful if she thought such passages taught very much wisdom. It was her comic plots that were intended to teach, and her scenes of humor seem closer to what we should call mere "comic relief" from the intensity of the moral lesson. The whole problem of the medieval attitude toward laughter is, as Curtius has indicated, a vexing one;[17] but in any event it is certainly not until the paradoxical concept of the wise fool is developed that we find any striking examples later than classical literature of comic laughter teaching. As wisdom and folly confront each other in the same person, sustained irony becomes possible for the first time since the classical age, and in the laughter of fools the voice of wisdom is heard.

All this can be better understood in the specific example of the first great Renaissance fool, that of Erasmus. In her we can see not only the prototype of all the fools to follow, but also the extent of the contrast between those of the Middle Ages and the Renaissance. She stands at the threshold of what Erasmus himself considered a new world, and she opens the door for the host of fools who parade across the sixteenth century. Of that infinite number of fools (to use the phrase from Ecclesiastes that all fools are fond of citing),[18] it is not my purpose to establish a comprehensive catalogue, but rather to concentrate on three important and representative ones: Erasmus' Stultitia, Rabelais' Panurge, and Shakespeare's Falstaff. What I wish to examine is the development of the concept of folly as it is related to its time and exemplified in these three figures. In order to do so, each fool must necessarily be considered in context, and this is only possible if the number of fools is manageable. To isolate the fool from his context would be to falsify his meaning; for the meaning of what he says, who he is, and what he stands for is inseparable from the mode of speech he adopts and the genre in which he is presented, and his cultural significance is incomprehensible without some reference to the historical currents that were dominant in that time.

[17] Ernst Robert Curtius, *European Literature and the Latin Middle Ages*, tr. Willard R. Trask (New York, 1953), pp. 417–35.
[18] Ecclesiastes, I.15.

The results of such an enquiry depend to a great extent upon which fools are chosen, of course; but Stultitia, Panurge, and Falstaff may be said to be among the most representative of their epoch. Certainly they are the creations of three of the greatest artists of the sixteenth century, and they themselves have become classics of the imagination. It may be objected that of these three only Stultitia wears the traditional cap and bells and that even she is not really a fool in the court-jester sense of the word. Yet that is part of the point I wish to make: the Festes and Touchstones of the sixteenth century are not the only "fools" of that time. They are the most medieval fools and hence the most traditional ones, but for that very reason they are less indicative of the humanistic, skeptical thought that the Renaissance added to the concept of the fool. Moreover, it was because of the concept of the fool developed in such non-jester types as Stultitia and Panurge that Shakespeare was able to give to his jesters the stature he did. The outlandish costume of motley assigned to the medieval fool distinguished him sharply from other human beings; but the contribution of the Renaissance to this figure was precisely that of making him just like everyone else, of claiming that folly was the quintessence of humanity and that all men were fools in one or another sense of that word.

There is one important fool who might have been added to this triad, and that is Ariosto's Orlando — who, in turn, would have necessitated inclusion of Astolfo. If I have excluded Orlando, it is only because he raises the whole problem of the fool in love, which is an entire tradition in itself. "El enamorado simple," as Don Quixote (a kind of one himself) calls him,[19] would have been a fitting companion for the fools I have chosen, but it would have been necessary to account for his very special genealogy and that would have taken us too far afield.[20]

For the same reason (as well as for the more obvious ones) I have mostly avoided the Falstaff whom Queen Elizabeth is said to have requested, the comic hero of *The Merry Wives of Windsor. Don Quixote*, on the other hand, though it also shares the tradition of the

---

[19] C V.217/II.xii.

[20] Two important works on this subject are B. Zumbini, "La Follia d'Orlando," *Studi di letteratura italiana* (Florence, 1906), and, more recent and more valuable, Rocco Montano, *Follia e saggezza nel Furioso e nell' Elogio di Erasmo* (Naples, 1942).

fool in love and is peculiarly indebted to *Orlando Furioso*, is even more closely related to the concept of folly in the *Moriae encomium*, the *Tiers Livre*, and *Henry IV*. In some senses, the Knight of the Mournful Countenance and his squire bring the tradition that we shall be tracing to its inevitable conclusion. In effect, they turn it inside out, as I shall suggest in some final observations. But because they are in this sense dissimilar and because they take us beyond the sixteenth century and into yet another country, I have decided to leave an extensive consideration of this last pair of fools for another occasion.

The fools whom I have chosen, in addition to their representativeness and magnitude, provide a certain neatness of distribution. Chronologically, the *Moriae encomium* (1509), the *Tiers Livre* (c. 1545), and the two parts of *Henry IV* (c. 1597–8) span the century at relatively equidistant intervals.[21] Since, as I hope to show, the *Encomium* is to a great extent the product of Italy, they may be said to follow the Renaissance geographically, northward across Europe from Italy to France to England. It is, indeed, almost as if the same figure moved through time and space with the Renaissance, getting progressively older as the years pass; for the young fool who comes out of Italy becomes the middle-aged fool in France and, finally, the old fool in the taverns of Eastcheap. To be sure, the figure of this fool does, like Virginia Woolf's Orlando, undergo a sexual metamorphosis in its successive reincarnations, but folly, as Stultitia points out, is the property of both men and women. Appropriately, the metempsychosis of Stultitia finally produces Ben Jonson's Androgyno,[22] who, when asked which body he would prefer, replies that none of them gives him any delight except that of the fool himself:

> Alas, those pleasures be stale, and forsaken;
>   No, 'tis your Foole, wherewith I am so taken,
> The onely one creature, that I can call blessed:
>   For all other formes I haue prou'd most distressed.[23]

Finally, in terms of genre, Stultitia, Panurge, and Falstaff represent three of the most significant Renaissance forms, the humanistic oration, the sustained prose narrative, and the drama, while at the same

---

[21] The dates given are the conjectural dates of composition.
[22] See Harry Levin, "Jonson's Metempsychosis," *PQ*, XIII (1943), 231–9.
[23] *Ben Jonson* [Works], ed. C. H. Herford and Percy and Evelyn Simpson (Oxford, 1925–52; 11 vols.), V, 29 (*Volpone*, I.ii.55–9). Cited hereafter as Jonson, *Works*.

time each of these forms is developed out of a medieval genre, the sermon joyeux, the fabliau, and the morality play.

To extend this brief introduction further, however, would be to incur the censure and ridicule of the first fool we shall meet; for she is especially impatient of lengthy introductions and eager to speak for herself. For this moment she is the protagonist to whom we must give our attention as she leads the action on what King Lear, in a more poignant context, called "this great stage of fools."

I ❧ ERASMUS' STULTITIA

I

THE PRAISE OF FOLLY

👑👑👑👑👑👑👑👑👑👑👑👑👑👑👑👑👑👑👑👑👑👑👑👑👑👑👑👑

IT WAS the wisest man of his age, Desiderius Erasmus of Rotterdam, who created the most foolish fool of all. Hailed by his contemporaries "sicut si esset miraculum Mundi," [1] he was honored everywhere for his vast learning and profound wisdom; and in the dawn of printing the shadow of his influence was cast across the whole of Europe, from Sweden to Spain, with a rapidity and ubiquitousness that had no precedent. The story of how, in a world that prided itself upon its revival of learning, this illegitimate son of an obscure father came to be courted by princes and popes and scholars is too well known to be told again, but we may recall that even so unlikely a figure as Jack Wilton once made a notable detour to see "aged learnings chief ornament, that abundant and superingenious clarke, Erasmus." [2] To be sure, by the time Nashe came to record the peregrinations of his unfortunate hero, Erasmus had already been dead for over half a century; yet this very fact would seem to anticipate the extent to which his reputation and esteem outlived him. For over two hundred years after his death, the great humanist remained one of the most widely read and respected of European authors, and as late as 1751 Samuel Johnson, who subsequently awarded him one of the crowns of the

[1] *Epistolae obscurorum virorum,* ed. and tr. Francis Griffith Stokes (New Haven, 1925), p. 213.
[2] *The Works of Thomas Nashe,* ed. Ronald B. McKerrow (London, 1904-10), II, 245.

Muses in a Greek epigram, proclaimed that "he will stand for ever in the first rank of literary heroes." [3]

Had Erasmus himself been able to read Johnson's tribute, he would have been the first to recognize it as an echo of the traditional Homeric epithet, *orchamos andrôn*. As such, Johnson's very phrasing may be seen as the product of that system of learning which Erasmus, perhaps more than any other individual, helped to establish in Europe and which, until yesterday, was the common heritage of educated men. Today, however, though he continues to occupy that rank of literary pre-eminence which Johnson predicted, his books, with one exception, go unread; and of all the paradoxes that inform Erasmus' life none is more ironic than that this man, whom Roger Ascham once called "the ornament of learning in our tyme," [4] should now be best remembered for his defense of ignorance. His other, more scholarly books lie interred in the pomp of folios, abandoned to the predacity of worms and scholars; and even the man himself stands as little more than a shadowy, uncertain ghost before us. But his fool Stultitia continues, year after year, to climb her pulpit and deliver her oration to new audiences in every language, as vivid and ridiculous as she was when she first appeared one morning in Chelsea over four centuries ago. Even those who may not have heard her speak *in propria persona* have, whether they knew it or not, listened to her accents and her ironic laughter echoing down the centuries, from Hamlet to H. C. Earwicker, from Don Quixote to Felix Krull. For the irony of her persistence, striking though it is, is no more striking than the persistence of her irony.

Irony is the invention of the Greeks; but when their day was over, that strange, wry laughter faded into silence, leaving later ages ignorant of the sound. Although late antiquity and the Middle Ages were fond of the antithesis between jest and earnest, they had somehow lost the ability to conceive of the two in synthesis, which is the pre-

[3] See *Boswell's Life of Johnson*, ed. George Birkbeck Hill and L. F. Powell (Oxford, 1934–35), V, 430. See also *The Works of Samuel Johnson* (London, 1810), V, 237 (*Rambler* 108): "Compelled by want to attendance and solicitation, and so much versed in common life, that he has transmitted to us the most perfect delineation of the manners of his age, [Erasmus] joined to his knowledge of the world, such an application to books, that he will stand for ever in the first rank of literary heroes."
[4] Roger Ascham, *English Works*, ed. W. A. Wright (Cambridge, Eng., 1904), p. 267.

requisite for irony.[5] "A better metaphor," according to J. A. K. Thomson, "would be to call Irony the trembling equipoise between jest and earnest," and Thomson has gone on to attribute the role of "master spirit in restoring to Europe the Greek thing, Irony," to Erasmus himself.[6] The nature and effect of Erasmian irony is something we shall consider in detail when we come to his fool, who may be said to make the first major use of irony since Lucian. For the moment, however, we may simply observe that whether or not Erasmus is actually the first author since classical antiquity (as Thomson claims) to use such irony is a question whose pedantry he himself would have abhorred: we cannot ask it without recalling his jeers at those grammarians who, like Browne's and Browning's, discovered the name of Anchises' mother and "settled" the eight parts of speech.[7] Some scholars have suggested that Erasmus may have learned his irony from Lorenzo Valla; yet to reread Valla with this in mind is to listen in vain for anything quite so subtle and acute as that which characterizes Erasmus. Nevertheless, even if Valla or some other author could be demonstrated to take chronological precedence in this matter — and there are, indeed, many examples of so-called irony in medieval literature — the significant fact is that Erasmus was the first post-classical author to employ irony in any *sustained* fashion and to perceive its infinite potentialities. Moreover, it is Erasmus who is largely responsible for the ironic smile that curled so many sixteenth-century lips, since his were the books that were translated and read all over Europe.

In much the same way, Erasmus may be said to have given Europe the paradox of the Wise Fool. For though that personified oxymoron is at least as old as Socrates and Christ, and though its medieval ancestors and apologists are legion, its first modern, and most influential, appearance is as the figure of Stultitia in the *Moriae encomium*. There,

[5] See Ernst Robert Curtius, *European Literature and the Latin Middle Ages*, tr. W. R. Trask (New York, 1953), pp. 417–35.

[6] J. A. K. Thomson, *Irony* (London, 1926), pp. 166, 233.

[7] ME 103 and 104. Cf. also the noble statement of this position by Pico della Mirandola in his celebrated letter to Ermolao Barbaro: "Viximus celebres, O Hermolae, et posthac vivemus, non in scholis grammaticorum et paedagogiis, sed in philosophorum coronis, in conventibus sapientum, ubi non de matre Andromaches, non de Niobes filiis atque id genus levibus nugis, sed de humanarum divinarumque rerum rationibus agitur et disputatur . . ." The text of this letter can be found in E. Garin, *Filosofi italiani del quattrocento* (Florence, 1942), pp. 428–44.

for the first time, the implications of an ironic and paradoxical drama-tization of Nicholas of Cusa's *docta ignorantia* were fully realized and, because of the book's popularity, given widespread currency. So widespread was it, in fact, that one may doubt if Viola could have observed of Feste that "This fellow is wise enough to play the fool,/ And to do that well craves a kind of wit," [8] had she not, like a good pupil of Ascham, read her Erasmus.

Just how much of Erasmus Shakespeare himself had read is impos-sible to determine, but it seems probable that his debt is greater than has been commonly supposed. It would be surprising, given the pop-ularity of certain Erasmian texts, if it were not. We now know, for example, that Ben Jonson and George Chapman, both of whom ad-mittedly had larger Latin than their rival from Stratford, read Eras-mus with care and profit; many of their most celebrated passages have, only within the present century, been revealed to be nothing more than gifted translations from Erasmus.[9] If the cases of Jonson and Chapman show us nothing else, they at least demonstrate that Erasmus was "in the air"; and we may infer that Shakespeare, who breathed that same air, must have been familiar with such current translations as Chaloner's, as well as with those Latin works he is likely to have read at the Stratford Grammar School.

With the exception, however, of Bataillon's brilliant study of Span-ish Erasmianism,[10] the entire question of Erasmus' influence on Euro-pean literature and thought remains to be examined in detail. There have been a few hints and guesses; there is a certain amount of spe-cific evidence; and the bibliography of the *Bibliotheca erasmiana*,[11] though incomplete and occasionally inaccurate, is of some help in providing a starting point. What evidence we do possess points to a phenomenally widespread dissemination of Erasmus' books, not only the "schoolbooks" (*Colloquia, Adagia, Copia, Apophthegmata, Si-milia*), but also especially the *Enchiridion militis christiani* and the *Moriae encomium*. It is, in short, no exaggeration to say, as one

[8] Shakespeare, *Twelfth Night*, III.i.67-8.

[9] See the commentary to Jonson, *Works*, and also the edition of *Volpone* edited by John D. Rea (New Haven, 1919); and Franck L. Schoell, *Études sur l'humanisme continental en Angleterre à la fin de la Renaissance* (Paris, 1926), *passim*.

[10] Marcel Bataillon, *Érasme et l'Espagne* (Paris, 1927).

[11] *Bibliotheca erasmiana. Bibliographie des oeuvres d'Érasme* in *Bibliotheca Belgica*, ed. F. van der Haeghen, R. van den Berghe, T. J. J. Arnold, and A. Roersch (Ghent, 1897-1915).

scholar has, that the figure of Erasmus dominated the cultivated world of Europe in the first two decades of the sixteenth century.[12] That influence continued, though not in quite so dominant a way, through the rest of the century and beyond. In 1628, over a century after its publication, the young Milton was to find the *Encomium* "in everyone's hands" at Cambridge.[13] His chance remark in the sixth *Prolusion* is a kind of augury: of all Erasmus' books, it is the *Encomium* that was destined to live and to have "a greater and more direct influence on European literature than any of the other works of Erasmus."[14] One small measure of this influence may be found in Voltaire, who, though no great admirer of Erasmus, felt obliged, when he came to write the entry Folie for the *Dictionnaire philosophique*, to begin by pointing out that "there is no question of renewing Erasmus' book, which today would be nothing more than a fairly insipid commonplace."[15]

Despite its popularity, the *Encomium* is the most difficult of Erasmus' works, precisely because of the nature of its irony and paradox; and if, like Machiavelli's *Principe*, few books have been more influential, few have been more misunderstood. The *Encomium's* first critic is in this respect typical of the many who followed him. When Martin Dorp suggested to Erasmus that he write a praise of wisdom as a corrective to *The Praise of Folly*, he made evident his total failure to comprehend what Erasmus had written.[16] One can only sympathize with the author's despairing sigh: "I wonder what has got into that man's mind!"[17] In England, Philip Sidney seems to have understood it better and speaks of it in conjunction with a verse adapted from Ovid, "ut lateat virtus proximitate mali," remarking that it has "another foundation then the superficiall part would promise."[18] Chaloner, Erasmus' first English translator, also recognized that "in

[12] Myron P. Gilmore, *The World of Humanism, 1453-1517* (New York, 1952), p. 223.
[13] *The Works of John Milton*, ed. Frank A. Patterson, et al., XII (New York, 1936), 220: "Et cuique jam in manibus est ingeniosissimum illud *Moriae* encomium non infimi Scriptoris opus . . ."
[14] Gilmore, *Humanism*, p. 227.
[15] *Oeuvres complètes de Voltaire*, XIX (Paris, 1879), 159n. This sentence occurs in the edition of 1764 but was later deleted.
[16] EE II.13 (304).
[17] EE II.243 (412).
[18] *The Complete Works of Sir Philip Sidney*, ed. A. Feuillerat, III (Cambridge, Eng., 1923), 26-7.

this booke, treatyng of suche a Theme, and vnder suche a person, he openeth all his bowget." [19] On the other hand, Ascham, though he urged Erasmus upon his students and explained that he "writeth rightlie, rightlie vnderstanded," would appear to have misread the book as badly as Dorp, if his one reference to it can be taken as exemplificative of his reading.[20] Indeed, one is finally forced to the reluctant conclusion expressed by Thomson that Erasmus' "contemporaries, with the almost solitary exception of his dear friend, Sir Thomas More, did not understand him; when More died, no one at all. They admired his scholarship; they applauded his wit; but they really understood neither his scholarship nor his Irony." [21]

The mode of irony which informs the speech of Erasmus' wise fool may be described, with the same phrase that Cusanus coined to describe the nature of learned ignorance, as a *coincidentia oppositorum*. Whether those opposites are jest and earnest, praise and censure, or wisdom and folly, it is the coincidentia — the synthesis, the equipoise, the concord — which produces the quality of irony. To be able to perceive such a coincidentia requires a certain type of mind, of which Erasmus' is one of the great examples. What is more, it may also require a certain type of historical epoch: only at certain moments in history has irony found a soil in which it could burgeon. Almost invariably these moments are moments of transition, when one epoch is in the process of dying and another is being born. Irony, then, is essentially a mode of thought that belongs to what Northrup Frye has evocatively called the "winter" of experience or to what Longinus, with reference to the Homer of the *Odyssey*, called the setting sun — to the hour, as T. S. Eliot describes it, "Between midnight and dawn, when the past is all deception, / The future futureless."

The age of Erasmus, as everyone knows, was such a moment in the course of history, a moment briefly poised between the moribund Middle Ages and the nascent Reformation. In this sense it is not, I think, too fanciful to see that epoch itself as an analogous kind of *coincidentia oppositorum*. The period comprising roughly the first two decades of the sixteenth century is characterized in its thought by an extraordinary confluence of disparate currents, Italian and

---

[19] "Sir Thomas Chaloner's Translation of *The Praise of Folie*," ed. Clarence H. Miller (diss., Harvard University, 1955; 2 vols.), I, 5.

[20] Ascham, *Works*, p. 271; see also p. 215.

[21] Thomson, *Irony*, p. 233.

northern, ancient and modern, naturalistic and idealistic, secular and
religious, pagan and Christian. It is the supreme moment of that synthesis we call Christian humanism. Jean Seznec has given a suggestive
description of it in terms of the pagan gods, and the iconographic
achievement he is concerned with is symptomatic of much else:

But beneath this gaiety and enthusiasm [of the fifteenth century] lurks a
stubborn disquiet; just because a "pagan" cult of life is now being pro-
fessed, with the gods as its incarnation, the need is felt of bringing that
cult into line with the spiritual values of Christianity — of reconciling the
two worlds. Humanism and art appear, for a brief moment, to have suc-
ceeded in accomplishing this result; the Renaissance, in its moment of
flowering, is this synthesis — or rather this fragile harmony. But the sixteenth century, as it advances, is forced to avow the discord it thought
had been successfully hidden. An era of crisis and reaction then dawns.[22]

This reconciliation of two worlds is apparent wherever we turn
in the early sixteenth century: we can observe it in the sculpture of
Michel Colombe and hear it in the polyphonies of Jannequin, and the
title of one of the books of Jean LeMaire de Belges, written at almost
exactly the same time as the *Encomium,* seems to state it emblemati-
cally as *La concorde des deux langages* — "the harmony of two cul-
tures." Visually, the finest flower of the hybridism of northern and
southern strains is the work of Erasmus' friend, Albrecht Dürer; and
with the same horticultural image Augustin Renaudet has described
the *Encomium* itself as a flower of Hellenism and humanism, nour-
ished by a sap that continues to be popular and gothic.[23] Written in
1509 and first published in 1511, the *Moriae encomium* stands in spirit
halfway between Pico della Mirandola and Martin Luther. That
Erasmus conceived of it as he journeyed from Italy to England, or
that he wrote it in "an Italianate England," [24] may be seen as equally
symbolic of the spirit of its epoch. Indeed, the more we examine Stultitia's speech, the more it seems to sum up — or rather, to synthesize
into the Janus-head of paradox — all of the contradictory tendencies
of her age. Not the least significant of these contradictions is the metamorphosis, at precisely the time of Stultitia's first popular success, of
the name of "the subtle doctor," Duns Scotus, into the commonly

[22] Jean Seznec, *The Survival of the Pagan Gods,* tr. Barbara Sessions (New York,
1953), p. 320.
[23] Augustin Renaudet, *Érasme et l'Italie* (Geneva, 1954), p. 101.
[24] Renaudet, *Italie,* p. 101.

accepted epithet for a fool. Stultitia herself will claim that the soul of Scotus "is more prickly than a porcupine or hedgehog," [25] and Rabelais' Epistemon will derive the name of Scotus from the Greek adjective *skoteinos*, meaning obscure or blind.[26] Thus, as one of the wisest men of the Middle Ages becomes the quintessence of folly for a new age, the stage is set for Erasmus' Stultitia; and the very etymology of the word *dunce* seems, coincidentally, almost to parody the title of Erasmus' book and its punning reference to Sir Thomas More.

[25] ME 159–60.
[26] R V.134–5n5.

2

THE EPISTLE DEDICATORY

❧❧❧❧❧❧❧❧❧❧❧❧❧❧❧❧❧❧❧❧❧❧❧❧❧❧❧❧❧❧❧❧❧

I⊤ was in More's house that the *Moriae encomium* was written; it was at his suggestion that it was expanded; and it is to him that it is dedicated. Like most Renaissance epistles dedicatory, Erasmus' letter to More is not only encomiastic of the recipient but programmatic of the work as well, and in it we are told when, why, and how the *Encomium* was composed. Any examination of Stultitia's oration ought therefore to begin with a consideration of this dedication. Because it is a letter to More, Erasmus' closest friend, some scholars have used it as important evidence about the composition and nature of the *Encomium*, assuming that if Erasmus were direct and accurate with anyone it would be with More. Read on the basis of this assumption, the epistle has been considered particularly valuable; for if, as some have assumed, Erasmus is here speaking without a mask, this would then be a far more "trustworthy" statement than anything he says after he dons the persona of Stultitia. Yet such an assumption fails to take into account the public nature of this epistle, which was, after all, specifically written to be printed at the head of the *Encomium*; and just as an autobiography is not the same thing as a private journal, so an epistle dedicatory and a letter represent two quite different genres. The epistle does indeed contain important evidence about the composition and nature of the *Encomium*, but much of that evidence lies between the lines; and this letter is not so ingenuous, nor its author so unmasked, as either would wish to seem.

In the epistle, the basic paradoxical device of the *Encomium*, the confusion of wisdom and ignorance, is set up. "I have called my book," says Erasmus to More, "*The Praise of 'Moria*' because of your name, which comes as near to the word for folly as you are far from the meaning of it." [1] The Ciceronian juxtaposition is a neat one — and yet not quite so neat as it appears thus isolated from context, for it follows hard upon a sentence in which Erasmus had deliberately confused similar concepts of nearness and farness.[2] Nonetheless, the irony of the title is at once made plain: it can be translated either as "The Praise of Folly" or "The Praise of More," and if Folly is rude and stupid, More is "wholly learned and wholly gracious." From the outset, the names of More and Moria and the concepts of wisdom and folly, like those of absence and presence, are intentionally confused. Setting out from this ambiguity and traveling via the well-worn Horatian road of "aut prodesse . . . aut delectare," Erasmus arrives at a position from which he can claim both frivolity and gravity for his little treatise. Others may judge me as they will, he says, but, unless self-love deceives me badly, I have praised folly in a way not wholly foolish.[3] It is upon this premise, of course, that the entire *Encomium* is based, and the possible seriousness of the joking to follow is hinted at several times in this prefatory epistle. Trifles may lead to serious things; fooleries may give profit; and while nothing is sillier than to treat serious things triflingly, nothing is more graceful than to treat trifling things in such a way that you seem to be less than trifling.[4] This playing with words is, like the constant use of the double (or triple) negative, a characteristic of the style Erasmus employs in the *Encomium*; and the style itself becomes in this way a reflection of the ironic paradoxes of the argument.

The position established with regard to trifles and serious things is a commonplace in Renaissance defenses of secular and "light" literature and was inevitably brought forth to meet objections against works deemed "more frivolous (*leviores*) than befit a theologian." Yet when

[1] ME II: "Primum admonuit me Mori cognomen tibi gentile, quod tam ad Moriae vocabulum accedit, quam es ipse a re alienus."

[2] ME I: "cuius equidem absentis absens memoria non aliter frui solebam, quam praesentis praesens consuetudine consueveram . . ."

[3] ME VI: "De me quidem aliorum erit judicium: tametsi, nisi plane me fallit Φιλαυτία, stultitiam laudavimus, sed non omnino stulte."

[4] ME V-VI: "maxime si nugae seria ducant, atque ita tractentur ludicra, ut ex his aliquanto plus frugis referat lector . . . Ut enim nihil nugacius, quam seria nugatorie tractare, ita nihil festivius, quam ita tractare nugas, ut nihil minus quam nugatus fuisse videaris."

it appears, however briefly or tentatively, before the paradoxical title *Moriae encomium*, it also serves to warn the reader that he should look below the surface of the joking that is to follow. Chaloner, who unlike many Renaissance translators seems to have understood the work he rendered, comprehended this fact and the verbal device, and to drive their implications home to his English readers he reiterated them in his own introduction:

A Folie it maie be thought in me to have spent tyme in englisshyng of this boke, entitled *the praise of Folie*, wheras the name it selfe semeth to set foorth no wisedome, or matter of gravitee: unlesse perhappes Erasmus, the autour therof, delited to mocke men, in callyng it one thyng, and meanyng an other.[5]

Despite these allusions, however, the esoteric aspects of the *Encomium* are little more than hinted at. Not only was it dangerous to be more explicit, but Erasmus was concerned with defending himself against the attacks he could foresee. The defensive arguments he employs here are those he was to return to and expand in such utterances as the famous letter to Martin Dorp and, later, after the attacks had in fact begun, in the adage *Ollas ostentare*.[6] His defense begins, in the best humanistic tradition, with a citation of classical precedents, and the catalogue he supplies is the usual one, such as we find, for example, in Nashe's *Praise of the Red Herring*.[7] Though Erasmus' list is, happily, briefer than Nashe's, it includes the most famous mock panegyrics — the pseudo-Homeric *Batrachomyomachia*, the pseudo-Virgilian *Culex*, Ovid's *Nux*, and that favorite of Renaissance authors from Spenser to Gelli to Montaigne, Plutarch's *Gryllus*.

This argument from precedent is buttressed by several moral arguments, all of them traditional and all of them repeated and elaborated in the letter to Dorp. I have, says Erasmus, censured only the general manners of men (*communem hominum vitam*) and have mentioned no one by name, thus attempting to teach rather than to "bite."[8] What is more, he claims that by attacking all classes of men he has

[5] Miller, "Chaloner, *Folie*," I, 1.
[6] EE II.90–114 (337) and LB II.460–461D.
[7] Nashe, *Works*, III, 176–8. For a discussion of this tradition and a more complete catalogue, see McKerrow's note, IV, 389–95. See also A. S. Pease, "Things without Honor," *Classical Philology*, XXI (1926), 27–42, and A. E. Malloch, "The Techniques and Function of the Renaissance Paradox," *SP*, LIII (1956), 191n.
[8] ME VI: "At enim qui vitas hominum ita taxat, ut neminem omnino perstringat nominatim, quaeso, utrum is mordere videtur, an docere potius, ac monere?"

shown that he was angry at no individual, but rather at all vices.[9] Finally, with a characteristic side-swipe at Juvenal,[10] he points out that he has deliberately avoided moving through "that occult sewer of vices." The English reader may remember Ben Jonson's statement of the same principle, and actually, as one might have guessed, Jonson is translating from Erasmus' letter to Dorp:

Whilst I name no persons, but deride follies, why should any man confesse, or betray himself? why doth not that of S. *Hierome* come into their mind; *Vbi generalis est de vitiis disputatio, ibi nullius esse personae injuriam?* Is it such an inexpiable crime in *Poets,* to taxe vices generally; and no offence in them who, by their exception, confesse they have committed them particularly?[11]

The moral tone of the *Encomium* is thus demonstrated to be a high one, and Erasmus later even boasted that some had thought the book more edifying than Aristotle's *Ethics* or *Politics*[12] — a "modernist" claim in defense of imaginative literature that one meets often in Renaissance authors, as in the celebrated passage where Milton asserts that Spenser is a better teacher than Scotus or Aquinas.[13] Erasmus' final argument is his insistence — from one point of view quite proper, from another quite specious — that the reader remember that the oration is pronounced by Stultitia, not Erasmus, and that the decorum of the persona had to be maintained.[14] This was perhaps his best defense, and he reiterated it for the rest of his life whenever the subject of the *Encomium* came up; in the edition of 1515 he emphasized the point often in the notes added to the *Encomium* by means of his amanuensis, Gerard Listrius.[15]

---

[9] ME VI: "Praeterea qui nullum hominum genus praetermittit, is nulli homini, vitiis omnibus iratus videtur."

[10] For example, the adage *Ollas ostentare,* LB II.461A.

[11] Jonson, *Works,* VIII, 633-4 (*Discoveries*).

[12] LB II.460F-461A: "Hoc quicquid est libelli, video candidis ingeniis, et iis qui bonis literis sunt initiati, magnopere probari; qui praeter jocandi festivitatem affirmant illic esse non pauca, quae ad corrigendos hominum mores magis conferant, quam Aristotelis Ethica, aut Politica dogmata, qui paganus plus quam paganice hisce de rebus praecepit."

[13] Milton, *Works,* IV, 311 (*Areopagitica*).

[14] ME VII: "decoro personae serviendum fuit." Cf. LB II.461C: "Denique non perpendunt id, quod in dialogis est potissimum personae decorum, et Erasmum imaginantur loqui, non Moriam."

[15] For example, LB IV.406E (Listrius' notes not given in ME): "Hoc ad Moriae personam referendum est, apud quam vocari sapientem contumelia est: veluti apud

These, then, are the main points in the epistle dedicatory that any casual reader comes away with. What is more, they are the points that Erasmus wished him to come away with. Yet if we examine the epistle with a more penetrating eye, certain questions present themselves, the answers to which bring us closer to Erasmus' intentions in writing it and lead us directly into the techniques of the *Encomium* itself. One may, for example, wonder why Erasmus should have felt it necessary to repeat the familiar clichés in defense of satiric and "frivolous" literature to More, of all people. Not only was More *doctissimus*, but it was he himself who had led Erasmus to Lucian. And it was Lucian who had fished the murex up for both of them. Erasmus' epistle dedicatory to his translation of Lucian's *Gallus*, written two years before, had been quite explicit about the nature of the game.[16] Certainly Erasmus knew — he says in the epistle that he knows—how much More enjoyed this kind of joke which the two of them had found in Lucian. Presumably, therefore, no one less needed a justification of the *Moriae encomium*, nor would anyone have been more familiar than More with the traditional defenses. Why, Erasmus asks at the end of his epistle, should I say these things to you? The answer, of course, is that More did not need the epistle, that, as I have already suggested, it was not written for More but for the *Encomium*, because Erasmus intended that the reader should be led into that work by way of this epistle.

Evident though these facts are, their corollary has not always been so easily perceived: that Erasmus is not here talking privately and frankly to a friend, but publicly to his readers and future critics. He is, therefore, wearing as much of a mask as he is in the encomium itself, though not quite the same mask.

It is to this mask that we may attribute the lie Erasmus tells in the very first sentence of the epistle. For the *Encomium*, as we know very well, was not composed by Erasmus as he traveled from Italy to England, but rather in More's own house after he had arrived there. Some scholars, confronted with what Erasmus says in the

aulicos, docti stulti vocantur, apud doctos vicissim aliud." On Listrius, see EE I.459 (222); *Bibliotheca erasmiana;* and A. Renaudet, "Érasme, sa vie et son oeuvre jusqu'en 1517," *Revue historique,* CXII (1913), 258.

[16] EE I.425-6 (193): "Tantum obtinet in decendo gratiae, tantum in inueniendo felicitatis, tantum in iocando leporis, in mordendo aceti, sic titillat allusionibus, sic seria nugis, nugas seriis miscet; sic ridens vera dicit, vera dicendo ridet . . ."

epistle and what he acknowledges in another letter,[17] have attempted to explain the discrepancy by claiming that, though he wrote his book in Chelsea, he thought it up while traveling.[18] Such an explanation is by no means implausible, but it is unnecessary. It also misses the point. What we must seek is not the explanation of the contradiction, but rather the reasons why Erasmus perpetrated the inaccuracy that his book was written on the journey. Equally unnecessary and misguided has been the long discussion of the dateline, "Ex Rure, quinto Idus Iunias, An. M.D.VIII," which Erasmus placed at the end of the epistle. Scholars have often debated what Erasmus meant by *rus*,[19] and P. S. Allen has conjectured that it does not necessarily mean Chelsea, as most have thought (why write to More from his own house?), but possibly St. Germain-des-Prés.[20] Yet surely what Erasmus means by the dateline is that the *Encomium* was written in the country rather than the city; and the point he is emphasizing is the same one Nashe is making when he writes at the beginning of his *Praise of the Red Herring*, "of my note-books and all books else here in the country I am bereaued." [21] All these devices, the *ex rure*, the trip on horseback, its parody later in the epistle as a hobbyhorse ride, and Erasmus' subsequent descriptions of how he wrote the *Encomium* in only a week, while ill, and without any books at his disposal,[22] are scholarly disclaimers. He protests too much, and we may be forgiven for wondering if there were no books in More's house that he could have borrowed. Erasmus is simply using these excuses to remove his book from the battleground of scholarship on which it could more easily be attacked. Thus, whenever an adversary might attempt to riposte Stultitia's thrusts, Erasmus could always explain that his sword was only a wooden toy, that he was only joking, that it was all simply

---

[17] EE II.94 (337): "Diuersabar id temporis apud Morum meum ex Italia reuersus . . ."

[18] See, for example, I. Bruns, "Erasmus als Satiriker," *Deutsche Rundschau*, CIII (1900), 192–3.

[19] See the *Bibliotheca erasmiana* for a résumé of these arguments.

[20] EE I.459 (222).

[21] Nashe, *Works*, III, 175–6.

[22] Cf. LB II.460F: "Lusimus et nos ante complureis annos, Μωρίας ἐγκώμιον, cui non plus septem dierum operam impendimus, idque nullis librorum adminiculis adjuti. Nam nostra sarcina nondum advecta tum erat." Cf. also EE II.94: "renum dolor complusculos dies domi continebat. Et mea bibliotheca nondum fuerat aduecta. Tum si maxime fuisset, non sinebat morbus quicquam in frauioribus studiis acrius agitare. Coepi per ocium Morias encomium ludere, nec in hoc sane vt aederem, sed vt morbi molestiam hoc velut auocamento leuarum."

a game. It is a trick that Falstaff, with his dagger of lath, also knew.

Of the many disclaimers which Erasmus proffers, the *en voyage* excuse is particularly interesting, since it helps us to locate the *Encomium* within a certain tradition. Perhaps the earliest Renaissance use of this particular antischolastic device is Petrarch's in his own book on folly. In the *De sui ipsius et multorum ignorantia* he is at pains to make the reader believe that his tract was written *en voyage* — specifically, while sitting in a boat going down the Po.[23] Thus, he carefully explains that his book could not possibly be scholarly (*non denique grauitatem* [*habet*]) and that it is no wonder if the hand and speech of the writer float a bit (*fluctuat*): for lucubration requires a lamp, scholarship a study. The theme of the *hortus conclusus* that we find in Boccaccio and others is, in its insistence upon removal from the world of hard fact and moral codes, an analogous device to disclaim a certain type of responsibility; and Marguerite de Navarre, in her imitation of Boccaccio, removes her characters from any scholarly responsibility as well by specifically excluding from the group "those who had studied and were men of letters." [24] Similarly, More's *Utopia* was not only put down on paper in spare moments ("onelye that tyme, whyche I steale from slepe and meate"), but it also claimed to be nothing more than a recounting of what he had been told, thus supposedly freeing him "of all the labour and study belonging to the invention of this work." [25] Finally, Petrarch's description of writing in a boat may remind us that Cusanus also claimed that his philosophy of learned ignorance came to him "at sea while returning from Greece," [26] while at the same time Petrarch's verb *fluctuat* anticipates Montaigne's explanation that he wrote down whatever came into his head, "divers et ondoyant," as he was attempting to describe his own ignorance.

[23] Petrarch, *De sui ipsius et multorum ignorantia*, ed. L. M. Capelli (Paris, 1906), p. 83: "Ego autem, amice, ne quid nescis, et ut noris unde et quo anime tibi hec scribo, *inter Padi uertices parua in naui sedeo*. Ne mireris si uel manus scribentis uel oratio fluctuat; *per aduersum hunc ingentem amnem tota cum ignorantia mea nauigo* . . ." (italics mine). See also the epistle dedicatory to this work, *Seniles* XIII.5, printed in the same volume, p. 15: "Liber quidem dicitur, colloquium est; nil de libro habet praeter nomen, non molem, non ordinem, non stilum, *non denique grauitatem, ut qui cursim in itinere approperante conscriptus est* . . ." (italics mine).

[24] Marguerite de Navarre, *L'Heptaméron*, ed. Michel François (Paris, 1950), p. 9.

[25] Thomas More, *Utopia*, tr. Ralph Robynson, ed. J. H. Lupton (Oxford, 1905), pp. 4, 1.

[26] See Ernst Cassirer, *Individuum und Kosmos in der Philosophie der Renaissance* (Leipzig and Berlin, 1927), p. 8n.

Just as Erasmus claims that he wrote her speech under the most casual conditions, so Stultitia will repeatedly point out that she is speaking extempore and that her author is a man who writes down whatever enters his head or falls from his pen, "dum nulla lucubratione." [27] Those nine Horatian years of study and revision during which, as he tells Arbuthnot, Pope urged writers to "keep your piece" are simply ridiculed by the unscholarly fool.[28] Erasmus' insistence upon the unscholarly conditions under which the *Encomium* was composed is matched by his equal insistence upon the lusory character of the book; and the verb *ludere* and its derivatives (not to mention words with analogous connotations such as *jocus, nugae, festivus, ridere, delectare*) appear eleven times in this brief epistle to establish the *Encomium* as a "game of wit" (*hunc ingenii nostri lusum*). Let my readers, says Erasmus, think that I have been playing a game of checkers for fun or riding a hobbyhorse.[29] For it is only a game, this little treatise — though, to be sure, Erasmus hints that such trifles may, as they do in Lucian, have serious implications (*maxime si nugae seria ducant*).

Now one of the defining characteristics of play is its formality, its established sequence of events and the accepted rules that govern those events.[30] One cannot play the game unless one knows the rules, and neither can one watch the game with any comprehension unless one is aware of the formal pattern and the strict laws that control and define it. Like all games, the *Encomium* also has its patterns and its rules, and one must know them in order to comprehend Stultitia's speech. Thus the "serious matters" at which Erasmus hints can be accurately apprehended only after the nature and function of the "trifles" have been comprehended. In the game that is Stultitia's speech, the formal pattern is that of classical oratory, the rules are those of Erasmian irony. We must know something of both before we can accurately interpret the message of the first fool.

[27] ME 107.
[28] ME 107.
[29] ME V: "Proinde si videbitur, fingant isti, me latrunculis interim animi causa lusisse, aut si malint, equitasse in arudine longa."
[30] See J. Huizinga, *Homo Ludens* (Boston, 1955), ch. 1. On Erasmus as *homo ludens*, see Alfons Auer, *Die vollkommene Frömmigkeit des Christen nach dem Enchiridion militis Christiani des Erasmus von Rotterdam* (Düsseldorf, 1954), pp. 18ff.

3

THE IRONIC
MOCK ENCOMIUM

THE rubric, *Stultitia loquitur*, that stands at the head of the *Moriae encomium* announces what is the most important single fact about Erasmus' book. It ought to come as something of a surprise, and surely it did to its first readers; for nothing in the title or the epistle dedicatory prepares us for the fact that this encomium of folly is to be delivered by Folly herself. There is, indeed, no precedent for it in the literary tradition. The title of the book, though intentionally somewhat oxymoronic, cannot have come as any great surprise to the intelligent, well-read reader of 1511. There would doubtless have been a certain amusement in finding that Brandt's ship, launched less than two decades before, had been sailed so triumphantly into port, but the mock-encomiastic genre was not unfamiliar, and the reader would probably have recalled at once that long tradition of works which praised "Busireses, Phalarises, quartan fevers, flies, baldness, and plagues of that sort." To have found that it is Folly herself who speaks may have occasioned some greater surprise, especially since in Brandt's book it was Wisdom who occupied the pulpit and preached admonishingly to the fools sitting beneath her. Moreover, as some readers may have remembered, the one time that one of Brandt's fools did mount to the pulpit, he was struck dumb.[1] Yet actually, for the

[1] Sebastian Brandt, *The Ship of Fools*, tr. Alexander Barclay, ed. T. H. Jamieson (Edinburgh and London, 1874; 2 vols.), I, 119; II, 273, 231.

ridiculous to speak was no less traditional than for the ridiculous to be praised: like the vicious and the bestial, the ridiculous and foolish had early won the right of speech in literature.

What would have been astonishing to the reader of 1511, however, is the fact that here the ridiculous is praising itself. Fools had spoken before this and foolishness had been praised; but never before had a fool praised foolishness. Erasmus' great originality, then, was to make Stultitia both the author and the subject of her encomium, to conceive of "Moriae" as being simultaneously both objective and subjective genitive. Thus, "The Praise of Folly" only translates half of the title: it might more accurately be rendered as "Folly's Praise of Folly."

As Erasmus' title thus doubles back on itself, it tends to cancel itself out in the fashion of a double negative. At least one is already tantalized by the doubt that it may cancel itself out. Or is it perhaps actually a triple negative? Does doubt cancel out doubt? To begin to examine the problem is to condemn oneself to a vertiginous semantic labyrinth. For the praise of folly, being a *mock* praise, is in fact the censure of folly; but if Folly is thus censuring folly, Wisdom would presumably praise folly. Or, to look at it from another angle, if the praise of folly is, by its mock-encomiastic nature, actually the praise of wisdom, Folly must be praising wisdom. But if Folly praises wisdom, then Wisdom would presumably censure wisdom. One is obliged to surrender to the manner of Gertrude Stein and say: to praise folly is fooling, but if Folly is foolish and Folly is praising folly, then the foolish is fooling — that is, wisdom is being praised. Yet, if the unwise is praising wisdom, it is folly to do so, and wisdom to praise folly. If the reader is by now thoroughly lost, I am not surprised. Nor, for that matter, would Erasmus be; for it is in just this way that he intended to confuse his reader. The simplest statement of his strategy — that Folly praises folly — propounds an insoluble dilemma of permanent uncertainty similar to the famous statement of St. Paul that Epimenides the Cretan said Cretans always lie.[2]

[2] The complex structure and effect of such ironic ambiguities have interesting and illuminating analogues in the visual arts; and insofar as the ironic mode dictates and is dependent upon a certain perspective or "point of view," it is perhaps not without significance that Erasmus develops this new type of irony at precisely the same time that Dürer and others are experimenting with the science of visual perspective. The work done by Panofsky and other art historians is indispensable for any examination of this relationship, and I should also like to refer the interested reader to the brilliant book by E. H. Gombrich, *Art and Illusion. A Study in the Psychology of Pictorial*

Erasmus' book is a mock encomium — but at the same time the mocking is mocked. I know of no other mock encomium before the *Moriae encomium* that employs this subtle device,[3] and after Erasmus only Swift successfully approximates it. Certain modern authors have at times done something analogous, and there are common dramatic devices that are often very similar, but, with the exception of Swift, no one has employed this particular strategy in quite the way Erasmus does. It would therefore seem likely that Erasmus did more than reintroduce sustained irony into European literature. He appears, in fact, to have invented a new kind of irony.

When this has been said, however, it must still be admitted that there is one particular probable inspiration, if not direct source, for the kind of irony Erasmus has created. Though we find nothing like it in other mock encomia, we do find something very similar in the thought of the most prominent pagan in Erasmus' hagiarchy, Socrates. There is a passage in the *Apology*, which will be examined in greater detail when we consider Rabelais, that comes astonishingly close to the technique of the *Encomium*: this is the passage about the oracle at Delphi, where Socrates claims he is the wisest of men because he knows that he is ignorant. It is not surprising that Stultitia herself gives evidence of having read this Platonic work and recalls this specific passage.[4] At one point in her eulogy, Stultitia observes that what she is saying may at first sight seem foolish or absurd, and yet it is really profoundly true.[5] Few single sentences in the *Encomium* demonstrate more clearly the puzzle of Chinese boxes that Erasmian irony contains. Stultitia says that what seem to be her absurdities are actually truths. Yet, because Stultitia says it, it may not be so, since the truth of Stultitia may be foolishness. But in that case, the foolishness of Stultitia ought to be truth; and perhaps what Erasmus is saying is: "What at first sight may seem true is really absurd." How can we tell which he means? The answer is that he means neither one nor

---

Representation (New York, 1960). Gombrich's third section, "The Beholder's Share" (pp. 181–287), offers particularly suggestive analogies to Erasmus' irony.

[3] For an ample collection of these, see Caspar Dornavius, ed., *Amphitheatrum Sapientiae Socraticae Joco-seriae, hoc est, Encomia et Commentaria Autorum, qua veterum, qua recentiorum prope omnium: quibus Res, aut pro vilibus vulgo aut damnosis habitae, Styli Patrocinio vindicantur, exornantur . . .* (Hanover, 1619).

[4] Plato, *Apologia Socratis*, 21A–22E. Cf. ME 38.

[5] ME 64: "Rem dicam prima fronte stultam fortassis atque absurdam, sed tamen unam multo verissimam."

the other, but both, and more than both. Once cannot reduce Erasmian irony, any more than one can Socratic irony, to a simple formula; even the complex statement of the mechanics of this irony two paragraphs above is a dangerous oversimplification. Folly is foolish and Folly is wise, but the head of Janus is greater than both of his faces. One might, indeed, propound as a general theory the fact that the highest tropes operate on a formula of one plus one equals three. Empson has demonstrated this to be true of ambiguity, and students of the drama know that the meaning of a play is greater than the sum of the "meanings" of the characters. So, in the same way, the greatest works of art (as Socrates seems to suggest at the end of the *Symposium*) incorporate both the comic and the tragic visions but inhabit a higher sphere than either. If Dorp, Erasmus' first critic, misread the *Encomium* by taking every statement literally, later critics have often misread it as badly by taking every statement for its opposite. Either position tends to miss the point; and we cannot really understand the *Encomium* until we see the truth and realize the implications of a recent critic's observation that in the *Praise of Folly*, irony "does more than affect the meaning. There theme and tone blend: the irony *becomes* the meaning." [6]

That Erasmus should have written his most famous book in this manner should not be surprising. The man who attacked both the Church and the Church's attacker at the same time, who urged that Luther be protected by the princes but refused to side with Luther, who placed Socrates in the same order of the blessed with St. Paul, obviously conceived that truth was rarely simple. His biographer Huizinga has emphasized:

If Erasmus so often hovers over the borderline between earnestness and mockery, if he hardly ever gives an incisive conclusion, it is not only due to cautiousness, and fear to commit himself. Everywhere he sees the shadings, the blending of the meaning of words. The terms of things are no longer to him, as to the man of the Middle Ages, as crystals mounted in gold, or as stars in the firmament. "I like assertions so little that I would easily take sides with the sceptics wherever it is allowed by the inviolable authority of Holy Scripture and the decrees of the Church." "What is exempt from error?" [7]

[6] C. R. Thompson, tr., *Ten Colloquies of Erasmus* (New York, 1957), p. xxii.
[7] J. Huizinga, *Erasmus of Rotterdam*, tr. F. Hopman (London, 1952), p. 116.

Georges Duhamel signalizes this same quality in Erasmus when he writes, "I would readily call him 'the king of *but*.' "[8] Surely such apparent vacillation is rather a quality of the maturest minds: the ability to see both sides of a question implies a particularly high order of wisdom.[9] Yet the tragedy of Erasmus' life lay exactly here, in this quality of mind that was incomprehensible to his contemporaries. One would not, of course, have expected comprehension, much less toleration, of Erasmus' position from either Luther at one extreme or the monks of Spain at the other; but even his friend Dürer one day entered in his journal the poignant cry, "O Erasmus roterodamus, wo willst du bleiben?"[10] The Luthers could assert, "Hier stehe ich!" but Erasmus, had he heard Dürer's question, could only have answered, "Here *I* stand — but also here, and here, and here." So, too, his mouthpiece Stultitia is ambiguously vacillatory, unsure even of what is folly and what is wisdom: "I wyst there was none of you all so wyse, or rather so foolysshe, naie wyse sooner, as wolde be of any other opinion."[11] The concepts are confused and blurred, until we cannot tell them apart. Even Listrius loses his customary confidence in interpreting this particular sentence.[12] Yet whatever conclusion we come to, the sentence still seems to say that to make a mistake is to be wise. But then, of course, this is said by Stultitia, a fool. And so we find ourselves once again lost in the labyrinth.

The substitution by the Renaissance humanists of rhetorical for syllogistic argumentation is a phenomenon which has often been

[8] Georges Duhamel, *Deux Patrons* (Paris, 1937), p. 33. H. R. Trevor-Roper has more recently given a sensitive appreciation of just this quality of equipollence in Erasmus' mind, in *Historical Essays* (London, 1957), pp. 35–60.

[9] Cf. Whitehead's interesting remark: "Now what, *exactly*, did Plato mean? He was at pains *never* to mean anything exactly. He gave every side of a question its due. I have often done the same, advancing some aspect which I thought deserved attention, and then in some later work, presenting its opposite. In consequence I am accused of inconsistency and self-contradiction." *Dialogues of Alfred North Whitehead as Recorded by Lucien Price* (New York, Mentor Books, 1956), p. 247.

[10] *Dürers Schriftlicher Nachlass auf Grund der Originalhandschriften und Theilweise neu entdeckter alter Abschriften*, ed. K. Lange and F. Fuhse (Halle am Salle, 1893), p. 164.

[11] ME 16: "Equidem sciebam, neminem vestrum ita sapere, vel desipere magis, imo sapere potius, ut in hac esset sententia."

[12] LB IV.412F: "Quanto cum decoro personae, variat correctionem? Porro quod aliis est desipere, id est Stultitiae, sapere."

attested to. It is enough merely to observe here that Stultitia's role
as orator and her claim that oratory is the least mendacious mirror
of the mind are indicative of her Erasmianism; indeed, her very phrase
(*oratio, minime mendax animi speculum*) is stolen from Erasmus'
Apophthegmata, where he derives the idea from Socrates via Xenophon.[13] Accordingly, when she steps up to the pulpit, Stultitia launches
into an oration which is classical in form, and no point is more labored
by her at the beginning of her speech than that she is *not* going to
give a scholastic dissertation. Hoyt Hudson demonstrated that the
form of her speech adheres closely to the paradigm of oratorical
structure expounded by Quintilian,[14] although, as we shall see, it is
even closer to Greek models for encomia than to Roman models for
public addresses. Accepting for the moment, however, the Quintilian
paradigm, we can observe how Stultitia's speech begins with an
exordium, moves through a narration and partition to the confirmation
(which comprises the main body of the speech), and ends with the
traditional peroration. In a typical gesture, Stultitia herself mocks the
same form later in her speech when she attacks the sermons of the
monks. Equally typical of her point of view are her substitution of
an anti-partition for the partition and her sarcastic attacks on those
who sprinkle such orations with Greek tags, a device which she
herself will employ throughout her encomium, even the Greek title
of which is also exposed to her ridicule.[15]

Discounting the partition, which is devoted to her refusal to give
a partition, the exordium and narration comprise an introduction. In
it she introduces the main themes that will inform the rest of the
work. She begins by describing herself, and it is doubtless significant
that the first thing she says — characteristically worded as a double
negative — is that she is not ignorant: *neque enim sum nescia*. The
opening sentence, in its Ciceronian length and elegance, introduces

[13] ME 6; cf. LB IV.162D (*Apophthegmata*). This idea will in turn be borrowed by
two later Erasmians, Juan Luis Vives, who expanded it in his *De Ratione Dicendi*
(*Opera* [Basle, 1555], pp. 103–5), and Ben Jonson, who Englished it out of Vives
to supply his *Timber* with the celebrated passage beginning "*Language* most shewes
a man: speake that I may see thee. It springs out of the most retired, and inmost parts
of us, and is the Image of the Parent of it, the mind. No glasse renders a mans forme,
or likenesse, so true as his speech" (Jonson, *Works*, VIII, 625).

[14] H. H. Hudson, tr., *The Praise of Folly by Desiderius Erasmus* (Princeton, 1941),
pp. 129–42.

[15] ME 108: "cum in omnium paginarum frontibus leguntur tria nomina, praesertim
peregrina . . ."

so many of the book's devices and techniques that it is worth considering in some detail.[16]

Howe so ever men commonly talke of me (as pardie I am not ignoraunt
what lewde reportes go on FÓLIE, yea even amonges those that are veriest
fooles of all) yet that I am she, I onely (I saie) who through myne influence do gladde both the Goddes and men, by this it maie appeare sufficiently: that as soone as I came forth to saie my mynd afore this your so
notable assemblie, by and by all your lokes began to clere up: unbendyng
the frounyng of your browes, & laughyng upon me with so merie a coun-
tinaunce, as by my trouth me semeth evin, that all ye (whom I see here
present) doe fare as if ye were well whitled, and thoroughly moysted
with the *Nectar* wine of the Homericall Goddes, not without a porcion
of the juyce of that mervaillous herbe *Nepenthes*, whiche hath force to
put sadnesse and melancholie from the herte: Where as before ye satte all
heavie, and glommyng, as if ye had come lately from Trophonius cave . . .

It is appropriate that this speech, which is to destroy so many
illusions, should thus begin with an *utcunque loquuntur* clause which
places Folly in direct opposition to commonly accepted opinions,
implies that those opinions are foolish (*stultissimos*), and insists upon
the intelligence (*neque enim sum nescia*), uniqueness (*hanc inquam
esse unam*), popularity (*hunc coetum frequentissimum*), and superiority (*meo numine deos atque homines exhilaro*) of Stultitia herself.
It is characteristic that she proves her argument with a dubious proof
which, upon further consideration, seems to have some validity after
all — as John Donne, who recalled it, also insisted;[17] for while we

---

[16] [In all cases where a passage is quoted in English and the original text is given
in the note, the footnote numbers for such texts are given just before the English
quotation so that the original text will begin at the bottom of the same page.] ME
1–2: "Utcunque de me vulgo mortales loquuntur, neque enim sum nescia, quam male
audiat stultitia etiam apud stultissimos, tamen hanc esse, hanc inquam esse unam, quae
meo numine deos atque homines exhilaro, vel illud abunde magnum est argumentum,
quod simulatque in hunc coetum frequentissimum dictura prodii, sic repente omnium
vultus nova quadam atque insolita hilaritate enituerunt, sic subito frontem expor-
rexistis, sic laeto quodam et amabili applausistis risu, ut mihi profecto quotquot
undique praesentes intueor, pariter deorum Homericorum nectare, non sine nepenthe
temulenti esse videamini, cum antehac tristes ac solliciti sederitis, perinde quasi nuper
e Trophonii specu reversi."
[17] John Donne, *Paradox X:* "I always did, and shall understand that *Adage;*
              per risum multum possis cognoscere stultum,
That by much *laughing* thou maist know there is a *fool*, not that the *laughers* are
fools, but that among them there is some *fool*, at whom *wise men* laugh: which
moved *Erasmus* to put this as his first *Argument* in the mouth of his *Folly*, that
she made Beholders laugh; for *fools* are the most laughed at, and laugh the least
themselves of any." *The Complete Poetry and Selected Prose of John Donne,*
ed. Charles M. Coffin (New York, Modern Library, 1952), pp. 286–7.

may question *amabili* (they are, obviously, laughing at her, not with her), we cannot question *risu* (they *are* laughing). It is typical that in one sentence she should employ a quotation from a Latin playwright (Terence), a Greek poet (Homer), and even one from Erasmus' own *Adagia*.[18] It is, finally, indicative of the message she is to propound that she should, at the very outset of her speech, take it for granted that gaiety and drunkenness are to be extolled and that sadness and the melancholy effects of religion (the Delphic oracle of Zeus Trophonius) should be deplored.

With the quasi-Lucretian description of spring in the next sentence, Stultitia introduces the images of sunshine, vernality, and pleasure with which she is repeatedly to characterize herself in her encomium. She then proceeds to announce that it is her pleasure to play the sophist for a while — not, she insists, the pedantic kind of sophist who is nowadays the bane of schoolboys, but that ancient kind who took the name Sophist to avoid the infamous name Wise.[19] Though Listrius gives his customary explanation of this remark by ascribing it to the *decorum personae*, we recognize the usual method in Stultitia's madness. Similarly when, several sentences later, she calls herself the true bestower of all good things, we may recall that in the *Enchiridion* Erasmus had applied an almost identical epithet, from the apochryphal *Wisdom of Solomon*, to "the wisdom of Christ which the world thinks folly." [20] Stultitia then explains that she is to praise herself in the speech she will make, and she takes a swipe at those wise ones (*sapientes istos*) who claim it is foolish for a person to praise himself. Even if it is, she asks wittily, what could be more in character (*modo decorum*)?

Following the traditional Quintilian order, Stultitia then proceeds to the partition. In the land of medieval oratory, this particular plot of ground was reserved especially for the encampment of the Schoolmen; the *genius loci* was Petrus Hispanus, the tourneys held there were combats by choplogic. All that the humanist spirit hated most

---

[18] See LB II.316E; Homer, *Odyssey*, IV.220-1; and LB II.292F–294B.

[19] ME 3: "Lubitum est enim paulisper apud vos Sophistam agere non quidem hujus generis, quod hodie nugas quasdam anxias inculcat pueris, ac plusquam muliebrem rixandi pertinaciam tradit, sed veteres illos imitabor, qui, quo infamem Sophorum appellationem vitarent, *Sophistae* vocari maluerunt."

[20] E 40: "De Christi vero sapientia, quam mundus stultitiam putat, ita legis: *Venerunt autem mihi pariter omnia bona cum illa et innumerabilis honestas per manus illius*" [*Sap.* 7.11].

seemed to be centered here in *divisiones* and *definitiones*, and it was the partition that was most commonly attacked or avoided in humanist oratory.[21] Stultitia's scornful passing nod at the partition may be quoted in full.[22]

> But at my hand, ye shall heare an unadvised, and sodeine tale tolde, thoughe so muche perhaps the truer, Whiche I woulde not ye shoulde thynke were saied of me for a colour, to advaunce therby the rypenesse of my witte, as commonly these learned men do. Who puttyng foorthe (as ye knowe) some boke more than whole .xxx. wynters had in cullyng, ye and that sometymes none of their owne doyng, will sweare yet, that they made it but for a recreacion of theyr graver studies, or rather as fast as penne coulde renne. For truly it hath ever best lyked me to speake streight what so ever laie on my tongues ende. But this, to the ende ye loke not for it, I doe warne ye of afore hande, that I in no wyse will, accordyng to these common Sophisters and Rhetoriciens maner, go about to shew by diffinicion what I am, and muche lesse use any division: In as muche as I holde bothe the one, and the other for unluckie tokens, either to comprehende hir under a certaine ende, or limite, whose influence stretcheth so universally, orels to divide hir, in whose observaunce all men dooe so wholly consent. And yet I can not tell to what purpose it shoulde serve, to represent a certaine shadow, or image of my selfe, where as presently ye maie discerne me with your eies. For I am here (as ye see) the distributrix and dealer of all felicitee, named Μωρία in Greeke, in Latine *Stultitia*, in Englishe Folie.

Stultitia here insists upon the spontaneous and unlabored quality of her oration, much as Erasmus had insisted upon those same qualities in his book. Indeed, she pokes fun at the very excuses Erasmus had used in the epistle dedicatory to More and was to use again in the letter to Dorp: "tamen triduo sibi quasi per lusum scriptam." What

---

[21] For all of this, one may now consult Father Ong's monumental treatise on Ramus; for the humanist attack on Peter of Spain, see esp. ch. 4. Walter J. Ong, *Ramus, Method and the Decay of Dialogue* (Cambridge, Mass., 1958).

[22] ME 5–6: "A me extemporariam quidem illam et illaboratam, sed tanto veriorem audietis orationem. Id quod nolim existimetis ad ingenii ostentationem esse confictum, quemadmodum vulgus Oratorum facit. Nam ii, sicuti nostis, cum orationem totis triginta annis elaboratam, nonnunquam et alienam proferunt, tamen triduo sibi quasi per lusum scriptam, aut etiam dictatam esse dejerant. Mihi porro semper gratissimum fuit, ὅττι κεν ἐπὶ γλῶτταν ἔλθοι, dicere. At ne quis jam a nobis exspectet, ut juxta vulgarium istorum Rhetorum consuetudinem me ipsam finitione explicem; porro ut dividam, multo minus. Nam utrumque ominis est inauspicati, vel fine circumscribere eam, cuius numen tam late pateat, vel secare, in cuius cultum omne rerum genus ita consentiat. Tametsi quorsum tandem attinet mei velut umbram atque imaginem finitione repraesentare, cum ipsam me coram praesentes praesentem oculis intueamini? Sum etenim uti videtis, vera illa largitrix ἐάων quam Latini STULTITIAM, Graeci ΜΩΡΊΑΝ appellant."

was an excuse from Erasmus, however, becomes a militant defense from Stultitia. At pains throughout this brief partition to insist that spontaneity is truth, she utters whatever enters her head and draws attention to what she had earlier called "the mere sight of me" (*solo statim aspectu*) rather than to any representation of herself. The function of this argument is the same as that of the epistle dedicatory: it obviates a riposte from the Schoolmen by refusing to compete on their grounds. It is all a game, and one can hardly deem the work serious enough to call for an answer. At the same time, there is a more positive aspect to this argument, for Stultitia is also claiming a certain value in naturalness, a certain truth in spontaneity.

Her next argument is akin to this. What is the point, she asks, of my even speaking, when you can see me for yourselves and my appearance is so unmistakable? "As if some one contendyng that I were Minerva, or Sophia, myght not straight with my onely loke be confuted . . . For in me (ye must thynke) is no place for settyng of colours [cosmetics], as I can not saie one thyng, and thynke an other." [23] Cosmetics (*fuci*) are as offensive to her as they are to Hamlet or Dean Swift or almost any of the great satirists. What is more, she pointedly implies that they are the property of Wisdom, as this world knows it. The suppositions, ampliations, restrictions, and appellations that we normally find in the partition are the cosmetics of the Schoolmen, and they are, as More wrote to Martin Dorp, not only inept but false. [24] The scholars, the Schoolmen, are said to be wise, but they are really hypocrites and *môrotatoi*, most foolish. May we not indeed, Stultitia asks, call them *môrosophoi*? — a word that Chaloner was to render for all time as "foolelosophers." Thus Stultitia uses a partition to refuse to deliver a partition, and more telling than her revelation of the hypocrisy of the Schoolmen is her demonstration of their futility. How, she asks, can you force into the bounds of a definition what is universal? How can you divide what is integral? She is speaking, of course, of the cult of folly. But — and the implica-

[23] ME 6: "aut quasi si quis me Minervam aut Sophiam esse contendat, non statim solo possit obtutu coargui, etiam si nulla accedat oratio, minime mendax animi speculum. Nullus apud me fucis locus, nec aliud fronte simulo, aliud in pectore premo."

[24] *The Correspondence of Sir Thomas More*, ed. E. F. Rogers (Princeton, 1947), p. 38: "in suppositionibus quas vocant in ampliationibus, restrictionibus, appellationibus, et vbi non quam ineptas, quam etiam falsas praeceptiunculas habet . . ." Cited in translation in Ong, *Ramus*, pp. 58–9.

tion is unmistakable — she might just as well be speaking of the *cultus Christi*. It is the more devastating that she should attack the Schoolmen with their own favorite weapon, the partition, since by rejecting that particular oratorical device she has rejected the very basis of all their endeavors.

It is not only the Schoolmen who find themselves under her attack, however. She makes equal fun of the "nostri temporis rhetores," the humanist scholars. In doing so, she ridicules by implication Erasmus himself. "I have thought good to borowe," she says of her coinage *môrosophoi*, "a littell of the Rhetoriciens of these daies, who plainely thynke theim selves demygodes, if . . . thei can shew two tongues." It is, she adds in one of her wittiest asides, a distinction they share with the horseleech.[25] Now, of all Erasmus' gestures, none is more human or more beguiling than that he places himself in the Ship of Fools as one of the passengers. Folly is as universal in this world as lying was among the Cretans; the author of a tract on folly is no more exempt than Epimenides. So Stultitia makes fun of Erasmus' excuses and his knowledge of Greek, and later, when she is attacking the cult of saints, she will make an equivocal attack as well on the worship of a saint named Erasmus (ME 78). Similarly, in the *Cyclops* colloquy, Polyphemus argues that the world must be nearing its end because evil and corruption are so widespread: "people whore, buy, sell, pawn, engage in usury, build; kings make war, priests study to make money, theologians make syllogisms, monks run up and down the world, the populace is in tumult, Erasmus is writing colloquies: there is no end to the evils that beset us."[26] If Stultitia extends her irony to include Erasmus, however, she also extends it to include, finally, herself as well. She may excuse her use of Greek terms at this juncture by claiming that she does it to make fun of the bilinguists; but she continues to employ the device throughout the rest of her

[25] ME 7–8: "Visum est enim hac quoque parte nostri temporis rhetores imitari, qui plane Deos esse sese credunt, si hirudinum ritu bilingues appareant, ac praeclarum facinus esse ducunt, latinis orationibus subinde graeculas aliquot voculas, velut emblemata intertexere, etiamsi nunc non erat his locus."

[26] LB I.883D–883E: "Quoniam, inquiunt, idem nunc faciunt homines quod faciebant imminente diluvio, epulantur, potant, commessantur, ducunt, nubunt, scortantur, emunt, vendunt, foenerant et foenerantur, aedificant: Reges belligerantur, Sacerdotes student augendis censibus, Theologi nectunt syllogismos, Monachi per orbem cursitant, populus tumultuatur, Erasmus scribit colloquia: denique nihil malorum abest, fames, sitis, latrocinia, bellum, pestilentia, seditio, rerum bonarum inopia."

speech, in precisely the manner of those who, as she says, weave into their Latin orations some little Greek words as ornaments, even though there is no place for them.[27]

The next section of Stultitia's oration, in which she discusses her birth, education, and companions, can be located only with difficulty in the Quintilian schema. Hudson assigns it to the commencement of the confirmation, yet it seems more like an introduction to the confirmation than an integral part of it. Hence, in Leonard Dean's translation,[28] it comes as a conclusion to what Hudson would call the narration-partition section. The difficulty arises from the fact that such a genealogy does not belong to an oration generally, but rather to an encomium specifically. In the paradigm for encomia established by T. C. Burgess on the basis of Menander, Aphthonius, Nicolaus Sophista, and others,[29] we find that the initial parts of an encomium are lumped together under the general heading *prooimion*, but that this is followed by a special section entitled *genos* or, by Anaximenes, *genealogia*. Under this genealogical section, there are generally four subsections: *ethnos*, the race whence the person praised has sprung; *patris*, his country; *progonoi*, his ancestors; and *pateres*, his parents. To these four may be added, if appropriate, a *genesis*, which refers to any special or unusual circumstances regarding the birth. Accordingly, Stultitia's discussion of her birth follows traditional precedent.

Her ethnos, progonoi, and pateres she describes negatively: "My father therfore was neyther Chaos, nor Orcus, nor Saturnus, nor any other of that olde and rustie race of Gods." Equally negative is the description of her genesis: she was not begotten out of her father's head, like Minerva, nor did he beget her in wedlock, but rather, as Homer says, "mingled in love." Therefore, the unusual thing about her birth is that it was not unusual. It was, indeed, so natural that, like Erasmus' own birth, it was not even legitimate. The father in whom she rejoices was Plutus, "the onely syre of Gods and men," author of *le monde renversé*. But lest the reader recall his Aristophanes, Stultitia quickly explains that her father was not the Aristophanic Plutus, worn-out and weak-eyed, but Plutus when he was young and

---

[27] See note 25.

[28] Leonard F. Dean, tr., *The Praise of Folly, by Desiderius Erasmus* (New York, 1949).

[29] T. C. Burgess, "Epideictic Literature," *University of Chicago Studies in Classical Philology*, III (1902), 89–261; see esp. pp. 157–66.

vigorous, "full of hote bloudde, but muche fuller of *Nectar* drinke."
This Plutus of whom Stultitia speaks with such filial devotion is the
god of wealth — wealth that upsets the world and governs wars,
marriages, and all human activities. But we must remember that this
is also Plutus the god of plenty, companion to Demeter, who is
responsible for the abundance of crops, good harvests, and the full
breadbasket that Hesychius calls *euplouton*.

Stultitia's mother was Neotês, Youth, by far the fairest and gayest
of the nymphs. Her *patris*, the mention of which provides one of
those rhetorical occasions for the description of a *locus amoenus* which
Curtius has traced through medieval literature,[30] was in the Fortunate
Isles themselves,[31]

where all thynges grow ["]unsowed and untilled["]. In whiche iles
neither labour, nor age, nor any maner sickenesse reigneth, nor in the
fields there dooe either Nettles, Thistles, Mallowes, Brambles, Cockle, or
suche lyke bagage grow, but in steede thereof Gyfloures, Roses, Lilies,
Basile, Violettes, and suche swete smellyng herbes, as whilom grew in
Adonis gardeins, dooe on all sides satisfie bothe the sente, and the sight.

These gardens that, as Shakespeare describes them, "one day bloom'd,
and fruitful were the next" and that served Milton as a kind of
prototype for Eden were a land that almost every Renaissance poet
was to rediscover. The original source for these isles is, of course,
the description of the land of the Cyclopes in the *Odyssey*, but one
wonders if Spenser may not have remembered Stultitia's own description of her fatherland, where nature is triumphant and luxuriant and
where "Ne needs there Gardiner to set, or sow,/To plant or prune"
(*F.Q.*, III.vi.xxxiv).

The rogues' gallery of attendants and companions that Stultitia
introduces after her description of the Fortunate Isles comes closest
to the category in the epideictic paradigm termed *anatrophê*, that
section of an encomiastic speech which deals with the special circumstances of the subject's youth. One might expect to find an extensive
and hilarious treatment of this, on the order of that which we find,

[30] Curtius, *European Literature*, pp. 183–202.
[31] ME 11: "ubi ἄσπαρτα καὶ ἀνήροτα omnia proveniunt. In quibus neque labor, neque
senium, neque morbus est ullus, nec usquam in agris asphodelus, malva, squilla, lupi-
numve, aut faba, aut aliud hoc genus nugarum conspicitur. Sed passim oculis, simul-
que naribus adblandiuntur moly, panace, nepenthes, amaracus, ambrosia, lotus, rosa,
viola, hyacinthus, Adonidis hortuli."

for example, in *Pantagruel;* but Stultitia, always more interested in the present than in the past and, indeed, still in that time of youth which would properly form part of the anatrophê, merely gives a list of her nurses (Drunkenness and Ignorance) and her companions (Self-Love, Flattery, Forgetfulness, Laziness, Pleasure, Madness, Sensuality, Intemperance, and Sound Sleep). If they sound more like a gang of juvenile delinquents than fit playmates for a goddess, that of course is intentional. Foolery and roguery go hand in hand, and it is only to be expected that the greatest fool of all should travel in the company of the deadly sins, now expanded from seven to eleven. Such "unrestrained loose companions," as Henry IV once described a similar band of rogues, call up stock antipathetic responses in our minds; and just as we ridicule the Fool, so we censure the rogues that attend her. On the other hand, we have already seen that Stultitia may not be as foolish as we may have expected, and the second of her nurses, Ignorance, has already been confused with Wisdom. The careful reader may therefore be properly skeptical of his response to this simple list of vices. By the time Stultitia has finished her speech, they, like everything else, will have been demonstrated to be something other than what they seem. It is too early in the speech for Stultitia to reveal the true nature of her companions here, for we would not believe her; but as they are swept along with her in the flood of rhetoric to come, they imperceptibly suffer a sea-change. With the exception of Philautia, they are hardly mentioned again; yet when Stultitia has descended from the pulpit, when the applause has died down and we think back to the companions she has had, we are suddenly aware that she has spent her youth not among vices, but virtues.

With this catalogue of companions, Stultitia finishes her introduction and moves into the central part of her speech, which may be divided into three sections roughly corresponding to Burgess' Aphthonian categories of *praxeis, synkrisis,* and *epilogos.* The first, the praxeis, concerns the achievements and attributes of Stultitia, or what Dean has labeled "The Powers and Pleasures of Folly." The second, which is more implicitly than explicitly a synkrisis, is an account of "The Followers of Folly." And the end of the speech, the epilogos, is the celebrated description of the "Christian Fool." Thus, the following outline may be set up to demonstrate the adherence of the

Encomium to the Aphthonian encomiastic scheme as well as to the Quintilian oratorical paradigm.

APHTHONIUS	ERASMUS	QUINTILIAN
	Folly's greeting	exordium
prooimion	Folly will praise herself extemporaneously	narration
	Folly will not deliver a partition	partition
genos	Folly's birth	
anatrophê	Folly's companions	
praxeis	The powers and pleasures of Folly	confirmation
synkrisis	The followers of Folly	
	The Christian Fool	
epilogos	Folly will not deliver a peroration	peroration

Although such a schematization is essentially of interest only to the specialist in epideictic literature, it does at least demonstrate the position that the *Moriae encomium* occupies in this particular tradition, a tradition that was most familiar to Erasmus as it manifested itself in Lucian. In emphasizing the Greek rather than the Latin prototype for Stultitia's speech, I have not wished to detract from Hudson's contribution to our understanding of the structure of this oration; what is important above all is to recognize, as he did, that Erasmus' work is classical in nature. But the Aphthonian paradigm, in exposing the component parts of what Quintilian calls the confirmation, does reveal the further important fact that it is the praxeis, not the synkrisis, that is the central section of Stultitia's speech. The praxeis, "The Powers and Pleasures of Folly," occupies not only the most predominant position, but something close to half of the length of the entire speech: in an edition of eighty-nine pages, the synkrisis takes up twenty-seven pages, whereas the praxeis takes up thirty-nine, or half again as many. This is highly significant for any understanding of the *Encomium*. When the average reader has remembered this book, he has been most likely to remember the synkrisis, the attacks on the clergy, the princes, the papacy, and other estates. This is the section most discussed by commentators, just as it was the section most notorious, because most scandalous, in Erasmus' own day. But if Erasmus' little book has been largely misunderstood, one of the main reasons is that too much attention has been focused upon his description of Stultitia's followers and not enough on Stultitia herself and what she stands for. To be sure, the synkrisis is easier to understand than the praxeis: the synkrisis is constructed out of a simple satire that is mere invective, whereas the subtler ironies of the praxeis are those of the introductory parts of the *Encomium*, many-faceted and often self-contradictory. One senses that the attack on the monks and princes was written in a different spirit, as well as in a different style and with a cruder satire, and it may even be that this was the part Erasmus added, almost as an afterthought, after his friends in Chelsea had urged him to continue the work he read to them.[32]

In any event, if the pages to follow seem to slight the description of Stultitia's followers and to concentrate more upon the description of Stultitia herself, the reason is simply that the former is better known and more easily understood, whereas the latter is not only more elusive but contains the central and most original part of Erasmus' argument. The figure of the Fool dominates her speech; the nature of her folly lies at the heart of her message. The jesting equivalent of the serious philosophy expounded in the *Enchiridion militis christiani* — which is what Erasmus claimed the *Encomium* was[33] — is to be found not so much in the plangent laments and angry denunciations of the folly of the sixteenth-century world as in the lambent ironies and laughing praise with which Stultitia describes her own true nature.

[32] EE II.94: "Operis incoepti gustum amiculis aliquot exhibui, quo iucundior esset risus cum pluribus communis. Quibus cum vehementer placuisset, instituerunt vti pergerem. Obsecutus sum . . ."

[33] EE II.93: "Nec aliud omnino sectauimus in Moria quam quod in caeteris lucubrationibus, tametsi via diuersa. In Enchiridio simpliciter Christianae vitae formam tradidimus. In libello De principis institutione palam admonemus quibus rebus principem oporteat esse instructum. In Panegyrico sub laudis praetextu hoc ipsum tamen agimus oblique quod illic egimus aperta fronte. Nec aliud agitur in Moria sub specie lusus quam actum est in Enchiridio. Admonere voluimus, non mordere, prodesse, non laedere; consulere moribus hominum, non officere."

4

THE TRANSVALUATION
OF VALUES: TECHNIQUE

⚜⚜⚜⚜⚜⚜⚜⚜⚜⚜⚜⚜⚜⚜⚜⚜⚜⚜⚜⚜⚜⚜⚜⚜⚜⚜⚜⚜

STULTITIA's encomium is outrageous. The curses of mankind she boasts of as her gifts; the frailties and failings of humanity she extols as desired achievements; and she lovingly contemplates the vices of her companions as though they were virtues. Laughing and jeering, coaxing and bullying, she dances us into a Land of Cockayne, a world of luxury and drunkenness, idleness and irresponsibility. Yet the farther we go, the graver the dance-step becomes. The voice, as we listen to it chattering on, imperceptibly modulates into tones of high seriousness and moral purpose. And at moments we even perceive tears behind all that laughter. The Land of Cockayne, when we get there, proves not to be the anticipated utopia of indolent illusion, but a religious world of terrible sincerity. How does she manage it? It is not merely that, as Duke Senior said of Touchstone, she uses her folly as a stalking-horse and under the presentation of that shoots her wit. Erasmus' irony does not work that way. What we initially tend to dismiss as a stalking-horse turns out to be a Trojan horse instead: a fowler does not lurk somewhere underneath; an armed adversary hides within.

The *Encomium*, as Erasmus never tired of explaining, is a game. Yet as we watch this game being played and listen to Stultitia push her joke so far that she jokes herself into seriousness, we become aware of how well it illustrates Huizinga's observation that "play can very well include seriousness." [1] In his profound study of the element of *lusus* in culture, he almost seems to have given a description of what happens in the *Encomium*: "Any game can at any time wholly run away with the players. The contrast between play and seriousness is always fluid. The inferiority of play is continually being offset by the corresponding superiority of its seriousness. Play turns to seriousness and seriousness to play. Play may rise to heights of beauty and sublimity that leave seriousness far beneath." [2]

William Blake believed that if the fool were to persist in his folly he would become wise,[3] and we hear Stultitia achieve wisdom in just that way. At the beginning, however, her folly is — or appears to be — absolute. She speaks in eulogy of foolish youth as opposed to wise age, of levity as opposed to gravity, of drunkenness and intemperance as opposed to sobriety and restraint. She advocates rashness and iconoclasm and license; she condemns prudence and reverence and discipline. If Self-Love is her closest companion, modesty is totally alien to her. As her speech progresses, illusion and deception triumph over reality and truth, and reason and Stoic honor are rejected for passion and Epicurean pleasure. It is as though the pursued and retreating vices in Mantegna's famous allegory in the Louvre had suddenly turned and won the field after all, routing the forces of Minerva. Yet it is more than a defeat that takes place; for, under the beguiling spell of Stultitia's rhetoric, a kind of metamorphosis has occurred. A later artist, Paul Klee, has painted a portrait of "Mephisto als Pallas," and it is that kind of transformation that Stultitia effects where, just as the playing turns into high seriousness, so what seems wise turns out to be evil and what had seemed evil becomes wisdom. Thus, in the course of her speech, rashness becomes prudence, passion becomes reason; the illusion, finally, is the reality, and ignorance is wisdom.

Such a process of transmutation has been described by Edgar Wind, who properly sees it as characteristic of certain trends of thought throughout the sixteenth century, as a "transvaluation of values." [4] Nietzsche's phrase is a convenient one to use in this connection, so long as we recognize that by *Umwertung aller Werte* he intended to

---

[1] Huizinga, *Homo Ludens*, p. 45.
[2] Huizinga, *Homo Ludens*, p. 8.
[3] William Blake, *The Marriage of Heaven and Hell*, "Proverbs of Hell."
[4] Edgar Wind, *Pagan Mysteries in the Renaissance* (New Haven, 1958), p. 69.

suggest something more drastically revolutionary and destructive than the ironic inversion of values which Stultitia performs. To be sure, there have always been thinking men who have questioned the accepted values of society; they are usually the martyrs of that society, and Socrates and Jesus are their prototypes. Skepticism, if it is not sterile, leads to revaluation, and out of the skepticism of the sixteenth century such trends emerged with sufficient predominance for us to speak of a movement.[5] The old accepted terms and standards and values came to be re-examined, revaluated, and redefined. Wisdom, honor, virtue — those concepts of the Stoics upon which humanism since Petrarch had built its foundations — were questioned and doubted.

Whitehead was fond of claiming that Western thought was a series of footnotes to Plato, and one may add as a corollary to this the observation that Western ethics is largely a series of footsteps after Zeno. For, from a certain point of view, our Western heritage may be seen as one of Stoicism, where *nomos* — custom, law, convention — informs all the aspirations and judgments of man. Yet at other moments in history an Epicurean standard of *physis* — nature — has been brought forth as a corrective to excessive Stoicism. The study of the transvaluation of values in the sixteenth century, when an increasing number of men were turning to Lucretius rather than to Cicero for their answers, is, in some senses, a study of the revival of Epicureanism — or pseudo-Epicureanism, as it may often more properly be labeled. A fuller examination of this trend must be deferred until the next chapter when its relationship to Erasmus will become more apparent, but it must be mentioned now as an integral part of Stultitia's device of turning values upside down.

Wind has given a brief description of this process and hinted at its relation to neo-Epicureanism:

So much has been written in recent years on the continuation of the Middle Ages into the Renaissance, and of mediaeval modes of thought in

[5] The late Theodore Spencer coined the phrase "counter-Renaissance" to characterize some aspects of this movement. The phrase, though not wholly a happy one, would perhaps be convenient had its coinage not been somewhat debased by the confusing and prodigal use of it in Hiram Haydn, *The Counter-Renaissance* (New York, 1950). The defects of this book have often been pointed out (most notably by P. O. Kristeller in *JHI, III* [1951], 468–72), but it must also be said that it remains a valuable book, not only for the many useful quotations it has assembled, but also because it helps to define the broad outlines of the major trends of skepticism in the late Renaissance.

Renaissance Platonism, that we are apt to underestimate the decisive "trans-valuation of values" which Ficino and some of his Florentine friends effected in the theory of morals. A noble form of irascibility, for instance, remained a contradiction in terms as long as *ira* was classed irrevocably as a deadly sin. Yet under the influence of Seneca's *De ira*, although the mediaeval classification continued, a "noble rage" was separated off from the common vice and defended as a virtue by Florentine humanists, in particular by Bruni, Palmieri, Politian, and Landino. By a similar trans-mutation the vice of sloth, the horrid *acedia*, was distilled into noble melancholy; for although *acedia* remained a deadly sin, an Aristotelian refinement of the affliction became the privilege of inspired men. It is with these Renaissance vindications of melancholy and rage as noble passions that the cult of noble *voluptas* should be compared. Like *acedia* and *ira*, the vice of *luxuria* continued to be classed as a deadly sin, and the vulgar *voluptas*, that is, incontinence, was pictured in her image. And yet, on the authority of Plotinus, sustained in this instance by Epicurus, a noble *voluptas* was introduced as the *summum bonum* of the Neoplatonists.[6]

It is precisely this sort of transmutation that Erasmus attempts to effect in the *Encomium*. To each of the Stoic virtues an Epicurean opposite is contraposed, not in order to destroy so much as to qualify the accepted Stoic value. The device itself is as old as Socrates, and its classic formulation was given by Chamfort when he observed that, to have a just idea of things, one must take words in the opposite sense from that given them by the world.[7] One of Castiglione's courtiers suggests a similar process when he refers to "covering a vice with the name of its neighboring virtue, or a virtue with the name of its neighboring vice." [8] Stultitia herself follows Chamfort's dictum, and we are always aware that what is being attacked is not only the accepted meanings of words, but also "the world" that gives such meanings their acceptance. Yet, at the same time, it is important not to misconstrue the significance of Erasmus' gesture or to miss its subtlety. It is the gesture, always, of the "king of *but*." He is not totally against those Stoic virtues which Stultitia attacks any more than he is totally for them; nor is he unconditionally in favor of those "Epicurean" virtues just because Stultitia extols them. Thus, when Stultitia praises drunkenness, we are certainly not to think that Erasmus is advocating Bacchanalian orgies. What we are to see is

[6] Wind, *Mysteries*, pp. 69–70.
[7] Nicholas-Sébastien de Chamfort, *Oeuvres complètes* (Paris, 1824), p. 393.
[8] Baldessar Castiglione, *Il Libro del Cortegiano*, ed. V. Cian (Florence, 1947), p. 38.

that he is redefining the nature of sobriety and happiness and truth itself. He *pretends* to espouse the most outrageous Epicurean licenses in order to show the fallacies of their Stoic restraints. He does so not to advocate without qualification the former, but rather to redefine the latter.

There is no passage more illustrative of this method or more characteristic of the book than that in which Stultitia discusses the Stoic concept of prudence. It is a passage that looks forward to Falstaff at Shrewsbury, and it is so important, so illustrative, and so self-explanatory that, despite its length, it must be quoted in full.[9]

Than sir, seyng I have this chalenged unto me the praise of fortitude, and of industriousnesse, what if I claime *Prudence* also? perhaps some will saie, as soone myght I goe about to mingle fyre and water. But for all that I hope to bringe it to passe, if as hitherto you have dooen, ye vouchsave me your eares, and attentivenesse. And fyrst of all, if *Prudence* consisteth in longe practise and experience of thynges, unto whether of these maie the honour of that name better square? Either to this wyseman, who partly for shame, and partly for dastardnesse of herte, attempteth nothyng, or els that foole, whom neither shame, beyng shameles, nor perill, beyng reckeles, maie feare from provyng any thyng. A wyseman reportes hym selfe to his bokes, and there learneth naught but mere triflyng distinctions of woordes. A foole in jeopardyng, and goyng presently where thynges are to be knowne, gathereth (unles I am deceived) the perfect true prudence. Whiche Homer seemeth, notwithstandyng his blindnesse, to have seen, whan he saied thus, "A foole knoweth the thyng, that is ones dooen." For there be two stronge lettes against suche knowlage of thynges to be gathered, that is to saie, shame and dreade: shame, that casts a mist before mens myndes: and dreade, that, shewyng the perilles, discounsaileth men from ventryng any enterprises. But I Folie maie, and am wonte to wype those lettes cleane awaie. Yea, few men consider, how many ways els it availeth to bloushe at nothyng, and dare dooe every thyng. But now

---

[9] ME 46–50: "Ergo posteaquam mihi fortitudinis et industriae laudem vindicavi, quid si prudentiae quoque vindicem? Sed dixerit aliquis eadem opera ignem aquae misceas, licebit. Verum hoc quoque successurum arbitror, si vos modo quod antehac fecistis, auribus atque animis favebitis. Principio si rerum usu constat prudentia, in utrum magis competet eius cognominis honos, in sapientem, qui partim ob pudorem, partim ob animi timiditatem nihil aggreditur, an in stultum, quem neque pudor quo vacat, neque periculum, quod non perpendit, ab ulla re deterret? Sapiens ad libros Veterum confugit, atque hinc meras vocum argutias ediscit. Stultus adeundis cominusque periclitandis rebus, veram, ni fallor, prudentiam colligit. Id quod vidisse videtur Homerus, etiamsi caecus, cum ait ρεχθὲν δὲ τε νήπιος ἔγνω. Sunt enim duo praecipua ad cognitionem rerum parandam obstacula, pudor qui fumum offundit animo, et metus, qui ostenso periculo, dehortatur ab adeundis facinoribus. At his magnifice liberat Stultitia. Pauci mortales intelligunt ad quam multas alias quoque commoditates conducat, nunquam pudescere, et nihil non audere. Quod si pru-

(loe) and if ye take prudence after the rate, as whan it resteth in judgement and discourse of thynges, herken ye (I praie you) howe farre they are wyde thereof, who dooe make it their chiefest profession. For fyrst it is not unknowen, how all humaine thynges lyke the *Silenes or duble images of Alcibiades,* have two faces muche unlyke and dissemblable, that what outwardly seemed death, yet lokyng within ye shulde fynde it lyfe: and on the other side what semed life, to be death: what fayre, to be foule: what riche, beggerly: what cunnyng, rude: what strong, feable: what noble, vile: what gladsome, sadde: what happie, unlucky: what friendly, unfriendly: what healthsome, noysome. Briefely the Silene ones beyng undone and disclosed, ye shall fynde all thynges tourned into a new semblance. If these woordes to some seme spoken to clerkly, goe to, I will expounde theim more plainely. I praie you, who is he that confessith not a prince to be bothe riche, and a great lorde? but set case he hath no good qualitees of the mynde, nor with all those gooddes he hath, can be satisfied: now is he not riche, but poorer than the poorest. Than againe admit he be gevin to sundrie vices: now is he no lorde, but more subjecte than a servaunt: and after this rate maie ye skanne also the others. But this is enough for exemple. Now it maie be, ye muse what I meane hereby, but geve me leave yet a little further. If one at a solemne stage plaie, woulde take upon hym to plucke of the plaiers garmentes, whiles they were saiyng theyr partes, and so disciphre unto the lokers on, the true and native faces of eche of the plaiers, should he not (trow ye) marre all the mattier? and well deserve for a madman to be peltid out of the place with stones? ye shoulde see yet straightwaies a new transmutacion in thynges: that who before plaied the woman, shoulde than appeare to be a man: who seemed youth, should shew his hore heares: who countrefaited the kynge, shulde tourne to a rascall, and who plaied god almightie, shulde become a cobler as he was before. Yet take awaie this errour, and as soone take awaie all togethers, in as muche as the feignyng and counterfaityng is it, that so deligteth the beholders. So likewise, all this life of mortall men, what is it els, but a certain kynde of stage plaie? wheras men come foorthe dis-

---

dentiam accipere malunt eam quae rerum judicio constat, audite obsecro, quam procul absint ab hac, qui hoc nomine sese venditant. Principio constat, res omneis humanas, velut Alcibiadis Silenos, binas habere facies nimium inter sese dissimiles. Adeo ut quod prima, ut ajunt, fronte mors est, si interius inspicias, vita sit: contra quod vita, mors: quod formosum, deforme: quod opulentum, id pauperrimum: quod infame, gloriosum: quod doctum, indoctum: quod robustum, imbecille: quod generosum, ignobile: quod laetum, triste: quod prosperum, adversum: quod amicum, inimicum: quod salutare, noxium: breviter omnia repente versa reperies, si Silenum aperueris. Id si cui forte nimis philosophice dictum videtur, age pinguiore, quemadmodum dici solet, Minerva, planius faciam. Quis Regem non et opulentum, et dominum fatetur? Atqui nullis animi bonis instructus est, atqui nihil illi satis est, jam videlicet pauperrimus est. Tum animum habet plurimis addictum vitiis, jam turpiter servus est. Ad eundem modum in caeteris quoque philosophari liceret. Sed hoc exempli vice posuisse satis sit. At quorsum haec? inquiet aliquis. Audite quo rem deducamus. Si quis histrionibus in scena fabulam agentibus personas detrahere conetur,

guised one in one arraie, an other in an other, eche plaiyng his parte, till at last the maker of the plaie, or bokebearer causeth theim to avoyde the skaffolde, and yet sometyme maketh one man come in, two or three tymes, with sundrie partes and apparaile, as who before represented a kynge, beyng clothed all in purpre, havyng no more but shyfted hym selfe a little, shoulde shew hym selfe againe lyke an woobegon myser. And all this is dooen under a certaine veile or shadow, whiche taken awaie ones, the plaie can no more be plaied. Here nowe if one of these wisemen, come (I wene) from heaven, did sodeinly appeare, and saie, "howe evin this great prince, whom all men honor as their god and soveraigne, deserveth skarce to be called man, seyng like the brute beastes, he is trained by affections, and is none other than a servaunt of the basest sort, seyng willyngly he obeith so many, and so vile vices his maisters. Or than againe, would bidde some other who mourned for his fathers or friendes decease, rather to laughe, and be merie, because suche diyng to this worlde is the beginnyng of a better life, wheras this here, is but a maner death as it were. Furthermore, wolde call an other gloriyng in his armes and auncestrie, both a villaine, and a bastarde, because he is so many discentes disalied from vertue, whiche is the onely roote of true nobilitee." And in suche lyke sorte woulde raile upon all the rest. I praie you, what shulde he prevaile therby, but make men take him for frantike & distraught? For surely as nothing can be more foolisshe than wisedome out of place, so is nothyng more fonde than prudence out of season. And dooeth he not out of season (trow ye) that plieth not him selfe as the world goeth?

ac spectatoribus veras nativasque facies ostendere, nonne is fabulam omnem perverterit, dignusque habeatur, quem omnes e theatro velut lymphatum saxis ejiciant? Exorietur autem repente nova rerum species, ut qui modo mulier, nunc vir: qui modo juvenis, mox senex: qui paulo ante Rex, subito Dama: qui modo Deus, repente homunculus appareat. Verum eum errorem tollere, est fabulam omnem perturbare. Illud ipsum figmentum et fucus est, quod spectatorum oculos detinet. Porro mortalium vita omnis quid aliud est, quam fabula quaepiam, in qua alii aliis obtecti personis procedunt, aguntque suas quisque partes, donec choragus educat e proscenio? Qui saepe tamen eundem diverso cultu prodire jubet, ut qui modo regem purpuratum egerat, nunc servulum pannosum gerat. Adumbrata quidem omnia, sed haec fabula non aliter agitur. Hic si mihi sapiens aliquis coelo delapsus subito exoriatur, clamitetque hunc quem omnes ut Deum ac dominum suspiciunt, nec hominem esse, quod pecudum ritu ducatur affectibus, servum esse infimum, quod tam multis, tamque foedis dominis sponte serviat. Rursum alium, qui parentem extinctum luget, ridere jubeat, quod jam demum ille vivere coeperit, cum alioqui vita haec nihil aliud sit, quam mors quaedam. Porro alium stemmatis gloriantem, ignobilem ac nothum appellet, quod a virtute longe absit, quae sola nobilitatis sit fons, adque eundem modum de caeteris omnibus loquatur, quaeso quid is aliud egerit, nisi ut demens ac furiosus omnibus esse videatur? Ut nihil est stultius praepostera sapientia, ita perversa prudentia nihil imprudentius. Siquidem perverse facit, qui sese non accommodet rebus praesentibus, foroque nolit uti, nec saltem legis illius convivialis meminerit, ἢ πίθι, ἢ ἄπιθι, postuletque, ut fabula jam non sit fabula. Contra, vere prudentis est, cum sis mortalis, nihil ultra sortem sapere velle, cumque universa hominum multitudine vel connivere libenter, vel comiter errare. At istud ipsum, inquiunt, stultitiae est. Haud equidem inficias iverim, modo fateantur illi vicissim hoc esse, vitae fabulam agere."

nor will not take the market as it ryseth? nor at least remembre the law of quassyng, "Other drinke thy drinke, or rise, and goe thy waie?" On the other side, it is a verie wysemans part to coveite to know nothyng beyond his bands, and either as the whole multitude of other men dooe, to dissemble gladly, or to erre, and be deceived with the most. But evin this is Foly (saie thei). And in good faieth I will not muche denie it, upon condicion againe they graunt me, that to dissemble, or erre so, is the right plaiyng of the pageantes of this life.

Fools rush in where angels fear to tread. Folly does not deny it; she rushes in with them, at the head of their ranks. But the question she asks is: is not such imprudent action precisely the source of prudence? How can one learn prudence except through experience? What is considered "in the world" to be wise and sagacious prudence is, in fact, nothing more than "shame, that casts a mist before mens myndes: and dreade, that, shewing the perilles, discounsaileth men from ventryng any enterprises." The wisdom and prudence displayed by the Poloniuses of this world are vicarious at best, "mere triflyng distinctions of woordes" (*meras vocum argutias*); and St. Paul, in a passage from the first chapter of I Corinthians which Erasmus quotes in the *Enchiridion* (E 39), had warned: "For it is written, I will destroy the wisdom of the wise, and will bring to nothing the understanding of the prudent." It is the heedless, imprudent fool who, "in jeopardyng, and goyng presently where thynges are to be knowne, gathereth (unles I am deceived) the perfect true prudence." No great action can be accomplished if a man is hamstrung by prudence, if he first — as Stultitia says in an earlier passage — "enquires prudently" (*prudenter exquireret* [ME 34]) into the antecedents or consequences of that action; but after the experience of the action he will have learned true prudence.

But what of prudence of judgment? It is here that Stultitia makes her most telling points and most clearly reveals her (and Erasmus') mind to us. The image of the Silenus extends far beyond her present argument to become emblematic of her entire speech and to typify a whole way of thought — a way of thought which was, significantly, attributed by Erasmus in both the *Enchiridion* and the *Adagia* to Christ himself.[10] The source of this imagery is, of course, Alcibiades' comparison of Socrates to a grotesque figurine of a Silenus which

[10] E 70; LB II.770C–782C.

opened up to reveal the image of god inside.[11] Erasmus popularized this image in one of his longest adages, where he explains that it may symbolize either an object which has a vile and ridiculous exterior concealing an admirable interior or a man whose ugly appearance conceals a noble soul.[12] He goes on to make the comparison between the Silenus and such ancients as Diogenes, who, though he looked something like a dog, was perceived by Alexander the Great to contain something of divinity.[13] Arcane literature is the same: on the surface it may seem ridiculous or trifling, but underneath it contains divine wisdom.[14] Finally, Christ himself, whose divinity expressed itself in poverty, simplicity of heart, and humble sayings, is a kind of Silenus.[15]

When Rabelais sat down to write *Gargantua* over twenty years later, he too, recalling this adage, invoked the image of the Silenus to hint at the arcane nature of his book, and later still, when he wrote the *Tiers Livre*, he remembered the Silenus aspect of Diogenes which Erasmus had pointed out.[16] To Erasmus' parallels, Rabelais added the homely comparison between the ancient Silenus and the apothecary's box which contains healing drugs. The image became a Renaissance commonplace, but Erasmus was its source. And when, at the beginning of the next century, Bacon refers bad-mannered scholars to "that which Plato said of his master Socrates, whom he compared to the gallipots of apothecaries," implying that he got the comparison direct from Plato, he is actually mistranslating Rabelais, who got it from Erasmus.[17]

All human affairs, Stultitia maintains, are like the Sileni of Alcibiades and have two aspects, so that for any given truth the opposite may

---

[11] Plato, *Symposium*, 215a-b.

[12] LB II.770C: "quo licebit uti, vel de re, quae cum in speciem, et prima, quod adjunt, fronte vilis ac ridicula videatur, tamen interius ac propius contemplanti, sit admirabilis: vel de homine, qui habitu vultuque longe minus prae se ferat, quam in animo claudat."

[13] LB II. 771B-C: "Hujusmodi Silenus fuit Diogenes, vulgo canis habitus. Verum in hoc cane divinum quiddam animadverterat Alexander Magnus . . ."

[14] LB II.773C: "Jam habent et suos Silenos arcanae Litterae. Si consistas in superficie, ridicula nonnunquam res fit: si penetres usque ad anagogen, divinam adores sapientiam."

[15] LB II.771D ff: "An non mirificus quidam Silenus fuit Christus? . . ."

[16] R I.3–6/I.Prol. and V.5–25/III.Prol.

[17] Francis Bacon, *The Advancement of Learning* (London and New York, Everyman's Library, 1950), p. 21.

be equally true. If you open the Silenus, you will find everything suddenly reversed. The entire concept of the transvaluation of values is postulated upon this simple assumption. It finds its authorities in Socrates, who claimed that ignorance was wisdom, and in Christ, who claimed that death was life. At the same time, the image of the Silenus has another function: it bears not only the implication of paradox but the hint of concealment as well. The internal truth is hidden behind the external façade, even as the seriousness is hidden within the jesting. When Erasmus and Rabelais refer their readers to the Silenus, they are throwing out the hint that there is an esoteric meaning to what they have written. Thus the image of the Silenus succinctly expresses those two characteristics of the Renaissance employment of the mixed style of the *Spoudogeloion* that were new: whereas the Middle Ages had tended to place jest and earnest in antithesis, for the Renaissance earnestness could be both contained and concealed within jest. In defining her concept of prudence of judgment, Stultitia employs the figure of the Silenus simply to point out that prudence consists in refraining from too summary a judgment. If all human affairs do, in fact, have a bifrontal quality, it is imprudent to judge them as though they did not; true prudence consists in refraining from noting such contradictions and disparities, in pretending not to notice.

Stultitia, however, is no less two-faced than her Silenus, and, as is so often the case, it is almost impossible to determine what is the victim of the double-edged sword she swings so heftily in this passage. When she refers to the ruler who is slave to his passions, or when she speaks of death as life, we hardly know how to interpret her remarks. For surely it *is* folly to look up to a ruler who is only a slave; surely it is folly not to accept the Christian truth that the real life begins at death. And yet at the same time it is just as great a folly to tax that ruler with his slavery or to insist so much on death as life that you make life seem death. Erasmian irony is epitomized in the concluding sentences of this passage on prudence; for almost everything Stultitia says can (and should) be taken in two ways. In a certain sense it *is* perverse not to accommodate oneself to things as they are; in another sense it is folly to accept the world as it is. The fool as satirist delights in stripping off the world's masks of hypocrisy; yet in her heart of hearts she knows as well as the preacher of Ecclesiastes that the number of fools is infinite, that the mask is a part of life.

In Stultitia's analysis of the true nature of prudence, we have a paradigm of the method Erasmus generally employs to effect a transvaluation of values. A value (prudence) is transvaluated by means of praising its opposite (rashness and self-deception); the fool's gold of both is refined by the alchemy of the fool into the pure gold of a new value (true prudence based on understanding). The reader is led into this transvaluation gradually and unwittingly, as satire turns to sympathy. For the Erasmian technique is to begin with satire; and on the simplest level, this advocacy of rashness and self-deception from the mouth of a fool is nothing more than satire. Rash, irrational acts are, after all, bad: they lead to wars and crime and sin, and the wise man is doubtless the Demosthenes who runs away to live and fight another day.[18] Similarly, certain masks and hypocrisies should not be accepted without question, and Erasmus spent most of his life stripping the masks off priests and princes. Therefore, as Stultitia begins her attack on prudence we are doubtless expected to read it as we should any other satire and reject what she ironically praises. Yet in the end the satire is spoiled, *manquée*. A humanity, a sympathy for human frailty inevitably enters in, as it does in the satires of Samuel Johnson,[19] and deflects the point of the satirical dagger. For rashness, looked at in a certain way, may actually be prudence. To live at all is a kind of rashness, but it is better to live than not to live. It is better, and finally more prudent, to accept experience and learn from it than to retreat to the so-called prudence of those who claim to learn about life in their libraries. Life itself, in Raleigh's phrase, is only "a play of passion." [20] We are all actors, all masked; but the mask is an essential, integral part of life, and, like Max Beerbohm's Happy Hypocrite, we are finally indistinguishable from our mask. By means of this argument, it is not so much rashness and self-deception that Erasmus advocates as a new kind of prudence, a prudence which is redefined and revaluated in the very process of praising, partly in satire, partly in sympathy, its opposite.

[18] ME 37. See also the accounts in the *Apophthegmata* (LB V.227E) and the *Adagia* (LB II.379C-E).

[19] I am indebted to Professor Walter Jackson Bate for pointing out to me this "Erasmian" aspect of Johnson's satire.

[20] *The Poems of Sir Walter Raleigh*, ed. A. M. C. Latham (London, 1929), p. 48. It is interesting to note that this poem, which employs the Erasmian stage imagery, ends with a reference to the earnest-jest trope.

This is the technique that is employed throughout the *Encomium* to upset the traditional values and concepts and to redefine such ideals as reason, sobriety, and wisdom. This is the heart of Erasmus' argument, and it is the nature of this transvaluation that must be examined and comprehended if we are to understand the message his fool delivers. Foolish youth, drunkenness, self-love, passion, madness, pleasure, illusions and self-delusion, and ignorance itself are Stultitia's main themes; and we must follow her through her panegyrics of these "vices" if we are to see who she is and what she stands for.

5

THE TRANSVALUATION
OF VALUES: APPLICATION

E<small>VER</small> her mother's daughter, Stultitia begins her self-portrait by eulogizing foolish youth, that time of life which would seem to incorporate all the ignorance and license that the wise man learns, as he grows older, to shun. Children, born of the folly of the bed, are witless and carefree, irresponsible and selfish; they are fools. Beardless and inexperienced, they stand in opposition to the bearded gravity and experience of age. Yet, as much a beard-hater as any of Julian's Corinthian Christians, Stultitia insists upon how lovable children are and points out how passionately men cling to their own youth. The cares and pains of life come with age and knowledge, and who would not prefer the insouciance and happiness of youth? As for those beards, she adds, stealing a joke from one of Lucian's epigrams,[1] they may be the sign of wisdom, but goats have them too; and Valla, who also used the same witticism, is even more explicit about whom he has in mind: "those goatish beards, I mean to say, the Stoics." [2] Childhood is the happiest time of life, but all too soon the shades of the prison house close about the growing boy and the happy songs of innocence are quickly replaced by the plaintive laments of experience. "The farther and farther he is retired from me, the lesse and lesse he

---

[1] *Anthologia Graeca*, XI.430.
[2] Lorenzo Valla, *Scritti filosofici e religiosi*, tr. Giorgio Radetti (Florence, 1953), p. 110.

liveth, untill at last, *tedious olde age* dooe crepe upon hym, not onely urkesome to others, but hateful also to him selfe." [3] Who could bear it, Stultitia asks, were it not for my final gift? For there is no childhood like a second childhood, and there is no fool like an old fool. As she had earlier seen herself bringing the flowers of spring after a hard winter, so now Stultitia sees herself bringing the pleasures of childhood back after bitter middle age. Following her oxymoronic bent, she proceeds to confer new dignity on the traditional figure of the *puer-senex*.[4] Are not old men babies? the satirical rogue asks. Do I not make them go backwards to childhood and once more have wrinkled faces, running eyes, toothless gums, and frail limbs? It is the lesson that Hamlet read to Polonius, and Harry Levin has conjectured that it may indeed have been the *Encomium* that Hamlet was reading.[5] It is, Stultitia claims, precisely by her gift of dotage (*delirare*) that she makes old age palatable: "That and if men had the grace to forbeare quite from medlyng with wisedome, leadyng foorth all theyr lyfe in my service, now (I wene) there shoulde be no olde age at all, but rather they shoulde enjoie a moste happie, and continuall youthe." [6] Youth, then, is foolish and thoughtless, and second childhood is even more so; Stultitia does not contest the point. On the contrary, she praises it *because* it is foolish and thoughtless and because she knows the melancholy truth that one of Webster's villains was to learn in death: "Thers nothing of so infinit vexation/ As mans owne thoughts." [7]

As Montaigne was later to do, Stultitia speaks of the "trois commerces" of life; but whereas Montaigne was to list them as women,

---

[3] ME 17–8: "Quoque longius a me subducitur, hoc minus minusque vivit, donec succedat τὸ χαλεπὸν γῆρας, id est, molesta senectus, non jam aliis modo, verum etiam sibimet invisa." It may be recalled that Erasmus wrote his most celebrated poem on the pains of old age: "Ad Gulielmum Copum medicorum eruditissimum de senectute carmen" in *The Poems of Desiderius Erasmus*, ed. Cornelius Reedijk (Leiden, 1956), pp. 283–90. On the same theme, see the "Elegia secunda, in iuuenem luxuria defluentem atque mortis admonitio," pp. 210–3.

[4] On this topos see Curtius, *European Literature*, pp. 98–101, and Wind, *Mysteries*, p. 165.

[5] Harry Levin, *The Question of Hamlet* (New York, 1959), p. 118.

[6] ME 20: "Quod si mortales prorsus ab omni sapientiae commercio temperarent, ac perpetuo mecum aetatem agerent, ne esset quidem ullum senium, verum perpetua juventa fruerentur felices."

[7] *The Complete Works of John Webster*, ed. F. L. Lucas (Boston and London, 1928), I, 189 (*The White Divel*, V.vi.206–7).

friends, and books, Stultitia naturally has a slightly altered catalogue. She replaces books with the bottle. Continually boasting of her addiction to wine and, like Rabelais, continually urging her followers to drink "à pleins guodetz," she would have approved wholeheartedly, one feels sure, of the imperative answer to all life's problems that issued from the Holy Bottle. Rejoicing to see her auditors looking flushed with wine, she tells them that she herself was conceived in drunkenness and brought up on wine. An old man, possessing her gift of dotage, is not a bad drinking companion. Bacchus is her first follower among the gods. And who, indeed, would not choose to be Bacchus, "ever merie conceited, ever younglyke, ever provokyng men to laughter with his sporte and pleasantnesse" (ME 23). Some of her followers, "especially the old ones," claim that wine provides the greatest of all pleasures, even more than women. And the first rule of conviviality, she remarks, remembering the *Adagia* again,[8] is, "Other drinke thy drinke, or rise, and goe thy waie" (ME 50).

Now this praise of wine may seem particularly foolish, and the reader may understandably be reluctant to admit that there could be anything serious, or Erasmian, about an eulogy of bibulousness. If anything in the *Encomium* would seem to be pure joking, it is this panegyric of drunkenness and drunkards. The sensible man has always acknowledged the curse of drink and its debilitating influence. But Stultitia perversely claims that it is a boon. Her only reservations are that this pleasure tends to turn to poison while the bee-mouth sips, that the anodyne of drink is only temporary,[9] and that good wine is hard to come by.[10]

In many ways, there is no more striking image for Erasmus' transvaluation of values than this symbolic use of wine. It succinctly demonstrates not only the iconoclastic gesture implied in rejecting sobriety, but also the humane common sense that creates the premises for the devil's advocate. Wine and drinking were, of course, commonly accepted symbols of the debasement of man's rational powers. The worst condition of man, Montaigne says, is when he loses self-

[8] LB II.381C-F.

[9] ME 92–3: "Proinde cum inter multas Bacchi laudes illud habeatur, ut est, primarium, quod animi curas eluat, idque ad exiguum modo tempus, nam simulatque villum edormieris, protinus albis, ut ajunt, quadrigis recurrunt animi molestiae . . ."

[10] ME 93: "Non ubivis nascitur generosum et lene merum, quod curas abigat, quod cum spe divite manet."

knowledge and self-control.[11] All the noble and divine potentiality inherent in man is negated and vitiated by his helpless, senseless condition when drunk; and when Michelangelo wished to illustrate on the Sistine ceiling the Neoplatonic theory that man could either rise to the level of God or sink to that of beasts, he did so by painting a picture of God in the whirlwind at one end and a picture of the drunkenness of Noah at the other. Adam, placed in the middle of the ceiling, has, so to speak, the potentiality of moving in either direction,[12] but if he chooses to descend the ladder of the states of being, he finds, propped against the bottom rung, the drunken figure of Noah, "in shape and life," as Spenser said of another drunkard, "more like a monster, then a man." [13] From the drunkenness of Noah to the drunkenness of that "most ridiculous monster" Caliban, over-indulgence has been a generally accepted symbol for this debasement and rejection of grace. Only a fool would praise drunkenness — and so Stultitia does.

When she speaks of wine, her language becomes appropriately Horatian, and it is doubtless from Horace that she derives much of her argument.[14] That argument is somewhat self-contradictory, but then she is a fool. On the one hand, she praises wine for its ability to conceal the truth of the pains of existence; on the other hand, she praises it because it reveals the truth within the drunkard. This latter position is of course based on the concept of *in vino veritas*, and Stultitia explicitly refers to Alcibiades' citation, near the end of the *Symposium*, of this very proverb.[15] This traditional freeing power of wine (*libera vina*), upon which Rabelais was also to insist, accords with Stultitia's insistence throughout her speech upon naturalness and spontaneity: the drunkard's truth represents the absence of that hypocrisy and Stoic reserve which are anathema to her. Wine is also implicitly praised for the conviviality it engenders. Just as, at the end of the scene on Pompey's barge in *Antony and Cleopatra*, the warring pillars of the world join hands in a drunken dance betokening at least a momentary concord, so in the sixteenth-century world of wars a

[11] M II.11/II.ii.

[12] Charles de Tolnay, *Michelangelo II*, "The Sistine Ceiling" (Princeton, 1945), *passim.*

[13] Edmund Spenser, *The Faerie Queene*, I.iv.xxii.

[14] See Steele Commager, "The Function of Wine in Horace's Odes," *Transactions and Proceedings of the American Philological Society*, LXXXVIII (1957), 68–90.

[15] ME 66; Plato, *Symposium*, 217e.

little drink, it seems to the fool, might bring a little peace. But Stultitia's main praise of wine is based upon its powers to hide truth, to enable us to forget the cares of the soul, to dissolve the melancholy of existence. For both Erasmus and Stultitia are aware, as Samuel Johnson was, that "Life is a pill which none of us can bear to swallow without gilding." [16]

Later in the same century, Montaigne was to take up Stultitia's argument again, and his essay *De l'yvrongnerie* serves as a gloss to these sections of her speech. To be sure, he says, drinking is a vice, "lâche et stupide," yet it is less vicious and harmful than others. It does provide pleasure, and it costs our conscience less than other "vices" that give pleasure.[17] The only problem for Montaigne, as for Stultitia, is that the pleasure does not last and that drinking too much leads to pain — for, as he says, "mon estomac n'yroit pas jusques là." Nevertheless, wine does give back joy to men and youth to the aged; "that good God" sweetens and softens the passions of the soul, as fire softens iron.[18] The pains of old age, as vivid to Montaigne as Stultitia's descriptions of them, are mollified by this last of pleasures.[19]

The incommodities of age, which need some helpe and refreshing, might with some reason beget in me a desire or longing of this faculty: for, it is in a man the last pleasure, which the course of our years stealeth upon us.

One is surely not to imagine that Erasmus is counseling a life of inebriation or that he seriously believes wine is the medicine for the world's ills. Even his fool is not that foolish. For both of them, wine is a symbol. Beneath their jocular praise of it, they are both able to expound the more somber truths that life, at the best of times, is difficult for all of us, that old age is a time of pain, that unnatural

[16] As cited in Walter Jackson Bate, *The Achievement of Samuel Johnson* (New York, 1955), pp. 51-2.

[17] M II.14/II.ii: "ie le trouue bien vn vice lâche et stupide, mais non moins malicieux et dommageable que les autres, qui choquent quasi tous de plus droit fil la societé publique. Et si nous ne nous pouuons donner du plaisir, qu'il ne nous couste quelque chose, comme ils tiennent, ie trouue que ce vice couste moins à notre conscience que les autres . . ."

[18] M II.17/II.ii: "Platon defant aus enfans de boire uin auant dishuict ans, [et] auant quarante de s'eniurer; mais, a ceus qui ont passé les quarante, il ordone de s'y plaire; et mesler largement en leurs conuiues l'influance de Dionisius, ce bon dieu qui redone aus homes la gayeté, et la iunesse aus uieillars, qui adoucit et amollit les passions de l'ame, come le fer s'amollit par le feu."

[19] M II.16/II.ii: "Les incommoditez de la vieillesse, qui ont besoing de quelque appuy et refrechissement, pourroyent m'engendrer auecq raison desir de cette faculté: car c'est quasi le dernier plaisir que le cours des ans nous dérobe."

abstinence is a crabbed philosophy, that men are afraid of truth, and that the comradeship of the symposium is a greater thing than the enmity of war. They clink their glasses and urge us to drink up, to forget for a moment the cares of the soul, explaining in jesting tones of utmost earnestness that where ignorance is bliss, it is folly to be wise.

Like her eulogy of wine, Stultitia's justification of her favorite companion, Philautia, is based upon an understanding and an acceptance of the frailties and cares of human existence. For her to champion self-love is as preposterous as everything else she does, and it may seem that it would not only be difficult but impossible for Erasmus to turn inside out a concept whose connotations are so totally pejorative. He himself, in such books as the *Enchiridion* and the *Adagia*, leaves no doubt about his disapproval of self-love, and certainly much of the time that Stultitia praises it we are meant to read this as sarcasm on Erasmus' part. What is unexpected, however, is the astonishing extent to which Erasmus is able, through the ironic mouthpiece of Stultitia, to render virtuous a kind of self-love. It is, in fact, the best example in the *Encomium* of how his ironic playing with words enabled Erasmus to illuminate certain facets of experience which he could not, or would not, otherwise have done. At times it almost seems that he has been led beyond his intentions by the nature of his irony and his involvement in the game Stultitia plays; for in none of his other writings, as far as I know, does he ever offer any positive, eulogistic evaluation of any kind of self-love.

Now not only is self-love a moral sin associated with pride, but a long tradition of medieval thought had made it an especially grave religious sin as well. The true Christian was characterized by his denial of self, his self-abasement, his self-abnegation — indeed, often by his self-hatred. Whether or not such self-hatred gave pleasure is hardly the question to ask; but it is just the question Stultitia does ask. "Finally, wheras it is the greattest parte of felicitee, for a man to desyre to bee, as he is in deede, that dooeth Selflove procure you by a redier waie." [20] If one is discontented with oneself, she argues, how can he have a happy life? It was this attitude that made Erasmus a

----

[20] ME 36: "Denique cum praecipua felicitatis pars sit, ut, *quod sis esse velis*, nimirum totum hoc praestat compendio mea Philautia . . ."

Pelagian in Luther's eyes. The Erasmian argument, however, does not rest finally upon self-contentment (though that is undeniably a part of the argument), but rather upon the happiness that a man who loves himself can give others. "Maie he please others, that is displeasant, and tedious to hym selfe?" (ME 35). It is true that nothing is so foolish as to admire and be pleased with yourself; yet can you do anything that is graceful or seemly or pleasing if you are not?[21] Philautia is, Stultitia explains, the source of all the arts that entertain us — oratory, music, drama, poetry, and the rest. It could also, she hints, be a deterrent to war, for if we are proud and complacent about our own country, why should we wish to acquire another? Her most telling point, however, is the question with which she begins this discussion: "I praie you, can he love any bodie, that loveth not hym selfe?"[22] Here Erasmus places the entire concept of self-love and the Manichaean condemnation of pleasure in a new context simply by asking how we can love our neighbor as ourselves, if we do not, in fact, love ourselves.

It is, then, a specific type of self-love that Erasmus advocates, a self-love turned outward, whose effect is largely selfless. He does not for a moment admit or imply that man is actually worth his self-esteem. He insists that self-love is self-deception, but he argues that it does at least make life more palatable. Similarly, the advantages derived from self-love that he emphasizes are not so much those advantages to ourselves (though they are not denied) as the advantages to others. Nevertheless, Stultitia's views on Philautia would not be by Erasmus if she did not present the other side of the question, and there is a bitter irony, as well as a plea for personal integrity, in the question she asks some pages later: "For what hurteth the, the peoples hissing, as longe as thou clappest thy selfe on the backe?"[23] There are types of self-love that are bad, or at least fatuous, and in redefining the value of self-love Erasmus does not hesitate to demonstrate the folly of one type as well as the wisdom of the other. By so doing, he makes his type of self-love all the more compelling. Thus, in a later passage he speaks of the ridiculous self-love of snobs, the conceit of artists, and

---

[21] ME 36: "Quid autem aeque stultum atque tibi ipsi placere te ipsum admirari? At rursum, quid venustum, quid gratiosum, quid non indecorum erit, quod agas, ipse tibi displicens?"

[22] ME 35: "Quaeso num quenquam amabit, qui ipse semet oderit?"

[23] ME 57: "Quid laedit, si totus populus in te siblet, modo tute tibi plaudas?"

the absurdities of chauvinism (ME 83–7). His treatment of Philautia's sister, Flattery (*Assentatio*), is equally ambiguous (ME 87–9). On the one hand, the malady of princes is summarily dealt with: "How be it there is in deede a certaine kynde of flaterie, wherby some traitours and deceitfull villaines, dooe traine simple folkes oftentymes to theyr undoyng." [24] On the other hand, there is another kind of flattery, derived from kindliness and candor (*ab ingenii benignitate candoreque*) rather than from asperity. It is this type of flattery that has a benign influence upon life itself and from which man derives both pleasure and virtue.[25]

This *Adulacion* encourageth a weake spirit, comforteth one droupyng in sadnesse, quickeneth a langwisshyng thought, wakeneth a dulle head, reiseth up a sicke mynde, mollifieth a stubbourne hert, getteth love, and ones gotten, reteineth it still, enticeth children with a good wil to lerne their bokes, gladdeth olde folkes, teacheth, and admonissheth princes of theyr duities, under coulour of praise, without offendyng: briefely, it maketh that eche man to him selfe is bothe dearer, and more acceptable: whiche effect maie well be taken for the chiefest membre of felicitee.

Thus, in this heartfelt passage, even the flattery of princes, condemned universally in humanist writing, is turned to good account and made an instrument of virtue rather than vice. And flattery itself becomes, in Stultitia's words, "evin the verie hony, and conserve of mans societee and companiyng together." (ME 89).

Ancillary to Stultitia's examination of the concept of prudence, and analogous to her acceptance of experience as a mode of knowing and a road to wisdom, is her brief consideration of the passions (*affectus*). Long the targets of the Stoics, especially of that "double Stoic, Seneca," the passions and emotions are traditionally the enemies of reason; Erasmus himself, in a long passage in the *Enchiridion*, discusses the "two parts of man," passion and reason or, as St. Paul, whom he quotes, calls them, the spirit and the body (E 47ff). Erasmus' exhortations for the Christian soldier to follow the way of reason and the

---

[24] ME 88: "Quanquam est omnino perniciosa quaedam adulatio, qua nonnulli perfidiosi et irrisores, miseros in perniciem adigunt."

[25] ME 88: "Haec dejectiores animos erigit, demulcet tristes, exstimulat languentes, expergefacit stupidos, aegrotos levat, feroces mollit, amores conciliat, conciliatos retinet. Pueritiam ad capessenda studia literarum allicit, senes exhilarat, principes citra offensam sub imagine laudis et admonet et docet. In summa facit, ut quisque sibi ipse sit iucundior et charior, quae quidem felicitatis pars est vel praecipua."

spirit seem to be flatly contradicted by Stultitia, who, though she acknowledges that " 'wisedome,' accordyng to the Stoikes diffinicion, 'is naught else, than to be ruled by reason: and folie, to be ledde as affection will,' " [26] nevertheless counsels the other, the foolish road of passion. Faced with this contradiction, we may well wonder if Stultitia's eulogy of the passions is to be read ironically. Yet this can hardly be the case. The passages describing the virtues of passion, and more particularly that describing the inadequacy of the man who follows reason alone, are too sincere — too "passionate" — to be rejected as the counsel of the fool. One must, as always with Erasmus, accept both statements as facets of his thought; and one should probably regard the passage in the *Encomium* as a qualification of that in the *Enchiridion* — as a dependent clause by the "king of *but.*" Thus, while the Christian soldier is told that reason is nobler and more divine than passion, Stultitia, wise fool that she is, adds to that precept the qualification that to be without passions is unnatural and inhuman.

At the beginning of her defense of them, Stultitia states the position of those who oppose the passions: everyone admits that all passions belong to folly; the fool and the wise man are distinguished by the very fact that emotions guide the former and reason the latter; the Stoics insist that the wise man be alien to emotional perturbations (ME 50–4). Her one attempt to counter these arguments is not very effective; for without expanding or explaining the basis of her claim, she merely states "that notwithstandyng, these affections are not onely sette in steede of pilottes to suche as woulde recover the porte of wysedome, but also in any acte of vertue, are lyke certaine pricks, or incitacions provoking a man to dooe well" (ME 41). One could extrapolate a justification for this from other parts of her speech, but she herself does not attempt to give one, and consequently her argument seems less compelling here than elsewhere. This temporary failure is rapidly redeemed, however, when she takes up her favorite and most effective position, that nothing human is alien to her, and points out that if you subtract these human emotions from a man, you have left not a human being, but a marble effigy (*marmoreum hominis simulacrum*). If her description of this petrified man, this "stone un-

[26] ME 27: "Stoicis definitoribus nihil aliud sit sapientia, quam duci ratione; contra stultitia, affectuum arbitrio moveri . . ." It is, one may note, a typical joke on the part of Stultitia that she should speak oxymoronically of the "*arbitrio* affectuum."

moved, cold, and to temptation slow," is familiar to us, it is because
we have met him often in literature, and nowhere more memorably
than in Shakespeare's Malvolio, Angelo, and Octavius.[27]

For whiche of you woulde not lothe, and blisse you from the company
of suche maner a man, "as were mortified, and benummed in all those
sensis and understandynges, that naturally other men are ledde by? that
had no affections reignyng in him? nor woulde no more bee sterred with
love, or compassion, than if he were a flint stone? that in nothyng could
overshoote him selfe, but rather lyke Argus, see and cast all thynges to
the uttermost? Forgeve no man? be onely pleased with him selfe? esteeme
him selfe onely to be riche? onely to be a kynge? onely to be a freeman?
briefly, onely all thynges, but in his owne conceite onely? that cared for
no friendes? friende him selfe to no man? Wolde not sticke to defie the
Gods? and what so ever is dooen of other men in this present life, to
laugh at it and dispise it as a verie madnesse?"

Is not such a "wise" man but a fool, an "ass unpolicied"? Is not anyone
from the middle rank of most foolish men, any *homme moyen fou,*
preferable to such a man? *Errare humanum est* — the man Stultitia
describes *nihil erret.* But the fool, the man who makes a mistake, would
not only be a delight to all mankind, to his wife, his friends, and his
hosts, but he would consider nothing human alien to him.[28]

Nothing is more informed by this acceptance of humanity than
Stultitia's discussion of the value of madness. Folly is indeed madness,
and Stultitia is prepared to admit it; but in doing so she insists, as
usual, upon a distinction that is to provide the means of upsetting the
value of sanity. Like Montaigne, she can claim that *"Distinguo* is the
most universall part of my logike," [29] and by now we should be sufficiently familiar with her methods to realize that when she starts to
observe that there are really two kinds of madness (ME 70) she is

---

[27] ME 52: "Quis enim non istiusmodi hominem ceu portentum ac spectrum fugitet
horreatque, qui ad omnes naturae sensus obsurduerit, qui nullis sit affectibus, nec
amore, nec misericordia magis commoveatur,
          quam si dura silex, aut stet Marpesia cautes,
quem nihil fugiat, qui nihil erret, sed ceu Lynceus quispiam nihil non perspiciat, nihil
non ad amussim perpendat, nihil ignoscat, qui solus se ipso sit contentus, solus dives,
solus sanus, solus Rex, solus liber, breviter omnia solus, sed suo solius judicio, qui
nullum moretur amicum, ipse amicus nemini, qui Diis quoque ipsis non dubitet
mandare laqueum, qui quicquid in omni vita geritur, velut insanum damnet rideatque?"
[28] ME 53: "nihil humani a se alienum putet." The source of this famous quotation
is Terence, *Heautontimorumenos,* I.77.
[29] M II.6/II.i: "DISTINGO est le plus vniuersel membre de ma Logique."

about to embark upon another transvaluation of values. She gives, characteristically, both sides of the argument.

On one side, there is that kind of madness loosed upon the world by the vengeful Furies, the cause of war and rapine, greed, parricide, incest, sacrilege, and all other plagues of this sort. A few moments later, Stultitia is to give an incriminating catalogue of those infected by this nefarious madness. There are the hunters, who take pleasure in seeing animals savagely butchered (ME 73-4) — a description that was to provide one of Holbein's best illustrations.[30] There are those who are mad for building luxurious homes, far beyond their means, until finally they become bankrupt and have neither house to live in nor food to eat (ME 74). Then there are those who, like the alchemists, waste their lives and fortunes searching for the fifth essence, doomed to defeat but always prepared to justify their lost years with the pious observation that at least they tried (ME 74-5). There are also the gamblers who wreck their lives on the promontory of (M)alea.[31] There are the snobs, surrounded by the busts and portraits of their ancestors;[32] the artists, who would rather lose their homes than their talent (ME 85); and the chauvinists, who claim that their land is the best of all possible lands (ME 85-7). Finally, there are the superstitious, those who burn candles to St. George's horse, make charms against toothache out of verses of the Bible, hang votive gifts on the walls of the churches — but this "sea of superstitions" is, she apologizes, too vast to take into account (ME 78-83). Stultitia, of course, praises them all, *decoro personae*, and even when Erasmus' true voice cries out through the mask she manages to make a joke of it.[33]

But now, if some one of these cumbrous wysemen shoulde ryse up, and saie (and saie truely) "thou shalt never die ill, as longe as thou livest well:

[30] On Holbein's illustrations, see F. Saxl, "Holbein's Illustrations to *The Praise of Folly* by Erasmus," *The Burlington Magazine*, LXXXIII (1943), 275-9.

[31] ME 75-6. Stultitia's rhetorical trick here is untranslatable. What she says is: "in aleae scopulum illisa nave, non paulo formidabiliorem Malea." The promontory of Malea, mentioned as dangerous in Strabo, is not far from Sparta. In saying the last two words, Stultitia elides the *m*'s, thus making it sound as though she had said *alea* (dice).

[32] ME 83-4. Cf. Clément Marot's poem, "Chant de Follie, de l'origine de Villemanoche," *Oeuvres complètes de Clément Marot*, ed. Pierre Jannet (Paris, 1873; 3 vols.), II, 103-5.

[33] ME 82-3: "Inter haec, si quis odiosus sapiens exoriatur, succinatque id, quod res est, *non male peribis, si bene vixeris: peccata redimis, si nummulo addideris odium*

Thou redeemest thy synnes, in case to one halfpennie gevin to the poore, thou addest repentaunce of thy misdeedes, together with teares, praier, and fastyng: and changest all the trade of thy lyfe: this sainct will helpe the, if thou livest as he did." These advertisementes, and such semblable, if this wyseman (I saie) shoulde barke unto the people: See than straight from howe sweete a felicitee, into howe great a trouble and confusion, he shoulde plucke backe the myndes of mortall men.

All these types of madness Erasmus condemns, though it is significant that of each of them Stultitia observes that they give their subjects a kind of happiness. It may ruin their lives, and it does: "forsouth a few yeres have they spent yet, in great wanhope, and pleasure" (ME 74).

But there is another type of madness, "farre unlike the former" and "most . . . to be embraced" (ME 70): it occurs "as often as a certaine pleasant raving, or errour of the mynde, delivereth the herte of that man, whom it possesseth, from all wonted carefulness, & rendreth it dyvers waies, much recreated with new delectacion" (ME 70–1). In fact, perhaps not every error of the mind or senses ought to be called madness. For there are illusions and self-delusions that nourish the spirit, as well as those that wither it; and if the Stoics will speak of those truths men live by, Stultitia is prepared to acknowledge those lies men live by. Even the most intimate of human relationships are often postulated upon or made happier by self-deception; one man is blind to his friend's faults (ME 31–3), another kisses the wart on his mistress' neck (ME 32), and even the cuckold is happier deceived than enlightened (ME 34).

In discussing the value of prudence, Stultitia had observed that life was a play and that prudence was to pretend not to notice the illusion — in truth, to remove the illusion is to ruin the whole play.[34] She returns now to the image of the play in her discussion of benevolent madness, this time from the point of view of the audience rather than of the players; for if the players are symbolic of man's illusions, the audience is symbolic of man's reliance upon self-delusion. She tells the story (which Montaigne will also recall) from one of Horace's epistles of the Greek who would sit all day in an empty theater, laughing, applauding, enjoying himself, because he thought

---

malefactorum, tum lacrymas, vigilias, precationes, jejunia, ac totam vitae rationem commutaris: Divus hic tibi favebit, si vitam illius aemulaberis. Haec, inquam, atque id genus alia, si sapiens ille obganniat, vide a quanta felicitate repente mortalium animos in quem tumultum retraxerit!"

[34] ME 48: "Verum eum errorem tollere, est fabulam omnem perturbare."

plays were being enacted on the bare stage.[35] When his family and physicians cured him of these delusions, he protested that they had killed him rather than cured him, that they had destroyed his pleasures with his illusions (ME 71). We all enact our part in the play, Stultitia says; we all, in one way or another, look upon the empty stage and see panoply and drama where there is nothing. Swift, who appears to allude to the same Horatian story in his "Digression on Madness," [36] bitterly concludes with his famous definition that happiness "is a perpetual Possession of being well Deceived . . . The Serene Peaceful State of being a Fool Among Knaves." [37] Unlike Stultitia, however, he would without hesitation strike through the mask of deception. Cosmetics, as we have seen, were as objectionable a symbol to Erasmus as they were to Swift; but Swift, in his overwhelming desire to remove them, flayed a woman alive, and, he wrily comments, "you will hardly believe, how much it altered her Person for the worse." [38] The mind so hot for certainties, so impatient of deception, has received only the dusty answer of death. "Doth any man doubt," Bacon was to ask a century after Erasmus, "that if there were taken out of Mens Mindes, Vaine Opinions, Flattering Hopes, False valuations, Imaginations as one would, and the like; but it would leaue the Mindes, of a Number of Men, poore shrunken Things; full of Melancholy, and Indisposition, and vnpleasing to themselues?" [39] Erasmus did not doubt it and would not deny that it is folly not to unmask hypocrisy. Yet at the same time that it is also "the right plaiyng of the pageants of this life" (*vitae fabulam agere* [ME 50]).[40]

But *Philosophers* saie "it is a miserable thyng to be begyled, and erre so." Naie, most miserable is it (I saie) not to erre, and not to be deceived. For too too are thei deceived, who wene that mans felicitee consisteth in

[35] Horace, *Epistolae*, II.ii.128–40. Montaigne's use of the story is found at M II.216–7/ II.xii.

[36] Jonathan Swift, *A Tale of a Tub, to which is added The Battle of the Books and the Mechanical Operation of the Spirit*, ed. A. C. Guthkelch and D. Nichol Smith (Oxford, 1930), p. 171n.

[37] *Tale of a Tub*, pp. 171, 174.

[38] *Tale of a Tub*, p. 173.

[39] Francis Bacon, *Essays* [ed. G. Grigson] (Oxford, The World's Classics, 1947), p. 6.

[40] ME 89: "Sed falli, inquiunt, miserum est, imo non falli, miserrimum. Nimium enim desipiunt, quit in rebus ipsis felicitatem hominis sitam esse existimant. Ex opinionibus ea pendet: Nam rerum humanarum tanta est obscuritas varietasque, ut nihil dilucide scire possit . . . Aut si quid sciri potest, id non raro officit etiam vitae jucunditati. Postremo sic sculptus est hominis animus, ut longe magis fucis, quam veris capiatur."

thinges selfe, and not rather in the opinion how the same are taken. "In as muche as in all humaine thynges there is so great darkeness and diversenesse, as nothyng maie be clerely knowne out, nor discovered" . . . Or if that ought maie be knowen, the same yet not seeldome disavaileth to the gladsomeness and pleasure of the lyfe. Lastly, so is mans mynde framed, as muche more it deliteth in thynges to the shew, than in suche as are in deede.

With a nod perhaps to Cicero, who says that nothing is more foolish than to think that happiness comes from opinion,[41] the arch-fool says that it *does* come from opinion, not from things as they are, from dreams, not realities; it is indeed the perpetual possession of being well deceived. And what is the difference, Stultitia rhetorically asks, between the inhabitants of Plato's cave who gaze on shadows and those who emerge to see reality? The answer she does not find it necessary to give is that those in the cave are happier (ME 91).

The concept of happiness is so frequently introduced in Stultitia's transvaluative discussions that, though at first it may have seemed an almost fortuitous apology, it comes to reveal itself as the essence of her teleology. Just as each of her policies is directed toward this end, so each of her arguments rests upon this ultimate justification — that pleasure will be the result. The words for pleasure and joy and happiness — *felicitas, laetitia, voluptas, oblectio, iucunditas, delectatio* — run as a kind of leitmotif through her oration. Like Montaigne, she delights to box the ears of the Stoics with this Epicurean value;[42] like a fool, she esteems it above all other values. It is considered so self-evident as to need no justification: she simply escorts the other values through her argument until she has brought them to a point from which she can demonstrate that they cause pleasure, and then she has done, as if convinced that there can be no uncertainty about the value of a value that leads to pleasure. In the syllogism that x leads to pleasure, pleasure is desirable, and therefore x is desirable, she enthymematically takes the second proposition for granted. It is one of the subtlest tricks of her stultiloquence.

No one but a fool would take it for granted. What is more, most

---

[41] Cicero, *De legibus*, I.17: "Ipsum enim bonum non est opinionibus, sed natura. Nam in ita esset, beati quoque opinione essent, quo quid dici potest stultius?"

[42] M I.101/I.xx: "Quoy qu'ils dient, en la uertu mesme le dernier but de nostre uises c'est la uolupté. Il me plait de battre leurs oreilles de ce mot qui leur est si fort a contreceur."

Stoics and Christians would never admit it. To say that pleasure is the *verum bonum*, as Lorenzo Valla did, or the *summum bonum* as Cosmo Raimondi did, was to mark yourself an Epicurean — a label that had guaranteed admission to the sixth circle of Dante's Inferno. For Dante, of course, Epicureanism was a heresy because it signified a disbelief in the immortality of the soul, and this was the primary Christian objection to Epicurus. But there was also a moral condemnation of the Epicurean teleology which found its essence in pleasure. We find it articulated in such a work of art as that fresco at Ferrara which, depicting the triumph of St. Augustine, shows Epicurus himself being vanquished by the allegorical figure of Temperance.[43] To be sure, the Middle Ages really knew very little about Epicureanism, with the result that for many centuries the philosophy suffered the fate that Machiavellianism was to suffer in a later age: its author, unknown and a pagan, became a bugbear; the concept, misunderstood and corrupted, became a dirty word. Thus, when Chaucer's Franklin is described as "Epicurus owene sone," he is scarcely being complimented; nor, for that matter, is the name of Jonson's character, Sir Epicure Mammon, intended to signify a morally righteous life. The observation of one of the characters in Erasmus' *Colloquia* sums up accepted opinion: "Of all sects, there is none so wholly condemned by universal consent." [44]

Never was a judgment made with less evidence. What knowledge the Middle Ages had of Epicureanism came largely from Cicero, who can hardly be considered a witness for the defense. The text of Lucretius' great poem was as good as lost, and it was not until more than a hundred years after Dante's death that Poggio Bracciolini "rediscovered" it. The first modern discussion of Epicurus that displays any real understanding of his thought occurs in a brief and, until recently, neglected letter by Cosmo Raimondi, written in 1431;[45] the

---

[43] See Roberto Longhi, *Officina ferrarese* (Florence, 1956), plate I.

[44] LB I.882D: "Atque inter omnes nulla damnatior, omnium suffragiis."

[45] Santini first discovered a manuscript of this letter in the Biblioteca Martini in Lucca and published a text in *Studi Storici*, VIII (1899), 153ff. Eugenio Garin has published that text with a translation in *Filosofi italiani del Quattrocento* (Florence, 1942), pp. 133-49. In 1950, Garin announced in *Rinascimento*, I (1950), 100-1, the discovery of another manuscript of the same letter in the Biblioteca Laurentiana (MSS. Ashb. 267) which contains many variant details. This second manuscript has now been published by Garin in his most recent volume, *La Cultura filosofica del rinascimento italiano* (Florence, 1961), pp. 87-92. On Raimondi himself, see the short bibliography in Garin, *Filosofi*, p. 133, n. 1, to which may be added, G. Saitta,

first printed text of Lucretius did not appear until late in the fifteenth century. Despite this, there are hints of a revival, earlier than one might expect, in the works of Petrarch and Boccaccio, and in the latter's commentary on the *Divina Commedia* he tends to mitigate the severity of the Dantesque judgment. Later in the fourteenth century, Coluccio Salutati and Leonardo Bruni (who actually called himself *Epicureu[s] Litterarum*)[46] manifest a renewed interest in Epicureanism, if not an unqualified approbation of it. But it is not until the first half of the fifteenth century, in Raimondi and Francesco Filelfo, that we find the first indications of that serious revival which was to culminate in the three major statements in defense of pleasure written in the same century by Lorenzo Valla, Marsilio Ficino, and Cristoforo Landino. The history of this revival has only been sketched in, but when the complete story is written it should reveal one of the great subversive movements in the history of ideas.[47]

By now it should come as no surprise to learn that Erasmus' position in this controversy, adumbrated as early as his *De contemptu mundi*, is often uncertain, occasionally equivocal.[48] Yet his most formal and extended treatment of it, the colloquy *Epicureus*, written in 1533, presents an eloquent defense of the philosophy of Epicurus which reaches its climax in the daring claim that the greatest Epicureans are those Christians who lead a pious and holy life (LB I.888C). We know from his correspondence that Erasmus himself had been called "Epicurus" by his enemies, and the colloquy is therefore very much of a self-defense as well (EE X.338[2936]). Erasmus' argument owes much to Valla,[49] and his Epicurean even refers obliquely to the title of Valla's treatise. Despite its fifteenth-century precedents, though, it would have remained an unconventional argu-

---

Il Pensiero italiano nell' Umanesimo e nel Rinascimento (Bologna, 1949), I, 233–6; V. Rossi, *Il Quattrocento* (Milan, 1956), p. 46; and E. Garin, *L'Umanesimo italiano* (Bari, 1952), pp. 66–8.

[46] Cited in Raymond Marcel, *Marsile Ficin* (Paris, 1958), p. 115, n. 2.

[47] The earliest important study of this is F. Gabotto, "L'Epicureismo italiano negli ultimi secoli del Medio Evo," *Rivista di filosofia scientifica*, VIII (1889), 552ff, and "L'Epicureismo di M. Ficino," *ibid.*, X (1891), 428ff. More valuable and recent are the various discussions of Saitta, Gentile, Garin, and Kristeller — to which may now be added the most recent discussion, "Ricerche sull'epicureismo del Quattrocento" in E. Garin, *La Cultura filosofica*, pp. 72–86.

[48] The passage in the *De contemptu mundi* may be found at LB V.1257Aff.

[49] See B. J. H. M. Timmermans, "Valla et Érasme, défenseurs d'Épicure," *Neophilologus*, XXIII (1938), 414–19.

ment for most sixteenth-century readers, and the tone of the dialogue manifests an intention to shock its readers into truth. In this respect it resembles Stultitia's strategy, and such shock tactics were doubtless justified in this boldest of all Erasmus' transvaluations.

Epicureus[50] is a dialogue between two men, Serious-Minded (Spoudaeus), who takes the position that the Stoics err least from truth and next after them the Peripatetics,[51] and Pleasure-Lover (Hedonius), who confesses that he likes no sect so well as the Epicureans.[52] Hedonius appropriately begins the dialogue by rejecting the authority of Cicero's *De finibus*, one of the most serious attacks on Epicurus, on the grounds that it is better to enquire after the beginnings of Good than the ends. Proceeding to state the Epicurean principles that the happiness of man lies in pleasure and that that life is the most blessed which has most pleasure and least pain, he accuses those who object to them of misunderstanding the words. Since God is the *summum bonum,* he is the greatest pleasure; since nothing is more wretched than a guilty conscience, nothing is happier than a clear conscience. Therefore, there are no greater Epicureans than those who are Christians (and thus rejoice in God) and live piously (and thus have a clear conscience). Hedonius takes care to point out the distinctions between true and false pleasure, between the true good (*bona*) of the mind and the false pleasures of the body. Thus, he makes Spoudaeus admit that the pleasures of a happy dog, for example, are not desirable, since the greatest pleasures come from the mind. Similarly, the rejoinder to those who claim that the pious lack the pleasures of such things as riches, honor, and society is that these are false pleasures and do, in fact, only cause anxieties. Those who follow what are commonly called pleasures actually stray from real pleasure; for what they follow are the pleasures of a disordered mind that proceed from a false Good. God is the fountain of highest good that alone makes man happy (*Deum summi boni fontem homini sola conciliat*). Convinced, Spoudaeus nevertheless argues that the pious deprive themselves of even those pleasures that are lawful. The answer he receives

[50] It is interesting to note that this colloquy is later quoted by Erasmus' countryman, Bernard de Mandeville, in *The Fable of the Bees,* ed. F. B. Kaye (Oxford, 1924), I, 147. On Mandeville's debt to Erasmus, see I, cviff.

[51] LB I.882D: "Mihi tamen Stoici videntur minus aberrare a vero; quibus proximum locum tribuo Peripateticis."

[52] LB I.882D: "At mihi nulla secta magis arridet, quam Epicureorum."

from Hedonius is a striking exposition of Erasmus' Christian humanism.[53]

The immoderate use of lawful pleasures is unlawful. If you except that, those who seem to lead an austere life excel all others [in pleasure]. What is a more magnificent spectacle than the contemplation of this world? Men who are dear to God take far more pleasure from this than others. For while others, with curious eyes, contemplate this wonderous work, their minds are vexed because they cannot comprehend the cause of many things. Sometimes, like Momus, they murmur against the workman, often calling Nature a stepmother; and though this insult is verbally directed against Nature, in fact it also attacks Him who created Nature, if indeed there is such a thing as Nature. But the pious man whose eyes are religious and pure looks upon the works of the Lord, his father, with joy in his soul, admiring everything, finding fault with nothing, but offering thanks for all, when he considers that all this was made for man. And thus he adores in each thing the omnipotence, wisdom, and goodness of the creator, whose imprint he perceives in the created things. Now suppose that there really were such a thing as that palace Apuleius made for Psyche, or even something more magnificent and elegant; and suppose there are two people looking at it, one a traveler who has come to see it and one the servant or son of him who built this edifice. Which of them will take the greater delight in looking at it? The stranger, who has no connection with the house, or the son, who sees with pleasure the genius, wealth, and magnificence of his dear father in that building, especially when he realizes that all this creation was made for him?

This optimistic, joyous humanism lies at the heart of Erasmus' thought. We must rejoice in the world, he says, because it is God's

---

[53] LB I.887: "Etiam licitarum voluptatum immodicus usus est illicitus: hunc si excipias, in caeteris omnibus superant, qui videntur asperam vitam degere. Quod potest esse magnificentius spectaculum, quam hujus mundi contemplatio? Ex eo longe plus capiunt voluptatis homines Deo cari, quam caeteri. Siquidem hi dum curiosis oculis contemplantur admirandum hoc opus, anguntur animo, quod multarum rerum causas non assequantur. In quibusdam ceu Momi quidam obmurmurant opifici; neque raro naturam pro matre novercam appellant: quod convicium verbo tenus quidem naturam ferit, sed re vera in eum redundat qui naturam condidit, si qua est omnino natura. At homo pius, religiosis ac simplicibus oculis magna cum animi voluptate spectat opera Domini, Patrisque sui, demirans singula, nihil reprehendens, sed pro cunctis gratias agens, cum reputat haec omnia propter hominem esse condita: atque adeo in singulis rebus adorat omnipotentiam, sapientiam, ac bonitatem conditoris, quarum vestigia perspicit in rebus conditis. Jam finge mihi esse aliquod palatium re vera tale, quale Psychae fingit Apulejus, aut si quod potes magnificentius elegantiusque: huc adhibe duos spectatores, alterum peregrinum, qui tantum visendi causa venerit; alterum, servum aut filium ejus, qui construxit hoc aedicifium; uter impensius delectabitur; hospes ille, ad quem illa domus nihil attinet; an filius, qui carissimi patris ingenium, opes ac magnificentiam in aedificio magna cum voluptate speculatur; praesertim cum cogitat totum hoc opus ipsius gratia factum esse?"

creation and was made for the pleasure of man; yet we must recognize at the same time that the only true pleasures are those of the mind, that the pleasures most people seek are more painful than pleasurable, that God is the fountain of joy. Epicurus is "the adorable prince of Christian philosophy," and Christ himself is not the sad and mournful figure that is often described to us.[54]

If those who live pleasantly are Epicureans, there are none more truly Epicurean than those who live in holiness and piety. And if we are careful with names, no one more deserves the name of Epicurus than that adorable prince of Christian philosophy. For in Greek *epikouros* means helper. When the law of nature was almost obliterated by vice, when the law of Moses stimulated rather than cured lusts, when the tyrant Satan ruled with impunity, he alone brought help to mankind. Therefore they are wholly in error who babble that the nature of Christ was rather sad and melancholic and that He invited us to an unpleasant kind of life. On the contrary, He offers us the sweetest life of all and the one most full of true pleasure.

The Erasmian philosophy of Christ is a religion of joy, not of sorrow, and it makes of pleasure a virtue, not a vice. Sadness, as Erasmus says in the *Enchiridion*, impedes and chases men from good.[55] This Christ, the enemy of sadness, stands behind all Stultitia's arguments from pleasure, and, taken together, Hedonius and Stultitia personify Erasmus' Christian humanism. For while Stultitia herself only vaguely adumbrates Hedonius' Christian arguments for pleasure, she is more explicit than he about the humanistic ones. She is poignantly aware that the life of man is not often gay and that humanity is shrouded in sadness from birth to death — that we leave, as Montaigne says, this world as we come into it, crying. Venus gives beauty to few, Mercury gives eloquence to fewer; Hercules does not give wealth to many, nor does Jupiter make many kings; Mars often favors neither side, and

[54] LB I.888C-D: "Quod si Epicurei sunt, qui sauviter vivunt, nulli verius sunt Epicurei, quam qui sancte pieque vivunt. Et si nos tangit cura nominum, nemo magis promeretur cognomen Epicuri, quam adorandus ille Christianae philosophiae princeps. Graecis enim ἐπίκουρος auxiliatorem declarat. Cum naturae lex esset vitiis tantum non oblitterata, cum Mosis lex magis irritaret cupiditates, quam sanaret, cum impune regnaret in mundo tyrannus Satanas, solus ille pereunti humano generi praesentaneam attulit opem. Proinde vehementer falluntur quidam, qui blaterant Christum natura fuisse tristem quempiam ac melancholicum, nosque ad inamoenum vitae genus invitasse. Imo is unus ostendit vitam omnium suavissimam, veraeque voluptatis plenissimam . . ."

[55] E 43: "dolor, fuga impedimentumque bonorum . . ."

Neptune drowns more than he saves; the tripod of Apollo sends many away sad, and Phoebus sends pestilence on his shafts; Jove often thunders.[56] But that felicity which Spenser's knights find only in sleep and Shakespeare's princes only in death, Stultitia offers us in life itself, if we will only accept all of life. Whether induced by wine or illusions or ignorance or folly itself, pleasure is there if we will but take it, and to take it is to play the comedy of life. "For as touchyng this life here, maie it woorthily be called a life (I praie you) if ye take pleasure and delight awaie?" she asks. Her audience applauds the rhetorical question.[57]

Thus the ancient psychomachy between *virtus* and *voluptas* is finally resolved by the fool. The way of virtue and the way of pleasure are no longer divergent, for pleasure, as Ben Jonson was later to present it in song and dance, has been reconciled to virtue. From Xenophon to Brandt, as Panofsky has demonstrated,[58] Herakles Prodikos, symbolic of Everyman, stood at the crossroads and was obliged to choose which road he would travel; but now a more humane humanism has mitigated the old, intransigent dualism with the understanding that it is not a matter of bifurcation but of intertwining. Into his masque, Jonson introduces the figure of Daedalus that he may explain to Hercules how virtue and pleasure are not a fork in the road, but a "curious knot," since "all actions of mankind are but a Laborinth, or maze." [59] It is an image that Stultitia herself might have used to embody her vision of a truth that neither rejects nor restricts, but accepts and frees, and her advocacy of a joyous Christian humanism that takes pleasure in the glory of God and the nature of man. When one thinks of the hard, controversial, peregrine life of Erasmus, one is moved by this plea for happiness and joy, knowing, as one scholar has put it, that though he understood the value of this ideal he never attained it. The great Erasmian scholar Augustin Renaudet

---

[56] ME 93: "Paucis contigit formae gratia, Veneris munus, paucioribus eloquentia, Mercurii donum. Non ita multis obtigerunt opes, dextro Hercule. Imperius non cuivis concedit Jupiter Homericus. Saepenumero Mavors neutris favet copiis. Complures ab Apollonis tripode tristes discedunt. Saepe fulminat Saturnius, Phoebus aliquando jaculis pestem immittit. Neptunus plures exstinguit, quam servat."

[57] ME 16: "Quid autem vita haec, num omnino vita videtur appellanda, si voluptatem detraxeris? Applausistis."

[58] On all of this, see Erwin Panofsky, *Hercules am Scheidewege und andere antike Bildstoffe in der neueren Kunst* (Leipzig and Berlin, 1930).

[59] Jonson, *Works*, VII, 488 (*Pleasure reconcild to Vertue*, 253ff).

has given a beautiful description of this ideal and quality of mind. It may stand as a conclusion to this examination of Erasmus' anti-Stoical Epicureanism: "Yet at the spectacle of so much misery, he does not agree to conclude with the Stoics in favor of an abstract, inhuman, almost barbarous ideal of indifference and insensibility. The rule of life that he proposes for man's misery is founded on a smiling resignation that hopes for very little from life, but accepts and knows how to savor its pale and rare satisfactions." [60]

[60] Renaudet, *Italie,* p. 102.

6

THE FOOL IN CHRIST

🏵🏵🏵🏵🏵🏵🏵🏵🏵🏵🏵🏵🏵🏵🏵🏵🏵🏵🏵🏵🏵🏵🏵🏵🏵🏵🏵🏵🏵🏵

BECAUSE she believes, as St. Paul did, that we are fools for Christ's sake,[1] Stultitia accepts and boasts of her motley. "Ut insipiens dico; plus ego" — I speak as a fool; I am more.[2] She, like St. Paul, is more than a fool, because she knows that it is the wisdom of this world that is really folly and that her foolishness is wisdom. The message she delivers to sixteenth-century Europe is precisely that given by St. Paul to first-century Athens: "Let no man deceive himself. If any man among you seemeth to be wise in this world, let him become a fool, that he may be wise."[3] It is this final paradox — that folly is wisdom and wisdom folly — that, with its Christian ramifications, informs the whole of Stultitia's speech. Even pleasure, which so often seems her final goal, is not an end in itself but a means to a further end, the wisdom of folly. With this paradox she begins her speech, when she claims that she is not ignorant; with the same paradox she ends it, when she quotes a lost play of Aeschylus to say that even a fool may speak in season.[4] It is, as we have seen, the basis of her irony, but it is also the burden of her message.

In order to prove her own wisdom, she demonstrates the folly of the wise — the folly, that is, of those upon whom the world bestows that epithet. Her position is stated most succinctly in one of the colloquies, where an innkeeper remarks,[5]

[1] ME 173; I Corinthians, 4.10.
[2] ME 165; II Corinthians, 11.23.
[3] ME 173–4; I Corinthians, 3.18.
[4] ME 189. See also LB II.220F–221E.
[5] LB I.742B-C: "illud scio, multos esse moriones, gestantes auriculas & tintinnabula,

this I know, that there are many fools wearing ears and bells who know more than those who wear fur-lined caps, hoods, and other insignia of the wise. Therefore, it seems to me most foolish to display more wisdom in dress than in fact. I saw a certain man who was more than a fool, who wore a gown that hung down to his heels and the hood of our Doctors; he even had the face of a grave theologian. He disputed in the presence of everyone with a great show of gravity. But he was no less amusing to the great than any fool; for he exceeded everyone in foolishness.

It is this that Stultitia sets out to prove when, having described the all-pervasiveness of her influence, she proceeds to enumerate the host of her followers. Let me turn, she announces maliciously, "to those, who amongs you, have a certaine reputacion of wisedom" (ME 101); and as she reviews the ranks, her pride in their number is exceeded only by her *Schadenfreude* in pointing out which estates and institutions are represented. Scholars, monks, kings, nobles, courtiers, popes, cardinals, bishops, poets, authors, lawyers, philosophers, theologians — all are examined and found wanting. In the words of St. Paul to the Romans, "professing themselves wise they became fools." [6] And these, of course, are only the most distinguished fools, the battalion leaders, so to speak. To enumerate all the other "animalculi," the little souls, who are fools would be an endless undertaking, so she simply takes their folly for granted. As it is, her catalogue becomes so large and all-inclusive that almost no one escapes. A few perhaps do, she says in one place, but so far as she knows no one has ever seen them (ME 161). "There is," Bacon was later to affirm, "in Humane Nature, generally, more of the Foole, then of the Wise," [7] and Cicero had written in one of his letters that "everything is full of fools." [8] Indeed, by the time Stultitia has finished her enumeration of the foolish, her audience can only agree with Feste that "Foolery, sir, does walk about the orb like the sun: it shines everywhere." [9]

It is this satirical catalogue, this distorted mirror for magistrates,

qui plus sapiant iis, qui gestant pilea suffulta pellibus, epomides, reliquaque sapientum insignia. Itaque mihi stultissimum videtur, sapientiam profiteri veste potius, quam ipsa re. Vidi quendam plusquam morionem, qui gestabat vestem usque ad talos demissam, epomidem Magistri nostri: aderat & vultus, qui videri posset gravis Theologi: disputabat apud omneis non sine specie gravitatis: magnatibus autem non minus erat jucundus, quem quivis alius morio cum stultitiae genere superaret omneis."

[6] Romans, 1.22.
[7] Bacon, *Essays*, p. 47.
[8] Cicero, *Epistolae ad Familiares*, IX.xxii.4.
[9] Shakespeare, *Twelfth Night*, III.i.42.

that earned the *Encomium* its initial notoriety, and it is this part of Stultitia's speech that is best remembered today. While it may be true, as Erasmus claimed, that no names are named, there is neverthe- less a bite to the passage that has lost little of its mordacity after four centuries, even though some of the institutions and abuses that the fool exposes have disappeared or lost their pertinence. Like all powerful satire of invective, it was guaranteed to have a *succès de scandale*. Yet another reason for its popularity may be its accessibility. No one can mistake Stultitia's attitude in these pages: in other parts of her speech we are often not sure where she stands or how we are meant to react to what she says, but here there is no question. The very style of her prose and the tone of her voice change as she begins to list her followers; for at that point the delicate chiaroscuro of her perplexing irony is replaced by the direct glare of merciless invective. Often she sounds more as though her author were Martin Luther than Desiderius Erasmus. One of Erasmus' most recent commentators, speaking of this shift in tone, has observed:

if we see in this first part the establishing of a point of view, we must admit that it is at the same time too radical and too fanciful to support a straight attack on specific actual abuses. For the idea of Folly as Nature makes all activity foolish: it does not matter whether the theologians con- tinue in the mediaeval way or give place to classical scholars of the new school, for they would be equally vulnerable from Folly's angle of shot. The comic spirit generated in the first part of the book could only expand in further exaggerations. Consequently, something peters out when we come to Erasmus' actual survey of society.[10]

At times, it is true, Stultitia attempts to shift back into her former irony, but never with much success. When, for example, after she has scarified the monks for all their follies, she observes that those follies have nevertheless made them happy, it is impossible to accept this happiness in the way that one could accept the happiness of the deluded Greek in the empty theater. The value of the monk's happi- ness is never convincing in the way the value of the Greek's was. Nor is this simply because the monk's happiness is malign and the Greek's harmless; it is also because the one is described in a context of blunt invective and the other in a context of many-edged irony. Stultitia

[10] H. A. Mason, *Humanism and Poetry in the Early Tudor Period* (London, 1959), p. 83.

herself is not unaware of the change that has come over her speech, and at the end of her catalogue she confesses that she may seem to have been composing a satire rather than delivering an eulogy.[11]

No one has ever commented upon the *Encomium* without commenting upon this section, and many have referred only to this section. By now it should be clear, however, that those who claim to possess Erasmus' book on the basis of an understanding of his catalogue of fools are as mistaken as those who think they possess Proust's novel on the basis of a reading of the atypical section, "Un Amour de Swann": they have taken the least characteristic and most traditional part for the whole. Because of its ready accessibility and the large amount of commentary on it already existing, we need not linger over this part of the *Encomium* but may pass on directly to the great conclusion of Stultitia's speech.

That wise fool Touchstone, in a moment of learning, sententiously quotes to William a saying he has heard. Whether he got it from the Bible or from the *Apology of Socrates* he does not say, but it would make little difference to Erasmus anyway, and the saying sums up Stultitia's speech: "The fool doth think he is wise, but the wise man knows himself to be a fool." [12] The first proposition of Touchstone's aphorism is demonstrated by Stultitia in her devastating catalogue; the second is expounded by her at the close of her speech where she describes the Fool in Christ. She moves into this description by way of citing many authors, some classical but most of them Christian, who have written on behalf of folly. Of course, many of her quotations are distorted and craftily lifted from context, but the fool has tried to make fools of her audience in this way before. By the time she starts quoting from St. Paul's great epistle on folly, however, a new and higher seriousness enters her jest. Now that she has finished her catalogue of fools, her tone changes once more; the blunt sarcasm of invective diminishes and irony comes back again. No longer complex and coruscating, it is now a simpler, quieter variety of irony that Stultitia employs, and even that fades away as she gets nearer to the climax of her speech. For as she talks about the Christian fool, Erasmus' face begins to show through her mask, as silver seeps through a

[11] ME 154: "satyram texere, non encomium recitare . . ."
[12] Shakespeare, *As You Like It*, V.i.33.

mirror; and it is Erasmus' own voice that we hear toward the end
when Stultitia puts on, as she says, the lion skin.[13]

It is toward this portrait of the Fool in Christ that all Stultitia's
foolery has been directed. The fool of fools is the pious Christian who
emulates the folly of Christ, who accepts, as Christ did, human
frailty.[14] He is a fool because, in accepting the wisdom of Christ, he
rejects the wisdom of this world, having learned the lesson taught in
the *Enchiridion* that "the foolishness of God is wiser than man." [15]
"To be ignorant of certain things," Erasmus wrote to Dorp about the
Encomium, "is a part of knowledge" (EE II.101[337]), and the
Erasmian Fool in Christ is ignorant of the presumption of science, the
pedantries of scholasticism, and the airy speculations of metaphysics.
To enquire into natural phenomena and to attempt to understand the
physical mechanism of God's universe is, he believes, impious: it is,
in the untranslatable pun of Aristophanes, *periphronein ton hêlion*.[16]
The anfractuous methodology of the Schoolmen he sees for what it
is — an issueless labyrinth that frustrates rather than aids one's progress toward truth. And those who claim to perceive essences and
ideas generally cannot see themselves or "a pitte, or a stone liyng in
theyr waie." [17] Any false use of human intelligence is abhorrent to
him, whether it is the perverted constriction of pedantry or the libertine incontinence of wild speculation. The Erasmian fool has often
been seen as merely another anti-Aristotelian, but, as Pineau has
pointed out, he is more: he takes his stand against the value of any
"defined or definable doctrines, because they are not found in the
Scriptures." [18] He is, rather, a follower of the school of Colet and
those who, as Stultitia describes them,[19]

---

[13] Cf. LB II.137D–138B, where the image of putting on the lion skin is defined as
signifying that one enters into an affair with higher faculties and "more magnificently"
than is his nature.

[14] ME 177: "ipsum quoque Christum, quo stultitiae mortalium subveniret, cum
esset sapientia Patris, tamen quodammodo stultum esse factum, cum hominis assumpta
natura, habitu inventus est ut homo . . ."

[15] E 65: "Et quod stultum est dei sapientius est hominibus."

[16] Aristophanes, *Clouds*, 225. B. B. Rogers' suggestion of "contemn-plate the sun" is
perhaps the best one can do in English. Stultitia tacitly refers to this celebrated
portrait of Sophocles at ME 111–12.

[17] ME 112: "cumque se ipsos ignorent, neque fossam aliquoties, aut saxum obvium
videant . . ." On all this, see Eugene F. Rice, Jr., *The Renaissance Idea of Wisdom*
(Cambridge, Mass., 1958), pp. 156ff.

[18] J.-B. Pineau, *Érasme, sa pensée religieuse* (Paris, 1924), p. 184.

[19] ME 123–4: "velut sacrilegii genus execrentur, summamque ducant impietatem, de

estem[e] it plaine wickednesse and impietee, to speake so unreverently by so hiegh secretes of *Scripture,* which rather we shoulde have in veneracion, than after suche rate goe about to expounde theim, or with so prophane *Ethnical problemes* to dispute upon theim, or arrogantly diffine theim, defilyng and bespottyng the majestee of holy scripture with so cold, naie rather filthie woordes and sentences.

These abuses in religion and learning (to use a Swiftian description equally applicable to the program of the *Encomium*) are what the world calls wisdom; it is of these that the Christian fool must strip himself to achieve a state of complete simplicity.

He must be simple because Christ, who "delited muche in . . . yongelynges, or women, or fisshers" (ME 176), was simple and taught with the examples of children, lilies, mustard seed, and sparrows, and because He "dooeth . . . blame and reprove these worldly sages, who fully cleve and stande to theyr owne wysedome" (ME 175). The errors committed in ignorance are more easily forgiven by heaven than those committed out of the vanity of knowledge. Christ preached not the crafty wisdom of the fox, but the gentleness, meekness, and peacefulness of the lamb: we think of sheep as foolish animals, but He is the *agnus Dei.* The point is, of course, that the wisdom of God will reside, as Ficino once argued, only in a fit receptacle,[20] and a fit receptacle is a mind that has been cleared of false wisdom. Not only did Christ suffer the little children to come unto Him, but it is the childlike who can best approach Him. We must be fools for Christ's sake, for the mind of the fool is not closed to Him by *sapientia mundana.* Finally, the mind must also be free of the restrictions of the body, and here (ME 182–6) Erasmus goes on to expound that quasi-Platonic dualism between spirit and matter which stands more explicitly at the heart of the *Enchiridion.* It is a dualism that seems strangely at war with much that Stultitia has said earlier, though it is not, I think, finally irreconcilable with the earlier parts of the speech.

The highest folly and, indeed, the Christian's greatest reward (ME 187) is a transcendent, mystical theolepsy: to be seized by God in

---

rebus tam arcanis et adorandis magis quam explicandis, tam illoto ore loqui, tam prophanis Ethnicorum argutiis disputare, tam arroganter definire, ac divinae theologiae majestatem tam frigidis, imo sordidis verbis simul et sententiis conspurcare." Cf. the passage in the celebrated adage *Dulce bellum inexpertis* (LB II.961C-D). For a convenient modern edition of the adage, see *Dulce bellum inexpertis,* ed. and tr. Yvonne Rémy and René Dunil-Marquebreucq (Brussels, 1953); this passage, p. 60.

[20] See Marsilio Ficino, *Opera omnia* (Basle, 1576; 2 vols.), II, 1282ff.

such a way that the whole man is outside of himself (*totus homo extra se futurus sit* [ME 188]) and becomes an ineffable part of the *summum bonum* is analogous to the life in paradise. Combining the mysticism of the *devotio moderna* in which he was brought up with the Neoplatonic *furor divinus* which he learned from the Italians, Erasmus carries his argument on behalf of folly to its logical conclusion by demonstrating that the final state of folly is to lose oneself in God. And so, having begun her speech with a total acceptance of man in all his mortality, Stultitia brings her oration to a close by raising man out of that human mortality into the Christian immortality of the soul. She has brought us from the sight of man in his daily misery to a mystical vision of man in eternal joy; she has taught us that the way to God leads through an acceptance of the absurd comedy of this life. As she turns to descend from the pulpit, her final words command us to applaud, live, and drink. To applaud, that is, because we have been amused and entertained; to live life to the full; to drink her beloved wine. But on a higher level she is also asking us to applaud because we approve of the lesson she has taught, to live the Christian life she has extolled, and to drink from "that large flowyng well of eternall felicitee" which is Christ.

7

THE FOOL OF NATURE

THE longer one studies Erasmus, the more one realizes the extent to which his was one of the seminal minds of the modern world. It is, however, the nature of seed, as Christ reminded his followers, that it should lose itself in the plant it forms; and Erasmus is no exception to this. Like many great teachers, he is forgotten when his pupils are not, and many who read Rabelais or Montaigne, Shakespeare or Jonson, Ariosto or Cervantes, have only heard of the scholar from Rotterdam who taught them all so much. Since Erasmus' own day, there has probably not been a time more given to translation than our own, yet modern translations of his work are rare, and even those made in the sixteenth century are seldom reprinted. "His day," J. A. K. Thomson says, "may be coming yet, but I doubt that . . . Irony of an intellectual kind can never be made popular." [1]

The *Moriae encomium* is the one exception to this general neglect, in that it continues to be read and translated; yet it remains a difficult book, and one comes to feel that few who have read it have understood it, that for every More there have been many Dorps. Those who have reached some understanding of Erasmus' message have found it difficult to restate that experience for others, precisely because Erasmian irony is even less submissive than most literary forms to paraphrase. To touch it is to upset its delicate balance; to try to distil its essence is to lose those subtleties of flavor that *are* its essence. Often, of course, it is utterly impossible to say what Stultitia means,

---

[1] J. A. K. Thomson, *Irony* (London, 1926), p. 234.

since, at least when she has on "the lion skin," she means both what she says and the opposite of what she says. Yet too many readers have been content merely to turn each of her remarks upside down, to assume that she (or Erasmus) meant simply the opposite of what she says. If the present reading has been able to do nothing else, I hope it has at least managed to demonstrate that many of her most outrageous remarks can stand on their own feet, as well as their heads, and mean exactly what they say, as well as the opposite.

In the course of this detailed examination of the *Encomium*, I have also tried to keep in mind certain larger questions, such as the nature and function of the irony and the pattern of the work as a whole. I have wished, for example, to show that the most important part of Stultitia's speech is that section where she describes herself, rather than the more famous section where she describes her followers; that it is in the former that the rapier of irony is forged for the purposes of defensive battle, whereas in the offensive action of the latter the weapon employed is the broadsword of invective. But Erasmus' legacy to European thought was more than a formal, stylistic one. If we are to perceive anything like the full extent of the vast influence that his little book had, we must look beyond the irony, seminal though that was, to the figure of the fool as he drew her. For it is, in the last analysis, Stultitia herself, standing at the threshold of the sixteenth century, who casts her shadow across the subsequent ages.

There had never been anyone quite like her before. But the moment we say that, we are committed to saying what she is like; and herein lies the difficulty. It is not that we do not know: she has spoken at such length, and we have watched her so closely and heard her voice so clearly, that we could not fail to recognize her were she to appear again. But to *say* who she is, to describe her and explain what she stands for, is still not easy. The difficulty of course is primarily the result of her irony; but in addition to that, and growing out of it, is the difficulty created by the fact that Stultitia describes her position negatively. Occupying as she does a middle position, she locates it by describing the extremes on either side, both of which she rejects, both of which border her position, and upon both of which her position depends. Thus, when she invectively condemns a kind of action or thought, she rejects one side, but, when she ironically praises an opposite kind of action or thought, she also rejects the other side. Moreover, the position she occupies between the two is not only derived from the extremes, but includes something from each extreme as well.

It is as though one attempted to describe the quality of the color green by describing in detail yellow and blue, observing that green was neither yellow nor blue but stood somewhere in between and partook of the qualities of both. Given such a description, it would still be hard for someone who did not know to say what green was; and we, who know that there are greens and greens, could not tell whether the green in question was more blueish or yellowish. As a polemical device, this method is not without its advantages; for you cannot easily be attacked if you do not reveal exactly where you are. Also, you have the advantage of mobility; for you can move, so to speak, now nearer blue, now nearer yellow. At the same time, as an offensive strategy this device has its liabilities: precision becomes impossible, and you have no fixed point from which to attack. You cannot, that is, define the middle position you wish to advocate. One sees this more clearly, perhaps, in *A Tale of a Tub*, where Jack and Peter are vivid personalities but the figure of Martin is always a little shadowy.

It is, however, this middle position that characterizes the mind of Erasmus. Looking at the problem in another way, one can say that Stultitia is simply a figuring forth of his personality. The truth she derives from polar opposites is the dynamic truth Erasmus believed in, and her irony is the logical mode of expression both for a quality of mind that perpetually perceived the qualifying *but* to any argument and for an empathy of heart that participated actively in all aspects of being without committing itself exclusively to any one. Such a truth is, properly speaking, objective truth, and, inasmuch as irony depends upon perspective, it is the perspective of objective distance.

Such rare "objectivity" has made Erasmus seem vacillatory, inconsistent, and even cowardly to many later readers, as it did to his contemporaries. Gabriel Harvey, for example, could not help linking Erasmus' name with that of his bête noire, Andrew Perne, and observing, "Erasmus, and Dr. Perne will teach a man to Temporise and

Localise at occasion."[2] And Horace Walpole later summed up a whole school of anti-Erasmianism when he wrote, with reference to Pope's *First Satire of the Second Book of Horace*, "*Good Erasmus's honest mean* was alternate time-serving."[3] He has always been what Pope called him, "that great injured name."[4] But to the Harveys and Walpoles of the world Erasmus' position has inevitably seemed intolerable, because its moderation has been inconceivable to them. Actually, it reflects a rare depth of wisdom and a moral commitment to an all-embracing truth that is supremely consistent and courageous, as Thomson has pointed out. Thomson goes on to compare Erasmus' position to the Greek idea of *sophrosyne*, a word that he defines with Erasmian paradoxicality as "a passion for moderation."[5] That a fool should have a passion for moderation may seem to be the final joke, but like all Stultitia's jokes it is a joke of the highest seriousness.

There is one further reason for the difficulty in trying to describe the nature of Stultitia, which is simply that she is as all-pervasive and as protean as nature itself. Indeed, in many ways she is a surrogate for nature, and often in the course of her speech we can read *natura* for *stultitia*, *naturalis* for *stultus*. She herself insists upon this in many places. Folly, whose corporal seat is in the penis, not the head (ME 14–5), creates a natural life; she informs it in such a way that the more there is of folly the more there is of life (ME 30–1); and she preserves it against suicidal urges, causing her fools to exclaim how good it is to be alive (ME 54–7). Christ himself, in accepting the "nature of man," accepted folly (ME 177); for human life, says Stultitia, "is naught els than a certaine great plaie of Folie" (ME 46). She, like nature, is immanent in all human affairs, and it is she who holds society together (ME 34–5), because, as Erasmus told Dorp,

[2] *Gabriel Harvey's Marginalia*, ed. G. C. Moore Smith (Stratford-on-Avon, 1913), p. 138.

[3] Letter to the Reverend Henry Zouch, 21 October 1758, *The Yale Edition of Horace Walpole's Correspondence*, ed. W. S. Lewis, XVI (New Haven, 1951), 18.

[4] Alexander Pope, "An Essay on Criticism," v. 693. See also, Letter to Jonathan Swift, 28 November 1729: "Yet I am of the religion of Erasmus, a Catholic; so I live; so I shall die . . ." (*The Correspondence of Alexander Pope*, ed. George Sherburn [Oxford, 1956], III, 81). Also, I, 128, and esp. I, 118 (Letter to John Caryll, 18 June 1711): "I will set before me that excellent example of that great man and great saint, Erasmus, who in the midst of calumny proceeded with all the calmness of innocence, the unrevenging spirit of primitive Christianity!"

[5] J. A. K. Thomson, "Desiderius Erasmus," in *Social and Political Ideas of Some Great Thinkers of the Renaissance and Reformation*, ed. F. J. C. Hearnshaw (London, 1925), p. 156.

she excepts no condition of humanity: one touch of folly makes the whole world kin.[6] The numen of Folly, she observes, extends everywhere; her cult unites everything (ME 5). And she asks, "Is there ought doen here amonges mortall men not full of foly, bothe by fooles, and afore fooles?" (ME 42). If it is therefore natural to be a fool, to be a fool is also to be natural. From the Stoic point of view, nature is foolish; from Stultitia's point of view, stoicism is folly because it denies nature. Stultitia rejects the Stoics, as well as the philosophers, the metaphysicians, the scientists, and the Schoolmen, because they employ antinatural means to understand nature, "and yet dooeth nature lowdely laughe theim to scorne, with all theyr conjectures" (ME 111–2).

It is this Erasmian advocacy of nature, this belief in the benevolence of the force of nature in man, together with its corollary postulate that the human will is free, that caused Luther to accuse Erasmus of Pelagianism. In one of his answers to Luther, the second *Hyperaspistes, diatribe adversus Servum Arbitrium Martini Lutheri*, Erasmus expounds his view of nature succinctly when he writes,[7]

I say that in those who are well born and well brought up there is the least inclination toward evil. The greatest part of the proclivity comes not from nature, but from corrupt institution, from bad companionship, from the habit of sinning and evilness of will.

If the passage sounds familiar to our ears, it is because we know it in its French translation as the rule of the Abbaye de Thélème.[8] In a sense, the *Moriae encomium* is nothing more than a series of variations on this theme, and the part that Stultitia plays as Mother Nature is derived from this principle. It is, then, not his own nature that

---

[6] EE II.98(337): "nullum enim mortalium genus praeteriit Moria."

[7] LB X.1454F–1455A: "Fateor in quibusdam ingeniis bene natis ac bene educatis minimum esse pronitatis [*scil.*, ad malum]. Maxima proclivitatis pars est non ex natura, sed ex corrupta institutione, ex improbo convictu, ex assuetudine peccandi malitiaque voluntatis."

[8] R II.430/I.lvii: "En leur reigle n'estoit que ceste clause:

FAY CE QUE VOULDRAS,

parce que gens liberes, bien nez, bien instruictz, conversans en compaignies honnestes, ont par nature un instinct et aguillon qui tousjours les poulse à faictz vertueux et retire de vice, lequel ilz nommoient honneur. Iceulx, quand par vile subjection et contraincte sont deprimez et asserviz, detournent la noble affection, par laquelle à vertuz franchement tendoient, à deposer et enfraindre ce joug de servitude; car nous entreprenons tousjours choses defendues et convoitons ce que nous est denié." This was first pointed out by Renaudet and is discussed at some length in Lucien Febvre, *Le Problème de l'incroyance au XVIe siècle* (Paris, 1947), pp. 338ff. Febvre slightly misquotes the passage and gives an erroneous reference.

corrupts man, but the man-made institutions, habits, and customs to which he subjects himself.

In advancing this belief, Erasmus takes his position in the eternal philosophical conflict, which was articulated as early as Pindar as the war between *physis* and *nomos*, between nature and law or custom. Erasmus saw the conflict clearly and took the side of nature — insofar as he can ever be said to take a side. It is significant that at least twice in the *Colloquia* he refers to custom (*mos* or *consuetudo*) as a tyrant. Once, in fact, when one of his characters asks who made a certain "barbarous law," the answer given is, "Custom, than whom there is no mightier tyrant." [9] Human wisdom, that *sapientia mundana* of which Stultitia is so impatient, tends to construct laws as an expression of its experience, a code for its conduct, and a confinement for the passions and emotions with which it is always at war. Initially such *nomoi* are abstracted directly from the experience of nature, but in their abstract immutability they lose touch with the organic mutability of nature and gradually come to contradict their source. Montaigne, in his magnificent last essay, exposes the failure of one of the greatest *nomoi* ever created by man, Roman Law, to deal with or comprehend the experience of nature, out of which the laws had been made and to which the laws were meant to apply. "Nature," he says, anticipating what Samuel Johnson was to say about Shakespeare, "gives them ever more happy than those we give our selves." [10] In the course of human history, whenever human intelligence has seemed most powerful and self-sufficient, whenever it has reached a kind of godlike apogee and tended to rely more and more upon itself and its creations, a figure like Euripides or St. Paul or Diderot has appeared to turn that intelligence back upon itself, to question itself, to ask with William Drummond of Hawthornden, "What is all wee knowe compared with what wee knowe not?" [11]

Bataillon is reported to have remarked at a recent conference that

[9] LB I.825C (*Synodus Grammaticorum*): "ALBINUS: Quis persuasit legem tam barbaram? BERTULPHUS: Consuetudo, quovis tyranno potentior." See also LB I.767B (*Puerpera*).

It has been claimed that Shakespeare took his phrase, "the tyrant custom" (*Othello*, I.iii.230), from this source. See T. W. Baldwin, *William Shakspere's Small Latine and Less Greeke* (Urbana, 1944), I, 740–1.

[10] M III.362/III.xiii: "Nature les donne tousiours plus heureuses que ne sont celles que nous nous donnons."

[11] Quoted in Douglas Bush, *English Literature in the Earlier Seventeenth Century, 1600–1660* (Oxford, 1945), p. 277.

the word *nature* poses no philosophical problems in Erasmus, and I think one can agree with this, even though, as A. O. Lovejoy and H. S. Wilson have demonstrated,[12] the term is always a complex one in any author, especially in the Renaissance. For Erasmus, the humanist and alumnus of Deventer, nature, and human nature in particular, was the creation of God and a force for good which, if uncorrupted and unrestricted, would lead man to God and the Christian life. It was the creations of man — the institutions, the sciences, the philosophies — which he felt tended to corrupt and restrict the force of nature. Any philosophy of life that denied nature, that, as Rabelais says, repressed and held down men by vile subjection and constraint,[13] whether it was called Stoicism or scholasticism, tended to lead men away from the good and the true. To be sure, the Stoics had based their code on the principle of *Sequere Naturam;* but to follow nature in the Stoic sense generally meant to restrict one's natural impulses, and in this respect the Stoic philosophy could be regarded as antinatural. In contrast to this attitude, Erasmus believed, as he puts it in the *Enchiridion,* that "those things turn out badly which you attempt to do against your nature." [14] Against such abstract, antinatural edifices of philosophy as Stoicism, the natural world itself always stands as a challenge and a corrective: it is the touchstone of reality that calls into question any "unnatural" conduct. A modern poet, using Erasmus' symbol of the Sorbonne, has expressed the same philosophy when he ironically claims that

> They will get it straight one day at the Sorbonne.
>
> We shall return at twilight from the lecture,
> Pleased that the irrational is rational,
>
> Until flicked by feeling, in a gildered street,
> I call you by name, my green, my fluent mundo.[15]

[12] See *Courants religieux et humanisme à la fin du XVe et au début du XVIe siècle. Colloque de Strasbourg, 9–11 mai 1957* (Paris, 1959), p. 138. See also A. O. Lovejoy and George Boas, *Primitivism and Related Ideas in Antiquity* (Baltimore, 1935), pp. 447–456; and H. S. Wilson, "Some Meanings of 'Nature' in Renaissance Literary Theory," *JHI,* II (1941), 468–72.

[13] R II.430/I.lvii.

[14] E 70–1: "fere enim infeliciter evenire, quae tentes invita Minerva." The idiom *invita Minerva,* which is found in Virgil, is a traditional way of saying *contra naturam.*

[15] Wallace Stevens, "Notes Towards a Supreme Fiction," *The Collected Poems of Wallace Stevens* (New York, Alfred Knopf, 1955), pp. 406–7.

It is the green, the fluent mundo, the world of nature, that will always deny any attempt to make the irrational rational, to force the mutability of nature into the abstraction of a code; it is the feeling in the human heart that will always correct the antihuman constructs of the mind.

One must not, however, regard this advocacy of nature as a form of simple, anarchic, antirational primitivism. Not only did Erasmus insist that human nature had to be *bene natus ac bene educatus*, but, in the best tradition of the Christian humanism he helped to found, he saw nature and reason as going hand in hand. Just as he would have man reject the *sapientia mundana* in order that the *sapientia Christi* may enter into his spirit, so he would have man reject the unnatural reason of the Stoics and scholastics, not in order that he be deprived of reason, but rather in order that man's natural reason may operate freely. In attacking perversions of reason, Stultitia by implication is extolling the right use of right reason.[16] Her point is that natural reason will teach us to act reasonably, that it is the Stoical, scholastic *nomoi* that tyrannically put down natural reason and lead to the unreasonable excesses of those philosophies. We know the Erasmian position on natural reason more clearly from his other writings, especially the *Enchiridion*, then we do from the *Encomium*. Again, this is the result of the inability of irony to expound such a matter; and, given the ironic nature of his book, Erasmus simply had to forgo the expression of his belief in the power of reason, rightly employed, to lead man to the threshold of faith and salvation.

Yet one may also wonder if it is not true that in writing the *Encomium* Erasmus led himself into greater doubts about the efficacy of reason than he ever experienced before or after. Toffanin has remarked that in the *Encomium* wisdom has the air of wanting to commit suicide, and indeed the thought is quite explicitly entertained.[17] But at times it almost seems that every kind of reason is negating itself, both right reason and wrong reason, *ratio sapientiae* and *ratio scientiae*. Perhaps the joke carried Erasmus farther than he intended to go, or perhaps his doubts were particularly great at that time, but it does seem, as Renaudet has said, that "he did not even attempt to hope that

---

[16] Though it neglects to treat Erasmus, whose position on reason is difficult to determine, to say the least, the best study of *recta ratio* is the recent book by Robert Hoopes, *Right Reason in the English Renaissance* (Cambridge, Mass., 1962).

[17] Giuseppe Toffanin, *Storia dell' Umanesimo*, III (Bologna, 1952), 65. Cf. ME 56.

man, wretched as he was, could redeem himself with the power of his intelligence." [18] In Erasmus' thought generally, there is an almost paradoxical, synoptic fusion of rationalism and fideism: nature is seen as the handmaiden, not the adversary, of grace, and reason leads up to faith. Yet in the *Encomium* one does not sense quite the same harmonious interaction. The extreme reliance upon faith and theolepsy implied at the end of Stultitia's speech and the concomitant absence of reason in her description of the Christian Fool may simply have been dictated by the ironic trope and the foolishness of Folly; nevertheless, even when that has been admitted, Erasmus seems to go farther here in a direction of what is almost antinomian pietism than he does in his other utterances.

When all has been said about the philosophy of knowledge and nature that Erasmus sets forth in the *Moriae encomium*, the most impressive thing about his fool remains her humanity, her optimistic faith in human nature and her realistic acceptance of the vicissitudes of mankind. In this she prefigures Shakespeare's greatest fool, who, for all his comic motley, faithfully follows his master into the tragic storm when folly is the only companion left. To mention Shakespeare, whose debt to Erasmus may well have been enormous, is to remember the essentially dramatic character of Erasmus' mind and to wonder that he never went further than the *Colloquia* in this direction. For his ability to empathize with all conditions of humanity, however high or however wretched, is Shakespearean in its intensity and magnitude, and his vision of truth as the dynamic interaction of opposites is the dramatist's vision. It is significant that one of Shakespeare's profoundest characters put on the antic disposition to reach truth and turned, for a moment, from the harsh world to walk in the corridor and read what was perhaps Stultitia's speech. Both Shakespearean and Erasmian irony are so wholly informed with this sense of humanity that railing satire is rarely a possibility for them: an afterthought of pity almost always mutes the cry of outrage. Even when Stultitia turns her invective against her followers, we are aware that it is done out of pity for the victims of such fools — and not wholly without pity for the fools themselves. Although in many senses Swift is the most Erasmian of English authors, his savage indignation is alien

[18] Renaudet, *Italie*, p. 102.

to Erasmus' humanitarianism; he could never have accepted Stultitia's deluded Greek in the theater or her painted old woman. Though he would have endorsed her eulogy of the man who broke away from Plato's cave, he could never have shared her sympathy for those who remained within watching shadows.

Erwin Panofsky has seen this humanity in the *Moriae encomium* as an indication of the Renaissance spirit, and it is fitting to bring this consideration of Stultitia's speech to a close with his comment:

If one wants to perceive, at a glance, the difference between the Middle Ages and the Renaissance, one may compare Sebastian Brant's *Fools' Ship* of 1494 with Erasmus of Rotterdam's *Praise of Folly* of 1512. Brant, without a trace of tolerance or irony inveighs against more than a hundred kinds of human folly, firmly convinced that he is right and that everybody else is wrong. Erasmus also ridicules folly. But he, the most intelligent man of the century, does this by pretending to speak in the name of Folly herself. Whatever is said must therefore be interpreted as his opinion as well as hers . . . In an ironical double-twist like this there does appear a humanism — and a humanity — utterly foreign to the Middle Ages. In the Middle Ages reason could question faith and faith could question reason. But reason could not question itself and yet emerge with wisdom.[19]

It is this wisdom and this humanity that enable the first and greatest of all fools to look about her at the troubled condition of man and to claim that[20]

I partly through ignorance, partly through unreckefulnesse, not seeldome through oblivion of peines passed, sometyme through hope of better fortune, yea and now and than savouryng theyr bittred taste with a little hony of pleasure, in so manyfolde evilles releve and succour theim.

[19] Erwin Panofsky, "Renaissance and Renascences," *Kenyon Review,* VI (Spring 1944), 234–5.
[20] ME 54: "Verum ego partim per ignorantiam, partim per incogitantiam nonnunquam per oblivionem malorum, aliquando spem bonorum, aliquoties nonnihil mellis voluptatibus aspergens, ita tantis in malis succurro . . ."

II ❧ RABELAIS' PANURGE

8

LE TIERS LIVRE

"It is interesting to notice," wrote the Italian critic Zumbini at the end of the last century, "how the major philosophical and moral concepts introduced during the first thirty years of the sixteenth century managed to achieve their exalted ends by assuming forms that were comic, strange, whimsical, and seemingly very remote from those purposes." As examples of this, he proceeds to cite Erasmus' *Moriae encomium*, Thomas More's *Utopia*, the *Epistolae obscurorum virorum*, Ludovico Ariosto's description of the moon, and the macaronics of Teofilo Folengo, and he concludes by observing that "last in time but not in merit among all these high intelligences, Rabelais sketched out his thought in the characters and customs of a fantastic abbey." [1]

The list is a suggestive one and quickly maps out a large section of the topography of early sixteenth-century thought. Though the works themselves represent a diversity of genres ranging from mock epic to pseudo-epistle, from parody to the mariner's tale, their similarities are more striking than their differences: all are satires with a certain debt to Lucian; all were written by humanist Latinists; all were bitterly attacked; and all are variations, in one way or another, on the Horatian theme, *ridentem dicere verum*. Moreover, each displays that intermixture of style and adaption of genre which are so characteristic of Renaissance literature and which, as one critic has put it, "seem to express the self-questionings of a traditional culture

---

[1] Bonaventura Zumbini, *Studi di letterature straniere* (Florence, 1907), pp. 369–70.

during an epoch of rapid and far-reaching change."[2] What is perhaps most significant, however, is that they are all Erasmian, and as such they give partial indication of the extent and variety of his influence upon European thought and literature. The debt of the *Utopia* to Erasmus is a commonplace, and it is well known that Erasmus himself was falsely accused of having written the notorious *Epistolae obscurorum virorum*; both Ariosto's *Orlando Furioso* and Folengo's *Baldus* exhibit the specific influence of the *Encomium*; and, as we have seen, the very inscription over the door to the Abbaye de Thélème is a translation of a sentence Erasmus wrote against Luther.

Of all these authors, none is more comic and none more devotedly Erasmian than François Rabelais. Indeed, one way of reading his story of Gargantua and Pantagruel is to see it as a restatement in fable of the great humanist's philosophy. Unfortunately, the two men never met, nor is there any indication that Erasmus ever read that part of his disciple's work which was published during his lifetime. Nevertheless, he knew of Rabelais, and they shared, in the best humanist tradition, a friendship in spirit and a common dedication to *litterae humaniores*. Rabelais' apostleship to Erasmus is confirmed by the one letter we have from him to Erasmus, in which he reveals a deep filial affection and respect, acknowledges the proportions of his debt, and, in imagery that only the eccentricities of Renaissance taste could have deemed decorous, claims that the sage of Rotterdam has been not only a father to him but also a mother, at whose "chaste breasts I have suckled your divine learning."[3]

It is this *divina doctrina* that nourishes and informs all of Rabelais' writing, and scholars have already pointed out an astonishing number of verbal parallels in the works of the two men. More recently, Lucien Febvre and Raymond Lebègue have examined the ideological similarities between the two, and it is now generally recognized that Erasmus supplies one of the best tools for breaking open what Rabelais called the marrow bone (*os médullaire*) of his work — for penetrating, that is, to the esoteric content of his story.[4] Yet despite these scholarly

[2] Harry Levin, *Contexts of Criticism* (Cambridge, Mass., 1957), p. 86.

[3] EE X.130: "castissimis divinae tuae doctrinae uberibus usque aluisti."

[4] See L. Delaruelle, "Ce que Rabelais doit à Érasme et Budé." *Revue d'histoire littéraire*, XI (1904), 220–62; W. F. Smith, "Rabelais et Érasme," *RER*, VI (1908), 215–64, 375–8; L. Thuasne, *Études sur Rabelais* (Paris, 1904), pp. 27–157; Lucien Febvre, *Le Problème de l'incroyance au seizième siecle. La Religion de Rabelais*

efforts, there is still much that we do not know about the Erasmian influences upon Rabelais; and though it is a matter which calls for a full-scale treatment that cannot be attempted here, nevertheless the nature of our subject does lead us inescapably into the relationship between the two men. For when Rabelais came to write his most serious book, he turned, as Erasmus had a generation earlier, to a kind of fool for his protagonist and created in the character of Panurge a brother for Stultitia.

Panurge's book is the *Tiers Livre*. In *Pantagruel*, where we first meet him, his role is that of the side-kick and his function is to provide the roguish amusement of which his name (*panourgos*) warns us; but in the *Tiers Livre* he moves to the center of the stage, where, abandoning the wit of the rogue for the ignorance of the fool, he directs the action in a quest for knowledge. Later, in the *Quart Livre*, he will again occupy a more subordinate role, and by then he will have sunk from the ignorance of the fool to the petulance of the coward. This is not to say, as many have, that his character is inconsistent: it is merely that experience changes him.[5] But our concern here is not so much with Panurge the rogue or Panurge the coward as it is with Panurge the fool, and it is in the book he dominates, the *Tiers Livre*, that he is specifically given this part to play.

When we turn from the Abbaye de Thélème at the end of *Gargantua* to the story of Diogenes at the beginning of the *Tiers Livre*, we move from one world into another. The giants of the first two books, as almost every reader has observed, shrink in stature to the size of mere humanity; the Gargantuan world of humanistic optimism and freedom is replaced by a world of philosophical doubt and fear; and the position as hero of the perfect prince Pantagruel is almost usurped by the imperfect fool Panurge. As we begin the *Tiers Livre*, we leave Gargantua's kingdom of Utopia behind us and set out on the long road that is to lead us across France to a harbor in Brittany and voyages beyond. There was an "uchronianism" about the utopian world of Gargantua, an idealistic remoteness of (in Marot's phrase) "le bon vieulx temps." But the world of Panurge

(Paris, 1942); Raymond Lebègue, "Rabelais, the Last of the Erasmians," *Journal of the Warburg and Courtauld Institutes*, XXII (1952), 193–204.

[5] See W. M. Frohock, "Panurge as Comic Character," *Yale French Studies*, XXIII (1959), 71–6.

exists in a time more urgently present and is pervaded with an awareness of what Ronsard was to call "les misères de ce temps." The very
center of the Gargantuan world, the Abbaye de Thélème, seems in
fact, like the cloud-capped towers and gorgeous palaces of Prospero,
to dissolve before our eyes, as if Rabelais had anticipated that his
Utopia could not last. For while his description of it begins in the
hopeful, predictive future tense, it moves quickly into the past-
imperfect and ends in the nostalgic past-perfect which describes the
enigma "qui fut trouvé," presumably long afterwards, in the foundations of the abbey that, five chapters before, had not yet been built.

The time, then, of the *Tiers Livre* is now, the place here. The
story is still funny and still a game, but the jest is shaded with deep
seriousness and the game has become one of high stakes. The prose
that describes it is more learned, richer, and more somber in tone.
The author is no longer the fantastic M. Alcofribas, "abstracteur de
Quinte Essence," who, quoting Aristotle, claimed that laughter was
the property of man; he is now M. Fran. Rabelais, "docteur en Medicine et Calloïer des Isles Hieres," who asks his benevolent readers to
defer their laughter until the seventy-eighth volume.

Twelve years of silence on Rabelais' part stretch between *Gargantua* and the *Tiers Livre*, and to understand the difference between
these two books one must understand what happened to Rabelais and
to France in those intervening years. That Rabelais suddenly fell silent
and that, over a decade later, he suddenly chose to speak again both
seem to be the result of significant events that took place in his world.
By perilous coincidence, the *Vie inestimable du grand Gargantua* had
appeared in the bookstalls less than a fortnight before the seditious
placards were nailed on walls and doors across France on the night of
October 17, 1534. The years that followed the Affaire des placards
were years in which it was imprudent to speak and even more imprudent to publish, and shortly after that event the author of *Gargantua* simply disappears. When we find him again, some five months
later, on his way to Rome with Cardinal Jean du Bellay, he has already
exchanged his pen for a scalpel and begun the long road, analogous
to that of Panurge, that was to take him for ten nomadic years from
Rome back to Paris, from Paris to Montpellier, from Montpellier to
Lyon and back again, to Aigues Mortes, to Turin, to Chambéry, to

Orléans, to Mans, to the îles d'Hyères. During this time profound transformations were taking place in France, and by 1545, when Rabelais presumably wrote the *Tiers Livre*, the world for which Gargantua and Pantagruel had originally been conceived no longer existed.

When Rabelais took up his pen again, the political situation of France seemed particularly grave. The ambitions of Charles VIII and François I had been checked by Charles V and Henry VIII, and François found himself almost alone and without allies in his struggle against the Empire and England. The Treaty of Crépy had just been signed, and the Treaty of Ardres was about to be signed; in both cases the provisions were unfavorable to France. The Venetian ambassador, invariably a careful and perceptive observer of the French scene, wrote home that "at the end of 1545, His Majesty found himself in a situation more uncertain than that at the beginning of the year; for he had gained nothing in the English question, while at the same time he had expended a great deal. The Scots were highly discontent; the Emperor very uncertain." [6] At the same time that France was losing ground in Europe and being forced back into what were to become its modern boundaries, the situation within those boundaries was not a wholly secure one for the throne. François was in serious financial difficulties because of the expenses of his wars, and the people of Paris were refractory about complying with his demands for money. In 1543 the town of La Rochelle had revolted against his representative, and in the same year the whole of the southwest (including the îles d'Hyères, where Rabelais was perhaps writing the *Tiers Livre* shortly afterwards[7]) had revolted against the *gabelle*. Royal power was being questioned and redefined, and a great reign was drawing to its close.

In religion, the reformation was reaching its climax. The split between Calvinism and Lutheranism, as well as that between Catholicism and Protestantism, had become irreparable, and the compromise positions of men like Lefèvre d'Étaples and Erasmus were becoming less and less tenable. Erasmus had died at Basle in 1536, a disappointed old man, and in the same year Lefèvre had died at Nérac, in exile from the persecutions that followed the Affaire des placards and with

[6] E. Lavisse, *Histoire de France depuis les origines jusqu'à la Revolution* (Paris, n.d.), V (II), 117.
[7] See R I.cxxxix.

the regret that he had not suffered for the Evangile.[8] As Erasmus lay dying in Basle, the first edition of the *Institutio religionis christianae*, with its significant epistle dedicatory to François I, appeared in the same city, written by a man who had visited both Lefèvre and Erasmus shortly before their deaths and of whom Lefèvre's colleague, Roussel, had sadly observed at the time that "such an old malice had fallen on such a young man." [9] As Calvin was establishing himself in Switzerland, the persecutions of the Protestants under François I continued with increasing vigor, until in 1545–46 it seemed as though the whole of France was ablaze with the bloody flames of the *bûchers*. Every sort of non-Catholic became fuel for these fires: "among the victims," according to one historian, "one finds Lutherans and sacramentarians, simple dissidents who have adhered to no sect but who do not regularly profess Catholicism; free-thinkers; preachers and book-pedlars. The Place Maubert in Paris is the theatre for these horrible executions: in 1546 Pierre Chappot and Gobillon, Michel, Gresteau, and Dolet. Books are burnt as well as men; the *Institutes* for lack of Calvin." [10] In the provinces, as well as in Paris, the persecutions became more violent; and in April 1545, as Rabelais was finishing the *Tiers Livre*, the terrible massacre of the Vaudois took place in Provence, where over eight hundred people were killed, the women and children burnt alive in a church, and Mérindol, Cabrières, and twenty-two villages obliterated.[11] A cry of horror went up all over Europe. The conflicts in religion were about to break into open warfare.

It was in such tumultuous circumstances that the *Tiers Livre* appeared. What is more, it was because he felt the gravity of such developments in religion and politics that Rabelais (as he tells us in his Prologue) decided to take up his pen again after so many years. To speak at all in such a time, when books were burned and men were burned for writing them, was extremely dangerous — and for no one more so than for Rabelais, whose allegiances were suspect and whose first two books had already been condemned more than once

[8] Henri Hauser et Augustin Renaudet, *Les Débuts de l'âge moderne* (Paris, 1946), p. 247.
[9] E. Amann, "Lefèvre d'Étaples," *Dictionnaire de théologie catholique* (Paris, 1923–50), IX (i), 154.
[10] Lavisse, *Histoire*, V (II), 386–7.
[11] Lavisse, *Histoire*, V (II), 121.

by the Sorbonne. Obviously, he himself was perfectly aware that his friendship with the king's sister (to whom he dedicates the *Tiers Livre*), his evangelism, and his nonconformist pacifism all laid him open to charges of heresy and sedition; and it is a measure not only of his passionate commitment to certain ideas, but also of his courage, that he decided to write and publish the book he did. For, properly understood, it is one of the most daring books of the century, and Rabelais had seen men martyred for much less. Fortunately for him, however, its message does not seem to have been very completely comprehended, at least by those in a position to persecute him. Indeed, it is only recently that critics have even perceived the true subject of the *Tiers Livre*, and it would seem, as I hope to show, that even they have failed to understand many of the things Rabelais says.

His message, to be sure, is concealed. Like Stultitia, Rabelais rarely speaks his mind openly. If Erasmus could claim that he was only playing a game, so too can Rabelais; he is, in fact, what Huizinga calls him, "the play-spirit incarnate." [12] Often it is hard to know when he is playing and when he is serious, so perfectly are the two blended and so easily does the playing turn into high seriousness. There are moments, as there were in the *Encomium*, when the tone of voice is unmistakably grave, but most of the time the earnestness lurks behind the jest. It could hardly have been otherwise. Given the perilousness of his position and the subversive nature of his ideas, he could scarcely have presented them with naked directness. From the beginning Rabelais had relied upon the principle of *fabula docet*, but by 1545 he had obviously come to see the possibilities of *fabula abscondet* as well. The story of the Pichrocholine war, for example, is a fable that teaches an Erasmian pacifism, arguing that only defensive warfare is justifiable and pleading for a tolerant and clement peace. On the other hand, the story recounted in the Prologue to the *Tiers Livre* of the siege of Corinth is a fable which conceals an even more extreme pacifism; but it conceals it so successfully that no one has yet seen it for what it is. In 1534, Erasmian pacifism was still a tenable position, but by 1545 the pacifism that Rabelais advances would have been considered treason. "The best thing to do with a great truth, as Rabelais discovered," observes one of Lawrence Durrell's *sosies*, "is

[12] J. Huizinga, *Homo Ludens* (Boston, Beacon Press Paperbacks, 1955), p. 181.

to bury it in a mountain of follies where it can comfortably wait for the picks and shovels of the elect." [13]

Rabelais had, of course, claimed an esoteric quality for his earlier books, most explicitly in the Prologue to *Gargantua*, where he borrows from Erasmus the Socratic image of the Silenus and from St. Jerome the image of the marrow bone with its "substantific marrow." Yet, like almost everything else, the nature of the esotericism in the *Tiers Livre* differs from that in the first two books. In *Pantagruel* and *Gargantua*, the esoteric doctrine is, so to speak, more accessible: the message is borne within the story, but when it is expressed it is expressed directly. Gargantua's letter is the example that probably comes first to mind. Its serious credo resides within the comic Silenus of the tale as a whole, yet that credo itself is explicitly stated. The same may be said of the Abbaye de Thélème. In the *Tiers Livre*, however, such statements are rare and never reach the proportions of the letter or the abbey. Here it is the action itself that is the meaning; the exoteric and esoteric themes are more inextricably interwoven, more organically interdependent. It is as though the *sending* of Gargantua's letter had been made more important than its contents. Thus it is Panurge's quest and the failure of that quest that are more central to the meaning of the book than the subject of the quest. The difference is somewhat analogous to the difference between irony and satire discussed in the preceding section. And just as irony is more difficult to translate into direct statement than satire, so the lesson of the *Tiers Livre* is more difficult to perceive than that of the first two books.

[13] Lawrence Durrell, *Clea* (London, 1960), p. 142.

9

THE PROLOGUE

Though Panurge is the fool par excellence, in one sense or another every character in the *Tiers Livre*, with the possible exception of Gargantua, is a fool. Folly, as Stultitia boasted and as Panurge will repeat, is universal and the number of fools infinite; and it is Stultitia's catalogue of fools which comes to life to provide the dramatis personae for Panurge's story. They pass in review, one by one, as Panurge goes to each of them for an answer none of them can supply, and the last character consulted, the court jester Triboullet, is actually a fool by nature and profession. It is not surprising, then, to find that the first person we meet in the *Tiers Livre* — the author, who personally ushers us aboard his ship of fools — should also appear as a kind of fool. Laughing and joking, playing like every fool upon the word, waving his bottle in the air, muttering obscenities, cursing the monks, he steps forward to deliver the Prologue to his book, and when he appears it is as the wise fool Diogenes. This book, which is about a question, he opens with a question, asking the reader if he has ever seen Diogenes, the cynic philosopher. The pertinence of the query becomes apparent a few pages later when he explains that he is like Diogenes, and this explicit comparison is the key to his much misunderstood Prologue, which, in turn, is the key to his book. Written probably in January 1546, it is as dense and cryptic as any pages from Rabelais' pen, but a careful reading of it provides many of the essential clues to the meaning of his book and the significance of his fool.

Whatever else it may contain, the Prologue is Rabelais' most eloquent and moving defense of his role as author. By 1546, as the author of two of the most widely read and controversial books in France, he had necessarily become extremely self-conscious about his position; he had not only been censured by the Sorbonne but had also been called into question unofficially by many individuals, including reformers like Calvin, who refers in a letter of 1533 to "that obscene book, *Pantagruel*." [1] It is in response to these strictures that Rabelais begins the *Tiers Livre* by imputing to himself the persona of Diogenes, "a rare Philosopher, and the chearfullest of a thousand"; for the story of Diogenes is more than a witty tale. It is also an autobiography and must be read as such: the portrait of Diogenes which Rabelais draws is, as he himself admits, a portrait of the artist as well.

Before proceeding to examine this story, it may be useful to recapitulate its bare outlines. Briefly recounted, the anecdote is this. Threatened by an attack from Philip of Macedon, the Corinthians took fright and began frenetic preparations to meet the attack. Everyone, men and women alike, rushed about doing something for the war effort. Only Diogenes had no employment: he simply stood and watched the frenzied activities. After observing for some time, he then picked up the barrel in which he lived, took it to a hill in Corinth named Cranium, and there, in full view of everyone, started to roll it wildly down the hill, beating it, abusing it, knocking it about, until he had almost destroyed it. When one of his friends asked him what he was doing, he replied that "not being employed in any other Charge by the Republick, he thought it expedient to thunder and storm it so tempestuously upon his Tub, that amongst a People so fervently busie, and earnest at work, he alone might not seem a loitering Slug, and lazye Fellow."

Now from the Diogenes story as Rabelais tells it we learn that the Sinopian philosopher does two essential things: he sees and he tells the truth. The images of sight and speech combine to form the central image pattern of the entire Prologue; for knowledge (sight) and communication (speech) are the two basic qualities of any author. The point of the play on words in the second sentence of the Prologue — "If you have seen him, you then had Eyes in your Head" [2] — is that if the audience has *seen* the truth, here personified

[1] See A.-L. Herminjard, ed., *Correspondance des réformateurs* (Geneva and Paris, 1870), III, 110.
[2] R V.5/III.Prol.: "Si l'avez veu, vous n'aviez perdu la veue . . ."

by Diogenes himself, they are also in possession of the truth. "It is a gallant thing to see the clearness of (Wine, Gold) the Sun," [3] he continues, identifying truth with wine, as Stultitia had, and with money, as Panurge will, but above all with the traditional symbolism of the sun as the source of enlightenment; at the same time, he means to remind his audience of the best-known anecdote about Diogenes — how he asked Alexander the Great not to stand between him and the sun. [4] On the other hand, as Rabelais goes on to say, if they have not seen it (and he doubts if they have), they can at least be told the truth by someone who has. As Pantagruel, recalling an adage of Erasmus, says later in the *Tiers Livre*. [5]

Nature, I am perswaded, did not without a cause frame our Ears open, putting thereto no Gate at all, nor shutting them up with any manner of Inclosures, as she hath done unto the Tongue, the Eyes, and other such out-jetting parts of the Body: The Cause, as I imagine, is, to the end that every Day and every Night, and that continually, we may be ready to hear, and by a perpetual hearing apt to learn: For of all the Senses, it is the fittest for the reception of the knowledge of Arts, Sciences and Disciplines.

Diogenes himself, in the anecdote about the siege of Corinth, is first represented as a spectator, as one who observes in order to perceive the truth. [6] He then goes out and rolls his barrel, which is his symbolic way of communicating to the Corinthians the truth he has seen; and they, *seeing* this, thus learn the truth. In the same way, says Rabelais, I have stood by, watching my countrymen. [7]

To the same Purpose may I say of my self,
>   Tho' I be rid from Fear,
>   I am not void of Care.

[3] R V.5/III.Prol.: "C'est belle chose veoir la clairté du (vin et escuz) Soleil."

[4] It was at this point that Alexander "soubhaytoit en cas que Alexander ne feust, estre Diogenes Sinopien" (R V.7/III.Prol.).

[5] R V.130/V.xvi: "Nature me semble non sans cause nous avoir formé aureilles ouvertes, n'y appousant porte ne clousture aulcune, comme a faict es oeilz, langue et aultres issues du corps. La cause je cuide estre affin que tousjours, toutes nuyctz, continuellement puissions ouyr et par ouye perpetuellement aprendre: car c'est le sens sus tous aultres plus apte es disciplines."

[6] R V.14/III.Prol.: "Diogenes, les voyant en telle ferveur mesnaige remuer et n'estant par les magistratz employé à chose aulcune faire, contempla par quelques jours leur contenence sans mot dire."

[7] R V.16/III.Prol.: "Je pareillement, quoy que soys hors d'effroy, ne suis toutesfoys hors d'esmoy, de moy voyant n'estre faict aulcun pris digne d'oeuvre, et consyderant par tout ce tresnoble royaulme de France . . ."

For perceiving no Account to be made of me, towards the Discharge of a Trust of any great Concernment, and considering that through all the Parts of this most noble Kingdom of France . . .

Yet to be an idle spectator is not enough; for it is shameful to possess the truth and not attempt to communicate it.[8]

In my opinion, little Honour is due to such as are meer Lookers on, liberal of their Eyes, and of their Purse parsimonious; who conceal their Crowns, and hide their Silver . . . who with their very Countenances in the depth of silence, express their consent to the Prosopopeie.

Therefore, he concludes, I too shall roll my barrel — that is, he will write his book and, by the action he describes, symbolically tell the truth. It is particularly significant to note the relationship to Diogenes of the last phrase quoted above. "Par mines en silence" might seem to be a precise description of his barrel rolling; yet in rejecting that course of action and allying himself with Diogenes, Rabelais tells us that Diogenes was doing more than performing a silent pantomime. He was, in fact, communicating something to the Corinthians.

Having thus compared himself with the philosopher who perceives the truth and is obliged to bring it to those who do not have it, Rabelais goes on to speak more directly and personally about his role as he conceives it. He is aware of both the difficulty of the role and the obstinacy of his audience, and there is an intimate note of sadness in his voice as he thinks on the disasters of his epoch and the personal disasters that epoch has caused him.[9]

Having made this Choice and Election, it seem'd to me that my Exercise therein would be neither unprofitable nor troublesom to any, whilst I should thus set a-going my Diogenical Tub, which is all that is left me safe from the Shipwrack of my former Misfortunes . . . my Luck or Destiny is such as you have heard.

After the ten years that he has stood and watched in silence as his countrymen fell in futile battle or were burnt at the stake, he has decided that the only course left for him is to write. Having made this courageous decision, he then proceeds to analyze the three tradi-

[8] R V.17–8/III.Prol.: "Car peu de gloire me semble accroistre à ceulx qui seulement y emploictent leurs oeilz, au demeurant y espargnent leurs forces, celent leurs escuz . . . et par mines en silence signifient qu'ilz consentent à la prosopopée."

[9] R V.18–9/III.Prol.: "Prins ce choys et election, ay pensé ne faire exercice inutile et importun si je remuois mon tonneau Diogenic, qui seul m'est resté du naufrage faict par le passé on far de Mal'encontre . . . telle est ou ma sort ou ma destinée . . ."

tional aspects of his art: its source, its purpose, and its nature. Its source is not the classical muse (*Helicon*) or Jewish lore (*fontaine caballine*) or the Neoplatonic poetic furor (*enthusiasme*): it is wine, for which God be praised! This praise of drinking is not merely the good joke or the betrayal of a natural proclivity it has always been assumed to be. It takes on the same philosophical significance for Rabelais that it did for Stultitia and plays a similar role in an Epicure-anistic transvaluation of values. As we shall shortly see, Rabelais goes even further than Stultitia and gives it a religious significance as well; but strictly in terms of his art, wine is the source of that art simply because it is a source of truth. Moreover, wine, "the said blessed and desired Liquor," is a *natural*, not a metaphysical or supernatural, source of truth, as Rabelais explains with punning garrulity.[10] And so inspired by wine, he writes, and writing, drinks, laughing all the while: "Drinking thus, I meditate, discourse, resolve, and conclude. After that the Epilogue is made, I laugh, I write, I compose, and drink again."[11] The formula, one may note, is as appropriate to Stultitia and her method of delivering the *Encomium* as it is to Rabelais.

The purpose of his art is, in the best neoclassical tradition, a moral one: "I will set myself to serve the one and the other sort of People."[12] Citing the traditional figure of Amphion,[13] he implies that he too will "rebuild" the city of Paris. In addition, he will provide those engaged in offensive as well as defensive war with a moral lesson more practical and suited to the times than Peter Lombard does in his *Sentences*[14] — a claim which recalls Erasmus' boast that the *Encomium* was more edifying than Aristotle. Now the moral lesson that Rabelais wishes to teach his readers is, precisely, Pantagruelism; and his hope, like that of Ptolemy in the anecdote he recounts, is that by showing them this natural truth he may "encrease the Affection which [the people] naturally bore him."[15] Ptolemy, according to Rabelais' Lucianic ac-

[10] R V.5–6/III.Prol.: "Vous item n'estez jeunes, qui est qualité competente pour en vin, non en vain, ains plus que physicalement philosopher et desormais estre du conseil Bacchicque, pour en lopinant opiner des substance, couleur, odeur, excellence, eminence, proprieté, faculté, vertus, effect et dignité du benoist et desiré piot."

[11] R V.18/III.Prol.: "Icy beuvant je delibere, je discours, je resoulz et concluds. Après l'epilogue je riz, j'escripz, je compose, je boy."

[12] R V.19/III.Prol.: "ma deliberation est servir et es uns et es autres."

[13] See, for example, J. Peletier du Mans, *L'Art poëtique*, ed. André Boulanger (Paris, 1930), p. 67.

[14] R V.20n168.

[15] R V.21/III.Prol.: "extendre l'affection qu'ilz luy pourtoient naturellement . . ."

count, once brought back among his spoils a black camel and a parti-colored slave, striped "in such sort, as that one half of his Body was black, and the other white." He thought that these novelties would please the people, but instead they became frightened and indignant at such mistakes of Nature. Whereupon, he came to understand "that they took more pleasure and delight in things that were proper, handsom, and perfect, than in mishapen, monstrous and ridiculous Creatures." The application of the story to Rabelais hardly needs to be pointed out. His art is concerned with just that, the ridiculous and monstrous ones — Gargantua, Pantagruel, Panurge, and the rest — and the people may not like them. It may be true, as Horace says, that nothing prevents laughter from telling the truth, but that is no guarantee that the people will accept it. The purpose of Rabelais' art is to portray those aspects of nature (the camel) and of man (the slave) that his audience has not yet seen and may, indeed, not wish to see. They may regard these aspects as infamous monstrosities created by an error of nature, but this is because of their limited possession of truth. For nature is sometimes like that. The whole truth, "if you have never seen [it], as I am easily induced to believe that you have not," is that there are camels that are black and that mankind is often not wholly black or wholly white. It is a message that Montaigne would have understood. Yet Rabelais fears that his audience may only wish to hear that part of truth which is "proper, handsom, perfect"; they may be so offended by the other, more difficult and less pleasing, part of truth that they will kill him, as they did Euclion's cock, for exposing it.

This, then, is Rabelais' interpretation of his role as author. The role is a didactic one, weighted with responsibility, fraught with dangers, but capable of great achievements; and so he vacillates between hope and fear. His final conclusion, however, is that his audience will accept his message. He is ultimately prepared to trust in the goodness of human nature and to believe that mankind will accept his lesson in the spirit in which it is given.[16]

So I perceive in them all one and the same specifical Form, and the like individual Proprieties, which our Ancestors call'd Pantagruelism; by virtue whereof, they will bear with any thing that floweth from a good, free,

[16] R V.22/III.Prol.: "Je recongnois en eulx tous une forme specificque et proprieté individuale, laquelle nos majeurs nommoient Pantagruelisme, moienant laquelle jamais

and loyal Heart. I have seen them ordinarily take Good-will in part of
Payment, and remain satisfied therewith, when one was not able to do
better.

When we recall that his books had been violently attacked and
forbidden, that he had been forced three times into exile and did not
dare to enter and live in Paris,[17] and when we remember that within
less than a year his friend Dolet was to be burned alive for what he
had written, this Pantagruelist "Jollity of Mind pickled in the scorn
of Fortune" [18] and this optimistic expression of faith in mankind
become one of the most touching passages in the whole of Rabelais.
The faith in mankind that it reveals is exceeded only by Rabelais'
even greater faith in Truth itself.[19]

Believe it if you will, or otherwise believe it not, I care not which of them
you do, they are both alike to me, it shall be sufficient for my Purpose to
have told you the Truth, and the Truth I will tell you.

The most famous part of the Prologue, however, is not that where
Rabelais defines his literary role, but that where he speaks of his
political role. That Rabelais had a political purpose in writing the
Prologue has never been doubted. In his great edition of Rabelais,
Abel Lefranc himself asks: "Can we fail to see, as well, in the patriotic
exaltation that characterizes this prologue, a political intention?" [20]
Specifically, the patriotic exaltation that Lefranc refers to is the
Ciceronian rhetoric of the following paragraph.[21]

To the same Purpose I may say of my self,
            Tho' I be rid from Fear,
            I am not void of Care.
For Perceiving no Account to be made of me, towards the Discharge of a
Trust of any great Concernment, and considering that through all the

---

en maulvaise partie ne prendront choses quelconques ilz congnoistront sourdre de
bon, franc et loyal couraige. Je les ay ordinairement veuz bon vouloir en payement
prendre et en icelluy acquiescer, quand debilité de puissance y a este associée."
[17] Surely it is to this that he is cryptically referring when he says, "car à chascun
n'est oultroyé entrer et habiter Corinthe." The sexual overtones of the phrase are
explained by Erasmus in LB II.150D–151E.
[18] R VI.20/IV.Prol.: "gayeté d'esprit conficte en mespris des choses fortuites."
[19] R V.370/III.lii.: "Croyez la ou non, ce m'est tout un; me suffist vous avoir dict
verité. Verité vous diray."
[20] R V.xxii.
[21] R V.16/III.Prol.: "Je pareillement, quoy que soys hors d'effroy, ne suis toutesfoys

Parts of this most noble Kingdom of France, both on this and the other side of the Mountains, every one is most diligently exercised and busied; some, in the fortifying of their own Native Country, for its Defence; others, in the repulsing of their Enemies by an Offensive War; and all this with a Policy so excellent, and such admirable Order, so manifestly profitable for the future, whereby France shall have its Frontiers most magnifically enlarged, and the Frenches assured of a long and well-grounded Peace; that very little withholds me from the Opinion of good Heraclitus, which affirmeth War to be the Father of all good things; and therefore do I believe that War is in Latin called *Bellum* not by Antiphrasis, as some Patchers of old rusty Latin would have us to think; because in War there is little Beauty to be seen, but absolutely and simply; for that in War appeareth all that is good and graceful, and that by the Wars is purged out all manner of Wickedness and Deformity. For Proof whereof, the wise and pacifick Solomon could no better represent the unspeakable Perfection of the Divine Wisdom, than by comparing it to the due Disposure and Ranking of an Army in Battle Array, well provided and ordered.

This, Lefranc cogently argues, is a reference to the work of fortification that was begun at the end of 1545 and continued throughout 1546 in anticipation of a new rupture with Charles V, and there can be little doubt that Rabelais is writing with reference to such an event. What is not only doubtful but incredible is Lefranc's interpretation — which has become the traditional and accepted one[22] — of Rabelais' attitude toward this preparation for a new war. Is it really conceivable, in view of the position on war he had taken in both *Pantagruel* and *Gargantua*, that Rabelais could be attempting to "persuade the people to bow before the superior necessities and contribute without objection to the security of the towns and the king-

hors d'esmoy, de moy voyant n'estre faict aulcun pris digne d'oeuvre, et consyderant par tout ce tresnoble royaulme de France, deça, dela les mons, un chascun aujourd'huy soy instantement exercer et travailler, part à la fortification de sa patrie et la defendre, part au repoulsement des ennemis et les offendre: le tout en police tant belle, en ordonnance si mirificque et à profit tant evident pour l'advenir (car desormais sera France superbement bournée, seront François en repous asceurez), que peu de chose me retient que je n'entre en l'opinion du bon Heraclitus, affermant guerre estre de tous biens pere: et croye que guerre soit en latin dicte belle non par antiphrase, ainsi comme ont cuydé certains repetasseurs de vieilles ferrailles latines, parce qu'en guerre gueres de beaulté ne voyoient, mais absoluement et simplement, par raison qu'en guerre apparoisse toute espece de bien et beau, soit decelée toute espece de mal et laidure. Qu'ainsi soit, le Roy saige et pacific Salomon n'a sceu mieulx nous repraesenter la perfection indicible de la sapience divine, que la comparant à l'ordonnance d'une armée en camp."

[22] For a typical example, see Abraham C. Keller, "Anti-War Writing in France, 1500–60," *PMLA*, LXVII (1952), 240–50, esp. pp. 244–8.

dom"? [23] Can we really say that "with this *sursum corda*, with this rallying cry (for that is what it is), Rabelais has therefore fulfilled once again his role as royal propagandist"? [24] On the surface that is what Rabelais is trying to make it sound like, and his eloquence is, to be sure, urgent. On the other hand, we must be careful about taking Rabelais at face value; for that is what he wished the censors to do, and that is what most of his critics have done. V. L. Saulnier is the only commentator I know who has pointed out that not only do all of Rabelais' other writings contradict this position, but the rest of the *Tiers Livre* itself, especially Panurge's decision to marry in order to give up soldiership, also contradicts it.[25] Yet Saulnier's interpretation is scarcely more satisfactory than Lefranc's: there is little evidence to claim, as he does, that Rabelais is urging "un combat religieux." [26] He is not, in fact, urging any kind of combat at all.

The first hint we have of the insincerity of this passage is in its tone. The style itself, with its hollow rhetoric and oversubtle logic, ought to imply irony at once. At times it sounds a bit too much like parody to be serious: "car desormais sera France superbement bournée, seront François en repous asceurez." The etymology which derives *bellum* from *bellus* is too obviously a joke for Rabelais to have expected any but the most literal-minded censor to take it seriously. The refutation of that derivation was, in fact, the subject of Erasmus' longest, most eloquent, and most famous adage, *Dulce bellum inexpertis*, and, considering the nature of the *Adagia*, it can be none other than Erasmus himself to whom Rabelais' epithet, "some Patchers of old rusty Latin" (*certains repetasseurs de vieilles ferrailles latines*), applies. That he could have meant either the etymology or the epithet seriously is inconceivable. And the bland statement that "in War appeareth all that is good and graceful, and that by Wars is purged out all manner of Wickedness and Deformity" is, to say the least, denied by all experience. The entire passage smacks too much of the *advocatus diaboli* to be considered a *sursum corda*; it is too similar to Stultitia's invective irony to be accepted at face value.

That this passage can so consistently have occasioned misreadings is the result of most readers' having forgotten the fable of Diogenes

[23] R V.xxii.
[24] R V.xxii.
[25] R V.73/III.vii: "respirer de l'art militaire, c'est à dire me marier."
[26] V. L. Saulnier, *Le Dessin de Rabelais* (Paris, 1957), p. 91.

and his barrel from which it is extracted. For the function of the fable, like the function of all fables, is to point toward a moral which the reader is then expected to apply to another situation. As such, the story of Diogenes controls both the structure and the meaning of Rabelais' Prologue. Concomitantly, any given statement in the Prologue, if it is to be properly understood, must be considered in its analogous relationship to that story. Now there are two aspects to an allegorical fable: its moral and its application. The writer can either state the moral and suggest the application, or he can state the application and suggest the moral. To be explicit about both would tend to vitiate the power of the device: to leave one implicit causes the reader to participate in the device to the extent of working out that half for himself. Rabelais chooses to state the application of the fable for the reader. "Je pareillement," he says: "I am like Diogenes." Similarly, he explains that France is like Corinth; for everyone is busy making preparations, offensive and defensive, against the threatened invasion. He only is doing nothing, merely watching; so he has decided to imitate Diogenes and roll his barrel.

To understand this application, therefore, we must first determine the moral of the Diogenes fable, which Rabelais leaves for us to supply. What does Diogenes do? He first watches the Corinthians and meditates on what he has observed. He then goes out and imitates their action in a ridiculous fashion by abusing "his Jolly Tub, which serv'd him for an House to shelter him from the Injuries of the Weather," until he comes very close to destroying that home.[27] Patently, he is demonstrating to the people of Corinth that their frenzied preparations are absurd, an absurdity which Rabelais emphasizes by means of the long catalogues of ludicrous verbs he applies to both the defense of Corinth and the rolling of the barrel. What is more, he is also showing them that their thoughtless activity is completely futile (*comme Sisyphus faict sa pierre*) and is endangering their home (*en telle ferveur mesnaige remuer*). The significance of the fact that all this is done on a hill called Cranium is too obvious to be labored. Thus, the action of Diogenes condemns the action of the Corinthians. Is it not logical, therefore, that when Rabelais compares the defense of France to the defense of Corinth, and himself

---

[27] R V.14 & 16/III.Prol: "le tonneau fictil qui pour maison luy estoit contre les injures du ciel"; "tant que peu s'en faillit qu'il ne le defonçast."

to Diogenes, he is trying to show the French how absurd they are and to what extent they are endangering France itself? The irony that he employs to do so — his excessive praise of France's bellicose preparations — is precisely the same as that Diogenes had employed: "I saw everyone so terribly busy that I felt I really ought to be doing something myself . . ."

One cannot seriously imagine Rabelais looking on at the events of 1545 with approval. He did not, and in the Prologue he is explaining that he does not. He can see the "clairté du Soleil." He can also see that France is engaged in an absurd comedy; but he perceives as well the ultimately tragic nature of that comedy and the tragic fate of those "Persons, who in the view and sight of all Europe act this notable Interlude or Tragi-Comedy." [28] He himself, having watched this disaster in silence and fear for ten years, refuses to be any longer an Ass of Arcady, whose ignorant silence implies consent. His book may seem as foolish as Diogenes' barrel rolling; but the foolishness of them both is actually the wisdom of folly.

In addition to its political commentary, the Prologue to the *Tiers Livre* also contains several important indications of Rabelais' religious position in 1546. The most obvious of these is the famous anti-monachal passage that comes at the end, where, like Raminagrobis driving the monks away from his deathbed, the author drives them away from his book. It is even possible to identify, by religious order or activity, the various types of monks he had in mind. Those who "sometimes counterfeit [beggars]" (*contrefacent quelques foys des gueux*) are the Franciscans.[29] Those who "jog hither, wagging your Tails, to pant at my Wine and bepiss my Barrel" (*Venez vous icy culletans mon vin et compisser mon tonneau*) are the Sorbonne priests who had drawn up articles of censure against Rabelais' former books.[30] The "Bustuary Hobgoblins" (*Ces larves bustuaires*) are the monks who were at that moment responsible for the burnings in France, for the deaths of those whom Panurge, imitating monachal zeal, is later to condemn as "combustible Heretick[s]." [31] And the "Cerberian

[28] R V.17/III.Prol.: "personnaiges, qui en veue et spectacle de toute Europe jouent ceste insigne fable et tragicque comedie . . ."
[29] R V.25/III.Prol. Urquhart mistranslates *gueux* as "Devotion."
[30] See the passage in *Pantagruel*, R IV.347/II.xxiv.
[31] R V.172/III.xxii: "haereticque bruslable."

Hell-hounds" (*mastins Cerbericques*) is possibly a reference to the popular pun on Dominicans, *domini canes*. In any case, Rabelais sends all of them, in a bitter, almost Miltonic attack on their pastoral pretensions, as hounds back to their sheep. If, he concludes, to be a Catholic is to countenance such scandals, and if his refusal to do so is offensive to the Church, "I renounce my part of Papimanie." Finally, in a savage condemnation that makes reference to their supposed sexual promiscuity, he sends the monks off to the tortures they perform on others.[32]

All of this is an attitude with which we are familiar in Rabelais. There is, however, a more significant passage that explains another aspect of Rabelais' religious attitude in 1546 which seems to have gone unnoticed by even such an assiduous commentator as Lucien Febvre. To be sure, it is obscurely worded, but Rabelais had no other choice.[33]

Having dispatch'd this point, I return to my Barrel. Up, my lads, to this Wine, spare it not: Drink, Boys, and trowl it off at full Bowls: If you do not think it good, let it alone. I am not like those officious and importunate Sots [*lifrelofres*], who by Force, Outrage and Violence constrain an easie good-natur'd Fellow [*lans*] to whiffle, quaff, carouse, and what is worse [*trinquer, voire caros et alluz, qui pis est*]. All honest Tiplers, all honest gouty Men, all such as are a-dry, coming to this little Barrel of mine, need not drink thereof, if it please them not: But if they have a mind to it, and that the Wine prove agreeable to the Tastes of their worshipful Worships, let them drink frankly, freely, and boldly, without paying anything, and welcome. This is my Decree, my Statute and Ordinance.

Now there are in this passage five words that are somewhat unusual and have occasioned etymological notes in editions of Rabelais: *lifrelofres, lans, trinquer, caros,* and *alluz.* The one thing they all have in common is Germanic origins, and all of them imply a reference to Germany or Switzerland. This is especially true of *lifrelofres,* and,

[32] R V.25/III.Prol.: "Davant davant! Iront ilz? Jamais ne puissiez vous fianter que à sanglades d'estrivieres, jamais pisser que à l'estrapade, jamais eschauffer que à coups de baston!"

[33] R V.22-3/III.Prol.: "De ce poinct expedié, à mon tonneau je retourne. Sus à ce vin, compaings. Enfans, beuvez à pleins guodetz. Si bon ne vous semble, laissez le. Je ne suys de ces importuns lifrelofres, qui par force, par oultraige et violence, contraignent les lans et compaignons trinquer, voire caros et alluz, qui pis est. Tout Beuveur de bien, tout Goutteux de bien, alterez, venens à ce mien tonneau, s'ilz ne voulent, ne beuvent; s'ilz voulent et le vin plaist au guoust de la seigneurie de leurs seigneuries, beuvent franchement, librement, hardiment, sans rien payer, et ne l'espargnent. Tel est mon decret."

according to Huguet,[34] in sixteenth-century usage *en lifrelofre* was synonymous with *à la manière allemande*. Because of this, the passage has always been taken as one of the commonplace sixteenth-century jibes at the excessive drinking of the Germans and Swiss.

Yet there is an urgency and gravity of tone here which should warn us that Rabelais is saying something more important. Why should he interrupt his exhortation to drink up in order to say that those who do not wish to drink are not obliged to and that he is not going to force people to drink the way the Germans do? The answer should be apparent. The immediate connotations that "German" and "Swiss" would have had to any of Rabelais' contemporaries would have been "Lutheran" and "Calvinist"; and in fact the passage is a reference to the so-called Utraquist controversy which was raging in Europe, especially in Protestant Germany and Switzerland, at this very time. The wine Rabelais is talking about is indeed the source of truth; it is indeed "benoist piot," for it is the blood of Christ. Luther had insisted that the laity, as well as the clergy, be given the Eucharist in both kinds, and the Catholic Church had condemned this as a Hussite heresy. Rabelais takes what may seem to be a curious position in the controversy, yet it is an eminently Rabelaisian one. And one of the typically Rabelaisian turns of phrase employed to express it, "s'ilz voulent et le vin plaist au guoust de la seigneurie de leurs seigneuries," is a remarkable anticipation of the famous provision, "cujus regio, ejus religio," which was to be written into the Peace of Augsburg less than ten years later.[35]

Actually the position is Erasmian, as one might expect; and, as one might also expect, Erasmus carefully avoided the central issue of whether or not communion in both kinds was necessary to salvation. His spokesman Eusebius in the colloquy *Convivium religiosum* may well be referring to this controversy and expressing Erasmus' own uncertainty when he says, "Everyone is allowed to drink wine these days; whether or not this is a good thing I do not know." [36] In general, however, Erasmus tended to avoid the question almost entirely[37] and,

---

[34] E. Huguet, *Dictionnaire de la langue française du seizième siècle* (Paris, 1925—), s.v.

[35] See Hauser and Renaudet, *Débuts*, p. 517.

[36] LB I.680C: "Nunc licet quidem omnibus bibere vinum; an expediat nescio."

[37] See A. Renaudet, *Études érasmiennes (1521–29)* (Paris, 1939), p. 232.

apart from two or three brief references to it in his letters,[38] his only pronouncement on this issue is to be found in the *Apologia adversus monachos quosdam Hispanicos* (1527). The monks had, in their attack against Erasmus, quoted a letter of his in which they claimed he had said: "Nevertheless, quite frankly I do wonder why it should seem necessary to change that which Christ established, when the reasons they have advanced do not seem very serious."[39] To this charge, Erasmus replied that it was true that originally the sacrament had been distributed in both kinds. He went on to say that earlier in the letter quoted he had claimed that the greater sin of the Utraquists was that they rejected the judgment and custom of the Church. But still he maintained that it was not impious per se to receive the sacrament in both kinds.[40]

And a little before: "And in this matter it seems to me that he sins more because of the fact that he hatefully rejects the judgment and custom of the Roman Church, rather than because he believes it to be holy to take the Eucharist in both kinds." There it is. On the other hand, it is essential that the reasons be important ones which argue, contrary to the tradition of Christ and contrary to the authority of the Holy Scripture, that they should take away half of the sacrament from the laity. I do not doubt that they have some, which they perhaps prefer to conceal because of some constraint. But it is not in itself impious to take communion in both kinds.

Rabelais adopts this Erasmian position of freedom of choice in the matter of the Eucharist. Although he implies that he believes in *utraque specie*, at the same time he is not prepared to force his views on anyone else: "Drink, Boys, and trowl it off at full Bowls: if you do not think it good, let it alone." For Erasmus, as we have seen,

---

[38] Most importantly in answering (EE IV.116) a direct question on the issue from John Slechta (EE IV.82ff), where he maintains the same position that he does with the Spanish monks. See also EE V.15 and VI.402.

[39] LB IX.1066A-B: "Tametsi, ut dicam ingenue quod sentio, demiror cur visum sit immutare quod a *Christo* fuit institutum, cum causae, quas adferunt, non admodum graves videantur."

[40] LB IX.1066B-D: "Item paulo superius: *Atque hac in parte, mea sententia, magis peccat secunda factio, quod odiose rejecit judicium et consuetudinem Ecclesiae Romanae, quam quod existimat pium esse sub utraque specie sumere Eucharistiam.* Haec ibi. Oportet autem gravissimas esse causas, quae persuaserint, ut praeter veterem totius Ecclesiae consuetudinem, praeter *Christi* traditionem, praeter auctoritatem Scripturae divinae, dimidium ejus sacramenti subtraherent Laicis. Nec dubito quin habuerint, quae fortassis ob offendiculum aliquod premere maluerunt. Neque enim per se impium est, sub utraque specie sumere."

Christ was the fountain of eternal joy. For Rabelais, the blood of Christ is "a true Cornu-copia of Merriment" (*un vray cornucopie de joyeuseté*). For both of them, His religion is one not of sadness but of joy, not of despair but of hope: "Good Hope remains there at the bottom, as in Pandora's bottle; and not Despair, as in the Punction of the Danaids."[41] Thus, indebted as he is to Erasmus, Rabelais attacks any restriction on the will, either from the *larves bustuaires* or the *importuns lifrelofres*, and he propounds a Thelemite Christianity of free will and hope.

The subject of the *Tiers Livre* is truth and not, as has so generally been said, marriage. Panurge the fool is not seeking a wife; he is seeking an answer. That answer and that truth cannot be supplied by the world, for they reside, as we shall see, within Panurge himself and are dependent upon his free will. Rabelais' Prologue, with its imagery of the sun, of seeing and hearing, and of wine, is also about truth. In the Prologue he implies that it is only when the will is free and unrestricted by customs or institutions — when neither Alexander (the State) nor the monks (the Church) stand between it and the sun — that it can perceive the truth, the "clairté du Soleil." It is this that Panurge is taught in the course of the *Tiers Livre*, and it is this that the reader, if he listens carefully to Panurge's story, will learn. "Remark well what I have said," admonishes Rabelais near the end of his Prologue, "and what manner of People they be whom I do invite."[42] They are, as the first two words of the Prologue (significantly, added later by Rabelais) describe them, "bonnes gens." "I have not pierced this Vessel for any else, but you honest Men, who are Drinkers of the First Edition, and Gouty Blades of the highest degree."[43] We hear the accents of Stultitia again as he speaks. His message is, in the literal and fullest sense of every word, the message

---

[41] R V.23/III.Prol.: "Bon espoir y gist au fond, comme en la bouteille de Pandora: non desespoir, comme on bussart des Danaides." For this we now have the important work of Dora and Erwin Panofsky, *Pandora's Box* (New York, 1956); see esp. chs. 2, 3, and 4. Rabelais' reading of *bouteille* (πίθος) rather than *boîte* (*pyxis*) is indicative of his source for the story, as the Panofskys demonstrate; this passage, however, is not actually cited by them.

[42] R V.23/III.Prol.: "Notez bien ce que j'ay dict, et quelle maniere de gens je invite."

[43] R V.24/III.Prol.: "je ne l'ay persé que pour vous Gens de bien, Beuveurs de la prime cuvée, et Goutteux de franc alleu."

— "Gloria in excelsis Deo, et in terra pax hominibus bonae voluntatis!"
— of the Evangile itself: that God should be praised a little bit
(*pourveu que du tout louez Dieu un tintinet*), that there should be
peace, not war, in the world (the story of Diogenes), and that men
should be of good will (*Je les ay ordinairement veuz bon vouloir*).

PANURGE
IN SALMIGUONDIN

❧❧❧❧❧❧❧❧❧❧❧❧❧❧❧❧❧❧❧❧❧❧❧

PANURGE is a fool. Unlearned, imprudent, irreverent, libertine, self-indulgent, witty, clever, roguish, he is the fool as court jester, the fool as companion, the fool as goad to the wise and challenge to the virtuous, the fool as critic of the world. In all of this he resembles his sister, Stultitia. Yet in the last analysis he is not so perfect a fool as she, for he lacks the ultimate wisdom of folly. Even when we first meet him, we are aware that he is incapable of becoming the Fool in Christ because, paradoxically, he is not foolish enough. He is unable, in Blake's phrase, to "persist in his folly." In one sense, the *Tiers Livre* is the *Enchiridion* that should help him to that final folly, because the experiences that Panurge has are meant to be didactic, and, ideally, at the end of the book he should have learned from those experiences and achieved that transcendent Stultitian folly which is the wisdom of Christ. To put it another way, the story told by Rabelais is a story of *l'éducation du fou*. Yet, as we shall see, Panurge never really learns the lesson given him. That final wisdom is, on the contrary, reserved for someone else. At the end of the book, as at the beginning, it is Pantagruel, not Panurge, who possesses Stultitia's highest wisdom.

Thus, in Rabelais' hands, the Erasmian fool is split up. By means of her irony, Stultitia was able simultaneously to be the foolish and the wise fool; but when, in the drama of Rabelais' narrative, these two contradictory types of fool confront each other, each is personified by a separate character. Foolish and wise folly are dynamically opposed in the dialectic between Panurge and Pantagruel, rather than organically united. Such a bifurcation does not, however, signify any substantial difference between Erasmus' and Rabelais' concepts of the fool: it is simply the artistic result dictated by two different modes of presentation. On the other hand, since each of the characters in the *Tiers Livre*, with the sole exception of Gargantua, is a fool of one kind or another, it is perhaps even more accurate to say that Rabelais' Stultitia is nothing less than the sum of all of them and that Raminagrobis and Her Trippa, Bridoye and Triboullet, and the host of other "fools" represent aspects of Stultitia no less than Pantagruel and Panurge. Yet it is essentially these two main characters who share between them Stultitia's basic premise — that fools in their folly are foolish, but that in their folly they are also wise.

Coleridge, who seems to have been the first critic to penetrate to Rabelais' philosophical meaning, perceived something of this relationship when, with characteristic Kantian terminology, he said:

Rabelais is a most wonderful writer. Pantagruel is the Reason; Panurge the Understanding, — the pollarded man, the man with every faculty except the reason. I scarcely know an example more illustrative of the distinction between the two. Rabelais had no mode of speaking the truth in those days but in such a form as this.[1]

To be sure, the Germanic concepts of *Vernunft* and *Verstand* cannot be strictly applied to these two sixteenth-century characters. Nevertheless, the distinction that this conceptual antinomy attempts to articulate is of the same order as the distinction that Rabelais tries to make between Pantagruel and Panurge. For Pantagruel does represent reason, in the humanistic, Erasmian sense of that word, while Panurge represents understanding, in the sense of natural wisdom as opposed to acquired knowledge. This distinction between Pantagruel and Panurge and the significance of their relationship is demonstrated most clearly by Rabelais in the first five chapters of the *Tiers Livre*. These chapters provide a transition from the end of *Pantagruel* to the beginning of Panurge's quest, and, before we can follow Panurge

---

[1] *Coleridge's Miscellaneous Criticism*, ed. Thomas M. Raysor (Cambridge, Mass., 1936), p. 407 ("Table Talk," 15 June 1830). Coleridge's most extensive pronouncement on Erasmus is to be found in the tenth of his philosophical lectures, delivered on 1 March 1819: *The Philosophical Lectures of Samuel Taylor Coleridge*, ed. Kathleen Coburn (New York, 1948), pp. 289–311, esp. pp. 305–8.

on that quest for knowledge, we must first observe him as he attempts to be a surrogate for Pantagruel in the land of Salmiguondin.

It is, as I have already suggested, one of the characteristics of the fool that he should stand outside the law. For the most part he seems to be, and would prefer to be, oblivious of it; he would live, if he could, in a world without rules or restrictions. But when laws are brought to bear upon him — when, that is, he is forced to take notice of them — then he must oppose them. It is for this reason that he is so frequently an iconoclast or (in the etymological sense of the word) an antinomian. The opposition between *nomos* and *physis* is absolute; and insofar as the fool is the embodiment of natural forces and instincts, he cannot be subjected to the unnatural codification or restriction of those forces without surrendering his essential foolishness. The only law he knows is the lawless law of nature. Yet it is one of the characteristics of nomos that it is always trying to control physis, and so physis is perpetually resisting that control. Nomos cannot refrain from pointing out the undisciplined excesses and errors of physis, but the invariable rejoinder of physis to this censure is the invocation of a higher law which nomos is unable, or unwilling, to comprehend or accept. Whenever the tyranny of law or custom attempts to make the fool conform, it always finds, as Defoe put it, that

> some stubborn Fools remain
> That ha' so little Wit, they won't be slain;
> That always turn again when they're opprest,
> And basely spoil the Gay Tyrannick Jest:
> Madly take Arms, and with their Masters Fight,
> And talk of Nature, Laws of God, and Right.[2]

This dichotomy lies at the heart of the "problem" in *Measure for Measure*, for example, and a conversation between Escalus and Pompey demonstrates it neatly:

Esc. How would you live, Pompey? by being a bawd? What do you think of the trade, Pompey? Is it a lawful trade?
Pom. If the Law would allow it, sir.
Esc. But the Law will not allow it, Pompey; nor it shall not be allowed in Vienna.

[2] Daniel Defoe, "Jure Divino," as quoted in Bonamy Dobrée, *English Literature in the Early Eighteenth Century* (Oxford, 1959), p. 41.

Pom. Does your Worship mean to geld and splay all the youth of the
city?   II.i.236–43

"You are a tedious fool," Escalus had said to Pompey, and Pompey
remains the fool by refusing to accept Escalus' law and asking if the
law expects men to forgo their nature.

Yet despite his inherent antipathy to the law, the fool may also
come to have ambitions with regard to it. He may hope to achieve
a position where he makes or administers the laws, and occasionally
his ambitions are realized. Thus, at the beginning of the *Tiers Livre*,
Pantagruel gives to Panurge the governorship of Salmiguondin, and
we witness the incongruous spectacle of the fool as ruler. Sancho
Panza will achieve a similar greatness when he is given the governorship of the island, and even Falstaff, though he foolishly aspires to
higher office, is given at least a charge of foot. But the irresponsible
fool, who cannot govern himself, is preordained to failure as a governor of others. At best, like Sancho, his natural sympathies may
enable him to administer a humane, if unconventional, justice; but
more often, like Panurge, his natural irresponsibility causes him to
lead the state into anarchy and ruin. The law of nature, that is, may
seem to be a more benevolent law, but its very permissiveness makes
it incapable of controlling society. So it is that Panurge, when he
takes over the governorship, manages to exhaust the revenues of three
years in only forty days by giving endless parties and feasts, by deficit
spending and unsound fiscal policy, and by consuming "son bled en
herbe." At the end of the forty days, he himself is badly in debt, and
when he leaves Salmiguondin to go on his quest he can say with
Sancho, "I came without crosse to this Government, and I goe from
it without a crosse, contrary to what Governours of other Ilands are
use to doe." [3]

Money is always a problem for the fool. He rarely has very much,
and he generally owes a great deal. It is always difficult to bring him
to a reckoning, and to ask where the money went is as futile as asking
what the devil he was going to do in that galley. He himself has no
compunction about either spending or borrowing, and when he meets
a likely creditor, he says with Falstaff, "I see no reason in the law of

[3] C VII.316/II.liii: "sin blanca entré en este gobierno, y sin ella salgo, bien al
revés de como suelen salir los gobernadores de otras ínsulas." The "crosse" of the
translation is, of course, a coin.

Nature but I may snap at him" (2:III.ii.330–1). The money, of course, goes for high living, for there is no economy in the law of nature. The world may cry, "mesnaige, mesnaige," but the counsel of the fool in the face of such exhortations to thrift is: "Set your Mind to live merrily in the Name of God and good Folks!" [4] And the fool Panurge is even able to argue with moronic sophistry that his prodigality is in obedience to the four cardinal virtues of prudence, justice, fortitude, and temperance. "But when," asks Pantagruel, "will you be out of Debt?" Panurge answers, like the fool he is, "At the next ensuing Term of the Greek Calends."

In the whole of Rabelais, no passage so closely resembles the *Moriae encomium* as Panurge's celebrated praise of debts and debtors which Pantagruel's question calls forth. It is, of course, the formalistic similarity that is most noticeable; in this instance Erasmus and Rabelais meet on the common ground of Lucianic adoxography.[5] They meet, as well, in the ironic amalgamation of jest and earnest. For Panurge's eulogy, like Stultitia's self-eulogy, is a mock one that is not wholly mocking. It is a failure to perceive the ambiguous Erasmian irony with which this encomium is delivered that has created the long critical argument over whether Rabelais is here speaking seriously.

Panurge begins his description of the pleasures of debt with a description of a prototype of Volpone, delivered in the relatively simple sarcastic invective that characterized Stultitia's catalogue of fools.[6]

You can hardly imagine how glad I am, when every Morning I perceive my self environed and surrounded with Brigades of Creditors; humble, fawning, and full of their Reverences: And whilst I remark, that, as I look more favorably upon, and give a chearfuller Countenance to one than to another, the Fellow thereupon buildeth a conceit that he shall be the first dispatched, and the foremost in the Date of Payment; and he valueth my Smiles at the rate of ready Money. It seemeth unto me, that I then act and personate the God of the Passion of Saumure, accompanied with his Angels

---

[4] R V.36/III.ii: "Pensez vivre joyeulx, de par li bon Dieu et li bons homs!"

[5] The work of Lucian that most closely resembles this is the *Parasite*.

[6] R V.44/III.iii: "Cuidez-vous que je suis aise, quand tous les matins autour de moy je voy ces crediteurs tant humbles, serviables et copieux en reverences? Et quand je note que moy faisant à l'un visaige plus ouvert, et chere meilleure que es autres, le paillard pense avoir sa depesche le premier, pense estre le premier en date, et de mon ris cuyde que soit argent content. Il m'est advis que je joue encores le Dieu de la passion de Saulmur, accompaigné de ses Anges et Cherubins. Ce sont mes candidatz, mes parasites, mes salüeurs, mes diseurs de bons jours, mes orateurs perpetuelz."

and Cherubims. These are my Flatterers, my Soothers, my Claw-backs, my Smoothers, my Parasites, my Saluters, my givers of good Morrows, and perpetual Orators.

One is also reminded of the passage in which Stultitia anticipates *Volpone*.[7] In both of them the sarcasm is unmistakable.

Yet as Panurge goes on with his argument his tone becomes more serious, and it is possible to take him in earnest as well. To be sure, the jest is always uppermost, and he is parodying the encomium by praising the despicable — just as he is also parodying, among other things, the expositions of the Schoolmen, the pseudo-scientific diagnoses of *Amor Hereos*,[8] the traditional descriptions of the Golden Age, and the proverbial imagery of Menenius Agrippa. But — such is the urgent sincerity of his eloquence — one is also aware that there is a note of seriousness in his description of debt as the Homeric chain of gold that holds the world together. For Stultitia, that *copula mundi* had been folly; but Panurge is just as serious and just as jesting when he defines it as debt. His picture of the horrors of a world without debt and the pleasures of a world with it might have come from Stultitia's mouth, and his claim for debt is the same as hers for folly — that no society or union in life can be pleasant or lasting without it.[9] For more serious-minded Ficino, however, the *copula mundi* was nothing less than love,[10] and he must be considered here as well because it is from his commentary on the *Symposium* that Panurge the fool is directly translating.[11] Indeed, as Panurge develops his argument, what he calls debt gradually becomes not only a pun on duty (*debvoir*)[12] but a synonym for love itself, that love which is *caritas*.

[7] ME 97–8.

[8] For *Amor Hereos* see John Livingston Lowes, "Lover's Malady," *MP*, XI (1913–4), pp. 491–546.

[9] ME 34: "In summa usque adeo nulla societas, nulla vitae conjunctio sine me vel jucunda, vel stabilis esse potest."

[10] *Commentarium Marsilii Ficini Florentini in Convivium Platonis, De Amore*, ed. Raymond Marcel (Paris, 1956), p. 165 (III.iii): "Quamobrem omnes mundi partes quia unius artificis opera sunt eiusdem machine membra inter se in essendo et vivendo similia, mutua quadam caritate sibi invicem vinciuntur, ut merito dici possit amor nodus perpetuus et copula mundi partiumque eius immobile substentaculum ac firmum totius machine fundamentum." See also R. Marichal, "Rabelais devant le Néoplatonisme," in *François Rabelais, Ouvrage publiée pour le quatrième centenaire de sa mort, 1553–1953* (Geneva-Lille, 1953), pp. 181–209, esp. pp. 185–6. (Referred to hereafter as *Quatrième centenaire*.)

[11] See C. A. Mayer, "Rabelais' Satyrical Eulogy: The Praise of Borrowing," in *Quatrième centenaire*, pp. 147–55.

[12] R V.58/III.iv: "dont est dict le debvoir de mariage."

The borrowing from Ficino is not simply coincidence or parody; it is a suggestion that for *debt* we may also read *love*, the taking and giving, borrowing and lending of the heart's devotion. Without this, says Panurge, the world would be no better than a dog kennel (*chienerie*); and as, in his description of the debtless world, the planets lose their motions and the sun and stars go out, one is reminded of Cleopatra, for whom a world without love was "no better than a sty." In such a world,[13]

Faith, Hope, and Charity would be quite banished . . . for Men are born to relieve and assist one another; and in their stead should succeed and be introduced Defiance, Disdain and Rancour, with the most execrable Troop of all Evils, all Imprecations and all Miseries.

Insofar as debt refers to the owing of money, Panurge is jesting, but, insofar as it refers to the owing of affection, he is serious. Pantagruel chooses to interpret it exclusively as the former (as well he might, in view of the financial debts Panurge has amassed) and he reproves Panurge by quoting the lesson from the Epistle to the Romans (13.8): "You shall owe to none any thing save Love, Friendship, and a mutual Benevolence."[14] You may talk from now to Pentecost, he says, but you will never convince me that debts are a good thing. At the same time, he qualifies his advice by adding, "I will nevertheless not from hence infer, that none must owe any thing, or lend any thing";[15] for, he explains, we all have to borrow at times and at times we all ought to lend. He too is preaching the lesson of *caritas*, but it is a more reasonable and a less self-indulgent charity. Just as Panurge will be told during the storm at sea in the *Quart Livre* that one must help himself before he asks God's help, so here Pantagruel explains to him, with a story from Plato, that a man must work for his own livelihood before he asks another's help. The story ends with Pantagruel offering to clear up Panurge's debts, and Panurge thanks him. But his thanks are a farcical parody of thanks, and, ungraciously, he bewails what it will be like now that he is out of debt, anticipating, with an anecdote from Poggio's *Facetiae*, scurrilous treatment from

[13] R V.48/III.iii: "seront bannies Foy, Esperance, Charité. Car les homes sont nez pour l'ayde et secours des homes. En lieu d'elles succederont Defiance, Mespris, Rancune, avecques la cohorte de tous maulx, toutes maledictions et toutes miseres."
[14] R V.59/III.v.
[15] R V.60/III.v: "Je ne veulx pourtant inferer que jamais ne faille debvoir, jamais ne faille prester."

those who might have been his obsequious creditors. For the first time, Pantagruel displays impatience with his castellan and abruptly terminates their discussion: "Let us wave this Matter (quoth Pantagruel) I have told it you over again." [16]

With this curt dismissal, Pantagruel comes as close as he ever does to anger; yet even here it is actually not so much anger as impatience. Pantagruel has explained to Panurge that, for all his clever arguments on behalf of debt, he is wrong, that Scripture (St. Paul) and the ancients (Plato) prescribe the proper charity and the proper occasion for debt and that their charity and debt are not Panurge's. Nevertheless, despite the fact that he has been so carefully taught this lesson, Panurge remains indocile and reverts to his original concept of a debtor's paradise. It is at this intractability that Pantagruel loses his patience. We might have expected downright anger when Pantagruel first discovered Panurge's conduct of his governorship. But Rabelais, in one of his rare and significant appearances in the first person, is quite explicit about the fact that Pantagruel does not get angry.[17]

Pantagruel being advertised of this his Lavishness, was in good sooth no way offended at the matter, angry nor sorry; for I once told you, and again tell it you, that he was the best, little, great Good-man that ever girded a Sword to his Side; he took all things in good part, and interpreted every action to the best Sense: He never vexed nor disquieted himself with the least pretence of Dislike to any thing; because he knew that he must have most grosly abandoned the Divine Mansion of Reason, if he had permitted his Mind to be never so little grieved, afflicted or altered at any occasion whatsoever. For all the Goods that the Heaven covereth, and that the Earth containeth in all their Dimensions and Heighth, Depth, Breadth, and Length, are not of so much worth, as that we should for them disturb or disorder our Affections, trouble or perplex our Senses or Spirits. He only drew Panurge aside, and then making to him a sweet Remonstrance and mild Admonition . . .

[16] R V.62/III.v: "Laissons (dist Pantagruel) ce propos, je vous l'ay ja dict une foys."
[17] R V.35/III.ii: "Pantagruel, adverty de l'affaire, n'en feut en soy aulcunement indigné, fasché ne marry. Je vous ay ja dict et encores rediz que c'estoit le meilleur petit et grand bon hommet que oncques ceigneït espée. Toutes choses prenoit en bonne partie, tout acte interpretoit à bien. Jamais ne se tourmentoit, jamais ne se scandalizoit. Aussi eust il esté bien forissu du deificque manoir de raison, si aultrement se feust contristé ou alteré. Car tous les biens que le ciel couvre et que la terre contient en toutes ses dimensions: haulteur, profondité, longitude et latitude, ne sont dignes d'esmouvoir nos affections et troubler nos sens et espritz. Seulement tira Panurge à part, et doulcettement luy remonstra . . ."

This calm, reasonable optimism and acceptance is nothing less than the philosophy of *pantagruélisme*, which Rabelais will define again in the Prologue to the *Quart Livre* as a "certain Jollity of Mind pickled in the scorn of Fortune." [18] Based on reason and directed toward pleasure, it postulates that state of mind which Epicurus termed *ataraxia* — impassiveness or calmness of mind.[19] In contrast to Panurge's uncertainties and worries, Pantagruel is throughout the *Tiers Livre* a calm and joyful fixed point of reason: in contrast to Panurge's folly stands Pantagruel's wisdom.

The story of Panurge in Salmiguondin defines the contrasts in this relationship. Panurge is not wise, yet at the same time he is not simply foolish. As his eulogy of debt demonstrates, he has an intuitive, though limited, possession of the truth and, as the *Tiers Livre* will finally show, he possesses more of it than anyone else except Pantagruel and Gargantua. It is Pantagruel who has the complete possession of truth after which Panurge is striving, and, as Panurge wanders through the *Tiers Livre* futilely asking his question, Pantagruel steps forward from time to time and gives him the answer. But, unhappily, even when he hears it told to him, Panurge the fool is incapable of seeing the truth.

[18] R VI.20/IV.Prol.: "certaine gayeté d'esprit conficte en mespris des choses fortuites."

[19] For *ataraxia*, see *Epicurea*, ed. Hermann Usener (Leipzig, 1887), pp. 30–1 (*Epistula* I.82); pp. 36, 41–2 (*Epistula* II.85, 96); p. 62 (*Epistula* III.128). See also, for example, Cicero, *Epistulae ad Familiares*, XV.xix.2–3. Cf. Montaigne's definition, based on Sextus Empiricus, *Hypotyposes*, I.xii: "Ataraxie, qui est vne condition de vie paisible, rassise, exempte des agitations que nous receuons par l'impression de l'opinion & science que nous pensons auoir des choses. D'où naissent la crainte, l'auarice, l'enuie, les desirs immoderez, l'ambition, l'orgueil, la superstition, l'amour de nouuelleté, la rebellion, la desobeissance, l'opiniatreté & la pluspart des maux corporels" (M II.226–7/II.xii).

II

THE QUEST

🏵 🏵 🏵 🏵 🏵 🏵 🏵 🏵 🏵 🏵 🏵 🏵 🏵

THE day after his return from Salmiguondin, Panurge, weary of war and the harness of battle, appears before Pantagruel without his codpiece, garbed in a Roman toga, and, quoting Cicero's "cedant arma togae," announces his intention to marry. In his ear he wears that flea which, from Charles d'Orléans to James Joyce has been what Sir Hugh Evans said it was, "a familiar beast to man, and signifies Love." [1] Joining a long line of Renaissance heroes, he forsakes the world of wars for the world of love, the life of action for a life of repose, and comes, the man of Mars, to the bower of Venus. In doing so, he joins as well the even longer line of warriors who have been fools in love — a line that stretches from Troilus and Orlando to Lucien Leuwen and is only finally extinguished by a prostitute in one of Balzac's antiheroic drawing rooms who, in reply to a lover's cry, "Je deviens fou!", effectively ends the tradition by remonstrating calmly, "Mon petit, Roland furieux fait très bien dans un poème; mais dans un appartement, c'est prosaïque et cher." [2] If the *Tiers Livre* were indeed about love and marriage, we might have seen Panurge as Aeneas or Sir Calidore, the man of action who plays truant for love, or as Achilles or Antony, the man of war who becomes a fool in love; but, since it is about the nature of wisdom, we see him instead as Socrates, who returned from the Peloponnesian War to seek truth among the Athenians.

---

[1] Shakespeare, *The Merry Wives of Windsor*, I.i.21.
[2] Balzac, *La Cousine Bette*, in *Oeuvres complètes de H. de Balzac*, X (Paris, 1879), 371.

At his trial, Socrates recounted to the jury the story of what the oracle at Delphi had said about him.[3] He related how his friend Chaerephon had once asked the oracle if there were anyone wiser than Socrates, to which the priestess had replied that there was no one. Knowing only that he was not wise, Socrates was puzzled by the oracle and determined to check the truth of it by questioning men reputed for wisdom to see if he could not find a man wiser than himself. He examined all degrees of men, politicians, poets, and artisans, but found none of them to be wiser than he; for while he found all of them to be as ignorant as he, all of them thought they possessed wisdom, whereas only Socrates knew that he did not. "My conclusion," he explained to the jury, "was this: as I went on my quest at the god's bidding, it seemed to me that the most respected men were very nearly the most deficient, while others, who were considered of less account, seemed to be more intellectually respectable." [4] Finally, Socrates explained to his jury that as a result of this enquiry he came to understand that

wisdom belongs to God alone, and with this oracle he is saying that human wisdom is of little or no worth. And it seems that, when he spoke of Socrates, he was merely using my name to make an example of me, as if to say, "The wisest of you, O men, is he who, like Socrates, knows that as far as wisdom is concerned, he is actually worthless." [5]

"Quis non stultus?" asked Horace: who is not a fool?[6] It is a question that the fool himself has always asked after he has been among those reputed for wisdom. For the fool who, like Socrates, goes abroad looking for wisdom invariably finds that the so-called wisdom of the world is only ignorance in disguise. With her wry humor, Stultitia told the same story and took the same lesson from it.[7]

Who how unmete thei be to serve for any commen affaire, or purpose amongs men, we maie be taught by the example of Socrates hym selfe, the onely wiseman, but unwysely judged by *Apollos oracle*. That wheras on

---

[3] Plato, *Apologia Socratis*, 20d–23b.
[4] *Apologia*, 22a.
[5] *Apologia*, 23a–b.
[6] Horace, *Satirae*, II.iii.158.
[7] ME 38: "Qui quidem quam sint ad omnem vitae usum inutiles, vel Socrates ipse unus Apollinis oraculo sapiens, sed minime sapienter judicatus, documento esse potest, qui nescio quid publice conatus agere, summo cum omnium risu discessit. Quanquam vir is in hoc non usquequaque desipit, quod sapientis cognomen non agnoscit, atque ipsi deo rescribit . . ."

a tyme he went about to have saied his minde in a certaine mattier to the commens of Athenes, he lefte of sodeinly, beyng all to laught to scorne. How be it this Socrates, as in one poinct (me semeth) was not all wyde, in that he wolde not take upon hym the name of a wyseman, but rather ascribed the same unto god onely.

It is the same lesson that Panurge will be taught as he goes on what a later fool, Jack of Dover (who enacts another kind of parody on the Socratic story), will call his "quest of inquirie." [8] Whether or not Rabelais deliberately patterned the *Tiers Livre* after this anecdote from the *Apologia Socratis,* no one can say. There can be no doubt that he knew the story, though, and it is hard to believe that he did not have it in mind when he sat down to write about Panurge and his search for an answer.

This search, however, is not only destined to be futile but is wholly unnecessary. Yet Panurge does not realize this. He has decided to marry and to give up war, but then, unexpectedly, he begins to have second thoughts and he turns to ask Pantagruel if he thinks marriage is advisable.[9] Pantagruel's response is straightforward: "seeing you have so decreed, taken deliberation thereon, and that the matter is fully determined, what need is there of any further Talk thereof, but forthwith to put it into execution what you have resolved." [10] Nevertheless, the fact is that Panurge has *not* firmly made up his mind. But he is talking to an Erasmian, who can see both sides of the question and whose echoing answers, patterned after one of Erasmus' colloquies,[11] give Panurge neither certainty nor satisfaction; he is only advised to do what he wishes — to marry or not to marry. To Panurge, however, such Erasmian, Thelemite freedom of the will is simply confusing, and his summary of Pantagruel's responses shows us what he would have made of Stultitia's oration.[12]

---

[8] See *Jacke of Dover, His Quest of Inquirie, or his Privy Search for the Veriest Foole in England* (London, 1604). Reprinted by the Percy Society, vol. VII, ed. T. Wright.

[9] R V.80/III.ix: "Seigneur vous avez ma deliberation entendue, qui est me marier, si de malencontre n'estoient tous les trous fermez, clous et bouclez; je vous supply, par l'amour que si long temps m'avez porté, dictez m'en vostre advis."

[10] R V.80/III.ix: "Puis (respondit Pantagruel) qu'une foys en avez jecté le dez, et ainsi l'avez decreté et prins en ferme deliberation, plus parler n'en fault, reste seulement la mettre à execution."

[11] LB I.817C-818C (*Echo*).

[12] R V.85/III.x: "Vostre conseil (dist Panurge), soubs correction, semble à la chanson de Ricochet. Ce ne sont que sarcasmes, mocqueries, et redictes contradictoires. Les unes destruisent les aultres. Je ne sçay es quelles me tenir." Urquhart erroneously

Your Counsel (quoth Panurge) under your Correction and Favour, seemeth unto me not unlike to the Song of Gammer Yeabynay; it is full of Sarcasms, Mockqueries, bitter Taunts, nipping Bobs, derisive Quips, biting Jerks, and contradictory Iterations, the one part destroying the other. I know not which of all [your] Answers to lay hold on.

Pantagruel's explanation, which Panurge is not equipped to comprehend, expounds the Erasmian philosophy that lies at the heart of the *Tiers Livre*:[13]

your Proposals are so full of ifs and buts, that I can ground nothing on them, nor pitch any solid and positive Determination satisfactory to what is demanded by them. Are you not assured within your self of what you have a mind to? the chief and main point of the whole matter lieth there: all the rest is merely casual, and totally dependent upon the fatal Disposition of the Heavens.

But the counsel is lost, and Pantagruel himself knows that Panurge is not sufficiently assured of his will to make a decision. The answer does lie within Panurge, but Panurge is not enough of a fool, in the Erasmian sense, to realize it. It is, therefore, to demonstrate that the answer cannot be found outside himself that Pantagruel suggests to Panurge that he consult the "authorities."

The quest begins, at Pantagruel's urging, with the consultation of two sources of truth recommended by the ancients, the *sortes virgilianae* and dreams. Pantagruel knows that neither is infallible, but he insists that both are preferable to dice or bones, which are "abusive, illicitous, and exceedingly scandalous," merely traps or "baited Hooks" for the unwary, and strictly forbidden by Gargantua in his kingdom. Yet neither sortition nor oneirology provides a clear answer; for while Panurge confidently interprets the results of both as being highly optimistic with regard to his marriage, Pantagruel reads them as meaning that his friend will be cuckolded, beaten, and robbed by a wife. This, of course, is the answer he will continue to get, and it is the interpretation — as unjustifiably optimistic about women as

attributes the last sentence to Pantagruel, and I have silently corrected his translation.
[13] R V.85/III.x: "Aussi (respondit Pantagruel), en vos propositions tant y a de si et de mais, que je n'y sçaurois rien fonder ne rien resouldre. N'estez vous asceuré de vostre vouloir? Le poinct principal y gist: tout le reste est fortuit et dependent des fatales dispositions du Ciel."

Chauntecleer's celebrated Latin translation — he will continue to give. The *chanson de Ricochet* is a melody he cannot escape.

In the course of his oneiromantic experiment, he is required by Pantagruel to observe a certain abstinence in food and drink in order that the images of his dreams not be obscured by "the fumish steam of Meat" previously eaten. We should pause parenthetically to consider his reaction to this request, if only to observe that, like all fools, Panurge finds dieting a distressing experience. Pantagruel invokes that *aurea mediocritas* to which the fool is always antipathetic and commands Panurge: "Mediocrity is at all times commendable; nor in this case are you to abandon it." [14] Panurge, surprisingly enough, does as he is told, but the experience leaves him disgruntled the following morning, and he comes to regret his abstinence of the night before. Claiming that he cannot think properly on an empty stomach (*le ventre affamé n'a poinct d'aureilles*), he goes off to a gigantic breakfast; and as he goes he invokes the law of nature to excuse his appetite and disposition. He speaks in accents that anticipate Falstaff.[15]

But not to Sup: A Plague rot that base Custom, which is an Error offensive to Nature. That Lady made the Day for Exercise, to travel, work, wait on and labour in each his Negotiation and Employment; and that we may with the more Fervency and Ardour prosecute our business, she sets before us a clear burning Candle, to wit, the Suns Resplendency: And at Night, when she begins to take the Light from us, she thereby tacitly implies no less, than if she would have spoken thus unto us: My Lads and Lasses, all of you are good and honest Folks, you have wrought well to day, toiled and turmoiled enough, the Night approacheth, therefore cast off these moiling Cares of yours, desist from all your swinking painful Labours, and set your Minds how to refresh your Bodies in the renewing of their Vigour with good Bread, choice Wine, and store of wholsom Meats; then may you take some Sport and Recreation, and after that lie down and rest yourselves, that you may strongly, nimbly, lustily, and with the more Alacrity to morrow attend on your Affairs as formerly.

[14] R V.110/III.xiii: "Mediocrité est en tous cas louée et icy la maintiendrez."
[15] R V.123/III.xv: "Mais ne soupper point? Cancre! C'est erreur! C'est scandale en nature. Nature a faict le jour pour soy exercer, pour travailler, et vacquer chascun en sa neguociation; et pour ce plus aptement faire, elle nous fournist de chandelle, c'est la claire et joyeuse lumiere du soleil. Au soir elle commence nous la tollir, et nous dict tacitement: 'Enfans, vous estez gens de bien. C'est assez travaillé. La nuyct vient: il convient cesser du labeur et soy restaurer par bon pain, bon vin, bonnes viandes; puys soy quelque peu esbaudir, coucher et reposer, pour au lendemain estre frays et alaigres au labeur comme davant.' "

Foolish though Panurge's penchant for excessive drinking and eating may be, there is a note of a more serious Stultitian folly in his charming description of Mother Nature putting her children to bed. Stoic abstinence is unnatural and wrong to the Epicurean fool, and stern codes of joyless hard work and frugal living are to him a crime against nature. He too will work hard, but in joy, under the clear light of the sun. But when the day is over and the night has come, he will take his repose with equal cheer, rejoicing in the fruits of his labor, which are "good Bread, choice Wines, and store of wholsom Meats."

His first two attempts having failed, Panurge, accompanied by Epistemon and Frere Jan, starts out on his journey to visit a series of "oracles" and repositories of wisdom. Significantly, Pantagruel does not accompany his friends. He does, however, suggest their first stop, the Sibylle de Panzoust, not so much because he thinks she will provide the answer as because he believes that Panurge should, for his own benefit, leave no stone unturned. "Truth," as Montaigne says, "is of so great consequence, that wee ought not disdaine any induction, that may bring us unto it." [16] When a man is in quest of knowledge, he must look for it everywhere, and there is always a chance that someone like the Sibylle de Panzoust may indeed prove to be "an Eleventh Sibyl, or a Second Cassandra." Even if she is not, explains Pantagruel, it can do no harm to consult her, and one should not make the mistake Alexander did when he refused to listen to a man who he thought could tell him nothing.[17] Nature, concludes Pantagruel, in a passage already quoted, has given us ears with which to listen and learn.[18]

The sibyl, of course, proves no more helpful to Panurge than his dream. Indeed, she turns out to be but a parody of the sibyls of classical antiquity: toothless, sniveling, ill-kempt, rheumatic, in rags, she is discovered stirring a pot of cabbage soup, reminding us of nothing so much as the inhabitants of that Lucianic purgatory which Epistemon had seen and which Webster's Flamineo anticipates in death.[19]

---

[16] M III.361/III.xiii: "mais la verité est chose si grande, que nous ne deuons desdaigner aucune entremise qui nous y conduise."

[17] R V.130/III.xvi: "Que luy eust cousté ouyr et entendre ce que l'homme avoit inventé? Quelle nuisance, quel dommaige eust il encouru pour sçavoir quel estoit le moyen, quel estoit le chemin que l'homme luy vouloit demonstrer?"

[18] R V.130/III.xvi.

[19] See R IV.306ff./II.xxx. Also, *The Complete Works of John Webster*, ed. Lucas, I, 187 (*The White Divel*, V.vi.108-13): "Whither shall I go now? O *Lucian* thy

Her phyllomantic doggerel, in answer to Panurge's question, is sufficiently cryptic to permit the usual contradictory interpretations, and
the unsatisfied Panurge goes on to consult the deaf-mute Nazdecabre,
the poet Raminagrobis, and the magician Her Trippa, all of whom
fail him in the same way. Nazdecabre's sign language, reminiscent of
Thaumaste and his debate with Panurge in *Pantagruel,* is ambiguous;
Raminagrobis' poetic fury produces a poem whose message is hopelessly equivocal; and Her Trippa, who employs metopomancy, chiromancy, and geomancy and offers to attempt any other of some thirty-
five branches of magic to provide an answer, simply makes Panurge
so angry that he loses his appetite.

The traditional game of seeking to identify which of his contemporaries Rabelais had in mind while drawing these portraits has at
best a limited value and is not germane to the enquiry here. Nevertheless, it is illuminating to consider the only one of these consultants
who can be identified with any certainty, Her Trippa. There has
never been any reason to question Lefranc's identification of this
character as the famous Henry Cornelius Agrippa of Nettesheim,[20]
for both his name and his reputation for occult philosophy are transparently parodied. Calvin himself spoke of Rabelais and Agrippa in
the same breath as being "stricken with the same blindness," [21] and
Lefranc has pointed out the curious parallels between the careers of
the two men: both were doctors who possessed a large, humanistic
acquaintance with the literature of antiquity, both spent many years
in extensive wandering, and both were condemned by the Sorbonne
for reformist heresy. Agrippa was, even in his lifetime, a legendary
figure, a kind of Friar Bacon, notable for his alchemical, prognosticative, and generally occult talents; he did horoscopes for royalty and
his *De occulta philosophia* was widely read.[22] Later he was to influence

---

ridiculous Purgatory — to finde *Alexander* the great cobling shooes, *Pompey* tagging
points, and *Julius Caesar* making haire buttons, *Haniball* selling blacking, and *Augustus* crying garlike, *Charlemaigne* selling lists by the dozen, and King *Pippin* crying
Apples in a cart drawn with one horse!"
[20] R V.lxxiv–lxxx.
[21] R V.lxxix.
[22] On Agrippa, see H. Morley, *The Life of Henry Cornelius Agrippa von Nettesheim* (London, 1856); A. Prost, *Les Sciences et les arts occultes au XVIe siècle:
Cornelius Agrippa, sa vie et ses oeuvres* (Paris, 1881–82); C. Sigwart, *Kleine Schriften*
(Freiburg-im-Breisgau, 1889); G. Rossi, *Agrippa di Nettesheym e la direzione scettica
della filosofia nel Rinascimento* (Turin, 1906); L. Spence, *Cornelius Agrippa, Occult
Philosopher* (London, 1921); Agrippa von Nettesheim, *Die Eitelkeit und Unsicher-*

both Marlowe and Goethe in their portraits of Faust.[23] As a magus, then, his relationship to Her Trippa is patent. But what Lefranc, with his concern for the problem of the *querelle des femmes*, finds particularly relevant to the *Tiers Livre* is the fact that Agrippa also wrote a treatise *De nobilitate et praecellentia foeminei sexus*, and certainly there is a significant connection between the two. Yet it is disappointing to find that Lefranc and his followers, having gone so far, stopped short of the most important connection between Agrippa and the *Tiers Livre*. For the *Tiers Livre* is in many respects a dramatization of yet another of Agrippa's works: the story of Panurge and his unsuccessful quest for wisdom among the sciences is, in effect, a fabulous rendition of Agrippa's famous *De incertitudine et vanitate scientiarum et artium, atque excellentia verbi Dei declamatio*.

Agrippa's is one of the most complex and confusing personalities of the sixteenth century, and a comprehensive study of his thought is only now in the process of being written. The legend and the man became so indistinguishable during his own lifetime that they have tended to remain so ever since. Despite Pierre Bayle's early attempt to separate the two in his article for the *Dictionnaire*, for many people he continued to be what he was for Samuel Butler: "Sir Agrippa, for profound/And solid lying much renown'd." [24] Sir John Harington had a particular reason for wishing to call him a liar because Agrippa himself, invoking a Renaissance commonplace, had called poets liars; and though Nashe seems to have read him (especially his *De incertitudine*) more carefully than most, it is the legendary Agrippa who appears in *The Unfortunate Traveller* to conjure up Cicero for Erasmus.[25] To be sure, Agrippa himself did everything he could to en-

---

heit der Wissenschaften, tr. Fritz Mauthner (Munich, 1913), introd.; P. Villey, *Les Sources et l'évolution des Essais de Montaigne* (Paris, 1908), *passim*, esp. II, 175ff; C. G. Nauert, Jr., "Magic and Skepticism in Agrippa's Thought," *JHI*, XVIII (1957), 161–82. The best studies of the *De incertitudine* are those of Mauthner, Nauert, and Rossi. There is also a work by Orsier which I have not been able to see (J. Orsier, *H. C. Agrippa, sa vie et son oeuvre* [Paris, 1911]).

[23] For Marlowe, see *The Works of Christopher Marlowe*, ed. C. F. Tucker Brooke (Oxford, 1953), p. 150 (*Doctor Faustus*, vv. 145–6). For Goethe, see *Goethes Sämtliche Werke*, Jubiläums Ausgabe, XXII (Stuttgart and Berlin, n.d. [1902]: *Dichtung und Wahrheit*, vol. I), 191: "Eins seiner Lieblingsbücher war *Agrippa de vanitate scientiarum*, das er mir besonders empfahl und mein junges Gehirn dadurch eine Zeitlang in ziemliche."

[24] Samuel Butler, *Hudibras*, ed. A. R. Waller (Cambridge, Eng., 1904), p. 17 (I.i.).

[25] For Harington, see Sir John Harington, *A Preface, or rather a Briefe Apologie of Poetrie, and of the Author and Translator* in G. Gregory Smith, *Elizabethan Critical*

courage the legend of his occult powers, for it was largely through them that he secured his patrons. Nevertheless, his belief in the occult sciences was a sincere one, and it is, therefore, not only paradoxical but also poignant that late in life, in 1526, he repudiated it all with a bitter denunciation of the uncertainty and vanity of the sciences and the arts. One can only conjecture what may have provoked such a dramatic volte-face, but surely the vicissitudes of his life, the troubling times in which he lived, and his involvement with such people as More and Lefèvre in the religious controversies of their day contributed to his skepticism of man's rational powers and his increased reliance upon faith. It is significant that, like Rabelais, he was a great admirer of Erasmus, to whom he sent a copy of the *De incertitudine*;[26] and their two names are curiously linked by Philip Sidney when, on the basis of a common but surely incorrect reading of Agrippa, he says, "Agrippa will be as merry in shewing the vanities of Science as Erasmus was in commending of follie."[27] It is only one of the many paradoxes in his life that both the *De occulta philosophia* and the *De incertitudine* should have been first published in the same year (1531), though the former had been written years before (c. 1510) and is explicitly contradicted by the latter.[28]

The *De incertitudine*, which later exerted a profound influence on such thinkers as Montaigne and Bruno,[29] was widely read throughout the sixteenth and seventeenth centuries. This is not the place for a detailed examination of either the book or its influence, but, since Rabelais so explicitly refers to Agrippa and since the parallels between the *Tiers Livre* and the *De incertitudine* are so numerous and significant, it is necessary to leave Panurge and his quest briefly and give at least a cursory description of this much-neglected book.

Though the form of the *De incertitudine* is probably derived from Sextus Empiricus, it is interesting to note that at the very beginning

Essays (Oxford, 1904), II, 199–200. For Nashe, see R. B. McKerrow, ed., *The Works of Thomas Nashe* (London, 1910), V, 115ff, esp. 118n, and II, 252–4.

[26] See Erasmus' letter to Agrippa, EE IX.352.

[27] Philip Sidney, *An Apologie for Poetry* in Smith, *Elizabethan Critical Essays*, I, 182.

[28] See Nauert, "Agrippa's Thought," for a possible explanation of this. See also the *De incertitudine*, ch. XLVIII.

[29] For Montaigne, see Villey, *Sources, passim*, esp. II, 175ff. For Bruno, see J. Lewis McIntyre, *Giordano Bruno* (London, 1903), pp. 131, 148–9.

of his book Agrippa compares his experience to that of Socrates in the story from the *Apologia*.[30] In the opening sentences of his first chapter, he succinctly establishes his basic position, which subsequent chapters confirm and reconfirm with a repetitious host of exempla.[31]

Ancient opinion and the unanimous agreement of almost all who philosophize hold any science to be such that men, on their own, are able in accordance with their intelligence and ability to achieve something of divinity, so that often they are able to raise themselves beyond their human limitations and to attain the realms of the blessed gods. It is from this belief that those many encomia of the sciences come — encomia in which each man praises with lengthy, ornate speech those arts and disciplines with which he has increased the power of his mind by long exercise, striving to place them not only before all other sciences, but above the heavens themselves. I, however, am persuaded by other reasons, and I believe that there is nothing more pernicious or harmful to the life of man and the salvation of our souls than those very arts and sciences.

They are harmful, he explains, because they make us think we are better than we actually are, because they pretend, like the serpent in the Garden of Eden, to give us knowledge and instead only give us false pride. Learning is especially dangerous if it is possessed by a bad man, who will put it to bad use. Indeed, says Agrippa, nothing is worse than an art or a science surrounded by impiety. On the other hand, he continues, if learning should fall into the hands of a fool, it will simply confirm him in his folly by giving him weapons with which to defend it. This passage is, in fact, a remarkable anticipation of Panurge and his false use of learning.[32]

For even if [learning] should not fall upon a bad man, but simply upon a fool, nothing will be prouder or more difficult than he; for, in addition

[30] *Henrici Cornelii Agrippae ab Nettesheym . . . Opera in duos tomos concinne digesta, et nunc denuò, sublatis omnibus mendis, in φιλομούσων gratiam accuratissimè recusa . . .* (2 vols.; "Lugduni," n.d. [false imprint: Strasburg? c. 1620?]), II.4: "Socrates, dum omnes fermè disciplinas perscrutatus esset, tunc primum ab oraculo sapientissimus omnium judicatus est, cùm se nihil scire palàm fateretur."

[31] Agrippa, II.1: "Vetus opinio est, et fermè omnium Philosophantium concors & unanimis sententia, qua arbitrantur scientiam quamlibet homini ipsi pro utriusque captu ac valore nonnihil divinitatis adferre, ita ut saepè ultra humanitatis limites in Deorum beatorū choros eos referre possint; hinc varia illa & innumera scientiarum encomia prodierunt, quibus unusquisque eas artes atque disciplinas, exacuit, non minus ornatu, quàm longo sermone nititur omnibus anteferre, et vel supra coelos ipsos extollere. Ego verò alius [*sic*] generis persuasus rationibus, nil perniciosius, nil pestilentius hominum vitae, animarumque nostrarum saluti posse contingere arbitror, quàm ipsas artes, ipsasque scientias."

[32] Agrippa, II.3: "Quod si etiam in non tam malum, sed stultum aliquem incidat, nil

to his own folly, which he will retain, the authority of doctrine will support him, and he will have literary weapons with which to defend his folly, lacking which other fools are more mildly foolish.

This, of course, is precisely what has happened to Panurge, who is able to cite authorities and precedents to defend his obstinate position, and this is also what makes it so difficult for Pantagruel to teach him the lesson he must learn. "For nothing is more fatal than a fool with reason." [33] The seat of truth, explains Agrippa, is not in the head but in the heart (II.2), and such is the spacious liberty of truth that rational judgment or argument or demonstration cannot comprehend it, but only faith (II.5). In a sentence which might have been written by Erasmus or Rabelais, he maintains that it is not learning that brings a man to God, but good will (*bona voluntas*), and that nature without doctrine has more often earned a man praise and virtue than doctrine without nature (II.4).

The greater part of Agrippa's treatise consists of an enumeration and refutation of those arts and sciences by the possession of which a man thinks he is wise. Some of them are occult disciplines and some of them moral and scholastic disciplines, but all fall under his scythe. Though he deals with many more disciplines than those represented by Rabelais' characters, for each of the personages in the *Tiers Livre* there is a corresponding passage in Agrippa — even for Her Trippa himself. As a typical example, one might cite this sentence, which aptly applies to the episode with Raminagrobis.[34]

There are, however, those who reach such a fury of madness that they think there are some divine prophecies [in poetry], because formerly spirits gave their responses in poetic verses. Thus they call them prophets and seers inspired by the divine spirits, and they use the trifling verses of poets as though they were oracles for divination.

"Is that to be called a Poetical Fury?" exclaims Panurge; "I cannot rest satisfied with him!" [35] Thus it is with all the branches of knowl-

---

illo insolentius ac importunum magis, nam praeter id, quod illi de cognata stultitia superest tuetur illum doctrinae authoritas, habetque literarum instrumenta, quib. suam defendat amentiam, quibus caeteri stulti carentes mitius insaniunt . . ."

[33] Agrippa, II.3: "Nihil igitur exitalius, quàm cum ratione insanire."

[34] Agrippa, II.15: "Sunt tamen, qui ad tantum insaniae furorem devinerint, ut illi nonnullas divinitatis sortes inesse putent, quia daemones olim poeticis versiculis response dederunt: hinc illos prophetas ac vates, divinoque spiritu afflatos vocat [sic], ac Poetarum nugacissimis versiculis, tanquam oraculis ad divinandum utuntur."

[35] R V.168/III.xxii: "Appellez vous cela fureur poëticque? je ne m'en peuz contenter!"

edge: all are rejected as worthless, unsure, or misleading, as erroneous, hubristic, or simply evil. To be sure, in the course of his repudiation of the arts and sciences, Agrippa himself paradoxically demonstrates an astonishing range of learning, and there are chapters like "De pastura" (LXXV) where he seems more interested in displaying that learning than in attacking the science under consideration. Yet for the most part the attack is so violent and the denunciation so bitter than one never doubts his sincerity. His conclusion is that none of these sciences is possessed "except by favor of the serpent," that the outcome of them is always bad, and that all learning is folly (*omnes scientes insanire* [II.240]).

The only key that will open the truth is the Word of God. Using the traditional imagery of the fountain that both Erasmus and Rabelais employ, Agrippa proclaims that "God alone contains the fountain of truth" (II.235). The fountain is there for all to drink from, he maintains, and his evangelistic sympathies are nowhere more evident than when he insists that it is to the Word and only to the Word that man must go for truth, relying upon no commentaries, no anagogical interpretations, nor even upon theology itself (II.234).[36]

The truth and understanding of these canonical scriptures depends solely upon the authority of God Who reveals them, and can be comprehended by no judgment of the senses, no discourse of reason, no syllogistic demonstration, no science, no speculation, no contemplation, no human powers, but only by faith in Jesus Christ which God, by means of the Holy Spirit, has placed in our soul.

It is because learning frustrates our approach to this truth that Christ was rejected by the learned scribes and pharisees and received by fools, idiots, and children. And it is because of their ability to approach the Word directly that Christ chose as his disciples ignorant common people, the unread, the unlearned, and the asses (*è rudi vulgo idiotas, omnis literaturae expertes, inscios et asinos* [II.241]).

The last word here provides Agrippa with the subject of his penultimate chapter, "Ad Encomium asini Disgressio" (CII), which was

---

[36] Agrippa, II.235: "Harum autem Scripturarum (dico Canonicarum) veritas & intelligentia à sola Dei revelantis authoritate dependet, quae non ullo sensuum judicio, nulla ratione discurrente, nullo Syllogismo demonstrante, nulla scientia, nulla speculatione, nulla contemplatione, nullis denique humanis viribus comprehendi potest, nisi sola fide in Jesum Christum, à Deo Patre per Spiritum S. in animam nostram transfusa."

probably suggested by Stultitia's concluding encomium of the Fool in Christ and which in turn may have suggested Giordano Bruno's encomium of the Asino Cillenico at the end of his *Spaccio della bestia trionfante*. The ass, of course, is nothing less than the Fool in Christ, with no pretense to learning but with a simplicity of heart, lack of pride, patience, and an endurance of persecution that make him, as Agrippa says, more than any other animal capable of divinity. It is upon this symbol of the fool, the ass, the pure in spirit, that Agrippa brings his long treatise to a close, extolling not the learned, but the "gens de bien" who are able to approach God. Just as Stultitia's message was summed up in her portrait of the Fool in Christ, so Agrippa's is finally contained in his evocation of that foolish creature who has challenged the imagination from Philo to Tolstoy, the ass of Balaam, symbol of the wisdom of ignorance:[37]

for when that prophet and learned man Balaam went forth to curse the people of Israel, he did not see the angel of the Lord, but his ass did and spoke to Balaam his rider with a human voice. Thus often a rude and simple idiot sees what the scholastic doctor, corrupted with human learning, is unable to see.

It is the scholastic doctor who is the simple idiot; it is Balaam, as Ronald Knox was fond of observing, who was the ass.

Like Agrippa's, Panurge's quest among the sciences and arts will bring him ultimately to an ass of Balaam, "nostre Morosophe, l'unicque non Lunaticque Triboullet" (V.326/III.xlvii). But to mention the fool Triboullet here is to anticipate, and we must return to where we left Panurge, traveling in the company of Epistemon and Frere Jan to consult the authorities. The sibyl, the mute, the poet, and the magician all fail to provide him with a clear-cut answer to his question; but Panurge is prepared to look everywhere, and so he puts his question to his two companions as well.

It is to Epistemon that he first turns to ask for some remedy for his "perplexity of spirit." Pragmatist that he is, Epistemon suggests that Panurge take a good dose of hellebore, the classical antidote for madness, and stop going about in such foolish attire. But Panurge, not

---

[37] Agrippa, II.243: "nam cum Balaam vir sciens & Propheta exiret, ut malediceret populo Israël, Angelum Domini non vidit, vidit autem asinus, & humana voce ad sessorem Balaam locutus est. Sic inquam saepissimè videt simplex & rudis idiota, quae videre non potest depravatus humanis scientiis scholasticus Doctor."

content with a mere purgative, replies that he has vowed not to put on a codpiece until he has got an answer to his question. Epistemon mutters that Panurge ought to come to his senses and not act as though he were eligible to wear the fool's cap (*chapperon verd et jausne à aureilles de lievre*). But Panurge persists: "Give me your Advice, and tell me your Opinion freely, should I marry or not?" The answer that Epistemon is obliged to give is that he is unable to answer.

Now Epistemon is a symbol of classical learning, of the wisdom of the ancients, and it is a melancholy moment when he confesses that this wisdom is insufficient. To be sure, Epistemon knows many opinions which might help, and there is a certain theory of the Platonics . . . But he is not convinced that they are right, and anyway he does not really understand their discipline; then, too, he always remembers the difficulties they once caused that gentleman student in Cambridge. Filled though he is with the lore of the ancients, Epistemon is forced to admit the futility of any attempt to answer Panurge's question on the basis of their authority; and he watches sadly as his learning disappears with the young man at Cambridge, who, like Robin Ostler, is one of the most memorable and evocative unseen characters in literature. Reminding us of the last oracle Delphi ever gave[38] and anticipating that Plutarchan threnody which is to figure so significantly in the *Quart Livre*, he explains that the great oracles of the classical world are dead.[39]

But you know that they are all of them become as dumb as so many Fishes, since the Advent of that Saviour King, whose coming to this World hath made all Oracles and Prophecies to cease; as the approach of the Suns radiant Beams expelleth Goblins, Bugbears, Hobthrushes, Broams, Schriech Owl-Mates, Nightwalking Spirits, and Tenebrions.

[38] These poignant verses may be found in *Corpus Scriptorum Historiae Byzantinae*, ed. B. G. Niebuhr, XXXIII (*Georgius Cedrenus Ioannis Scylitzae Ope*, ed. Immanuel Bekker [Bonn, 1838], I), 532, where they read:

εἴπατε τῷ βασιλῆι, χαμαὶ πέσε δαίδαλος αὐλά.
οὐκέτι Φοῖβος ἔχει καλύβαν, οὐ μάντιδα δάφναν,
οὐ παγὰν λαλέουσαν, ἀπέσβατο καὶ λάλον ὕδωρ.

[Say this to the king: the cunning temple is fallen into dust. No more does Phoebus hold his shrine, no more the laurel of his oracles, no more the voice of the chattering brook: for the babbling spring has shrunk away.]

[39] R V.186/III.xxiv: "Mais vous sçavez que tous sont devenuz plus mutz que poissons, depuys la venue de celluy Roy servateur on quel ont prins fin tous oracles et toutes propheties, comme, advenente la lumiere du clair soleil, disparent tous lutins, lamies, lemures, guaroux, farfadetz et tenebrions."

Just as Dante must finally say farewell to Virgil, so Epistemon must finally reject his classical learning. The advent of Christ has vitiated its powers.

Panurge turns later to Frere Jan and his *matiere de breviare* for counsel. The friar advises marriage by all means, and as soon as possible; but his reason is lest Panurge's spermatic ducts should dry up. Panurge's world is indeed turned upside down when it is the pagan philosopher who bows before the coming of Christ and the man of God who praises sexual potency and the joys of copulation. Frere Jan's only nod to Christianity is to warn Panurge that the Day of Judgment is at hand and that unless he gets married in time he will find himself "with thy Genitories full in the Day of Judgment." [40] For Frere Jan, the passing of the *gloria mundi* seems to be the equivalent of sexual impotence, and, pointing to Panurge's grey hairs, he advises him to prepare, for the night is coming. As for cuckoldry, he takes it as a blessing: he claims (anticipating the witty argument of Donne's second *Elegie*) that at least it means his wife will be beautiful. His attitude is that if the Fates have decreed it, so it will be. This annoys Panurge, and he loses his temper, to the extent that he even asks if the monks know any remedy. [41] But the only remedy the man of God can think of is the one in the ribald story of Hans Carvel's ring. And with that their conversation and their journey come to an end: "Icy feut fin et du propous et du chemin."

[40] R V.206/III.xxvi: "Vouldrois tu bien qu'on te trouvast les couilles pleines au Jugement, *dum venerit judicare?*"

[41] R V.222/III.xxviii: "Digne vertus de Dieu, je commence entrer en fascherie. Vous aultres, cerveaulx enfrocquez, n'y sçavez vous remede aulcun?"

12

THE SYMPOSIUM

T HE first part of Panurge's quest is over, and he returns home empty-
handed. The fool, like Socrates, has gone among the wise and found
that they were more foolish than he. Pantagruel, who knew it all the
time, is not surprised; and when Panurge recounts the episode of
Raminagrobis, the prince's interpretation of the poet's verses provides
an occasion for him to repeat the advice he had initially given.[1]

I have not as yet seen any Answer framed to your Demand, which
affordeth me more Contentment: For in this his succinct Copy of Verses,
he summarily, and briefly, yet fully enough expresseth, how he would
have us to understand, that every one in the Project and Enterprise of
Marriage, ought to be his own Carver, sole Arbitrator of his proper
Thoughts, and from himself alone take counsel in the main and peremptory
closure of what his Determination should be, in either his assent to, or
dissent from it. Such always hath been my opinion to you; and when at
first you spoke thereof you scorned my Advice, and would not harbour
it within your mind. I know for certain, and therefore may I with the
greater confidence utter my conception of it, that Philauty, or Self-love,
is that which blinds your judgment and deceiveth you.

There are, however, other sources of wisdom that Panurge has not
yet consulted, and Pantagruel proposes to assemble them in a Socratic

---

[1] R V.225/III.xxix: "Encores n'ay je veu response que plus me plaise. Il veult dire
sommairement qu'en l'entreprinse de mariage chascun doibt estre arbitre de ses
propres pensées et de soy mesmes conseil prendre. Telle a tousjours esté mon opinion,
et autant vous en diz la premiere foys que m'en parlastez; mais vous en mocquiez
tacitement, il m'en soubvient, et congnois que philautie et amour de soy vous deçoit."

symposium to debate the issue. Recalling Cicero's tripartite division of *bona* into the soul, the body, and property,[2] he proposes that they invite a theologian, a doctor, and a man of law. But because he anticipates that there may be some disagreement among them, he also suggests that they add a fourth, a philosopher, since he would be able to resolve "assertively" any doubts.[3] Panurge agrees enthusiastically and offers to go himself to fetch the man of law, Bridoye — to which Pantagruel answers characteristically, "Faictez comme bon vous semblera."[4] It later appears, however, that he did not go after all but rather sent Epistemon.[5] The following Sunday they all assemble except, for reasons that are made clear later, the man Epistemon went to get. Attended by Panurge, Pantagruel, Epistemon, Frere Jan, Ponocrates, and Carpalim, Hippothadée the theologian, Rondibilis the physician, and Trouillogan the philosopher begin the long symposium which is at the center of the *Tiers Livre.*

With Hippothadée, Rondibilis, and Trouillogan, Rabelais brings his fool face to face with those representatives of knowledge who have the most serious claim to knowledge. There is no occultism or frenzy here, and there is no question of making fun of these authorities. The seriousness of their discourse is not only apparent in what they say and how they say it, but is symbolically confirmed by the personal attendance of Pantagruel and, later, of Gargantua himself. It is the very respectability of the learning represented by Hippothadée, Rondibilis, and Trouillogan which poses the most serious question in the *Tiers Livre* about the nature of wisdom and folly. To determine just what is meant by this colloquy is one of the most difficult problems in the whole of Rabelais, requiring that one be especially careful to keep in mind not only what is said and upon what authority, but who says it, in what tone of voice it is said, and what relation it bears to the action of the book.

Panurge opens the symposium by announcing its subject.[6]

[2] Cicero, *Partitiones Oratoriae*, XI.35; *De finibus*, II.18, V.23.
[3] R V.227/III.xxix: "attendu mesmement que le philosophe perfaict, et tel qu'est Trouillogan, respond assertivement de tous doubtes proposez."
[4] R V.228/III.xxix.
[5] Cf. R V.270/III.xxxvi.
[6] R V.229/III.xxx: "Messieurs, il n'est question que d'un mot. Me doibs je marier ou non? Si par vous n'est mon doubte dissolu, je le tiens pour insoluble . . ."

Gentlemen, the Question I am to propound unto you, shall be uttered in very few words; Should I marry, or no? If my Doubt herein be not resolved by you, I shall hold it altogether insolvable.

It is Hippothadée the theologian who, "exceeding modestly," rises to speak first. Almost echoing Pantagruel, he begins by saying that Panurge must first take counsel with himself, and he asks Panurge if he feels in his body "the importunate stings and pricklings of the Flesh." Panurge answers that he does indeed and, in reply to a further question, admits that he does not possess "from God the Gift and special Grace of Continency." Hippothadée's advice, in that case, is brief and clear: "My Counsel to you in that Case (my Friend) is, that you should marry" (*Mariez vous donc, mon amy*). Panurge, overjoyed to have received the answer he wanted, thanks the theologian and invites him to his wedding. But he suddenly remembers that he has another question to ask (*un petit scrupule à rompre*): will he ever be cuckolded? "You will indeed, my friend," is Hippothadée's answer, "if God so pleases."

This last response, as uncertain as all the others he has received, sends Panurge into a fury of mockery.[7]

Whither are we driven to, good Folks? To the Conditionals, which, according to the Rules and Precepts of the Dialectick Faculty, admit of all Contradiction and Impossibilities. If my Transalpine Mule had Wings, my Transalpine Mule would fly. If it please God I shall not be a Cuckold, but I shall be a Cuckold if it please him. Good God, if this were a Condition which I knew how to prevent, my Hopes should be as high as ever, nor would I despair: But you here send me to God's Privy-Council, to the Closet of his little Pleasures. You, my French countrymen, Which is the Way you take to go thither?

He rescinds his invitation to the wedding. But Hippothadée patiently explains that all depends upon God's benignity and that it is to Him that one must turn. He has shown us His will in the Bible, and it is by means of Scripture that one may "consult with those of his Celes-

---

[7] R V.230-1/III.xxx: "Où me renvoyez vous, bonnes gens? Aux conditionales, les quelles en dialectique reçoivent toutes contradictions et impossibilitez. Si mon mulet transalpin voloit, mon mulet transalpin auroit aesles. Si Dieu plaist, je ne seray poinct coqu; je seray coqu si Dieu plaist. Dea, si feust condition à laquelle je peusse obvier, je ne me desespererois du tout; mais vous me remettez au conseil privé de Dieu, en la chambre de ses menuz plaisirs. Où prenez vous le chemin pour y aller, vous aultres François?"

tial Privy-Council, or expresly make a Voyage unto the Empirean Chamber, where Order is given for the effectuating of his most holy Pleasures." [8] And, Hippothadée continues, there He has said that you will never be cuckolded if you take your wife[9]

descended of honest Parents, and instructed in all Piety and Virtue: Such a one as hath not at any time haunted or frequented the Company or Conversation of those that are of corrupt and depraved Manners; one loving and fearing God, who taketh a singular delight in drawing near to him by Faith, and the cordial observing of his Sacred Commandments: And finally, one who standing in awe of the Divine Majesty, of the Most High, will be loth to offend Him, and lose the favourable Kindness of his Grace, through any defect of Faith, or transgression against the Ordinances of his Holy Law, wherein Adultery is most rigorously forbidden, and a close adherence to her Husband alone most strictly and severely enjoin'd; yea, in such sort, that she is to cherish, serve, and love him above any thing, next to God, that meriteth to be beloved.

The language, we may note, is that of the rule of Thélème, and it is to an inhabitant of the Abbey that Hippothadée seems to commend Panurge. But Panurge, recognizing the source of the biblical passage, recognizes also the impossibility of fulfilling such conditions. "You would have me then," he comments in despair, ". . . espouse and take to Wife the prudent and frugal Woman described by Solomon: Without all doubt she is dead, and truly, to my best remembrance, I never saw her; the Lord forgive me." [10]

Thus dismissing Hippothadée, Panurge turns to the doctor, Rondibilis, and asks his question again. Citing a host of classical medical authorities, Rondibilis offers Panurge five ways of curbing his concupiscence: an immoderate use of wine, certain anti-aphrodisiac drugs, hard labor, long study, and copulation. As Rondibilis' descriptions of them (at times reminiscent of some of Stultitia's similar descriptions)

[8] R V.232/III.xxx: "consulter son conseil privé et voyager en la chambre de ses très sainctz plaisirs."
[9] R V.232/III.xxx: "issue de gens de bien, instruicte en vertus et honesteté, non ayant hanté ne frequenté compaignie que de bonnes meurs, aymant et craignant Dieu, aymant complaire à Dieu par foy et observation de ses sainctz commandemens, craignant l'offenser et perdre sa grace par default de foy et transgression de sa divine loy, en laquelle est rigoureusement defendu adultere et commendé adhaerer unicquement à son mary, le cherir, le servir, totalement l'aymer après Dieu."
[10] R V.233/III.xxx: "Vous voulez doncques (dist Panurge, fillant les moustaches de sa barbe) que j'espouse la femme forte descripte par Solomon? Elle est morte, sans poinct de faulte. Je ne la veid oncques, que je saiche; Dieu me le veuille pardonner. Grand mercy toutesfoys, mon pere."

make plain, all are restraints against nature except the last, which is a concession to nature. It is not hard to imagine which of the five Panurge chooses: "There did I wait for you," he exclaims at the mention of the fifth, "and shall willingly apply it to my self." The doctor proclaims Panurge physically fit for marriage, and, his question apparently answered, Panurge joyfully invites Rondibilis to his wedding. Yet there does remain a little "Roman" (*Si Peu Que Rien*) point to be settled — and, once again, Panurge voices his worries: "Shall I not be a Cuckold?"

Rondibilis is as astonished as Hippothadée was at the naïveté of the question, but his answer refers not to the will of God but to the law of Nature.[11]

Cuckoldry naturally attendeth Marriage; the Shadow doth not more naturally follow the Body, than Cuckoldry ensueth after Marriage, to place fair Horns upon the Husband's Heads. And when you shall happen to hear any Man pronounce these three words: He is married: If you then say he is, hath been, shall be, or may be a Cuckold, you will not be accounted an unskilful Artist in framing of true Consequences.

Introducing the Virgilian theme of *varium et mutabile semper femina*,[12] Rondibilis proceeds to expound the nature of woman, explaining that she is by nature a fragile, mutable, inconstant, and imperfect creature. No matter how virtuous or chaste a given woman may be, she is still a woman — "voy là tout." As Stultitia said, a woman is always a woman, that is, a fool.[13] Therefore she is governed by the changing moon and subject to the inordinate desires of that insatiable organ nature has put in her body. Continuing the discussion, Rondibilis, assisted now by Carpalim and Ponocrates, cites various examples from Eve onward to prove the further point that women generally desire what they are forbidden. It was upon this assumption that the permissive rule of Thélème had been formed: "for it is agreeable with the nature of man to long after things forbidden, and to desire what is denied us."[14] Panurge, however, does not really

[11] R V.243/III.xxxii: "Coqüage est naturellement des apennages de mariage. L'umbre plus naturellement ne suyt le corps que Coqüage suyt les gens mariez, et, quand vous oirez dire de quelqu'un ces trois motz: "*Il est marié*," si vous dictez: "*Il est doncques, ou a esté, ou sera, ou peult estre coqu*," vous ne serez dict imperit architecte de consequences naturelles."

[12] Virgil, *Aeneid*, IV.569–70.

[13] ME 28: "ita mulier semper mulier est, hoc est stulta."

[14] R II.431/I.lvii: "car nous entreprenons tousjours choses defendues et convoitons ce que nous est denié."

understand or accept the basis of the rule of Thélème, and he quickly gets fed up with Rondibilis' discussion of the nature of woman. He ends the discussion by bringing it back to the subject and observing that[15]

your Words being translated from the Clapper-dudgions to plain English, do signifie, that it is not very inexpedient that I marry, and that I should not care for being a Cuckold. [I'll be damned if you haven't turned clubs.]

And he rescinds his invitation to Rondibilis, as he had with Hippo-thadée.

With each of his first two counselors, Panurge is dissatisfied; he will not have them attend his wedding. Though both of them have implied that he will probably be a cuckold, it is not so much that which offends him as the fact that neither has been able to give him a definite answer. Hippothadée has sent him "aux conditionales"; Rondibilis has "rentré de treufles noires," that is, he has missed the point in telling Panurge not to worry about cuckoldry. The remedy that Hippothadée has offered is that Panurge should marry a perfect woman; Rondibilis' is that Panurge should not try to keep his wife faithful.[16] The fool, however, can see the impossibility and folly of both these suggestions that wisdom has made to him. He punctures Hippothadée's idealism with the realistic observation that such a woman does not exist; yet at the same time he has a higher ideal of a wife than Rondibilis' almost cynical, laissez-faire acceptance of the frailty of woman.

Now both Hippothadée and Rondibilis speak in tones of high seri-ousness, and their arguments are well-reasoned and cogent, buttressed on the one hand by the authority of scripture and on the other by the authority of science. Neither is ridiculous, and each is a *porte-parole* for Rabelais; for if Hippothadée may be seen as an expression of Rabelais' evangelistic faith and fideistic tendencies, Rondibilis may also be seen as a representative of Rabelais' medical beliefs and natu-

---

[15] R V.257/III.xxxiv: "Vos parolles, translatées de barragouin en françois, voulent dire que je me marie hardiment et que ne me soucie d'estre coqu. C'est bien rentré de treufles noires." For the expression "rentré de treufles noires," see R V.367/I.xlv, "rentré de picques," which, according to Clouzot, means "Parlé bien mal à propos." Urquhart understandably mistranslates this difficult idiomatic phrase, and I have supplied a more literal translation.

[16] Cf. the tale of Messer Coqüage, R V.251–3/III.xxxiii.

ralistic attitudes. Each, from his point of view, has the truth, and each represents a truth in which Rabelais believed. Yet — and it is *this* that is significant — each directly contradicts the other. The diptych they form can be easily described. Hippothadée is the idealistic theologian, whose wisdom is from Scripture and whose faith is in the will of God; Rondibilis is the realistic scientist, whose wisdom is from experience and whose faith is in the law of Nature. The one postulates a perfect woman, but her existence is denied by experience; the other postulates an imperfect woman, but her existence denies faith. The two of them together represent nothing less than that ubiquitous and troublesome Renaissance dichotomy, the realm of Grace and the realm of Nature. In the optimistic early decades of the sixteenth century, Rabelais had managed to resolve this dichotomy in the Erasmian Abbaye de Thélème, where Nature led directly up to Grace. But by the middle of the century Thélème, like the woman of Solomon, was dead; optimism had given way to doubt; and the dichotomy had reasserted itself. Will Panurge ever be a cuckold? Neither Grace nor Nature can give a definite answer, and the remedy of either by itself is contradictory to the other and unacceptable to the fool.

Though Panurge is merely annoyed at the responses he has received, Pantagruel is aware of the gravity of the philosophical impasse they have reached. Confronted by an open conflict between the wisdom of the body and the wisdom of the soul, he turns, as Erasmus in the *Enchiridion* had advised, to the wisdom of the mind for arbitration and calls upon Trouillogan, the philosopher, to resolve the problem. It was for this purpose, in anticipation of some disagreement, that Trouillogan had been added to the original triad in the first place, and now it is expected that he will be "able positively to resolve all whatsoever Doubts" (V.227/III.xxix). Addressed always as "nostre féal," he is the faithful servant and loyal subject; for he represents that human reason which, as Gargantua explains in his famous letter, has led their world out of the dark age of Grandgousier into "the light and dignity" of the present. Thus the fool Panurge, faced with the conflict between the wisdom of Grace and the wisdom of Nature and unable to accept either, is led to the wisdom of Reason.

Trouillogan has barely begun to speak, however, before an unexpected event occurs. Gargantua's little dog runs in, "quasi nuncius adveniens blandimento suae caudae gaudebat," as his prototype is described in the Book of Tobit.[17] "Our King is not far off," announces Pantagruel, "let us all rise" (V.261/III.xxxv). Preceded by this herald, the company all standing, Gargantua the king makes a ceremonial entrance to attend upon the conclusion of the long debate. The mythic, almost ritual symbolism of his regal presence signifies the importance of the moment that has arrived. Like Tobias, he brings the power of sight, that is, of wisdom. Not wishing to interrupt the discussion, he sits unobtrusively at the end of the table and, begging them to continue their discussion, asks only for a brief résumé of what has already been said. Trouillogan, he is informed, has answered Panurge's question of whether or not he should marry by saying that he should do neither one nor the other. Gargantua makes a joke about such a paradox, which is seconded by Pantagruel; but then Rondibilis more seriously explains its application in the realm of Nature.[18]

[Thus (quoth Rondibilis) do we make] a Neuter in Physick; as when we say a body is Neuter, when it is neither sick nor healthful; and a Mean in Philosophy; that by an Abnegation of both Extreams, and this by the Participation of the one and the other: Even as when lukewarm Water is said to be both hot and cold; or rather, as when Time makes the Partition, and equally divides betwixt the two, a while in the one, another while, as long, in the other opposite extremity.

To this, Hippothadée submits his own parallel from the realm of Grace.[19]

The holy Apostle (quoth Hippothadée) seemeth, as I conceive, to have more clearly explained this Point, when he said, Those that are married, let them be as if they were not married; and those that have Wives, let them be as if they had no Wives at all.

In interpreting this, Pantagruel, though no one realizes it at the time, manages to achieve precisely what they are seeking, the resolution of the conflict between Nature and Grace; for he reads the sentence of St. Paul in such a way that Nature and Grace go hand in hand.[20]

[17] Book of Tobit, II.9.

[18] R V.262/III.xxxv: "Ainsi (dist Rondibilis) mettons nous neutre en medicine et moyen en philosophie, par participation de l'une et l'aultre extremité, par abnegation de l'une et l'aultre extremité et, par compartiment du temps, maintenant en l'une, maintenant en l'aultre extremité." I have corrected Urquhart's mistranslation of "mettons nous."

[19] R V.262/III.xxxv: "Le Sainct Envoyé (dist Hippothadée) me semble l'avoir plus apertement declairé, quand il dict: 'Ceulx qui sont mariez soient comme non mariez; ceulx qui ont femme soient comme non ayans femme.'"

[20] R V.262–3/III.xxxv: "Je interprete (dist Pantagruel) avoir et n'avoir femme en

I thus interpret (quoth Pantagruel) the having and not having of a Wife. To have a Wife, is to have the use of her in such a way as Nature hath ordained, which is for the Aid, Society, and Solace of Man, and propagating of his Race: To have no Wife is not to be uxorious, play the Coward, and be lazy about her, and not for her sake to disdain the Lustre of that Affection which Man owes to God; or yet for her to leave those Offices and Duties which he owes unto his Country, unto his Friends and Kindred; or for her to abandon and forsake his precious Studies, and other businesses of Account, to wait still on her Will, her Beck, and her Buttocks. If we be pleased in this Sense to take having and not having of a Wife, we shall indeed find no Repugnancy nor Contradiction in the Terms at all.

"Vous dictez d'orgues," comments Panurge upon this explication, employing an idiom which has troubled all commentators. Plattard suggests a pun on *dire d'or*, but it seems likely that Sainéan is more correct in comparing it to the Provençal *canta coume un orgue* and interpreting the phrase to imply that Pantagruel has spoken as perfectly and harmoniously as an organ.[21] Whatever its precise meaning, there is no doubt but that it is a comment of approbation on Panurge's part; for the fool has understood the truth of Pantagruel's "harmonious" combination of Nature and Grace. He also knows that he is close to his answer, to the truth, though he cannot see where it is. Invoking, as Pantagruel had before him,[22] the adage *en buthô he alêtheia*, he claims that he is lost in the dark depths where truth is hid.[23] With the sense of the fool, however, he knows that the answer is near at hand. So he turns to Trouillogan.

But the memorable dialogue between Panurge and Trouillogan, which Molière was to mimic in *Le Mariage forcé* a century later, leads to Panurge's final defeat. Modest doubt, as Hector claims in *Troilus and Cressida*, is often the beacon of the wise, and out of the doubts created by Hippothadée and Rondibilis we expect that Trouil-

---

ceste façon, que femme avoir est l'avoir à usaige tel que Nature la créa, qui est pour l'ayde, esbatement et societé de l'homme; n'avoir femme est ne soy apoiltronner au tour d'elle, pour elle ne contaminer celle unicque et supreme affection que doibt l'homme à Dieu, ne laisser les offices qu'il doibt naturellement à sa patrie, à la Republicque, à ses amys, ne mettre en non chaloir ses estudes et negoces, pour continuellement à sa femme complaire. Prenant en ceste maniere avoir et n'avoir femme, je ne voids repugnance ne contradiction es termes."

[21] See Jean Plattard, ed., *Oeuvres complètes de Rabelais* (Paris, 1946–8), III, 284; and L. Sainéan, *La Langue de Rabelais* (Paris, 1922), I, 365–6.

[22] Cf. R IV.211/II.xviii: "et en chercherons la resolution jusques au fond du puis inespuisable auquel disoit Heraclite estre la verité cachée."

[23] R. V.264/III.xxxvi: "Mais je croy que je suis descendu on puiz tenebreux onquel disoit Heraclytus estre Verité cachée."

logan will provide the beacon of wisdom. On the contrary, however, he can only formalize that doubt into the ultimate skepticism of Pyrrhonism. It is true that at one moment he repeats the advice of the rule of Thélème and tells Panurge that he should do what he wishes (V.265/III.xxxvi), but his counsel is based not upon a will that is free, but rather upon a will that is lost, vacillating between two alternatives. He can advise Panurge, as he admits, nothing; he can only guess or conjecture, in the subjunctive or the conditional, and he is unable even to admit a hypothesis. Indeed, he does not even know whether he is or has been married himself. It is the *chanson de Ricochet* all over again, rewritten now as the rules for a game of tennis.[24] Reason alone is as insufficient as either Grace or Nature alone, and when it attempts to adjudicate between the latter two, it is simply confounded. "Que sais je?" it asks with Montaigne; and the answer is silence. Panurge admits his defeat. Trouillogan was his last possibility for an answer, but he has failed him: "Il m'eschappe."

Then an extraordinary, moving thing happens.[25]

At these words Gargantua arose, and said, Praised be the good God in all things, but especially for bringing the World into that height of Refinedness, beyond what it was when I first came to be acquainted therewith, that now the learnedest and most prudent Philosophers are not ashamed to be seen entring in at the Porches and Frontispieces of the Schools of the Pyrronian, Aporetick, Sceptick, and Ephectick Sects: Blessed be the Holy Name of God, veritably, it is like henceforth to be found an Enterprize of much more easie undertaking, to catch Lyons by the Neck, Horses by the Main, Oxen by the Horns, Bulls by the Muzzle, Wolves by the Tail, Goats by the Beard, and flying Birds by the Feet, then to entrap such Philosophers in their words. Farewel, my worthy, dear, and honest friends.

"Have we come to this?" he asks in a phrase Urquhart neglects to translate: "En sommes nous là?" It is the same question the fool had asked upon hearing Trouillogan's first answers (V.260/III.xxxv). All

---

[24] R V.269/III.xxxvi: "Je diz: vous qui estez icy; je ne diz pas: vous qui estez là bas au jeu de paulme."

[25] R V.269/III.xxxvi: "A ces motz, Gargantua se leva et dist: 'Loué soit le bon Dieu en toutes choses. A ce que je voy, le monde est devenu beau filz depuys ma congnoissance premiere. En sommes nous là? Doncques sont huy les plus doctes et prudens philosophes entrez on phrontistere et escholle des pyrrhoniens, aporrheticques, scepticques et ephectiques? Loué soit le bon Dieu. Vrayement, on pourra dorenavant prendre les lions par les jubes, les chevaulx par les crains, les boeufz par les cornes, les bufles par le museau, les loups par la queue, les chevres par la barbe, les oiseaux par les piedz; mais jà ne seront telz philosophes par leur parolles pris. Adieu, mes bons amys.'"

the learning and wisdom of the world have failed, and the only thing that seems to be left is doubt. For Gargantua, who had had such hopes for the world his son was to inherit and who himself inhabits a god-like realm of wisdom above that world, it is not enough. With a mythic gesture, he rises from the table and forsakes the symposium, rejecting the conclusions at which it has, at long last, arrived. "Adieu mes bons amys," he says, and though they wish to follow him he will not permit it. They have not yet reached the truth and must stay behind to search for it further.

With the departure of Gargantua, Panurge's symposium comes to a close. In his convocational remarks, he had told the participants that they represented his last hope of obtaining an answer: "If my Doubt herein be not resolved by you, I shall hold it altogether insolvable." [26] But now that hope has been disappointed, and Panurge is like the man Montaigne will describe when he observes that "Whosoever searcheth all the circumstances and embraceth all the consequences [of truth], hindereth his election." [27] The members of the symposium have brought him to the heart of the problem: they have led him into the dark depths where truth lies hidden; but, unable to give him the light to find it, they have provided only the greater darkness of Pyrrhonic despair.

It is not difficult to imagine that Rabelais himself had, in the years after Thélème, experienced a similar philosophical despair and that he is here dramatizing his own "war between the mind and sky." [28] The optimism of the ideal humanity of Thélème must have seemed, in the years after 1534, too easy, too idealistic; the real world of men and events would have seemed to contradict it at every stage. The mind, questioning itself, has asked what it could know and has received the empty answer of nothing. Rabelais' compatriot, Montaigne, was later to be brought to the same impasse, and his *Apologie de Raymond Sebond* reads like a commentary on Panurge's symposium. And yet, just as Montaigne was finally to find a way out of those straits, so Rabelais manages to lead us beyond the doubt of Trouillogan. Like Pilate, Trouillogan had asked, "what is truth?" and, being

[26] R V.229/III.xxx.
[27] M II.267/II.xx: "Qui [de la verité] recherche et embrasse toutes les circonstances et consequences, il empesche son election."
[28] The phrase is Wallace Stevens', from "Notes Toward a Supreme Fiction."

one of those who (as Bacon says) "delight in Giddinesse," would not stay for an answer.[29] Gargantua, however, has insisted that the others stay for that answer, and it is his son who brings them to it. The wise, as Pantagruel knew they would, have failed Panurge, and so at last he takes his companion to two fools.

[29] Francis Bacon, *Essays* (Oxford, 1947), p. 5 ("Of Truth").

13

BRIDOYE AND TRIBOULLET

After the symposium is over, Pantagruel comes upon Panurge wandering distractedly in the gallery, shaking his head from side to side, overcome with despair at his failure. It is the first time we have seen him so defeated, but, of course, it now seems to him that there can be no issue from his doubt. Invoking a Greek proverb that is at least as old as Demosthenes,[1] Pantagruel tells Panurge that, like a mouse in a trap, the more he struggles to free himself, the more enmeshed he becomes. That is, the more he consults *sapientia mundana*, the more his doubts increase. Pantagruel, who has known from the beginning that this would happen, now comes forth with his final suggestion.[2]

I have often heard it said in a vulgar Proverb, The Wise may be instructed by a Fool. Seeing the Answers and Responses of sage and judicious men have in no manner of way satisfied you, take advice of some Fool; and possibly by so doing, you may come to get that Counsel which will be agreeable to your own Heart's desire and contentment. You know how by the Advice and Counsel and Prediction of Fools, many Kings, Princes, States, and Commonwealths have been preserved, several Battels gained, and divers doubts of a most perplexed Intricacy resolved: I am not so

---

[1] Demosthenes, *Orationes*, L.26. Though the adage is preserved in this form by Erasmus (LB II.511F–512C) and Montaigne (M III.364/III.xiii), it is more familiar to us in the Ovidian, avian form that Ariosto and Hamlet's uncle remembered (Ovid, *Metamorphoses*, XI.73–5; Ariosto, *Orlando Furioso*, XXIII.105; Shakespeare, *Hamlet*, III.iii.68–9).

[2] R V.272–3/III.xxxvii: "J'ay souvent ouy en proverbe vulguaire qu'un fol enseigne bien un saige. Puys que par les responses des saiges n'estez à plein satisfaict, conseillez vous à quelque fol. Pourra estre que, ce faisant, plus à vostre gré serez satisfaict et content. Par l'advis, conseil et praediction des folz vous sçavez quants princes, roys et republicques ont esté conservez, quantes batailles guaingnées, quantes perplexitez dis-

diffident of your Memory, as to hold it needful to refresh it with a Quotation of Examples; nor do I so far undervalue your Judgment, but that I think it will acquiesce in the Reason of this my subsequent Discourse. As he who narrowly takes heed to what concerns the dextrous Management of his private Affairs, domestick Business and those Adoes which are confined within the streight-lac'd compass of one Family: who is attentive, vigilant, and active in the oeconomick Rule of his own House; whose frugal Spirit never strays from home; who loseth no occasion, whereby he may purchase to himself more Riches, and build up new heaps of Treasure on his former Wealth; and who knows warily how to prevent the inconveniences of Poverty, is called a worldly wise Man, though perhaps in the second Judgment of the Intelligences which are above, he be esteemed a Fool. So on the contrary, is he most like (even in the thoughts of all Coelestial Spirits) to be not only sage, but to presage Events to come by Divine Inspiration, who laying quite aside those Cares which are conducible to his Body, or his Fortunes, and as it were departing from himself, rids all his Senses of Terene Affections, and clears his Fancies of those plodding Studies, which harbour in the Minds of thriving Men: All which neglects of Sublunary Things are vulgarly imputed Folly.

It is to this that the whole of the *Tiers Livre* has been leading, and with this succinct but complete description Pantagruel reveals the goal of Panurge's quest. All of the themes of the paradoxical *docta ignorantia* are here brought together: the foolishness of worldly wisdom and the wisdom of folly, the ignorance of prudence and the prudence of ignorance, the blindness of wisdom and the vision of folly, heaven's favors to fools and rejection of the wise. Panurge, having journeyed from one source of wisdom to another with his question and having failed each time to find an answer, is at last convinced, as Socrates was, that those who are reputed wise are really fools. Will he not now, asks Pantagruel, try the obverse of that paradox and see if those who are reputed fools are not really wise? "By my Soul," answers Panurge, "that Overture pleaseth me exceedingly well." But, he suggests, since we have tried the wisest of the wise, let us now

---

solues. Jà besoing n'est vous ramentevoir les exemples. Vous acquiescerez en ceste raison; car, comme celluy qui de près reguarde à ses affaires privez et domesticques, qui est vigilant et attentif au gouvernement de sa maison, duquel l'esprit n'est poinct esguaré, qui ne pert occasion quelconque de acquerir et amasser biens et richesses, qui cautement sçayt obvier es inconveniens de paoûreté, vous appellez saige mondain, quoy que fat soit il en l'estimation des intelligences coelestes, ainsi fault il, pour davant icelles saige estre, je diz sage et praesage par aspiration divine, et apte à recepvoir benefice de divination, se oublier soymesmes, issir hors de soymesmes, vuider ses sens de toute terrienne affection, purger son esprit de toute humaine sollicitude et mettre tout en non chaloir, ce que vulguairement est imputé à follie."

try the most foolish of fools.[3] What about Triboullet?, asks Pantagruel: he "is compleatly foolish, as I conceive." "Yes, truly, (answer'd Panurge) he is properly and totally a Fool." And so Carpalim is sent off to bring to them Triboullet the fool.

Before he arrives on the scene, however, the rest of the company has one more journey to make. Bridoye the judge, who had been invited to the symposium, had been unable to come, having been summoned before the Senate to defend a judgment he had handed down. Upon hearing this, Pantagruel expresses concern for the good judge of Fonsbeton. In the more than forty years, explains the prince, that Bridoye has been judge he has handed down more than four thousand definitive sentences, and, while they have often been appealed, the appeals have never been sustained. And, he goes on,[4]

that now in his old Age he should be personally summoned, who in all the foregoing time of his Life, hath demeaned himself so unblamably in the Discharge of the Office and Vocation he had been called unto; it cannot assuredly be, that such a change hath happened without some notorious Misfortune and Disaster: I am resolved to help and assist him in Equity and Justice to the uttermost extent of my Power and Ability. I know the Malice, Despight, and Wickedness of the World to be so much more now-a-days exasperated, increased, and aggravated by what it was not long since, that the best Cause that is, how just and equitable soever it be, standeth in great need to be succoured, aided and supported. Therefore presently, from this very instant forth, do I purpose, till I see the event and closure thereof, most heedfully to attend and wait upon it, for fear of some under-hand tricky Surprizal, Cavilling, Pettifoggery, or fallacious quirks in Law, to his detriment, hurt, or disadvantage.

Once again we hear in Pantagruel's voice that haunting note of pessimism which lurks behind all the frivolity of Rabelais' story. Since the days of the Abbaye de Thélème, human maliciousness has so increased that one can no longer be sure that right will triumph. Thus, accompanied by Panurge, Epistemon, Ponocrates, Frere Jan, Gym-

[3] R V.277/III.xxxviii: "Mais, ainsi comme avons choizy la fine creme de Sapience pour conseil, aussi vouldrois je qu'en nostre consultation praesidast quelqu'un qui feust fol en degré souverain."

[4] R V.270-1/III.xxxvi: "Que maintenant doncques soit personnellement adjourné sus ses vieulx jours; il, qui, par tout le passé, a vescu tant sainctement en son estat, ne peut estre sans quelque desastre. Je luy veulx de tout mon povoir estre aidant en aequité. Je sçay huy tant estre la malignité du monde aggravée que bon droict a bien besoing d'aide, et praesentement delibere y vacquer de paour de quelque surprinse."

naste, Rhizotome, and the others, he goes off to investigate the matter of Bridoye.

Bridoye has been accused of giving an unfair judgment. His only excuse to the Senate in defense of his decision is that, having grown old and subject to the miseries and calamities that age brings with it, his sight is perhaps not as good as it has been in the past, that he may have misread the dice and perhaps mistook a four for a five, especially since in this particular judgment he was using his little dice. But, he pleads, invoking the ancient antinomy of *nomos* and *physis*, the infirmities of nature should not be considered a crime by the law. Upon hearing his excuse, the President of the Senate, Trinquamelle, immediately asks the obvious question: "What dice, my friend, are you talking about?" Unaware that his procedure is irregular, Bridoye explains that, of course, just like all the other judges, after he has heard a case argued at great length and has pondered carefully the arguments of both sides, he rolls his dice and bases his decision upon the result. He has always done this and, in doing so, "I do the same as you others, Gentlemen, and act in accordance with judicial custom." [5] When the case is relatively simple, he uses his big dice; but when it is more complex and difficult to determine, he then resorts to his little ones.

Patiently concealing his astonishment at such irregular practices, Trinquamelle asks why it is necessary to hear the case at all if it is going to be decided by dice anyway. Bridoye alleges three reasons. The first is to preserve the formalities, which are the essence of the law and which often manage to destroy the materialities and substance of the case;[6] and as he says this we are reminded of his namesake, the judge Brid'oison in Beaumarchais' *Mariage de Figaro*, who is also wont to plead, "la forme, voyez-vous, la forme!" The second reason for hearing the case is that it gives Bridoye good exercise; for there is no bodily exercise, he claims, like emptying briefcases, leafing through papers, examining portfolios, and filling wastebaskets (V.293–5/ III.xl). Finally, his third reason is that time, which ripens all things,

[5] R V.288/III.xxxix: "Je fays comme vous aultres, messieurs, et comme est l'usance de judicature."

[6] R V.292/III.xl: "Premierement pour la forme, en omission de laquelle ce qu'on a faict n'estre valable prouve tresbien *Spec.*, *tit. de instr. edi. et tit. de rescrip. praesent.*; d'advantaige, vous sçavez trop mieulx que souvent en procedures judicaires les formalitez destruisent les materialitez et substances . . ."

is the father of truth. *Veritas filia temporis,* that favorite Renaissance motto (which was carved on the chimney of the Ronsard family home), calls to Bridoye's mind the example of Dendin père et fils.

Pierre Dendin, he recounts, formerly the judge at Parthenay, had been, as Shallow was to Falstaff, an old friend of his at law school. He was a great chap, claims Bridoye, and there is indeed something of Justice Shallow's reminiscences in his marvelous description:[7]

a very honest Man, careful Labourer of the Ground, fine singer in a Church-Desk, of good Repute and Credit, and older than the most aged of all your Worships, who was wont to say, that he had seen the great and goodly Man the Council of Latran, with his wide and broad brimmed red Hat: As also, that he had beheld and looked upon the fair and beautiful Pragmatical Sanction, his Wife, with her huge Rosary or Patenotrian Chaplet of Jeat-beads, hanging at a large Sky-coloured Ribbond.

He too had heard the bells at midnight and was famous for his carousing and parties; he never talked to the litigants in a case without first having a drink with them in a tavern. Now his son, Tenot Dendin, wanted to be a judge as well, but he had little success in his calling and, eager though he was, never managed to settle a case. His father explained to him that he was *too* eager, that he moved in too fast on a case; for the son decided cases at the beginning, when they were still green and hard, whereas the father took them at their end, when they were ripe and easily digestible. The father explained to his son that one must wait until the litigants were all worn out with arguing, and then the cases could be easily settled.

That, explains Bridoye, is why he always lets them argue out their cases before he casts his dice. "Yea, but," mutters Trinquamelle, "how do you proceed (my Friend) in Criminal Causes, the culpable and guilty Party being taken and seized upon, *Flagrante Crimine?*" (V.307/III.xlii). "Even as your other Worships use to do (answered Bridlegoose:) First, I permit the Plaintiff to depart from the Court, enjoyning him not to presume to return thither, till he preallably should have taken a good sound and profound Sleep." For there is nothing like sleep, he explains, for settling legal cases, and he proceeds

[7] R V.297/III.xli: "homme honorable, bon laboureur, bien chantant au letrain, homme de credit et aagé autant que le plus de vous aultres, messieurs, lequel disoit auoir veu le grand bon homme Concile de Latran, avecques son gros chappeau rouge; ensemble la bonne dame Pragmaticque Sanction, sa femme, avecques son large tissu de satin pers et ses grosses patenostres de gayet."

to recount another tale to prove his point. A Gascon gambler had wanted to fight, but no one would fight with him. Then he fell asleep. While he slept another man who wanted to fight came along and woke him up. The Gascon, however, wanted to go on sleeping and told the other man to have a nap himself and then they would both fight. But when they both awoke, they no longer wished to fight: "they, instead of fighting, and possibly killing one another, went jointly to a Sutler's Tent, where they drank together very amicably, each upon the pawn of his Sword. Thus, by a little Sleep, was pacified the ardent Fury of two warlike Champions." [8]

Upon these explanations Bridoye rests his defense and leaves the courtroom. Trinquamelle asks Pantagruel to decide the case, not only because of his noble rank, but especially because the case is so paradoxical and presents so many new elements that it is only fitting that the prince should determine it — because of "that excellent Wit . . . prime Judgment, and admirable Learning wherewith Almighty God, the Giver of all Good Things, hath most richly qualified and endowed you" (V.311/III.xliii). Pantagruel pleads for leniency on the grounds of Bridoye's age, his simple-mindedness, and all the equitable judgments he has given in the past.[9]

Truly, it seemeth unto me, that in the whole Series of Bridlegoose's Juridical Decrees, there hath been, I know not what, of extraordinary savouring of the unspeakable Benignity of God, that all those his preceding Sentences, Awards, and Judgments, have been confirmed and approved of by your selves, in this your own Venerable and Sovereign Court: For it is usual (as you know well) with Him whose Ways are inscrutable, to manifest his own ineffable Glory, in blunting the Perspicacy of the Eyes of the Wise, in weakening the Strength of potent Opressors, in depressing the Pride of rich Extortioners, and in erecting, comforting, protecting, supporting, upholding and shoaring up the poor, feeble, humble, silly, and foolish Ones of the Earth.

So saying, and after making arrangements for the correction of Bridoye's error, Pantagruel and his companions leave. As they are

---

[8] R V.310/III.xlii: "en lieu de se batre et soy par adventure entretuer, ilz allerent boyre ensemble, chascun sus son espée. Le sommeil avoit faict ce bien et pacifié la flagrante fureur des deux bons champions."

[9] R V.312/III.xliii: "Et me semble qu'il y a je ne sçay quoy de Dieu qui a faict et dispensé qu'à ses jugemens de sort toutes les praecedentes sentences ayent esté trouvées bonnes en ceste vostre venerable et souveraine Court: lequel, comme sçavez, veult souvent sa gloire apparoistre en l'hebetation des saiges, en la depression des puissans et en l'erection des simples et humbles."

riding home, Pantagruel recounts the story to his companions, and, as if to confirm that the stories Bridoye had told were not senile babble, Frere Jan tells Pantagruel that he used to know Pierre Dendin, and Gymnaste recounts that he was there when the Gascon had his altercation.

Epistemon is puzzled, however, and expresses incredulity that Bridoye's dice could have been without error for so many years, especially in cases that were in themselves ambiguous, intricate, and obscure. As an example of such a difficult case, he[10] tells the story of a case brought before Dolabella for judgment. A woman, who had had a child by a first marriage, married again and had a second child; her second husband and his son killed her first son, and in revenge she killed them. Dolabella found the case so ambiguous that he didn't know what to decide, for while the woman's crime was great, her revenge was justified. Finally, he sent for advice to the Areopagites in Athens; but their response was that the parties involved should appear before them in a hundred years, as much as to say that they were so confused by the case that they didn't know what to decide. Epistemon concludes,[11]

Who had decided that Plea by the Chance and Fortune of the Dice, could not have erred nor awarded amiss, on which side soever he had past his casting and condemnatory Sentence: If against the Woman, she deserved Punishment for usurping Sovereign Authority, by taking that Vengeance at her own hand, the inflicting whereof was only competent to the Supream Power, to administer Justice in Criminal Cases: If for her, the just Resentment of so atrocious Injury done unto her, in murthering her innocent Son, did fully excuse and vindicate her of any Trespass or Offence about that Particular committed by her. But this continuation of Bridle-goose for so many Years, still hitting the Nail on the Head, never missing the Mark, and always judging aright, by the meer throwing of the Dice, and the Chance thereof, is that which most astonisheth and amazeth me.

Pantagruel, however, is able to explain this curious fact,[12] and it is toward his explanation that the entire episode has been leading:

---

[10] It is Epistemon, not Pantagruel, as the R text, following the edition of 1552, indicates. See note 12.

[11] R V.315/III.xliv: "Qui eust decidé le cas au sort des dez, il n'eust erré, advint ce que pourroit. Si contre la femme, elle meritoit punition, veu qu'elle avoit faict la vengence de soy, laquelle apartenoit à Justice. Si pour la femme, elle sembloit avoir eu cause de douleur atroce. Mais en Bridoye la continuation de tant d'années me estonne."

[12] The explanation of Bridoye's success, which is the culmination of this episode, is given by Epistemon — or at least so it is in the generally accepted text; but there

Bridoye's success for so many years with the dice is the result of the benevolence of God. Many of the cases the judge heard were complex, confused, and beyond his understanding. He also knew that the devil is capable of disguising himself as a messenger of light and, using the mouths of corrupt lawyers, of persuading human reason that black is white (*tourne le noir en blanc* [V.315–16/III.xliii]). Stultitia had also warned of the same thing: "Wheras these wisemen are thei, that ar 'double tounged,' as the aforesaid Euripides telleth us, with the one of whiche they speake the trueth, with the other, thynges mete for the tyme and audience. Theyr propretee it is to chaunge blacke into white." [13] Accepting, then, the inadequacy of his own wisdom to determine such cases, Bridoye put his trust in the wisdom of God.[14]

He did in these Extremities, as I conceive, most humbly recommend the Direction of his Judicial Proceedings to the Upright Judge of Judges, God Almighty; did submit himself to the Conduct and Guideship of the Blessed Spirit, in the Hazard and Perplexity of the Definitive Sentence; and

---

is a serious textual confusion here which ought to be cleared up. The answer, of course, ought not to be given by Epistemon at all, but rather by Pantagruel, who is throughout the *Tiers Livre* the repository of wisdom. There is no other episode in the entire book where the prince is unable to understand something and has to turn to one of his companions for an answer. Furthermore, the religious basis of the answer is wholly inappropriate to Epistemon, for his knowledge, as we have seen, is derived from classical learning. And, finally, since one of the reasons for Pantagruel's plea for clemency was that Bridoye had always been right in the past, why should he now be astonished at that record? The only consistent thing for Rabelais to have done would have been for him to give the final speech to Pantagruel, in which case the former speech, the story of Dolabella, would have had to be made by Epistemon, since Pantagruel could hardly answer his own question. And that is precisely what Rabelais originally did, as an examination of the apparatus criticus in the R text shows. In the original text of 1546, chapters XLIII and XLIV formed one whole chapter, and the later title of chapter XLIV (*Comment Pantagruel raconte une estrange histoire de jugement humain*) did not exist. There the story of Dolabella was told, not by Pantagruel, but by Epistemon as an example of the ambiguous type of case he mentions at the end of chapter XLIII—and, one may add, in keeping with his allegorical role as classical learning. It was, therefore, Pantagruel who appropriately gave the final opinion on Bridoye. Though it may well have been Rabelais himself who changed this in the corrected edition of 1552, where the present chapter division was made, the change produces an unacceptable inconsistency which is perpetuated by Lefranc's text (R). If Rabelais did it, Homer nodded. Whatever the cause of the error, the text should be properly amended.

[13] ME 66–7: "At sapientum sunt duae illae linguae, ut idem meminit Euripides, quarum altera verum dicunt, altera, quae pro tempore judicarint opportuna. Horum est nigrum in candida vertere . . ."

[14] R V.316/III.xliv: "se recommenderoit humblement à Dieu, le juste juge, invocqueroit à son ayde la grace celeste, se deporteroit en l'esprit sacrosainct du hazard et perplexité de sentence definitive, et par ce sort exploreroit son decret et bon plaisir que nous appellons arrest . . ."

by this Aleatory Lot, did, as it were, implore and explore the Divine Decree of his Good Will and Pleasure, instead of that which we call the final Judgment of a Court.

Bridoye was unable to appear at Panurge's symposium not simply because he was busy elsewhere, but because he had already progressed beyond the Pyrrhonism in which that symposium culminated. We see him only after the symposium, because he represents an ideal beyond Pyrrhonism, and his episode prepares us for the final conclusions of the *Tiers Livre*.

In the story of Bridoye there are three main themes which must be considered in further detail. The first of these is the inadequacy of the law. As we have already seen, the concept of law (*nomos*) is basic to an understanding of the fool: the law would seem to contradict all that the fool represents. This is the reason why Rabelais must take us into the law courts, to show us what the law is really like. We find it, as Montaigne described it, clotted with citations and commentaries and opinions of learning, blown up with pride at its accomplishments and wisdom, and yet wholly inadequate to judge the complexity of human nature — "There is but little relation betweene our actions, that are in perpetuall mutation, and the fixed and unmoveable lawes." [15]

If the *Apologie de Raymond Sebond* may be said to represent the conclusion of Panurge's symposium, it is Montaigne's final and greatest essay, *De l'experience*, with its rejection of the law as a mode of comprehending human experience, that may serve as a gloss upon the story of Bridoye. Montaigne had been, like Bridoye, a judge, and he himself must have witnessed the futility of the endless and contradictory briefs and citations and codes of the court. He too must have seen that the customs and formalities of law, which gather like barnacles upon the cases, often destroy the very substance of those cases; that the nomos of law often bears no relation to the physis of experience; and that, as he says, nature gives laws "ever more happy, then those we give our selves." [16] For Bridoye, the best thing about the laws is, significantly, the *physical* exercise they give him. His speech, with its invidious and relentless repetition of "comme vous

---

[15] M III.362/III.xiii: "Il y a peu de relation de nos actions, qui sont en perpetuelle mutation, avec les loix fixes et immobiles."

[16] M III.362/III.xiii: "Nature les donne toujours plus heureuses que ne sont celles que nous nous donnons."

aultres, Messieurs" and with its proliferation of senseless citations, is a devastating parody of legal argumentation, where the glosses, as Montaigne says, only increase our doubts and ignorance.[17] Indeed, as we read them, it is Montaigne's own despair that we share: "There's more adoe to enterpret interpretations, than to interpret things: and more bookes upon bookes, then upon any other subject. We doe but enter-glose our selves." [18] Stultitia herself had made exactly the same point.[19]

Next these now, *Civilians*, and *Canonistes* chalenge no meane place amongs learned men. And who than they stande depelier in *Selflikyng*? For whiles continually thei turne, and retourne *Sisyphus stone* in rehersyng up an hundred *lawes* and Paragraphes all with a breath, it skilleth not howe littell to purpose, and whiles they adde *glose* upon *glose*, and *opinions* upon *opinions*, they make as though theyr law science were most hard, and difficult to be atteined to.

The second theme that runs through the Bridoye episode is that of *veritas filia temporis*. The story of Pierre Dendin is postulated upon the same assumption as "The Prioress' Tale" and Shakespeare's last plays, that time will reveal the truth. It is a theme that counsels against precipitous action and advises us to lie down, like the Gascon gambler, and sleep first. The Areopagites of Athens called for the principals of Dolabella's case to appear in a hundred years, not only because they could not see the truth of the case, but because they knew that in a hundred years the truth would be apparent. The law, however, feels that it must come to a decision at once, when it may not possess all the facts, when truth may be hopelessly obscured, and when the judgment may be made in error. Montaigne speaks of the same lesson when he recounts the story of the men in his time who were hanged by mistake. It is true that if, as in Philippus' court, a man is unjustly fined, retribution can be made; but, says Montaigne, "my poore slaves were hanged irreparably." [20]

---

[17] M III.363/III.xiii: "les glosses augmentent les doubtes et l'ignorance."

[18] M III.365/III.xiii: "Il y a plus affaire à interpreter les interpretations qu'à interpreter les choses, et plus de livres sur les livres que sur autre subject: nous ne faisons que nous entregloser."

[19] ME 109–10: "Inter eruditos Jureconsulti sibi vel primum vindicant locum neque quisquam alius aeque sibi placet, dum Sisyphi saxum assidue volvunt, ac sexcentas leges eodem spiritu contexunt, nihil refert quam ad rem pertinentes, dumque glossematis glossemata, opiniones opinionibus cumulantes, efficiunt ut studium illud omnium difficillimum esse videatur."

[20] M III.368/III.xiii: "les miens furent pendus irreparablement."

The third theme, and the most important, is that of reason and faith; and Bridoye's account of how he hears and decides the cases is a paradigm of the proper relation between the two. Senile though he may be, the judge of Fonsbeton is a wise and virtuous man. He takes the greatest care to assemble and hear out all the facts in any given case; he ponders all aspects of the case and attempts rationally to adjudicate it. His reason tells him that the laws are inadequate to comprehend human experience, that precipitous decisions are often erroneous, and that time will eventually reveal the truth. But finally his reason also demonstrates to him that reason itself is often insufficient to the task given it. It is his own reason that leads him to understand that he is ignorant; it is that same reason which causes him to become distrustful of his own powers and aware of the antinomies and contradictions in laws.[21] At that moment, having gone as far as he can with reason, he turns to faith. Humbly recommending himself to the only just Judge and confessing his own weakness, he asks for divine help and guidance — and casts his dice. To be sure, dice are explicitly rejected at the beginning of the *Tiers Livre*,[22] but the difference here should be obvious. The dice that Panurge resorts to at the outset of his quest constitute gratuitous chance and are based neither upon an acceptance of the limitations of human reason nor upon faith in the judgment of God. It is through no reliance upon chance that Bridoye turns to his dice; it is in the firm belief that they will be guided by the hand of God.

In Panurge's symposium, reason and faith, represented by Rondibilis and Hippothadée, stood irreconcilably opposed. In attempting to reconcile them or to adjudicate between them, human wisdom, represented by Trouillogan, was simply confounded. As a judge, Trouillogan is as perplexed as Bridoye; but Trouillogan is left only with the question *que sais je?* whereas Bridoye is able to go beyond that to the answer. As Montaigne himself learned, it is simply *ce que je sais*: "What do I *know*?" is answered by "that which *I* know." To be sure, that is very little. The most that one knows is oneself and the fact that one is ignorant; yet that is a great deal to have plucked out of the nettle of Pyrrhonism. "A man must learne," says

[21] R V.315/III.xliv: "soy deffiant de son sçavoir et capacité, congnoissant les antinomies et contrarietez des loix."

[22] See R V.92–3/III.xi.

Montaigne, "that he is but a foole." [23] It is the lesson of Socrates and of Christ, and it is the lesson that Bridoye represents. In that knowledge there is wisdom; in that wisdom there is salvation. At the very moment of the impasse, the acceptance of that impasse opens a way out; for Montaigne the way out is postulated upon a kind of phenomenological transcendence,[24] but for Rabelais it is based upon faith itself. Gargantua left the banquet because it culminated in doubt, and he insisted that the others stay behind until they perceived the way beyond. It is in the story of Bridoye and his dice that they are shown it.

Bridoye is Stultitia's Fool in Christ, and his is the example Panurge must emulate if he is ever to get out of his mousetrap. The lesson is that human reason cannot resolve his doubt and that time alone will provide the answer to his question about cuckoldry. He has gone as far as he can by reason, but the wisdom of the world has provided him not with certainty but only with the dusty answer of Pyrrhonism. He must accept the fact that he does not and cannot know, and leave the rest to God; but God will not assist him until he has achieved the wisdom of knowing that he is a fool. As long as he rests in the doubt of worrying whether or not he will be cuckolded, he is an unfit receptacle for the grace of God. That is what Pantagruel had told him at the outset: that he should make up his mind whether or not he wishes to get married and then follow his will, prepared to leave the question of cuckoldry to God and equally prepared to accept whatever God determines. The problem is, of course, that he cannot make up his mind and cannot be "assured of his will" about getting married until he is able to accept his own ignorance about the future. As long as he tries to determine the future, so long will the future worry him and prevent his will from being free.

Panurge never learns the lesson that the events of the *Tiers Livre* ought to teach him, however, and his final appearance, when he confronts the fool Triboullet, is intended to show us that. Triboullet is a "natural" fool, a witless individual with no more capacity for

[23] M III.373/III.xiii: "il faut aprandre qu'on n'est qu'un sot."
[24] See Paul de Man, "Montaigne et la transcendance," *Critique*, December 1953, pp. 1011–22.

reason than Bridoye's dice. But like Bridoye's dice he is capable of being a receptacle for the wisdom of God — a potentiality that Pantagruel made clear when he first suggested him, explaining that a fool could be "not only sage, but [able] to presage Events to come by Divine Inspiration." [25] For Panurge to consult Triboullet, then, is theoretically equivalent to Bridoye's consultation of his dice. Like Bridoye, he is perplexed by a problem and has found no answer to it in human reason, so he turns to someone devoid of reason for his answer. During the consultation Triboullet does indeed receive the divine afflatus that Pantagruel had predicted. [26]

Did you not take heed (quoth he) a little before he opened his Mouth to speak, what a shogging, shaking, and wagging his Head did keep? . . . such a brangling Agitation and Moving . . . proceed[s] from, and [is] quickned and suscitated by the coming and Inspiration of the Prophetizing and Fatielical Spirit.

Yet the consultation with Triboullet is a failure: the fool's message is cryptic; Panurge refuses to accept Pantagruel's obvious interpretation of it; and he dismisses Triboullet with the observation that, after all, he is only a fool. It fails because Panurge is too foolish to be the fool he must be. He does not accept his own ignorance and the impossibility of knowing. The very way that he approaches Triboullet is an indication of this — he comes to him in exactly the same spirit in which he had approached all the others, waiting for guidance from some putative source of wisdom rather than being prepared to receive the decree of heaven. The difference is subtle, but it is important: one attitude asks "what is Thy will?" while the other accepts, "Thy will be done." Thus also, when the divine decree has been given, Panurge refuses to accept it. Not only does he give it a perverse interpretation, but he determines to go on with the quest.

Triboullet perceives all this from the beginning, from the very way that Panurge poses his question in all the pride of rhetoric and elegance. That is why Triboullet does not even wait for him to finish, but interrupts with a cry of despair and begins to beat Panurge,

[25] R V.273/III.xxxvii: "sage et praesage par aspiration divine et apte à recepvoir benefice de divination."
[26] R V.319/III.xlv: "Avez-vous consideré comment sa teste s'est, avant qu'il ouvrist la bouche pour parler, crouslée et esbranlée? . . . ce mouvement estoit suscité à la venue et inspiration de l'esprit fatidicque . . ."

shouting at him, "By God, God; mad Fool!" [27] It is the old *tu quoque*. Triboullet the fool calls Panurge a fool, and Panurge's retort is that Triboullet is a fool indeed and that he, Panurge, is a fool for ever having bothered to ask him his question. To be sure, both are fools, but they are quite different kinds of fools. Triboullet is a natural fool, but Panurge is a "mad Fool" — a "fol enraigé." That is to say, Panurge has been made foolish by his rage, by his stubbornness, by his unwillingness to become the true fool that Triboullet represents. Later, when Pantagruel repeats Triboullet's accusation, Panurge, remembering the *Encomium*, will agree that he is a fool, but only insofar as everyone is a fool.[28]

Not that I would impudently exempt myself from being a Vassal in the Territory of Folly; I hold of that Jurisdiction, and am subject thereto, I confess it; and why should I not? For the whole World is foolish. In the old Lorrain Language (*fou* for [*t*]*ou*) All and Fool were the same thing. Besides it is avouched by Solomon, that infinite is the number of Fools: From an Infinity nothing can be deducted or abated, nor yet by the Testimony of Aristotle, can any thing thereto be added or subjoyned. Therefore were I a mad Fool, if being a Fool I should not hold my self a Fool.

But this is too easy a way out. It is the rhetoric and sophistry that have characterized Panurge's arguments from the beginning; it is the frivolous display of learning with which he has perverted learning and wisdom all along and of which Agrippa had warned when he said that, if learning falls upon a fool, nothing will be prouder or more difficult than he. There is none of the humility of Agrippa's ass here: Panurge cannot accept being a fool himself, except insofar as he can join everyone else. When, finally, he becomes patronizing to Triboullet and, with insincere magnanimity, forgives him all (V.325/III.xlvi),

---

[27] R V.318–9/III.xlv: "Depuys [Panurge] luy exposa son affaire en parolles rhetoriques et eleguantes. Davant qu'il eust achevé, Triboullet luy bailla un grand coup de poing entre les deux espaules, luy rendit en main la bouteille, le nazardoit avecques la vessie de porc, et pour toute response luy dist, branslant bien fort la teste: 'Par Dieu, Dieu, fol enraigé, guare moine, cornemuse de Buzançay.'"

[28] R V.324/III.xlvi: "Non que je me vueille impudentement exempter du territore de follie; j'en tiens et en suys, je le confesse. Tout le monde est fol. En Lorraine, Fou est près Tou par bonne discretion. Tout est fol. Solomon dict que infiny est des folz le nombre; à infinité rien ne peut decheoir, rien ne peut estre adjoinct, comme prouve Aristoteles, et fol enragé serois si, fol estant, fol ne me reputois." Urquhart, without the benefit of the Lefranc edition, misunderstands the reference to *Tou*, which is geographical, not philological. See R V.324 (note 5): "*Fou* est un village à trois lieues de *Toul* (Meurthe-et-Moselle), sur la route de Ligny."

it is simply the last straw. He has not reformed, he has not been humbled, he has not accepted his own ignorance, he has not deferred to the will of God: he remains the silly fool he always was.

In bringing Panurge and Triboullet face to face, Rabelais illustrates vividly the two kinds of folly, the good and the bad. Each calls the other a fool, and each is a fool, but Panurge is a fool in the bad sense. Saulnier, who has written some brief but important pages comparing the *Tiers Livre* and the *Moriae encomium*, has perceived this essential fact, and it is worth noting what he has to say:

Panurge is a fool, in the bad sense of the word, because he refuses to be "foolish." Do you want to be wise? Be careful, then. That is precisely the least contemptible degree of folly and of attachment to oneself. Because in reality, one *must* be "foolish" — in the eyes of the world. To want to be wise according to the world's laws is essentially folly. One must be "foolish." It is not a question here of a folly of the Cross, but simply of an anticonformism; and that is already something. The undertaking is that of a quest for truth, conducted by oneself.[29]

But why, one may ask, is Panurge so stubborn? Why does he benefit so little from all of his experiences in the *Tiers Livre*? The answer is given by Pantagruel when, remembering Stultitia's favorite companion, he says to Panurge: "Philauty, or Self-love, is that which blinds your judgment, and deceiveth you." [30] He has been blinded by Philautia, by his egotistical overconcern with himself and his future. It is Philautia who takes him on his long quest; it is she who causes him to interpret every answer in a way favorable to himself. Triboullet, on the other hand, represents just the opposite of self-love; for he is, as Pantagruel describes him, the kind of fool who is able to "[forget] himself, [rid] all his Senses of Terene affections, and [clear] his Fancies of those plodding Studies, which harbour in the Minds of thriving Men: All which neglects of Sublunary Things are vulgarly imputed Folly." [31] It is precisely this inability to forget himself, to accept his own frailty, that frustrates Panurge through the whole of the *Tiers Livre*. He is told throughout to do what he wants to do; yet he is never able to accept himself as he is.

The Renaissance, with its humanistic concern for teaching, is filled

---

[29] Saulnier, *Le Dessin de Rabelais*, pp. 209–10.
[30] R V.225/III.xxix: "philautie et amour de soy vous deçoit."
[31] R V.273/III.xxxvii. See note 2 for text.

with examples of what education can do, but the *Tiers Livre* is the only example I know of an education that fails. As such, it is an object lesson on the order of *The Mirrour for Magistrates*: we ourselves are meant to learn from Panurge's failure. Panurge himself is by no means wholly despicable, and, indeed, we find ourselves coming to love him as much as Pantagruel does, who "[l'] ayma toute sa vie." He is more than merely irresistible, though. He is wiser and better than almost everyone he meets in the *Tiers Livre*: he sees through the sham wisdom of the world, and he rejects without hesitation that wisdom and its pretenses. He is also the joyful optimist that the good Pantagruelist ought to be, meeting defeats cheerfully, hoping always for better luck next time. But as his quest takes him farther and farther into the labyrinthine ways of truth, he becomes lost and loses as well his joy and optimism. The final problems defeat him wholly because, although he represents many of the best qualities of the fool, he is incapable of accepting the final folly. He goes with his sister Stultitia through the nature of folly and the ranks of fools, but he falters at the threshold of that transcendent folly with which she closes her speech.

At a certain moment in Max Beerbohm's parody of Shakespearean tragedy, '*Savonarola*' *Brown*, Lucretia Borgia, after listening to her fool babble on, wittily exclaims, "Methinks the Fool is a fool!" It is this judgment that, in all seriousness, we must finally make of Panurge. Lovable though he is and wise though he is in many things, he is, in the end, simply foolish; for he rejects the wisdom of folly. Pantagruel has told him all along what he must do, but he cannot understand it. Having failed to become the wise fool, he regresses to become a more foolish fool than he ever had been before. When we see him again, in the *Quart Livre*, he is still a clever enough rogue to outwit the bovine Dindenault, but in the Erasmian tempest he himself is reduced to a bovine, lachrymose coward.[32] He leaves the *Tiers Livre* as he entered it, harassed by doubt and menaced by fear, and, instead of having achieved the joy of Pantagruelism, he has acquired only the grief of folly.

[32] *Quart Livre*, chs. XVIII–XXIII.

14

PANTAGRUELISM

❦❦❦❦❦❦❦❦❦❦❦❦❦❦❦❦❦❦❦❦❦❦❦

THE perfect fool is Pantagruel. Yet it is the imperfect fool, Panurge, who is given the leading role in the *Tiers Livre* because it it through his experience that Rabelais shows us the vanity of worldly wisdom and the necessity for fooldom. These are truths that Pantagruel has known from the beginning, and, while he can and does state them throughout the book, his author knows that for Pantagruel to tell us is not as pedagogically effective as for Panurge to show us. Diogenes was also aware of this, which is why he performed his mimetic action "sans mot dire" instead of simply telling the Corinthians what their errors were. Nevertheless, as Panurge is acting out his tragicomic epic, Pantagruel is always there, commenting on and explaining the action, standing for that truth that Panurge seeks but cannot find.

That truth, of course, is Pantagruelism, and Pantagruelism, as should be evident by now, is a profounder philosophy than the indulgent libertinism that Rameau's nephew and so many others have thought it was.[1] Postulated upon the Pauline knowledge that the wisdom of this world is folly and that what this world calls folly is true wisdom, Pantagruelism counsels us to become fools. By so doing, we may become fit receptacles for God's wisdom, which is the only true *sapientia*, and thus we become able to accept His will without fear or doubt. At the same time, our own will is freed by our very acceptance of God's will; for to enter into what Rabelais calls the "Divine Mansion of Reason" (*deificque manoir de raison* [V.35/III.ii]) is to

---

[1] See Denis Diderot, *Le Neveu de Rameau*, ed. Jean Fabre (Geneva, 1950), p. 9. Also, Diderot's letter to Général Betzky, 21 March 1774, cited by Fabre, pp. 126–7.

achieve that state of ataraxy in which our will is no longer frustrated by doubts and worries. That is to say, if we accept our own ignorance and place our faith in the wisdom of God, then no wordly things can trouble us. Pantagruel explains,[2]

all the Goods that the Heaven covereth, and that the Earth containeth in all their Dimensions and Heighth, Depth, Breadth, and Length, are not of so much worth, as that we should for them disturb or disorder our Affections, trouble or perplex our Senses or Spirit.

This is so because, with God's wisdom, external things become in themselves indifferent, neither good nor bad except as our mind or heart deems them good or bad. As Hamlet tells Rosencranz, "there is nothing either good or bad but thinking makes it so." [3] Therefore, Pantagruelism advises us, as St. Paul did the Romans, "Let every man be fully persuaded in his own mind," [4] a phrase which, as M. A. Screech has recently pointed out, is translated by Pantagruel.[5]

[Let every man be fully persuaded in his own mind:] Yea, in Things of a Foreign Consideration, altogether extrinsical and indifferent, which in and of themselves are neither commendable nor bad, because they proceed not from the Interior of the Thoughts and Heart, which is the Shop of all Good and Evil. Of Goodness, if it be upright, and that its Affections be regulated by the pure and clean Spirit of Righteousness; and on the other side, of Wickedness, if its Inclinations straying beyond the Bounds of Equity, be corrupted and depraved by the malice and Suggestions of the Devil.

It is for this reason that Panurge is constantly told that he must make up his own mind, be "assured of his will," and act thereupon. Once the will has determined what it wishes to do, then one must not hesi-

---

[2] R V.35/III.ii: "Car tous les biens que le ciel couvre et que la terre contient en toutes ses dimensions: haulteur, profondité, longitude et latitude, ne sont dignes d'esmouvoir nos affections et troubler nos sens et espritz."

[3] *Hamlet* II.ii.255–7. Cf. Melville's interesting and pertinent marginal comment on this passage, as quoted in F. O. Matthiessen, *American Renaissance* (New York, 1941), p. 406. Cf. also Herman Melville, *Pierre*, ed. H. A. Murray (New York, 1957), p. 159.

[4] Romans, 14.5: "Unusquisque in suo sensu abundet."

[5] R V.70/III.vii: "Chascun abonde en son sens: mesmement en choses foraines, externes et indifferentes, lesquelles de soy ne sont bonnes ne maulvaises, pource qu'elles ne sortent de nos coeurs et pensées, qui est l'officine de tout bien et tout mal: bien, si bonne est, et par le esprit munde reiglée l'affection; mal, si hors aequité par l'esprit maling est l'affection depravée." I have corrected Urquhart's mistranslation of the crucial phrase from Romans.

tate in doubt about the future, but proceed to act, trusting in God.[6]

It is therefore expedient, seeing you are resolved for once to make a trial of the state of Marriage, that, with shut Eyes, bowing your Head, and kissing the Ground, you put the business to a Venture, and give it a fair hazard in recommending the success of the residue to the disposure of Almighty God.

But it is because Panurge is incapable of becoming the perfect fool and because in his imperfect folly "the malignant Spirit misleads, beguileth, and seduceth" him that he cannot make up his mind.[7] Therefore he cannot act. The answer to his question can never be found in the repositories of worldly wisdom; it can only be found within himself. But he does not know himself, as Epistemon saw at the very outset of the quest when he exclaimed: "to have the understanding, providence, knowledge and prediction of a Man's own mishap is very scarce and rare to be found any where!"[8] The rule of Pantagruelism is that of the Abbaye de Thélème; but Panurge cannot do what he wishes, since he is incapable of determining what he does wish.

Because he cannot satisfy the conditions that make Pantagruelism possible, Panurge is thereby denied the supreme reward of that philosophy, which is *joyeuseté*. Unlike Pantagruel, he moves through the *Tiers Livre* with his brow wrinkled by doubt and worry and fear; the prince, on the other hand, is the smiling idea and example of all joyous perfection.[9] He is the Fool in Christ, and Christ, as Stultitia explained, is the true fountain of joy. Just as Stultitia's final folly led her to an Epicurean *voluptas*, so Pantagruel is the living image of Epicurean *joie et volupté*. Back in Salmiguondin, Panurge had said to his prince, "pensez vivre *joyeulx*, de par li bon Dieu et li bons homs!" but he is counseling a false joy, and, as the book progresses, we see that it is he and not Pantagruel who lacks the true happiness, which is Christian folly. The laughter that pervades all of Rabelais'

[6] R V.85–6/III.x: "Il se y convient mettre à l'adventure, les oeilz bandez, baissant la teste, baisant la terre, et se recommandant à Dieu au demourant, puys qu'une foys l'on se y veult mettre."

[7] R V.147/III.xix: "l'esprit maling vous seduyt." Cf. Screech, *Marriage*, p. 112.

[8] R V.126–7/III.xv: "Mais ô que chose rare est son malheur propre praedire, congnoistre, praevoir et entendre!"

[9] R V.363/III.li: "comme Pantagruel a esté l'Idée et exemplaire de toute joyeuse perfection . . ."

work is not simply the thoughtless, drunken guffaw that so many readers have thought it was; it comes from and is informed by the serious philosophical assumptions of that Christian Epicureanism which Erasmus expounded. The "laughing philosopher" is first of all a philosopher.

By its very nature, the story of Gargantua and Pantagruel does not so much expound as demonstrate that philosophy, and we extrapolate it from the "jolly chearful Quart of Pantagruelick Sentences," testing our extrapolations against the Erasmian sources of those "sentences." In fact, however, we also possess a carefully reasoned statement by Rabelais himself in defense of this philosophy of joy, though for some reason it has never been given much serious attention. In a little-known book entitled *Les Dialogues de Loys Le Caron Parisien*, first published in Paris in 1556, the third dialogue is entitled "Valton, de la tranquillité d'esprit, Ou du souuerain bien," and the last of the three speakers in this dialogue is Rabelais himself.[10] Lucien Pinvert, who first called attention to this interesting speech, maintains that the words attributed to Rabelais are not an invention by Le Caron, but a transcription of a conversation that actually took place, "reproduced with the scrupulous fidelity that was customary in a time when the oral tradition had a much greater importance than it does today and often constituted, for lack of the many facilities available in modern life, the sole means of propagating thought."[11] This claim sounds a little exaggerated, and it is in fact somewhat contradicted by what Le Caron himself says at the beginning of the dialogue.[12]

[10] This was printed by Pinvert in *RER*, I (1903), 193–201. A recent edition, which I have been unable to see has been prepared by Jacques Saint Germain and was published for the Compaignie des Bibliophiles Gastronomes at Paris in 1949. The present quotations are taken from *Les Dialogues de Loys Le Caron Parisien* (Paris, Jean Longis, 1556), a microfilm copy of which was kindly provided by the Newberry Library, Chicago. On Le Caron himself, see L. Pinvert, "Louis Le Caron, dit Charondas," *Revue de la Renaissance*, II (1902), 1–9, 69–76, 181–8; and F. Gohin, *De Lud. Charondae (1534–1613) vita et versibus* (Paris, 1902).

[11] L. Pinvert, in *RER*, I (1903), 194.

[12] *Les Dialogues de Loys Le Caron Parisien*, Sig. 81v: "Me pourmenant quelquefois auec mon oncle en vn parc spatieux & plaisant pour la diuersité des couleurs de la fleurissante prérie, apres plusieurs propos nous entrâmes en la dispute de la tranquilité d'esprit & du souuerain bien. Il lui resouuint de ce que peu auparauant il auoit oui reciter à monsieur l'Escorché d'vn mesme question, discouruë entre lui, Cotereau & Rabelais, & humainement me la declaira toute. Depuis repensant à ces discours il m'a semblé de les traitter plus amplement, faisant parler ceux, desquelz les sentences estoit propres, & exprimant sous le nom de mon oncle nostre comune pensée."

Strolling one day with my uncle in a park that was spacious and pleasing for the diversity of colors on its flowering fields, we entered, after several other discussions, into the dispute over the tranquillity of the mind and the sovereign good. He recalled that he had recently heard the same question argued before M. l'Escorché by himself, Cotereau, and Rabelais, and he kindly recounted it to me. Since then, I have thought about these arguments and have decided to treat them more fully, giving to each participant the words that belonged to him, and expressing under the name of my uncle our mutual thoughts.

According to what he says, therefore, Le Caron was not present at the discussion, but learned about it from his uncle, who was one of the participants. Furthermore, he claims to have expanded what he was told and given to each of the interlocutors "the words that belonged to him" (*faisant parler ceux, desquelz les sentences estoient propres*). This last phrase is a bit unclear: it may mean that he gave to each of the speakers the words that Valton said he had spoken, or, more likely, it may imply a Thucydidean *ta deonta* — a supplying of appropriate words. Whatever the case, it seems unlikely that this is a verbatim transcript. Nevertheless, it does follow closely what Rabelais would have said — and indeed seems to follow his probable words more closely than one might expect. For in his speech there are two significant verbal parallels to passages in his book. One contains the familiar rule of Thélème, which would in any case have been well known to anyone interested in Rabelais.[13] But the other is more important as a confirmation of the resemblance between what Rabelais is made to say in the dialogue and what he must actually have said; for it is a citation of the adage *en buthô he alêtheia* which preserves the same surprisingly erroneous attribution of the phrase to Heraclitus rather than to Democritus that Rabelais makes in his two other citations of the image.[14]

It would seem, then, that we are able to take Le Caron's dialogue as an accurate representation of Rabelais' thought. It becomes for his descriptions of Pantagrueline joy what Erasmus' colloquy *Epicureus*

---

[13] *Les Dialogues*, Sig. 116v: "Les hommes noblement instituez & frequentants les compaignies de leurs semblables ont de nature vn instinct & eguillon, qui tousiours les pousse & incite à faits vertueux, & retire de vice, lequel plusieurs appellent honneur." Cf. R II.430–1/I.lvii.

[14] *Les Dialogues*, Sig. 113r: "la claire verité: laquelle à céte cause ie veux maintenant decouurir, & tirer ou plustost arracher du noir puîs Cimmerien, ou Heraclite la disoit estre cachée . . ." Cf. R V.264/III.xxxvi, IV.211/II.xviii.

was for Stultitia's joy — a reasoned statement of the philosophical bases for that *voluptas*. Because it is so important and yet so little known, it may be helpful to summarize the argument contained in these pages.

Interestingly enough, Rabelais begins his speech by disclaiming any debt to the Epicureans: "If any one of you thinks that I have taken from the school and disputations of Epicurus the discourse that I have undertaken to give, let him change his opinion at once. For I assure him that I have never been obligated or dedicated to that sect or to any other." [15] What this means, of course, is simply that he is claiming intellectual independence and disclaiming any possibility that he is a pagan heretic. He is also making it clear that he is not to be associated with those libertine Epicureans whom La Noue, who has given the most complete account of them, was to call "les enfans sans soucy." [16] At the same time, however, Rabelais' disclaimer is an unintentional confession that what is to follow is close to the Epicurean point of view. He begins, then, with the premise that if our actions and thought had no goal, no *telos*, nothing could be certain or happy in this life. That goal, he maintains, is contentment; for everything aspires to its last and final contentment and, having obtained it, desires nothing more but finds in itself the sum of all good. What is it that can render a man content? That is a question we must refer to the judgment of nature, which is common to all men. Now when the understanding (*l'Entendement*) has reached truth, it is content, filled with a marvelous ease and pleasure, and in that contentment no grief, however sharp or vehement, can perturb it. Rabelais then goes on to draw an analogy between the contentment of the understanding and the contentment of the body, but he is careful to conclude that one cannot compare the joys of the body with those of the mind, because no joy approaches that of the understanding content with its intelligence, that is, with itself (*l'Entendement content de son intelligence, c'est à dire de soi-mesme*).

[15] *Les Dialogues*, Sig 112v: "Si aucun de vous me pense auoir apporté de l'eschole & disputations d'Epicure le discours que i'ai entrepris, qu'il change de premiere face son opinion. Car ie l'asseure que ie ne me suis iamais obligé ne dedié à céte secte n'à autre quelconque."

[16] See François de La Noue, *Discours politiques et militaires* (Lyon, 1595), p. 714. The entire passage on the "Épicuriens aux Cours, aux Armées, et aux Villes" in the twenty-fourth discourse (pp. 704–54) is relevant.

Following these introductory premises, he moves into the main body of his argument. Pleasure (*volupté*), he says, is nothing but the enjoyment and contentment of that which is desired. At the same time, nothing can bring us pleasure which is not by nature good. All virtues, the arts, and the sciences place their entire goal in pleasure.[17]

For everything which is of man or in him or belongs to his life only tends to keep and make him happy, and to this end lead prudence, justice, fortitude, temperance, and all honorable things. Prudence lies in the search after truth. But why is it that one directs so many studies to the knowledge of this, if it is not that delight accompanies it and always excites this wonderful pleasure in knowing and understanding the cause and truth of things hidden in nature? Justice, for the pleasure in human company, is exercised to give each man his right, to keep faith in promises, to benefit those who merit it, and to receive the benefit worthily presented. What causes fortitude constantly to support and put up with labors and dangers but pleasure, which frees and delivers man from all pain? Moreover, is temperance anything else but pleasure, which makes the appetite wholly obedient to reason and thus gives to man a peace, contentment, and tranquillity so full of pleasure that he lacks nothing to live according to nature? Of the pleasures of the body I have already spoken; and they must be inseparably joined to those of the mind to constitute the true pleasure of the whole man. For one cannot live joyously if not also wisely, honestly, and justly; and for the same reason, neither can one live wisely, honestly, and justly, if not joyously. The fruit and reward of virtue is this same pleasure.

He concludes this part of his argument by saying that man, endowed with understanding, only desires *naturally* that pleasure which does

[17] *Les Dialogues,* Sig. 114v–115r: "Car tout ce qui est de l'homme, ou soit en lui, ou appartienne à sa vie, ne tend qu'à le conseruer & rendre heureux: & à céte mesme fin la prudence, la iustice, la force, la temperance, & toutes les especes de l'honnesteté se rapportent. La prudence gist en la recherche du vrai: mais pourquoi est ce qu'on emploie tant d'estudes à céte congnoissance si non qu'vne delectation l'accompagne & excite tousiours ce merueilleux plaisir de sçauoir & entendre la cause & verité des chose cachées en nature? La Iustice pour la volupté de la compagnie humaine, s'exerce à rendre à châcun son droit, garder la foi des choses promises, bienfaire ceux, qui le meritent, & receuoir le bienfait dignement presenté. Qui pousseroit la force à soûtenir & porter constamment les trauaux & dangers, si non la volupté, qui afranchit & deliure l'homme de toute douleur? Dauentage qu'est-ce autre chose la temperance, que la mesme volupté, laquelle fait que l'appetit obeïsse entierement à la raison: & ainsi accorde en l'homme vne paix, conuenance & tranquilité pleine de si grand plaisir, que rien ne lui defaut pour viure selon nature? De la delectation du corps i'ai dés ia parlé: aussi doit elle estre inseparablement coniointe auec celle de l'Esprit pour constituer la vraie volupté de tout l'homme. Par ce qu'on ne peut viure ioieusement, si non aussi sagement, honnestement & iustement: ne par mesme raison sagement, honnestement & iustement, si non ioieusement. Et le fruit & guerdon de la vertu est icellemesme volupté."

not corrupt but agrees with and supports the order of nature, and thus that pleasure is called reasonable — a position which, we may remember, was the basis for the rule of Thélème.

Rabelais goes on to tell his auditors that there are other things that are called by the name of *volupté* but they are false pleasures, and we must beware of them. He then cites the rule of Thélème already quoted, in which he maintains that men are naturally drawn toward the good and that this quality is called honor. Its goal is nothing other than this praiseworthy pleasure.[18]

The beginning, cause, and origin of this pure pleasure is the knowledge of divine and most excellent things, and its proper task is to make man content according to his perfect nature (which we have often said to be reason or virtue) and to moderate his affections according to its order and judgment that they may enjoy a firm and lasting pleasure — which pleasure would otherwise, if not thus tempered, engender more grief than joy. For to constitute, like the Stoics, an apathy, that is (if I may be permitted the word), an impassionateness, is to make the spirit lazy and cowardly so that it cannot even be stirred to virtue. On the contrary, they seem to me to be too impudent and bold who abuse the favor of the sciences by restlessly working to write and publish their languishing inventions of amorous agonies — as though they proposed to shatter the ease of our natural tranquillity and force us to obey even passions. Noble pleasure never accompanies such labors; and I may say frankly that the work of writing and bringing one's thoughts to the public does not merit any great praise, but ought rather to be suppressed as vain and wholly useless. For those who formerly followed and still today follow such a course cannot convince me that they have not diminished for me the

[18] *Les Dialogues*, Sig. 116v-117r: "Le commencement, la cause & l'origine de céte pure volupté est la congnoissance des choses diuines & plus excellentes: & son propre deuoir de rendre l'homme content selon la parfaite nature (laquelle souuent auons dit estre la raison ou vertu) & moderer les afections selon l'ordre & iugement d'icelle: afin qu'elles iouissent d'vn ferme & durable plaisir: lequel autrement si n'estoit ainsi temperé, engendreroit plus de douleur, que de ioië. Car de constituer comme les Stoiciens vne apathie, c'est à dire (s'il m'est permis d'vser de ce mot) impassionneté, c'est faire l'esprit si lâche & couard, que mesment il ne se puisse émouuoir à la vertu. Au contraire ceux me semblent estre trop impudents & temeraires, lesquelz abusans de la faueur des sciences trauaillent sans repos à mettre en escrit & publier à touts leurs inuentions languissantes d'amoureuses angoisses: comme s'ilz se proposoient de rompre en nous l'aise de nostre tranquilité naturelle, & nous contraindre à suiure mesmes passions. De telz labeurs la noble volupté ne s'accompagne iamais: & puis dire franchement que le trauail d'escrire & éuenter au public ses pensées, ne merite grande louange: ains plustost doit estre reprimé comme vain & entierement inutile. Car ceux & qui ont anciennement suiui & suiuent encores auiord'hui tel train, ne se peuuent excuser, qu'ilz m'aient diminué de la grandeur & excellente gloire de la science: par ce que de leurs priuées conceptions ilz ont voulu brider les estudes & pensées des autres: ce que font encores ceux de nostre eage au grand tort & mespris de la posterité."

grandeur and great glory of knowledge. For they have wished to harnass the study and thought of others with their private concepts. Even the men of our day do this in disdain, and to the harm of posterity.

In this final passage, where the vanity of learning is rejected for the "order and judgment" of nature, Rabelais has expressed the essence of the *Tiers Livre*. Stutitia had said it before him.[19]

Wherfore lyke as amongs mortall men they are fardest removed from blisfulnesse, that geve theim selves to the studie of wysedome, yea, twise foolishe in this, that beyng borne men, they woulde possiblie if they could, usurpe the state of the immortall *Gods*, and (as poetes feigne the *Geantes* did) "with theyr engins of science move warre against Nature."

What Renaudet has written of Pulci is equally appropriate as a description of Rabelais, that God, principle of joy and light, seems to be mingled for him with the soul of nature and her eternal laws.[20] For it is the acceptance of man's nature, and not pretension to worldly wisdom, that leads man to God and His final joy. "Nihil scire felicissima vita," claimed Agrippa, quoting Sophocles, in the epigram to his book, and Stultitia had claimed the same thing: "But the good simple people of the olde *golden worlde*, without any disciplines at all, lived onely as *Nature* taught, and instincted theim . . . For Nature abhorreth counterfeityng, and farre more towardly doeth it flourisshe, that with least arte and cure is tended to." [21] In acquiring knowledge, man attempts to rise above himself, but wisdom is the property of God alone. This advocacy of nature is also the conclusion of Montaigne.[22]

As [Nature] hath given us feete to goe withall, so hath she endowed us with wisedome to direct our life. A wisedome not so ingenious, sturdy, and pompous, as that of their invention; but yet easie, quiet and salutarie. And that in him who hath the hap to know how to employ it orderly and sincerely, effecteth very well what the other saith: that is to say naturally.

___

[19] ME 63: "Ut igitur inter mortales ii longissime absunt a felicitate, qui sapientiae student, nimirum hoc ipso bis stulti, quod homines nati cum sint, tamen obliti conditionis suae Deorum immortalium vitam affectant, et gigantum exemplo, disciplinarum machinis, naturae bellum inferunt . . ."

[20] Augustin Renaudet, *Érasme et l'Italie* (Geneva, 1954), p. 64.

[21] ME 58, 60–1: "Siquidem simplex illa aurei seculi gens, nullis armata disciplinis, solo naturae ductu instinctuque vivebat . . . Odit natura fucos, multoque felicius provenit, quod nulla sit arte violatum."

[22] M III.372/III.xiii: "Comme [Nature] nous a fourni de pieds a marcher, aussi a elle de prudance a nous guider en la uie; prudance, non tant ingenieuse, robuste et pompeuse comme celle de leur inuantion, mais a l'auenant facile et salutere, et qui faict tres bien ce que l'autre dict, en celuy qui a l'heur de sçauoir s'employer naifue-

For a man to commit himselfe most simply unto nature, is to doe it most wisely. Oh how soft, how gentle, and how sound a pillow is ignorance and incuriosity to rest a well composed head upon.

Nothing, as Stultitia said, can be unhappy if it expresses its true nature.[23] But Panurge will never know this joy, for he possesses only the folly of the fool; his quest will be endless. Pantagruel, on the other hand, has no quest at all. The joyful ease with which, near the end of the *Tiers Livre*, he makes up his mind to marry is in explicit contrast to Panurge's worried indecision through the book. Pantagruel will first accompany Panurge on their sea voyage, but when he returns he will be married to a wife whom his father will have chosen for him. One doubts, however, if Panurge will find a wife; it is unlikely that he will ever be able to make up his mind. The flea still in his ear, he boards ship at Thalassa with Pantagruel, Epistemon, and Frere Jan, accompanied by his new hope Xenomanes, and they sail forth to lands of allegory. And when, later, Pantagruel recounts the fable of the rivalry between Physis and Antiphysie,[24] of natural as opposed to artificial truth, this will be merely another way of explaining what Rabelais has been demonstrating all along with his Diogenic barrel of wine.

As they sail forth to find the Holy Bottle, the holds of their ships are filled with a cargo of a plant called Pantagruelion, and it is with a lengthy description of this allegorical plant that the *Tiers Livre* is brought to a close. The structure of Rabelais' book is that of a triptych: in the center panel the story of Panurge and his quest is told, while on each of the wings is painted an emblem that represents the goal of that quest — on one side the barrel of Diogenes, on the other the plant Pantagruelion. Whatever else they may stand for, both are symbols of that courageous, optimistic, joyful, natural truth which is Pantagruelism. It is truth that is the wine in the barrel "pierced for you" by Rabelais at the beginning of his book, that truth which is

ment et ordoneement, c'est a dire naturellement. Le plus simplement se commettre a nature, c'est s'y commettre le plus sagemant. O que c'est un dous et mol cheuet, et sain, que l'ignorance et l'incuriosite, a reposer une teste bien faict."

[23] ME 57: "Nihil autem miserum, quod in suo genere constat."

[24] *Quart Livre*, ch. XXXII. [The following article, of considerable pertinence to this discussion of Rabelais, appeared after this book had been set in type: Stanley G. Eskin, "Physis and Antiphysie: The Idea of Nature in Rabelais and Calcagnini," *Comparative Literature* XIV (1962), 167–73.]

"a true Cornu-copia of Merriment and Raillery." [25] It is truth that grows, "green without and whitish within," at the end of his book, that truth which is "odious and hateful to Thieves." [26] "Believe it if you will, or otherwise believe it not," says Rabelais: "I care not which of them you do, they are both alike to me, it shall be sufficient for my Purpose to have told you the Truth, and the Truth I will tell you." [27] "For," as he says earlier, "the Lord forbid that we should make use of any Fables in this a so venerable History." [28]

With extensive botanical accuracy, Rabelais describes the nature and properties of this plant, which has been identified by the commentators as flax. It seems likely that behind each bit of scientific description Rabelais meant to signify cryptically a moral quality, but for the most part it is impossible to penetrate to his hidden meaning with any assurance. On the other hand, he may be trying to give nothing more than accurate detail in order to ensure our belief in the existence of such a plant. Yet there are moments when, in his descriptions of the plant, he seems to be describing man himself. Whatever he may have meant (if he meant anything) by the botanical descriptions, his account of the properties of this plant is less opaque. Here we can definitely see through to a more profound level of meaning. There is no question, for example, about his allusions to the hangman's rope which is made out of Pantagruelion, which is used to hang liars and robbers, and which, significantly, takes none by the throat except those who have refused to drink (V.363/III.li). Nor is there any question about the passage in which, imitating Stultitia's "sine me" (ME 34), Rabelais describes the world "sans elle" — without Pantagruelion (V.365-7/III.li). For Stultitia the *copula mundi* was folly; for Panurge it was debt; for Ficino it was love; for Rabelais it is the truth of Pantagruelion.

Beloved by nature (*tant l'a cherie nature*), Pantagruelion has all the virtues of Pantagruel himself.[29]

For as Pantagruel hath been the Idea, Pattern, Prototype and Exemplary of all Jovial Perfection and Accomplishment, (in the truth whereof, I believe

[25] R V.23/III.Prol.: "un vray Cornucopie de joyeuseté et raillerie."
[26] R V.358/III.li: "abhorré et hay des larrons."
[27] R V.370/III.liii: "Croyez la ou non, ce m'est tout un: me suffist vous avoir dict verité. Verité vous diray."
[28] R V.358/III.li: "car de fable jà Dieu ne plaise que usions en ceste tant veritable histoire."
[29] R V.363/III.li: "car, comme Pantagruel a esté l'Idée et exemplaire de toute joyeuse

there is none of you, Gentlemen Drinkers, that putteth any question) so in this Pantagruelion have I found so much Efficacy and Energy, so much Compleatness and Excellency, so much Exquisiteness and Rariety, and so many admirable Effects and Operations of a transcendent Nature, that if the Worth and Virtue thereof had been known, when those Trees, by the Relation of the Prophet, made Election of a Wooden King to rule and govern over them, it without all doubt would have carried away from all the rest the Plurality of Votes and Suffrages.

Since it is truth, if Pantagruelion is poured into the ears all falsehood therein will be destroyed: "I shall forbear to tell you, how the Juice or Sap thereof, being poured and distilled within the Ears, killeth every kind of Vermin, that by any manner of Putrefaction cometh to be bred and ingendred there; and destroyeth also any whatsoever other Animal that shall have entred in thereat." [30] It is capable also of acting as a filter to separate right from wrong, as one might separate wine from water (V.370/III.lii). What is more, with it scientific (V.267-8/III.li) and geographic (V.368/III.li) discoveries are made, and man is able to accomplish things undreamt of. It is, indeed, *this* truth, and not *sapientia mundana* as some have claimed, that enables man to "be Deify'd" (V.369/III.li).

The most miraculous quality of Pantagruelion, however, is that it is indestructible. Time, which destroys all things, cannot destroy it, for truth is the daughter of time. Because it is a natural, living plant — because, that is, it is a truth that exists within nature — it dies each year; yet from the stem spring new branches. Rabelais does not dwell on this aspect of Pantagruelion, but we, in retrospect, can see that he was close to that acceptance of the permanent impermanence of nature that Edmund Spenser was later to describe so beautifully in his cantos on Mutability and the gardens of Adonis. The truth of Pantagruelion, like man himself, will persist, even though individual plants and individual men die. As Gargantua explained to Pantagruel in his famous letter, human nature can acquire a kind of

---

perfection (je croy que personne de vous aultres, beuveurs, n'en doubte), aussi en Pantagruelion je recongnoys tant de vertus, tant d'energie, tant de perfection, tant d'effectz admirables, que, si elle eust esté en ses qualitez congneue lors que les arbres (par la relation du prophete) feirent election d'un roy de boys pour les regir et dominer, elle sans doubte eust emporté la pluralité des voix et suffrages."

[30] R V.364/III.li: "Je laisse à vous dire comment le jus d'icelle, exprimé et instillé dedans les aureilles, tue toute espece de vermine qui y seroit née par putrefaction, et tout aultre animal qui dedans seroit entré."

immortality and, in the course of a transitory life, perpetuate its name and seed (III.99/II.viii). So also the truth of Pantagruelion, which grows plantlike within man, renews itself year after year. Nor can it be destroyed. For, says Rabelais, thinking of the dead in Provence and the Place Maubert, truth cannot be burnt out by fire. Pantagruelion has an asbestine quality, and fire, rather than destroying it, merely purifies it: "O how rare and admirable a thing it is, that the Fire which devoureth, consumeth and destroyeth all such things else, should cleanse, purge and whiten this sole Pantagruelion." [31] This quality of flax is described in Pliny, from whom commentators have assumed Rabelais took it; yet he may have had in mind as well a passage from Erasmus which all commentators have overlooked. Significantly, flax is also described in these terms in the colloquy *Epicureus*, whose relevance to the *Tiers Livre* and the concept of Pantagruelism cannot be overestimated.[32]

HEDONIUS: I call that evil which breaks the friendship between God and man. SPOUDAEUS: But I believe that very few are pure of this kind of evil. HEDONIUS: Yet I think that those who are purged are pure. Those who with the lye of tears, the soap of repentence, and the fire of charity have washed away their sins, are not only harmed by no sins, but very often they yield matter of greater good. SPOUDAEUS: I understand about lye and soap, but I have never heard of fire purging stains. HEDONIUS: But if you should go to a silversmith's, you will see gold purged by fire. And there is a certain sort of flax which, cast into the fire, is not burned but shines more brightly, as clear as water; and it is for that reason called *Living Flax.*

As Rabelais wrote this, there were fires burning all over France, and the fuel was human flesh; but out of his horror and despair he was able to maintain the optimism of Pantagruelism and to claim that those fires could not destroy the truth, but would only purify it. He even adds, with great daring, a minatory prediction.[33]

[31] R V.372/III.lii: "O chose grande, chose admirable! Le feu, qui tout devore, tout deguaste et consume, nettoye, purge et blanchist ce seul Pantagruelion . . ."
[32] LB I.882E-883A: "HEDONIUS: Malum appello, quod dirimit amicitiam inter Deum e hominem. SPOUDAEUS: Et ab hoc mali genere puto perpaucos esse puros. HE: Ego vero et purgatos habeo pro puris. Qui lixivio lacrymarum, ac poenitentiae nitro, aut caritatis igni maculas absterserunt, eis non solum nihil nocent peccata, verum etiam frequenter in majoris boni materiam cedent. SP: Equidem nitrum et lixivium novi; igni purgari maculas, nunquam audivi. HE: Atqui si adeas argentarias officianas, videbis aurum igni purgari. Quanquam et lini genus est, quod conjectum in ignem non exuritur, sed nitidius splendescit, quam ulla possit aqua; eoque *vivum* appellant."
[33] R V.372/III.lii: "Ne me parragonnez poinct icy la salamandre, c'est abus. Je

Do not think to overmatch me here, by paragoning with it, in the way of a more eminent Comparison, the Salamander. That is a Fib; for albeit a little ordinary Fire, such as is used in Dining-Rooms and Chambers, gladden, chear up, exhilerate and quicken it, yet may I warrantably enough assure, that in the flaming fire of a Furnace, it will, like any other animated Creature, be quickly suffocated, choaked, consumed and destroyed. We have seen the Experiment thereof . . .

Luckily for Rabelais, none of his censors understood this reference or he too might have been fuel for those fires. It was, of course, proverbial that the salamander lived in fire, and Falstaff refers to this fact in describing Bardolph's face (*1 Henry IV*, III.iii.52–4). But to the early sixteenth century that animal had another, more immediate meaning: the salamander, as his heraldry proclaimed it on every royal monument in France, was the king himself. There is a daring irony in intimating that François I lived in the fires of his own *bûchers*; there is an even more daring warning, analogous to that delivered three centuries later by Dickens with the image of spontaneous combustion, that if the persecutions and intolerance are allowed to go unchecked they will eventually destroy the throne and France. You cannot burn out the truth, and, as the verses which close the *Tiers Livre* have it,[34]

> If in your Soil it takes, to Heaven
> A thousand thousand Thanks be given;
> And say with France, it goodly goes
> Where the Pantagruelion grows.

The story of the *Tiers Livre* is the story of a quest for truth, here symbolized by a growing plant, symbolized earlier by a barrel of wine. That truth is, quite simply, the joyful, optimistic philosophy of Christ which Rabelais calls Pantagruelism. It is the philosophy of every wise fool.

---

confesse bien que petit feu de paille la vegete et resjouist. Mais je vous asceure que en grande fournaise elle est, comme tout aultre animant, suffoquée et consumée. Nous en avons veu l'experience."

[34] R V.377/III.lii:
> "Puys, si chez vous peut croistre, en bonne estrene,
> Graces rendez es cieulx un million:
> Et affermez de France heureux le regne
> On quel provient Pantagruelion."

III ❦ SHAKESPEARE'S FALSTAFF

15

THE FOOL IN DRAMA

🏵🏵🏵🏵🏵🏵🏵🏵🏵🏵🏵🏵🏵🏵🏵🏵🏵🏵🏵🏵🏵🏵🏵🏵🏵

Aｌｔｈｏｕｇｈ the ideological premises for the Renaissance concept of folly derive from the thought of Italian humanism and Pauline evangelism, the origins of the figure of the fool lie elsewhere. He is descended from the humbler background of the popular drama of the Middle Ages. In the same way that the earliest secular theatrics grew out of a spirit of festive play, of "fooling around," the fool, carefree, gay, irresponsible, became the characteristic product of that spirit. Born in a moment of truancy from the working-day world, he is the most playful creation of *homo ludens;* and he comes to us, as Breughel painted him, out of the village festival and the dramatic antics of rude mechanicals.[1] He is the spirit of Carnival. For it is precisely when (according to Panurge) Mother Nature says to her children, "You have wrought well to day, toiled and turmoiled enough . . . desist from all your swinking painful Labours . . . then may you take some Sport and Recreation," [2] that the fool appears to help man laugh at his troubles and forget his labors, to release him from the cares of the soul, and to urge him to eat, drink, and be merry. In a dramatic as well as an alcoholic sense, the fool is a sot; and if we would discover the prototypes of Stultitia and Panurge, we must look to the *sottie* of medieval France and to its two outstanding characters, *la mère Sotte* and *le Prince des sots.*[3] Like Stultitia, Mother Folly is a satirical

[1] See the studies listed in the bibliography by C. L. Barber, Olive M. Busby, Willard Farnham, R. H. Goldsmith, Barbara Swain, and Enid Welsford.
[2] R V.123/III.xv: "C'est assez travaillé . . . il convient cesser du labeur . . . puys soy quelque peu esbaudir."
[3] See Welsford, *The Fool, passim.*

scourge of princes and popes who presides over a general transvaluation of values under the impunity of jest: her theme song is that melody to which General Cornwallis surrendered, "The World Turned Upside Down." Like Panurge, the Prince of Fools is the author of roguish tricks and irresponsible conduct in a world whose only law is nature, whose only goal is gaiety: he cavorts to the music of Tyl Eulenspiegel. The freedom of each is the anarchy of a holiday humor; their jests are the comic release of the heart's longings.

But — such is the condition of mankind — every day is not playing holiday; Lent follows Carnival, and the ash-marked forehead of penitence supersedes the wine-suffused cheek of license. When the laughter of the dramatic antics in the street gave way to the awesome mystery of the spiritual dramas enacted in the church, the fool had to be left behind. But halfway between the devotion of the miracle play and the sacrilege of the sottie stood a third type of drama: equidistant, so to speak, from the altar and the street, the morality play on the village green depicted the pilgrimage of Everyman through life to God. Somewhat later, near the end of the fifteenth century in England, the morality play moved indoors, not to the church, but rather to the banquet hall; and there it is called a moral interlude. Basically, the interlude and the morality have the same structure, but the interlude incorporated more realistic local color. As Edmund Chambers says, "from the moral the interlude drew abstractions; from the farce social types." [4] And, insofar as folly is a part of the life through which Everyman makes his pilgrimage, the fool is given a role to play in the moral interlude.

It is not, however, the same role. In the moral interlude he no longer enjoys the liberty of the all-licensed fool that was his in the truancy of the sottie and farce. Men are, as Dante explained in the greatest of all morality dramas, subjected in their freedom to the greater power and better nature of God,[5] and it is God who, in the morality, calls the fool to that reckoning he had managed to avoid in the sottie. The principle of nature upon which the fool operates is no longer the carefree, harmless jest it was: under the law of God it becomes a serious moral temptation. Thus, where in the sottie the

[4] E. K. Chambers, *The Medieval Stage* (Oxford, 1903), II, 205.

[5] See esp. the speech of Marco Lombardo, *Purgatorio*, XVI.79–81: "A maggior forza ed a miglior natura/liberi soggiacete; a quella cria/la mente in voi, che 'l ciel non ha in sua cura."

fool's actions were implicitly understood to be free from consequences or punishment, in the morality they are explicitly held responsible for the gravest of all consequences and punishments, spiritual damnation. The greatest of all fools is the great tempter himself, Satan, and it is his surrogate, the Vice, who has the fool's role in the moral interlude. In the war between God and the Devil for the soul of man, it is he who tempts man with the indulgences of nature to surrender to the Prince of Darkness. And though he may, and invariably does, have his moment with Everyman, ultimately he must be rejected for the way of salvation.

Now if the figures of Stultitia and Panurge come from the sottie, the figure of Sir John Falstaff, the last of the great fools of the sixteenth century, comes from the morality play. As we turn from the *Moriae encomium* and the *Tiers Livre* to the *History of Henry the Fourth*, we come back to the fool in his natural habitat, the drama; and it is, appropriately enough, the greatest of all dramatists who has given us the biggest fool. In Falstaff we have the fattest, the oldest, the funniest, the most natural fool of the three. One might say that in his huge girth he embodies both Stultitia and Panurge. Like Erasmus' fool, he is a stultiloquent jester who overturns all the accepted values; like Rabelais', he is the incorrigible rogue who serves as companion to the youthful prince. Yet in terms of the structure of the two parts of *Henry IV* he takes from the moral interlude still another role — that of the fool as tempter. For "that reverend vice, that grey iniquity, that father ruffian, that vanity in years," who threatens to beat the prince out of his kingdom with a dagger of lath, is self-avowedly the fool as Vice.

The relationship of Falstaff to the personified vice of the moral interlude — and in particular to the Vice as Gluttony[6] — has already been carefully examined by various hands.[7] The most important fact

[6] See esp. J. W. Shirley, "Falstaff, An Elizabethan Glutton," *PQ*, XVII (1938), 271–87.
[7] For example, S. L. Bethell, *Shakespeare and the Popular Dramatic Tradition* (London, 1944); D. C. Boughner, "Traditional Elements in Falstaff," *JEGP*, XLIII (1944), 417–28; L. W. Cushman, *The Devil and the Vice in the English Dramatic Literature Before Shakespeare*, Studien zur Englischen Philologie, VI (Halle, 1900); Eduard Eckhardt, *Die lustige Person im älteren englischen Drama* (Berlin, 1902); Katherine H. Gatch, "Shakespeare's Allusions to the Older Drama," *PQ*, VII (1928), 27–44; J. W. McCutchan, "Similarities between Falstaff and Gluttony in Medwall's *Nature*," *SAB*, XXIV (1949), 214–19; James Monaghan, "Falstaff and his Forebears," *SP*, XVIII (1921), 353–61; John W. Spargo, *An Interpretation of Falstaff*, Washington Univer-

is that it is the element of the Vice in his character that largely determines both Falstaff's function and his fate in the plays of *Henry IV*. We find many striking similarities, even in phraseology, and a recurrent general pattern if we compare Prince Hal's companion to the tempters in such early moralities as *Everyman, The Castle of Perseverance,* and *Mankind,* and more particularly with the Vices in such typical moral interludes as Medwall's *Nature,* the anonymous *Mundus et Infans, Youth,* and *The Nice Wanton,* Wever's *Lusty Juventus,* Lewis Wager's *Life and Repentance of Mary Magdalene,* Fulwell's *Like Will to Like,* and William Wager's *The Longer Thou Livest the More Fool Thou Art* (to take a representative sampling that stretches from c. 1490 to c. 1568). In all cases, the role of the Vice is that sung by Feste in *Twelfth Night:*

> I am gone, sir,
>   And anon, sir,
> I'll be with you again
>   In a trice,
>   Like to the old vice,
> Your need to sustain;
> Who, with dagger of lath,
> In his rage and his wrath,
>   Cries, "ah ha!" to the devil,
> Like a mad lad,
> "Pare thy nails, dad."
> Adieu, goodman devil.   IV.ii.130–41

The theme of these plays is commonly a variation on the popular theme of the prodigal son, an admonitory tale which Autolycus says he presented in a marionette show (*W.T.,* IV.iii.102–3), which Falstaff, himself accompanied by a whole army of prodigals, urges Hostess Quickly to have painted on the walls of her tavern, and which finally does appear on the walls of his chamber at the Garter Inn in *The Merry Wives of Windsor.* Indeed, the subject would appear to have been a favorite one for tavern décor, and Drayton speaks of another fool who

sity Studies, IX (1921–2), 119–33; Bernard Spivack, *Shakespeare and the Allegory of Evil* (New York, 1958); J. Dover Wilson, *The Fortunes of Falstaff* (Cambridge, Eng., 1943); and Robert Withington, "The Development of the 'Vice,'" *Essays in Memory of Barrett Wendell* (Cambridge, Mass., 1926).

> In all his life . . . ne'r saw
> Painting: except in Alehouse or old Hall
> Done by some Druzzler, of the Prodigall.[8]

In *Lusty Juventus,* one of the most famous of the moral interludes, Good Counsell refers explicitly to

> The prodigall sonne as in Luke we reede,
> which in vicious liuing hys good had wast,
> As soone as his liuing he had remembred,
> To confess his wretchedness he was not agast,
> Wherefore his father louingly him embrast,
> And was right ioyful the text sayeth playne,
> Because his sonne was returned agayne.   Sig. [E.iv.]v[9]

This play, published in 1565, represents the moral interlude in its fully developed form, is generally typical, and bears the closest resemblance to the story of Prince Hal and his tempter companion; one can easily substitute for the three main characters, Juventus, Hypocrisy, and Good Counsell, the names of Hal, Falstaff, and the Lord Chief Justice.

Though the play is not divided in the text, it readily falls into four main scenes, which may be rapidly summarized. Before the play begins, however, there is the customary prologue in which, quite contrary to the moral theology of Erasmus and Rabelais, man is said to be "naturally prone,/to euil from his youth." The prologue prescribes, on the basis of this assumption, that man from his youth onward should be constantly restrained: "Bowe downe his neck, and keepe him in good awe." It concludes by describing the action the audience is about to witness (Sig.[A.i.]v).

Scene I. Enter Lusty Juventus, singing a carefree song whose refrain is, "In youth is pleasure." Not seeing his companions about, he longs for their "merry company"; but Good Counsell enters and tells Juventus that he must live by God's rules and not in riot. Impressed by his speech, Juventus urges him to teach him further. At this point Knowledge comes to aid Good Counsell, and together they give the youth various theological and moral lessons, all of which

---

[8] Michael Drayton, "Of his Ladies not coming to London," vv. 86–8, in *Works,* ed. J. W. Hebel et al. (Oxford, 1932), III, 205.

[9] All references to moral interludes are to the Tudor Facsimile Texts and are indicated in the text rather than in the footnotes.

Juventus accepts, promising to remain in the company of Good Counsell and Knowledge always.

Scene II. Enter the Devil. Observing what has happened to Juventus, he summons his son Hypocrisy to help him tempt the young man. After Hypocrisy has delivered himself of a typical anti-Catholic tirade (he boasts of his influence over popes and priests), Juventus enters, and Hypocrisy introduces himself as Friendship. Juventus explains that he is on his way to "heare a preachyng" (Sig. [C.iii.]v), but Hypocrisy persuades him to accompany him instead to a tavern for breakfast. Hypocrisy says that he will pay[10] and promises that "We shall haue a pudding" (Sig. D.i.v). To this temptation Juventus replies, "By the masse that meate I loue aboue all thyng:/You may draw me about the towne with a puddyng," and they go off together.

Scene III. Enter Fellowship, a companion of Hypocrisy, who helps him to urge Juventus toward the tavern, holding out another temptation of the flesh in the form of "litle besse" (Sig. D.ii.v). Little Bess, however, when they meet her at the tavern door, turns out to be Abhominable Lyuing in disguise, though she is called Unknown Honesty by Hypocrisy. She ushers them into the tavern and persuades Juventus to kiss her. The change in his character is immediate and evident in his language as well as his action, for, once inside the tavern, he begins to swear, using the oaths of Doll Tearsheet: "by the mas . . . by dogs precious wounds . . . horson villain . . . by gogs precious blood . . . by the blessed mass" (Sig. [D.iii.]v). Soon Juventus, Hypocrisy, and Fellowship get into an altercation over who is to enjoy the favors of Abhominable Lyuing, and, like Pistol, Juventus begins to swagger. Finally, however, the argument settled, they all go out singing a foolish song of *carpe diem*:

> Why should not youth f[u]lfyll his owne minde
>   As the course of nature doth him binde,
>   Is not euery thing ordained to do his kind?
>   Report me to you, report me to you.
> Do not the floures spring fresh and gay,
>   Pleasant and swete in the month of May?
>   And when their time commeth they vade away,
>   Report me to you, report me to you . . .

---

[10] Similarly, in *Youth*, Riot invites a youth to a tavern and promises to pay, though the young man, like Prince Hal, eventually does.

What should youth do with the fruits of age,
   But liue in pleasure in the passage,
   For when age commeth his lustes will swage,
   Reporte me to you, report me to you.   Sig. E.i.r

Scene IV. Enter Good Counsell, lamenting the fall of Lusty Juventus and, in terms of *ubi sunt,* the general depravity of the age. Juventus comes in, and they argue in a scene which, in language and attitudes, resembles closely the interchanges between Falstaff and the Lord Chief Justice. Juventus repents and, falling to the ground, bewails his sins. Good Counsell assures him that God will forgive repentant sinners, and, in confirmation, a character with the unwieldy name of Gods Mercifull Promises enters and extends mercy to the youth. He rises and pronounces a hymn of repentance, and, with an appropriate tribute to the queen by Good Counsell, the play ends.

The pattern of the plot is roughly the same in all moral interludes, though sometimes, as in *Henry IV,* the story begins with the temptation, reserving the powers of virtue for later. Nevertheless, even in *Henry IV* reference is constantly made to an earlier (and legendary) chastisement of the prince by the Lord Chief Justice, and this may be considered the equivalent of the first scene of *Lusty Juventus.* Often, as in *Youth,* the hero of these plays is an heir apparent, either to a kingdom or to some noble title. It affects, of course, not only an individual but the whole of good government if the ruler is counseled by evil powers — a common medieval and Renaissance theme found in all literatures and, perhaps most vividly, in the largest series of secular medieval paintings, the Lorenzetti frescos in Siena. It is especially typical of these interludes that the Vice and his companions should give themselves the names of virtues, a commonplace technique which Stultitia cleverly reverses when she gives her companions the names of vices.[11] When they are not carousing, the favorite sport of the Vices and the heroes they have misled (though it is not mentioned in *Lusty Juventus*) is often to take, as a character says in *Youth,* "a mans purs in the night" (Sig. [A.iii.]r). And the temptation to which the hero succumbs is invariably a natural temptation; for, as the Prologue to *Lusty Juventus* explains,

---

[11] There is a curious parallel to Stultitia's device in *Mundus et Infans,* where the word "couetous" is played with eulogistically ([B.ii.] r-v).

youth is frayle and easy to draw,
By Grace to goodness, by Nature to yll:
That Nature hath ingrafted, is hard to kyll.   Sig. [A.i.]v

When the Vice is finally rejected, it is usually against all his expectations, and the blow is a bitter one. The rejection of Falstaff is often prefigured in these interludes, as in *Like Will to Like*, where a judge named Seueritie comes in, like Justice Gascoigne, at the end of the play (Sigs. B.iii.r–C.[i.]r). But nowhere is it so closely prefigured as in *Youth:*

> Ryot: I am sure thou wylt not forsake me
>   Nor I wyll not forsake thee
> Youth: I for sake you also
>   And wyll not haue with you to do
> Ryot: And I forsake the vtterlye
>   Fie on the caytife fye
>   Once a promise thou dyd me make
>   That thou wolde me neuer forsake
>   But nowe I se it is harde
>   For to truste the wretched worlde
>   Fare well masters euerychcone.   Sig. [C.iv.]r

There are many verbal anticipations of *Henry IV* in these plays, many of which have been registered by former critics, and I shall note but a few that are most pertinent to the themes we shall take up. The theme of time, which is so important in *Henry IV*, is anticipated almost everywhere, and such lines as Juventus' "To pas the tyme away in pleasure" (Sig. A.ii.v) is only one example. The same youth's lament at the absence of his companions, "What shal I do now to pas away the day?" (Sig. A.ii.r), is echoed by Prince Hal when he says to Poins, "But, Ned, to drive away the time till Falstaff come." Similarly, the important themes of debt and reckoning in *Henry IV* are anticipated in *Mundus et Infans*. Debt, of course, is one of the obvious situations into which the Vice leads his victim, and Infans, in later life (when he is called Age), laments that "I thought to borowe and neuer pay" (Sig. [C.v.]r). The reckoning, however, is always more than a monetary one, as Conscyence makes clear:

> Men thynk not on the grete Jugement
> That the sely soule shall haue at the last
> But wolde god all men wolde haue in mynde
> Of the grete daye of dome

How he shall gyue a grete rekenynge
Of euyil dedes that he hathe done.   Sig. [C.iv.]r

In *Youth*, Riot has the same pathetically ill-founded hopes for future
preferment that Falstaff has, looking always for better days in the
future when the person he has corrupted takes over the government:
"Ye syr I truste to God all myght/At the next cessions to be dubbed
a knight" (Sig. B.i.r). And Infans, at the stage of life in which he is
called Manhode, is as much the *miles gloriosus* as Falstaff ever is,
though much more alliteratively so:

> I am worthy and wyght wytty and wyse
> I am ryall arayde to reuen vnder the ryse
> I am proudely aparelde in purpure and vyse
> As golde I glyster in gere
> I am styffe stronge stalworthe and stoute
> I am the ryallest redely that renneth in this route
> There is no knyght so grysly that I drede nor dout
> For I am so doughtly dyght there may be no dint me dere.
>   Sig. [A.v.]v

As one might expect, the same theological texts are introduced over
and over again. In *Lusty Juventus*, Good Counsell advises the youth
to

> Reade the .v. to the Galathians, and ther ye shall see
> That the flesh rebelleth agaynst the spirite,
> And that your own flesh is your most vtter enemye,
> If in your soules health you do not delight.   Sig. [E.iii.]r

It is the same passage to which Falstaff is referring when he remarks,
"His Grace says that which his flesh rebels against" (2:II.iv.380).
That Falstaff should so constantly quote the Bible has troubled some
critics, and others have explained it as a vestige of the puritanism of
Oldcastle; but it is also typical for the hypocritical Vice to quote
Scripture to his own purpose. Juventus himself, under the influence
of Hypocrisy, adopts this trick when he argues with Good Counsell,
and Good Counsell rebukes him for being "a great Gospeller in the
mouth" (Sig. [E.iii.]r). And if Falstaff has a whole school of tongues
in his belly (2:IV.iii.20) with which to make such pronouncements,
a laughable character in *Like Will to Like* is told: "Why Haunce thou
hast latin in thy belly me think,/I thought there was no room for
latin, there is so much drink" (Sig. C.[i.]r). Finally, just as Falstaff

is said to have need of a physician for his immortal part, so the Magdalene in her play is told by Knowledge of Synne that "The body is whole, but sick is the conscience,/Which neither the law nor man is able to heale" (Sig. F.ii.r).

There are many other similarities that one could point to, but I think I have given enough to make my point: it is not that any one of these resemblances or anticipations represents a specific borrowing on Shakespeare's part, but rather that he took a great deal in terms of plot and theme and even phraseology from his general knowledge of these moral interludes. Most important of all, perhaps, is his use of the tavern scene, but before considering this there is one more passage from the interludes which ought to be pointed out, simply because it is so unusual. It is from the Magdalene play and begins as follows:

> All things he doth by the power of the great deuill,
> And that you may see by his conuersation,
> He kepeth company with such as be euyll,
> And with them he hath his habitation:
> A frende of sinners, and a drynker of wyne,
> Neuer conuersant with suche as be honest,
> Against the law he teacheth a doctrine,
> All holy Religion he doth detest . . .   Sigs. [D.iv.]v–E.i.r

It is, of course, a precise description of Falstaff or, for that matter, of any of the sixteenth-century Vices. The man described is under the influence of the devil, keeps bad company, indulges in drink, and disobeys the law. Yet when we put this passage back in context, we find that the verses come from a speech delivered by a character called Malicious Iugement, and the friend of sinners and drinker of wine referred to is none other than Jesus Christ. It is a shocking irony and not without dramatic effect: one can almost hear the hisses from the audience. But it is also a most unusual irony, and if we would find anything like it we must, I think, go all the way back to Erasmus. Appropriately so, for the Christ described is Stultitia's Christian Fool, the Fool of God. It is a daring thing to describe the Christ as the Vice, but that is what Wager has Malicious Iugement do; that it can be done also implies that, conversely, the Vice can be described (and not merely named) as a Virtue. Falstaff himself will be subjected to just such a Stultitian transvaluation of values.

When the Vice leads Everyman astray in these dramas, he invaria-

bly leads him straight into the tavern, and it is in the milieu of the
tavern, the home of English realism, that the Christian soul is threatened. Even Mary Magdalene knows, *in gaudio*, its roaring boys and
swaggerers and tosspots, for she herself becomes one of the loose
women who frequent the taverns. The temptation of the Vice in
Youth is typical:

> Youth I pray the haue a doo
> And to the tauerne let vs go
> And we will drynke diuers wine
> And the cost shall be mine
> Thou shalt not pay one penny iwis.   Sig. B.i.r.

Once there, the victim invariably becomes a great drinker, boasting
of his prowess and paying for rounds; and, though it is said by Moros
in *The Longer Thou Livest the More Fool Thou Art*, any of the
youths from these plays might have said: "We will haue drinke if you
be thurstie,/For I loue to drinke without measure" (Sig. F.ii.r).

In addition to drink, the tavern also offered opportunities for sex,
and the two were commonly associated in the medieval mind. Rabelais'
Limousin scholar, in describing a typical day of the student in Paris,
says that he would go from the bawdy houses into the taverns of the
Pineapple, the Castle, the Magdalene, and the Mule;[12] and a song from
the *Carmina Burana* begins:

> Dum caupona verterem
> vino debachatus,
> secus templum Veneris
> eram hospitatus.[13]

The typical rake's progress is described by Infans:

> By my feyth syr into London I ran
> To the tauernes to drynke the wyne
> And than to the Innes I toke the waye
> And there I was not welcome to the osteler
> But I was welcome to the fayre tapester
> And to all the householde I was ryght dere
> For I haue dwelled with her many a daye.   Sig. [C.i.]v

[12] R III.62–4/II.vi: "Certaines diecules nous invisons les lupanares, et en ecstase vene-
reique inculcons nos veretres es penitissimes recesses des pudendes de ces meritricules
amicabilissimes, puis cauponizons es tabernes meritoires de la Pomme de Pin, du Castel,
de la Magdaleine, et de la Mulle."

[13] *Carmina Burana. Lateinische und deutsche Lieder und Gedichte einer Handschrift
des XIII. Jahrhunderts*, ed. J. A. Schmeller (Breslau, 1894), p. 138.

Hostess Quickly's establishment is only the last of many where men found wine, women, and sin — and, finally, the punitive arm of the law. The tavern stands symbolically in opposition to the moral justice of the lawcourt and the divine justice of the church. On the pilgrimage of life, it is permitted that man should take refreshment and repose at the Tabard Inn, but to choose to dally there until death (which was the wish of Golias), instead of going on to Canterbury, is pure apostasy. To turn to Bacchus instead of Christ is heresy, and, in time of national crisis, to prefer one's tavern to one's drum is political heresy. Even though the tavern reckoning may go unpaid, there are other and greater reckonings that a man cannot escape.

Falstaff's ancestry, then, is made up of men who loitered in the taverns to tempt the youth of Christendom, and his fate is theirs. There is, however, one important corollary to this fact of ancestry which is of considerable importance in terms of Falstaff's place in the tradition of folly. Since his prototype, the Vice, is inevitably a representative of the powers of damnation (he is usually, as Feste sang it, Satan's son), Falstaff himself is thereby automatically prevented from ever attaining or even aspiring to that Pauline folly which is the goal for Stultitia and the putative answer for Panurge. That is, insofar as he must play the tempter to Prince Hal, he cannot become the Fool in Christ; for Falstaff is, as Hal says, "far in the devil's book." Stultitia's advocacy of folly and exposure of the world's foolishness culminate in the reward of the folly of Christ. Panurge's conflict with the foolishness of the world could be resolved by the Christian folly that Pantagruel proffers, but he is unable to accept it. But for the "old, white-bearded Satan" that final and redeeming folly is never a possibility, and the topos of the Fool in Christ, which informs both the *Encomium* and the *Tiers Livre*, is simply irrelevant to any consideration of *Henry IV*. Falstaff's ancestry and the role it dictates for him make it impossible: he is "a devil . . . in the likeness of an old fat man."

At the same time, this would have been improbable as a conclusion for Shakespeare anyway, and in comparing him to Erasmus and Rabelais one must not fail to keep in mind that his greater secularity always distinguishes his thought from that of the other two. We shall never know the precise nature of the poet's religious views, but the very fact that he is so inexplicit about them implies a mind far more secular than either Erasmus' or Rabelais'. While some recent scholars have tended to give increasing emphasis to the Christian aspects of Shakespeare's thought, even they have generally taken greater comfort in a few of the later plays. In the case of *Henry IV*, it is true that God plays an important part in the history of kings, and Shakespeare alludes to the parallel between the youth of Hal and the parable of the prodigal son; yet beyond this, toward any sort of theoretical, dogmatic formulation, he does not go. Accordingly, it would be wrongheaded to attempt to read a specifically Christian lesson into the story of Shakespeare's prince and his fool — not because one would argue that the story is anti-Christian, but simply because Shakespeare's thought here, like Boccaccio's in the *Decameron* and Montaigne's in the *Essais*, tends to restrict itself to the life of this world.

Thus, though Falstaff's ancestral home is in the morality play and the moral interlude, and though his role is that of the spiritual tempter, he comes to us in quite another context. His story is a secular version of the morality play, where God the Father becomes the paternal King of England. Similarly, Falstaff's "victim" is not the abstract Humanum Genus or Juventus or Everyman, but specifically the Prince of Wales. The prototype for such a secularization is, of course, Skelton's *Magnyfycence*, written to admonish the young Henry VIII against evil counselors and misguided liberality. Falstaff, then, is a protagonist not in the cosmic war between heaven and hell, but in the mundane conflict between government and anarchy; his temptations affect the salvation of the throne rather than that of the soul. What is more, these very conditions are part of the reason why he is defeated at the end. He is, to be sure, defeated because he is the Vice; but, purely as the fool, he has no escape. For the fool, who inevitably finds himself at odds with the world, can only triumph when he is able to exempt himself from the conditions of the world — when he is able, in some way, to go beyond. That "beyond" may be the eternity of the bosom of Christ or it may simply be the ephemerality of the holiday of Carnival, but in either case the fool's triumph is made possible because the world has been, whether for the moment or for all time, rejected and turned upside down. In this respect the triumph of Christ and the triumph of Carnival are parallel, and, as Enid

Welsford and others have shown, the medieval Feast of Fools was explicitly conceived of as a kind of parody on the Day of Judgment — when the mighty are put down from their seats and those of low degree are exalted.

Yet the difference between Christ and Carnival remains: paradise is forever and Carnival is for a day. So long as Falstaff can preserve that day, he can triumph; for then he is able to daff the world aside and bid it pass, to cry with Pistol, "A foutra for the world and world-lings base!" If all the year were playing holidays, his triumph would be complete. But it is not, and the only satisfactory way to go beyond the inimical world is to become the Fool in Christ. Thus it is that Stultitia escapes from that world by being, in the end, theoleptically lifted out of it. Pantagruel's escape is not quite so mystical, but it is equally efficacious: his retreat is that symbolized by his father's Abbaye de Thélème and kingdom of Utopia — that is, a retreat into himself and his own free will. Whether it is Stultitia's paradise or Pantagruel's paradise on earth, both are paradise, and both Fools in Christ enjoy an unassailable triumph. Only the old lad of the castle is, for all his tricks and devices and starting holes, unable to escape permanently from his world because he, the Lord of Misrule, is dependent solely upon the momentary paradise of Carnival. When that moment is past, he is left defenseless, face to face with the hostile world. And that world calls him to a reckoning.

16

FALSTAFF AND STULTITIA

✿✿✿✿✿✿✿✿✿✿✿✿✿✿✿✿✿✿✿✿✿✿✿✿✿✿✿✿✿✿✿

WHEN Falstaff appears on the English stage at the end of the six-teenth century, he brings to a climax the tradition of the fool that Stultitia had started at the beginning of the same century. He is Stulti-tia's perfect fool come to life: his mountain of flesh is the living incar-nation of the paradigm she had presented in the first half of her oration. He has, it is true, grown old and gray with the passage of years, and he has become fat and broken-winded with drinking of old sack and unbuttoning after supper and sleeping on benches after noon; but Stultitia had always said that there was no fool like an old fool. He is, indeed, just what she claims an old man under her dominion will be — "moste happy, beyng also deare, and welcome to theyr friendes, amongs other respects, for this, that commonly they are verie pleasant in company, and merily bespoken." [1] His vision of life is Stultitia's, though deprived of its Christian overtones and pushed to its most outrageous conclusions; and she and her band of companions — especially her two male companions, Intemperance and Sound Sleep — find themselves reborn in him.

In view of their similarity, it is surprising that an examination of the relationship between Shakespeare's fool and Erasmus' has not been made before. If we would determine what Falstaff stands for and what unexpressed assumptions inform his conduct, no one can better tell us than Stultitia. This is not to claim that Shakespeare took

[1] ME 19: "At interim meo beneficio felix, interim amicis gratus, ne congerro quidem infestivus."

his idea of Falstaff directly from Erasmus, even though it would seem likely that he had read the *Encomium*. Even if he had not, Erasmus' ideas had filtered down through the century and become a part of the ideological climate of Shakespeare's world. If the facts were known, his fools might well owe more to Stultitia than one would dare to conjecture; but the facts simply are not known. It remains true, however, that the similarities between Falstaff and Stultitia are so basic and so striking that, once they have been perceived, they can hardly be avoided. We can learn a great deal about Shakespeare's fat old fool if we consider him in relation to the prototype Stultitia has provided.

As he plays his role in Shakespeare's dramatic account of the reign of Henry IV, Falstaff is constantly paired off and contrasted with other characters — with the prince, of course, most explicitly and with the king implicitly, but also, in *Part One*, with Hotspur and, in *Part Two*, with the Lord Chief Justice. This arrangement of characters figures forth the dialectical pattern that lies at the heart of the plays' ideological structure; the two plays are, in effect, built upon a system of thesis and antithesis, and for every thesis offered, whether Hal's or the King's or Hotspur's or Justice Gascoigne's, Falstaff represents the antithesis. The resolution of these dichotomies is achieved finally in the character of Hal when he becomes Henry V. Before considering "this same fat rogue" in relation to the characters who stand opposite him, however, we must first look at him alone for a moment, as he stands before us in all his bulk, and endeavor to see just who the old fool is.

We find him, in every way, the faithful follower of Stultitia, but he has another Erasmian prototype as well. If Stultitia may be said to provide a paradigm for Falstaff's nature, a character called Nestor in one of the colloquies may equally well be said to provide the pattern for Falstaff's conduct. The colloquy,[2] a satire upon the license that nobility gives to men who are often no better than knaves, is only one of many Renaissance treatments of this theme, but Erasmus' method is somewhat unusual. He cleverly performs his satire by having a knave called (after Alexander the Great's embezzling treasurer)

---

[2] LB I.834D-837F. The colloquy is punningly titled: Ἱππεὺς ἄνιππος, *sive Ementita Nobilitas*. The Greek pun can only be roughly rendered in English as "The Unknightly Knight" or "The Horseless Horseman"; a romance language, of course, can do it better—"Le Chevalier sans Cheval."

Harpalus ask his friend Nestor how he can counterfeit being a knight when he has neither nobility nor money. Nestor (a name associated not only with advice but also, as Joyce remembered, with horses) provides that advice, but in the course of doing so he manages to give a biting satire on the abuses of knighthood. The conduct prescribed for Harpalus is so close to Falstaff's own that it is tempting to imagine that Shakespeare may have read this colloquy as a schoolboy.

Nestor begins with a few simple rules. Harpalus is told that he should insinuate himself into the company of young noblemen, that he should be sure to wear silks and fine clothes, not wool, that he should make a point of inquiring after nobility as though he were acquainted with it, that he should be accompanied by a page who will call him "my lord," and so on.[3] Falstaff, of course, follows all this advice to the letter: he insinuates himself into the company of Prince Hal; he orders a satin cloak from Master Dommelton and is fond of "new silk and old sack"; he asks Justice Gascoigne about the king's health; and he enters "with his Page bearing his sword and buckler." Nestor goes on to advise Harpalus to have his servants rob for him from merchants on the road or people staying at inns, and he further suggests that he send out his servants as soldiers that they may return with plunder got under the law of war.[4]

The satirical description of perfect knighthood offered by Nestor reads like a description of Sir John himself.[5]

Unless you are a good dicer, an excellent cardshark, a depraved whore-master, a mighty drinker, a bold prodigal, a spender and borrower of other people's money, and adorned as well with the French pox, scarcely anyone will believe you are a knight.

[3] LB. I.834E-835E: "Ingere te in convictum juvenum vere nobilium . . . Ne vestis sit lanea, sed aut serica, aut, si deest qui emas, fustanea . . . Si quis ex Hispania veniat hospes, roga quomodo conveniat Caesari cum Pontifice, quid agat affinis tuus Comes a Nassauen, quid caeteri congerrones tui . . . Deinde sodales aliquot adsciscendi sunt, aut etiam famuli, qui tibi cedant loco, et apud omnes te Joncherum appellent." The word *Joncherum*, etymological source for the Elizabethan word *younker*, is glossed as follows in the LB edition: "Joncherus vox Germanica et Belgica, idem designans quam juvenem Dominum, composita ex *Jong* juvenis et *Heer* Dominus. Vulgo autem nobilium filii ita dicuntur."

[4] LB I.837A: "E famulis tuis interdum aliquem emandes, in bellum scilicet. Is spoliatis templis aut monasteriis quibuslibet, redibit onustus praeda bello parta."

[5] LB I.836A: "Ni sis bonus aleator, probus chartarius, scortator improbus, potator strenuus, profusor audax, decoctor et conflator aeris alieni, diende scabie ornatus Gallica, vix quisquam te credet equitem." There is, of course, a pun in the phrase *conflator aeris* on *aer* and *aes*.

The necessity and method of going into debt in order to become a counterfeit knight is discussed at some length in a passage that provided a source for Panurge's praise of debtors; and the would-be knight is urged to borrow large sums from great men, to do it brazenly (*ne quid puteat*), and generally to understand that "after many people have come to believe that you are of the nobility, you will easily find find fools who will give you credit; some will be ashamed to deny you, others will fear to do so. There are a thousand arts by which you can delude creditors." [6] We may remember Falstaff's boldness in trying to get a loan from the Lord Chief Justice and the thousand pounds he does borrow from foolish Justice Shallow. The theme of debt, which is treated at such length in the colloquy, is, as we shall see, one of the main themes of *Henry IV*. Harpalus is finally given advice about what he must do if his hypocrisy is discovered, and the devices Nestor prescribes are also used by old Jack.[7]

In this case you must remember to put on a bold front. And such boldness has never passed so easily for wisdom in any time more than today. You must invent excuses . . . Finally, if all else fails, run away to the army or to a riot. For as the sea conceals all evils of men, so war hides all sins . . . Pretend you are called by the king on some important business and that you will soon have an army.

"My lord," says Falstaff to the Lord Chief Justice, "I will not undergo this sneap without reply . . . I say to you, I do desire deliverance from these officers, being upon hasty employment in the King's affairs" (2:II.i.133–40).

All of these Falstaffian characteristics will be considered in greater detail later, and I do not wish to dwell at length upon what may only be a coincidental resemblance to Erasmus' colloquy. But the passage which closes it has a special relevance to Falstaff, his attitudes, his actions, and his fate.[8]

[6] LB I.836A-B: "Postquam apud multos confirmata fuerit nobilitatis opinio, facile reperies fatuos qui tibi credant; quosdam etiam pudebit negare, quidam metuent. Jam ut ludas creditores, mille sunt artes."
[7] LB. I.837C–D: "Heic oportet meminisse perfrictae frontis. Illud in primis, quod nullis unquam temporibus magis licuit audacia pro sapientia uti, quem hodie. Comminiscendum est aliquid quod excuses . . . Postremo, si nihil aliud, profugiendum est aliquo in bellum, in tumultum. Quemadmodum κλύξει θάλασσα πάντα τ' ἀνθρώπων κακά operit omnium scelerum sentiam . . . Adsimula te vocari in aulam Caesaris ad res magnas, brevi te adfuturum cum exercitu."
[8] LB I.837E-F: "NE. Quid est, cur tantopere affectes falsam opinionem nobilitatis? HA. Nullam aliam ob caussam, nisi quod his omnia licent impune. An hoc tibi leve

NESTOR: Why are you so eager to have a false reputation for nobility? HARPALUS: For no other reason than that all things are permitted to the nobility with impunity. And does this seem to you a matter of small importance? NESTOR: Even if the worst should happen, we all owe nature a death, even though you live as a Carthusian. And they die more easily who are broken on the wheel than those who die of the stone, gout, or palsy. But it is like a soldier to believe that nothing of a man survives after death except his corpse. HARPALUS: I share that opinion.

The resemblance between Falstaff and Stultitia is as close and even more profound; for they share the same nature. In fact, both Stultitia and Falstaff are, above all, stewards of Nature, and they represent her importunate claims in her eternal struggle against law and custom. Like Stultitia, Falstaff puts the case for the natural functions of the body and the natural affections of the heart, and he is forced to defend them in a world that would control and restrict both. Just as nature itself knows no bounds, so Falstaff lives out of all order, unyoked (1:I.ii.220) and surfeit-swelled (2:V.v.54), and his very fatness is the palpable symbol of his natural excesses. "Why," exclaims Bardolph, "you are so fat, Sir John, that you must needs be out of all compass — out of all reasonable compass, Sir John" (1:III.iii.24–6). The "fat fool," as Doll Tearsheet calls him, has more flesh than another man because he is more like nature itself than any other man. Indeed, there are moments when this globe of sinful continents seems greater even than nature's globe, when the very earth appears lean in comparison with him. Though, typically, he claims that he is swelled up with sighing and grief, we are of course aware that all this bulk is simply the result of enormous consumption; his bibulousness and gourmand-izing are legendary even to his contemporaries. We may say of him what is said of one of his most recent reincarnations, that "obviously this kingly man had an uncommon need of refreshment." [9] His pro-fuse sweating, with which he lards the lean earth, is nothing more than the natural result of all the liquid he imbibes. Though capons are dear to him, he would appear to eat less than he drinks, but only

videtur momentum? NE. Ut pessime cedat, mors una debetur naturae, etiamsi vixisses in Carthusia. Et levius moriuntur in rota, quam qui moriuntur calculo, podagra aut paralysi. Nam militare est, credere, nihil hominis superesse post mortem, praeter cadaver. HA. Sic opinior."

[9] Thomas Mann, *Der Zauberberg*, in *Gesammelte Werke* (Berlin, 1925), VIII, 358. Not only is Mynheer Peeperkorn a kind of reincarnation of Falstaff, but Falstaff may actually have been, in one of his aliases (1:III.iii.10), Peeperkorn's eponym.

because drinking is the more important to him and, on his limited credit, there are times when he apparently can afford only a half-pennyworth of bread if he is to have his usual intolerable deal of sack. Even then, however, he is able to squeeze a capon and some anchovies out of his budget;[10] and it is not surprising that when his friends think of him — or when he thinks of himself — it is as a carbonado, a shotten herring, a roasted Manningtree ox, a Bartholomew boar-pig, or some other form of food.

He is, as he says, the fellow with the great belly (1:I.ii.165), a belly of no indifferency (2:IV.iii.23); for, as Doll Tearsheet remarks, "There's a whole merchant's venture of Bordeaux stuff in him. You have not seen a hulk better stuff'd in the hold" (2:II.iv.68–70). It is the belly that Falstaff worships, like one of those of whom St. Paul says that "their belly is their god." [11] And appropriately, in Boito's brilliant libretto for Verdi's great opera, as the music becomes mock-religious, Falstaff punningly prays to his *Domine*, his Lord, to preserve his *addomine*, his belly. Epicurean belly-worshipper that he is, one can almost hear him joining in the Goliardic chorus,

> Alte clamat Epicurus:
> venter satur est securus;
> talem deum gula querit,
> cuius templus est coquina,
> in qua redolent divina.[12]

Galen, whom Falstaff claims to have read (2:I.ii.133), says that a big belly does not produce a subtle mind,[13] but the subtlety of Falstaff's wit would seem to belie this dictum. He has, as he claims, a whole school of tongues in his belly (2:IV.iii.20) — all of them, we might add, witty. As we watch him waddling across the stage he seems rather to confirm Persius' statement that the belly is the master of arts and the bestower of wit[14] — a proposition that Ben Jonson

[10] See the interesting observation of William Empson, "Falstaff and Mr. Dover Wilson," *The Kenyon Review*, XV (Spring 1953), 231n: "A similar ambivalence can be felt I think in the incessant metaphors of heavy meat-eating around Falstaff compared to 'one half-pennyworth of bread to this intolerable deal of sack,' where it is assumed (already in Part I) that the drunkard has no appetite."

[11] Philippians 3.18.

[12] *Carmina Burana*, p. 72.

[13] *Medicorum Graecorum Opera quae exstant*, ed. D. C. G. Kühn (Leipzig, 1823), V, 878: παχεῖα γαστήρ λεπτὸν οὐ τίκτει νόον.

[14] Persius, *Choliambi*, vv. 10–11.

remembered when he wrote his hymn to the bouncing belly in the masque of *Pleasure reconcild to Vertue,* where the belly is called the "Prime master of arts, & ye giuer of wit."[15] Perhaps Jonson even had the ventripotent old fool in mind when he wrote his speech for the Bowl-bearer.[16] Certainly he is an Epicurean, as are the pleasure-loving characters in Jonson's masque — indeed, he is just what Ford calls him in *The Merry Wives of Windsor,* "a damn'd Epicurean rascal" (II.ii.-299). And though he does not have the religious justification for following that doctrine that Erasmus' Epicurean or Le Caron's Rabelais had, he would, had he known it, have subscribed to Epicurus' own lesson that "the pleasure of the belly is the beginning and the root of all good; and even wisdom and culture must be referred to this."[17] Thus, though the virtuous may think there will be no more cakes and ale, Falstaff, who wonders at times if there is no virtue extant except the "virtue in that Falstaff," would claim with Epicurus that there was virtue in the pleasure of the belly. "If sack and sugar," he says, "be a fault, God help the wicked!"

It is because of this belief that he is able, perversely, to condemn the thinness of Justice Shallow as a vice and even go so far as to transfer his own role of the morality-play Vice to the squire of Gloucestershire and call him "this Vice's dagger" (2:III.ii.344). He is wary of thin men, and even the name of John of Gaunt occasions his derision (1:II.ii.70). When he thinks that he himself may have lost weight, he is genuinely alarmed: "am I not," he asks despairingly, "fallen away vilely since this last action?" (1:III.iii.1–2). It is for this reason that he cannot abide apple-johns, which bear his name and yet are no longer plump but withered; they are the only thing in either of the plays that makes him truly angry:

1 Draw.: What the devil hast thou brought there? Apple Johns? Thou knowest Sir John cannot endure an apple John.

2 Draw.: Mass, thou say'st true. The Prince once set a dish of apple Johns before him and told him there were five more Sir Johns, and, putting off his hat, said, "I will now take my leave of these six dry, round, old, withered knights." It ang'red him to the heart.   2:II.iv.1–9

---

[15] Jonson, *Works,* VII, 479.

[16] Jonson's masque also recalls the island of Messer Gaster that Panurge and Pantagruel visit in the *Quart Livre,* chs. LVII–LXII.

[17] *Epicurea,* ed. Hermann Usener (Leipzig, 1887), p. 278: Ἀρχὴ καὶ ῥίζα ταυτὸς ἀγαθοῦ ἢ τῆς γαστρὸς ἡδονῇ· καὶ τὰ σοφὰ καὶ τὰ περιττὰ ἐπὶ ταύτην ἔχει τὴν ἀναφυράν.

The taunt sticks in his mind, and he remembers it again in his persona of Monsieur Remorse (1:III.iii.5). He has need, it is true, of a physician rather for his immortal part, but it is bodily health that concerns him (2:II.ii.111–4); his life, which is his virtue, is dependent upon his belly. He claims that he is a virtuous man because he is "a goodly portly man, i' faith, and a corpulent" (1:II.iv.459–64).

The surrogate for nature, Falstaff is, like Stultitia, by nature an Epicurean, and Stoical restraint is anathema to him because he knows as well as Stultitia that the Stoics do not really live. So he continues to eat and drink with the "Ephesians . . . of the old Church" (2:II.ii.164). A voice is always calling in his ear: "It is thine host, thine Ephesian, calls" (*MWOW*, IV.v.19). Now, as Good Counsell tells Lusty Juventus,

> Sainct Paul vnto ye Ephesians geueth good exhortacion
> Saying, walke circumspectly, redeming the time,
> That is to spend it well, and not to wickedness enclyne.

> A.iii.r

Specifically, St. Paul had admonished the pleasure-loving Christians of Ephesus as follows: "See then that ye walk circumspectly, not as fools, but as wise, redeeming the time, because the days are evil. Wherefore be ye not unwise but understanding what the will of the Lord is. And be not drunk with wine, wherein is excess." [18] But Falstaff *is* a fool and, drunk with wine in evil days, he does not even know what the time is. The first words he utters are to ask what time it is, but the prince justly replies, "What a devil hast thou to do with the time of day?" Falstaff is concerned only with the moment as it passes, and, like one of Plautus' parasites in a fragment of a lost play preserved by Aulus Gellius, his only clock is his belly. [19]

Time, which plays such a major role in these plays, is of no concern to Falstaff. The moment of Carnival is timeless, and the fool is exempt from time just as he is exempt from the world. It is because the time is upset that Falstaff gets away with his roguery, and the Lord Chief Justice, borrowing a descriptive phrase from Hall's *Chronicle*, tells him as much: "You may thank th' unquiet time for your quiet o'erposting that action" (2:1.ii.170–1). The fool has his own

[18]Ephesians, 5.15-18.
[19] Plautus, *Comoediae*, eds. G. Goetz and F. Schoell (Leipzig, 1896), VII.140 (Aulus Gellius, *Noctes Atticae*, III.iii.5).

time, and the Pantagrueline fool knows it as well as Falstaff. It was for this reason that there were no clocks in the Abbaye de Thélème, because, as Gargantua said, "the greatest losse of time, that I know, is to count the hours, what good comes of it? nor can there be any greater dotage in the world then for one to guide and direct his courses by the sound of a bell, and not by his owne judgement and discretion." [20] Pantagruel himself, on the Isle of Chaneph, confirms this philosophy when he cites the usage of the Persians according to which each person's appetite and belly served as his clock,[21] and Jonson, in his masque, calls the belly "the truest clock i' the world to goe by." [22] For time, of course, is a form of *nomos*, a code that seeks to control and guide nature; but the belly is the servant of *physis*, and its hunger and thirst are not determined by the hour of the day. Prince Hal has seen that Falstaff's clock is his belly, which is why he says to him,

unless hours were cups of sack, and minutes capons, and clocks the tongues of bawds, and dials the signs of leaping houses, and the blessed sun himself a hot wench in flame-colored taffeta, I see no reason why thou shouldst be so superfluous to demand the time of the day.   1:I.ii.7–13

And so Falstaff, who has no concern for time, is unable to perform that redemption of time that St. Paul calls for in his Epistle to the Ephesians; he is an Ephesian of the old, not the new, church. It is the prince, not his Epicurean companion, who, aware that they are playing "fools with the time" (2:II.ii.154), will perform the role of redeeming time when men think least he will.

To attempt to exempt oneself from time and history, from the world and its passage, is vain — in both senses of that word. It is futile because time will bring an end and demand a reckoning. It is also egotistical because to exempt yourself from the world implies that you have a higher opinion of yourself than you have of the rest of the world. Falstaff is vain in both senses, and the theme of vanity, as Dover Wilson and others have observed, is associated with the prince's companion throughout the plays. One of the epithets that the prince applies to his aged jester is "that vanity in years" (1:II.iv.499); and at the end of the first part, when Hal thinks that Falstaff has been

---

[20] R II.400–1/I.iii: "la plus vraye perte du temps qu'il sceust estoit de compter les heures — quel bien en vient il? — et la plus grande resverie du monde estoit soy gouverner au son d'une cloche, et non au dicte de bon sens et entendement."

[21] *Quart Livre*, ch. LXIII.

[22] Jonson, *Works*, VII, 482.

killed in the battle of Shrewsbury, he looks on the inert hulk of his body and exclaims, "O, I should have a heavy miss of thee/If I were much in love with vanity!" (1:V.iv.105–6). At the end of the second part, when he wishes to call the attention of the Lord Chief Justice to Falstaff, he says, "My Lord Chief Justice, speak to that vain man" (2:V.v.48). It is his own pleasure and his own gain that Falstaff thinks of always, and his conduct in any action, whether borrowing money or running from battle or eluding the law, is determined by the effect it will have on him personally. The one letter that he sends to the prince is the essence of vanity (2:II.ii.118–47), even though the world-wide reputation to which he so vainly refers there is based upon a lie. He is vain of his girth, of his wit, of his amatory prowess, of his military strategy, of his charge of foot, of his youth — even of his "virtue." Finally, he is vain enough to claim that he himself is the whole world, that to banish plump Jack is to banish all the world (1:II.iv.527).

Stultitia had also claimed that the world could not exist without her; and Falstaff's vanity, though it is also in keeping with his role as the Vice, is even more in keeping with his role as a follower of Erasmus' fool. For Vanity, though it also signifies emptiness, is first of all simply the English name of Stultitia's favorite companion, Philautia. The self-love with which Stultitia praises herself is shared by Falstaff, and the claims of both of them are the same: each is the source of wit, the cause of love, the leader in battle — the world itself. Even the formal nature of their self-encomiastic remarks is the same, and a scholar has recently demonstrated that Falstaff's encomia, like Stultitia's, are indebted to Aphthonius.[23] As we have seen, however, Stultitia's Philautia was not wholly vicious. Seneca summed up the positive virtue of self-love when he remarked that "he who is a friend to himself is a friend to all the world."[24] This is what Stultitia means when she asks if a man can be pleasing to anyone if he is not pleasing to himself, and this is equally the source of Falstaff's charm and his ability to make people love him. The old fat rogue is selfish and vain, to be sure, but out of his vanity flowers a love for his fellow man and a commitment, however self-centered, to his friends. He is indeed Jack Falstaff with his familiars, John with his brothers and sisters, and Sir

[23] W. C. McAvoy, "Shakespeare's Use of the 'Laus' of Aphthonius" (diss., University of Illinois, 1952).

[24] Seneca, *Epistulae morales*, I.vi.7.

John with all Europe: in his name is his vanity, but his name is loved. A great part of the poignancy of his rejection is the defeat of that vanity as symbolized by the loss of that name; for the prince refers to him, in the end, only as "that vain man" and claims that he knows him not. As he loses his name and his friend, Falstaff loses not only his vanity but also his identity and his very being.

Part of Falstaff's vanity is his undeviating commitment to the pleasure principle; even in his old age, he is the personification of youthful gaiety. But he is a fool, and Stultitia had prescribed folly as the nostrum that would preserve youth: "That and if men had the grace to forbeare quite from medlyng with wisedome, leadyng foorth all theyr lyfe in my service, now I wene there should be no olde age at all, but rather they should enjoie a moste happie, and continuall youthe." [25] "Vivez joyeux," Rabelais had commanded, and Falstaff invariably does his best to obey, seeking, like every fool, his pleasure at the table and in the bed. That we see him mainly at night is because night is the time of pleasure, as opposed to the duties of the day. "La nuyct vient," said Panurge's Mother Nature to her children as she urged them to turn from labor to sport, and even laconic Silence adds his word to hers: "If we shall be merry, now comes in the sweet of the night" (2:V.iii.52–3). And Falstaff, seeking pleasure, has heard the chimes at midnight with Shallow (2:III.ii.228) and seen the seven stars with Pistol (2:II.iv.201); he has frolicked with the minions of the moon (1:I.ii.30) and wenched with the bona-robas of Turnbull Street (2:III.ii.217, 329); he has walked with Bardolph in the night betwixt tavern and tavern (1:III.iii.49). When the sun comes up on the morning of battle, far from Eastcheap, he can only turn to the prince and say, "I would 'twere bedtime, Hal, and all well" (1: V.i.125); and when, finally, he is rejected near the Abbey in the early afternoon, he still hopes that he will "be sent for soon at night" (2:V.v.96).[26] Like Mynheer Peeperkorn, whenever he is faced with any unpleasant situation or thought, Falstaff thinks of night and invokes what the Dutchman from Java calls "the sacrament of pleasure." [27]

Because he has what Samuel Johnson called "the most pleasing of

[25] ME 20: "Quod si mortales prorsus ab omni sapientiae commercio temperarent, ac perpetuos mecum aetatem agerent, ne esset quidem ullum senium, verum perpetua juventa fruerentur felices."
[26] "At night" here means, of course, "secretly."
[27] Mann, *Zauberberg*, VII, 419.

all qualities, perpetual gaiety," Falstaff also possesses "an unfailing power of exciting laughter." [28] For he is, as he boasts, the inventor of anything that tends to laughter, not only witty in himself, but the cause that wit is in other men (2:I.ii.8–12). It is his spirit that brings joy into history and pleasure into troubled times because his Epicureanism gives joy and pleasure to others as well as to himself. Rare is the man, like Prince John, whom he cannot cause to laugh (2:IV.iii.95), and that a man does not laugh at Falstaff is invariably an indictment upon that man. "He," remarks Johnson, commenting upon Prince John, "who cannot be softened into gayety cannot easily be melted into kindness." [29] It is what Stultitia herself had always claimed. Were it not for laughing, we should pity Falstaff (1: II.ii.117); but the point is that we do laugh. We laugh at him because he is fat and fatuous; we laugh with him because he is able to outwit the world in the way we should like to. But most of all we simply laugh, because Falstaff creates a climate which is free for laughter. One critic has summed up this extraordinary quality very well when he writes that

the greatest comedy, the comedy of Shakespeare or Rabelais or Dickens, for instance, is sympathetic comedy. We do not laugh at Falstaff or Panurge or Mr. Micawber because life sets booby-traps for them. We do not laugh at them because they are more like machines than the rest of us; in a fine play of fancy, in rash resourcefulness, they are less like machines than the rest of us . . . What the great sympathetic comic characters seem to do is to communicate enjoyment, to induce in us a certain playfulness and relaxation, and a certain genially critical attitude towards the stiff outer show of things.[30]

It is that spirit of enjoyment and playfulness which Falstaff personifies, as do Stultitia and Panurge, and it is upon our participation in that spirit that Falstaff depends. For his very existence is postulated upon laughing friends; when his friends desert him and that laughter ceases, he himself is destroyed.

"Give me life," says Falstaff, and it is an appropriate demand from one who is nature's surrogate. Life is more important to him than anything else — more than honor, fame, money, or greatness. Only

[28] *Johnson on Shakespeare*, ed. Walter Raleigh (Oxford, 1946), p. 125.
[29] *Johnson on Shakespeare*, p. 121.
[30] Anon., "Hamlet and the Clown," *Times Literary Supplement*, 16 October 1959.

sack and capons does he value as much, but then they are the sustainers of life for him. His quest for pleasure is also related to his demand for life because, as Stultitia had observed, life is not life without pleasure; and if Falstaff is a fool, to be a fool is, after all, to act the play of life.[31] Representing the life force of nature, he stands opposed to all the death forces in the world, whether the deathly restrictions of Stoical conduct or the mortal outcome of combat, and there is a mythic significance to his "resurrection" on the battlefield (1: V.iv.111). "Falstaff riseth up," reads the stage direction, and he comes to life again like St. George in the Mummers Play and like Epistemon revived after the battle by Panurge's penis.[32] Stultitia had said that she came to men like the soft breath of spring after hard winter,[33] and Falstaff himself is called by the Prince (in imagery to which we shall return), "thou latter spring" (1:I.ii.177). Just as winter is not the permanent death of nature, so Falstaff cannot be permanently put down, either in armed or verbal skirmish, and even Shakespeare found the old man difficult to kill off. What some critics have considered Falstaff's callousness about human life may actually be quite the opposite. His reference to men as "food for powder" and his pun on "pitiful" and "fill a pit" (1:IV.ii.70–4) may be the bitter sarcasms of a man who perceives the full absurdity of war and who values life more than anything else. Men who are about to be married he encourages to buy their way out of service (1:IV.ii.16–7) — for his own profit, of course; but it is also true that they will be left free to propagate life. His final selection of the feeble and infirm for cannon fodder resembles, from one point of view, nothing so much as eugenics.

When, after his supposed death, Falstaff appears before the prince bearing the body of Percy, the prince exclaims in astonishment, "thou art not what thou seem'st!" To this, Falstaff replies: "No, that's certain! I am not a double man; but if I be not Jack Falstaff, then am I a Jack" (1:V.iv.141–2). The expression "double man" has caused the commentators a good deal of vexation. Johnson thought that Falstaff was referring to the fact that he was carrying Hotspur on his back, but most editors have assumed that Falstaff is using the word in

---

[31] ME 16: "Quid autem vita haec, num omnino vita videtur appelanda si voluptatem detraxeris?" ME 50: "Haud equidem inficias iverim, modo fateantur illi vicissim hoc esse, vitae fabulam agere."
[32] R IV.304/II.xxx.
[33] ME 2: "post asperam hyemem, novum ver blandis Favoniis."

its sense of an apparition or wraith. Johnson's reading is obviously a part of what Falstaff has in mind, but the other reading is extremely dubious, especially since, as Samuel Hemingway has pointed out, Falstaff's use of *double* in the sense of *wraith* is considerably earlier than any registered in the Oxford Dictionary.[34] Although he was hesitant to accept it, R. P. Cowl saw what Falstaff really means when he suggested "a play, perhaps, on other meanings of 'double' as counterfeit, deceitful." [35] It is precisely in the sense of counterfeit and deceitful that Falstaff is using the word. He is, in fact, employing a traditional adage, and once again it is Erasmus who provides the explanation.[36]

Those men who are untrustworthy and insincere, now commonly called "two-tongued," used to be called, with a proverbial witticism, "double men." Virgil himself called the men of Tyre "two-tongued." It is also said, however, in allusion to the fact that the names of many men are disyllables, especially those of servants, who are thought to be deceitful and fraudulent types. Accordingly, the sense is ambiguous, and it is possible [for the phrase] to refer either to those who sit on two stools or to those who have disyllabic names.

Falstaff arrives, therefore, claiming that he is not a deceitful counterfeit — that it is really he, alive. He may also be anticipating an objection to the claim that he has killed Hotspur. When the prince subsequently claims that it was he who killed Hotspur, Falstaff can then wag his head and sigh, "Lord, Lord, how this world is given to lying!"

First and foremost, however, he means to say that he is still alive, that he is not counterfeiting life, that he is no imitation of a man. As the representative of nature and life, he hates nothing more than an imitation man; for, as Stultitia put it, "Nature abhorreth counterfeityng." [37] It is, as she said, the "wise" and not the foolish who are

---

[34] Shakespeare, *Henry the Fourth, Part I*, ed. Samuel B. Hemingway, New Variorum Edition (Philadelphia and London, 1936), p. 331.

[35] Shakespeare, *The First Part of King Henry the Fourth*, ed. R. P. Cowl and A. E. Morgan, Arden Shakespeare (London, 1914), p. 198.

[36] LB II.719B-C: "*Duplices viros* proverbiali joco vocabant, qui essent lubricia et insincera fide, quod nunc vulgo etiam *bilingues* appellant. Et Virgilius *Tyrios* bilingues appellat. Dictum est autem per allusionem, quod pleraque virorum nomina dissyllaba sint, praesertim servorum, quorum genus vafrum et fraudulentum habetur. Unde sensus ambiguus est, potest enim accipi vel de eo, qui duabus sederit sellis, vel cui nomen sit dissyllabum."

[37] ME 61: "Odit natura fucos."

two-tongued;[38] and the world of wise men in which Falstaff is condemned to live does seem filled with counterfeits, from the counterfeits of the king on the battlefield (1:V.iv.27–38) to the "counterfeited
zeal of Heaven" displayed by the Archbishop (2:IV.ii.27). Of course,
these counterfeiting wise men consider, not without reason, that Falstaff is the counterfeit, that he is not simply a drunken knight but an
old white-bearded Satan in disguise. Yet he claims that he is simply
himself and that others, like the prince, are mistaking the real thing
for an imitation. "Never call a true piece of gold a counterfeit," he
admonishes Hal (1:II.iv.539–40). Life itself, according to Falstaff,
can never be a counterfeit, but anything opposed to life is. Compare,
he would say with Stultitia, the life of a wise man with that of a fool;
the former, pale and sickly with too much study, has never really
known life (ME 69). It is the Epicurean man who is the true piece
of gold, for he values life. And the greatest counterfeit of all is the
dead man. Thus it is that the fool, if he has to, will counterfeit death
in order not to be a counterfeit of life:

'Sblood, 'twas time to counterfeit, or that hot termagant Scot had paid me
scot and lot too. Counterfeit? I lie; I am no counterfeit. To die is to be a
counterfeit; for he is but the counterfeit of a man who hath not the life
of a man; but to counterfeit dying when a man thereby liveth, is to be no
counterfeit, but the true and perfect image of life indeed.1:V.iv.113–27

Yet by its very nature life is mortal, and death finally comes to this
true and perfect image of life; for we all owe God a death. Falstaff,
who for so many years has heard the chimes at midnight, expires hearing those chimes once more, tolling now the end of holiday: "'A
parted," says the hostess, "ev'n just between twelve and one, ev'n
at the turning of the tide" (Henry V, II.iii.12–14). The fool, who was
wont to come on singing, "When Arthur first in court" (2:II.iv.36),
goes to Arthur's bosom crying, "God, God, God!" The hostess bids
him not think of God, but Falstaff knows that the time has come when
he must think of nothing else. When he dies, a part of nature dies
with him, and it is more than his limbs that become cold as any stone;
the warmth and sunshine of Martlemas are over, and the winter has
come. But surely it is appropriate that even in the moment of death
this foolish child of nature should have smiled, played with flowers,
and babbled of green fields.

[38] ME 66–7: "At sapientum sunt duae illae linguae."

17

FALSTAFF AND HOTSPUR

In the same way that the laughter of Stultitia was from time to time interrupted by the sobering thought of man's misery and his mortal cares, so across the world of Carnival the working-day world always casts its shadow, reminding man of what he attempts to forget. Personified by the puritan or the cynic or the virtuous, the world of duty, as it stands glowering at the folly of holiday, becomes the bugbear, the spoil-sport, the kill-joy. Whether he is called Malvolio or Jaques or Octavius, he warns us that man's responsibilities may not be put off indefinitely for his pleasures, that the remorse of Lent will succeed the abandon of Carnival. Like the morning sun through the windows of the tavern or the bedchamber above, he comes to mock the fool in his nocturnal pleasure and to present that reckoning which the world outside demands.

Beguiled though we are by the pleasures of Falstaff, we are always aware that they cannot last and that the other world will have its due. Even when we first come upon him asleep on the tavern bench, we have already heard the claims and criticisms of the world outside and know that they cannot be indefinitely denied. The prince is aware of it also, from the very beginning, and realizes that when the son is obliged to become the sun he will have to scatter the base contagious clouds of Falstaff's tavern world. Only Sir John Sack and Sugar foolishly assumes that the other world can be put off forever. But in fact it is with him already, its frown lurking behind all the laughter at the Boar's Head. For, from out of the cold north, the angry figure of young Henry Percy has risen to haunt the warm, convivial hearth-side in Eastcheap.

Though "the gallant Hotspur" is always explicitly contrasted to Prince Hal, his true opposite is Falstaff, and the prince stands between the two extremes represented by the young and the old knight. The contrast in their ages is symbolic of the contrast between the men themselves. Not only is Falstaff old with the skepticism of experience, whereas Hotspur is young with the daring of hope, but, paradoxically, Falstaff is a young old man and Hotspur an old young man. Falstaff, who never knows the time of day, confuses in his very person the time of age. He is the latter spring, the All-hallown summer, the Martlemas — the confusion of the seasons, bringing warmth and sun when there should be cold and dark. But if, unconscious of the time, he is approaching the second childhood of Stultitia's fool, Hotspur, who is ever conscious of the time of life, equally confuses the time of age by being Stultitia's other fool, the prematurely old and "wise." For though he is in fact very young and is so presented in contrast to his father, his uncle, and Glendower, he is also old before his time, having forsaken the carefree joys of youth for his crabbed concepts of honor and duty. Falstaff's beard should have the effects of gravity, but it displays only gravy; on the other hand, it is the beardless Hotspur who "beards" all those who cross his path. His only reference to the seasons is to disdain precisely that season which Falstaff represents, "the sun in March" (1:IV.i.111), yet he himself is, one might say, like snow in April, with his chill longing for horses and deathly combat rather than for wine and amatory sport. It is only the prince who knows how to frolic in the truancy of youth and yet accept, in the perfectness of time, the responsibilities and gravity of age. And when Hotspur, dying, says to Hal, "Oh Harry, thou hast robb'd me of my youth," part of the poignancy of the cry lies in our knowledge that the theft was of something he never really possessed.

That youthful holiday which Falstaff represents is, in its language (1.I.iii.46) and its games (1:II.iii.94–5), offensive to the "child of honor and renown," who will not play with mammets or tilt with lips but must have bloody noses and cracked crowns. If Falstaff, in his senility, is all for love, Percy, in his virility, is all for war; and while "old Jack" would gladly forsake the moment of battle for the bed, the "northern youth" leaves his bed crying, "to horse!" Hal makes as much fun of the latter (1:II.iv.114ff) as he does of the former (1:II.iv.286); and the horse itself is, as Harry Levin has pointed out, another kind of symbol shared by this contrasted pair.[1] For Falstaff, who is a "horseback-breaker" (1:II.iv.269), is unhorsed at Gadshill (1:II.ii.10) and given only a "charge of foot," though he wishes "it had been of horse" (1:III.iii.209–10); like Erasmus' Harpalus, he is literally a horseless knight. But Hotspur, who tends to compare everything to horses (as in 1:III.i.134–5, 159–60), seems even to prefer his horse to his wife. There is an ironic ambiguity in his response to Lady Percy's question, "What is it that carries you away?" for he answers, "Why, my horse, my love, my horse!" (1:II.iii.78–9). Similarly, the old fool wishes that his tavern were his drum, for he would waste the time of life drunk with sack; but the young fool shortens the time of life on the battlefield, drunk only "with choler" (1:I.iii.129). Stultitia had claimed that drunkenness brings harmony and friendship into the world. Rabelais had prescribed the same panacea for war. But they were talking of wine — the wine, for example, that Lancaster offers when he says:

> and here, between the armies,
> Let's drink together friendly and embrace,
> That all their eyes may bear those tokens home
> Of our restored love and amity.   2:IV.ii.62–5

The spiritual drunkenness of Hotspur creates rebellion and war. There are no capons and sack or cakes and ale for him, and the only use he can think of for a pot of ale is the Machiavellian device of poisoning (1:I iii.233). Falstaff says that love is worth a million pounds (1:III.iii.155–6), but Hotspur says, "Love? I love thee not" (1:II.iii.93). Both are jesting, yet the jests contain a seriousness as well.

As Falstaff and Hotspur thus square off on the issue of love, they reveal most clearly the nature of their passions. For both are passionate men, and in both of them passion governs reason. They are, therefore, according to Stultitia, both fools, because wisdom is to be led by reason, whereas folly is to be moved by the power of the passions.[2] Stultitia goes on to say that there are two predominant passions which stand as enemies to reason, anger (*ira*) and lust (*concupiscentia*), and in Hotspur and Falstaff we seem to have the personifications of these

---

[1] Harry Levin, "Falstaff Uncolted," *Modern Language Notes*, LXI (1946), 305–10.
[2] ME 27: "Etenim cum Stoicis definitioribus nihil aliud sit sapientia, quam duci ratione; contra stultitia, affectuum arbitrio moveri."

two passions. Young Percy is "govern'd by a spleen" (1:V.ii.19). In love with fighting and war, he is, as Samuel Johnson put it, "cholerick and quarrelsome," with a proud passion for high deeds. A man crosses him at his own peril, and Hotspur is quick to seek a quarrel at the slightest provocation. Glendower has only to open his mouth to provoke him, and anyone who does not share his passion for battle, like the unfortunate courtier (1:I.iii.29–69), arouses his passionate wrath. Though he makes a pretense to love, his real love is war. Falstaff, who makes a pretense at being a man of war but is really in love with love and drinking, is of course just the opposite. He is governed by his lust for women, wine, and comradeship — those "trois commerces" that Stultitia said she made possible. And although Stultitia lumps anger and lust together as man's two greatest passions, there is no question about her loathing of the one and her endorsement of the other. As we have seen, she makes a careful distinction between good and bad passions. Falstaff and Hotspur are both fools, but one she would welcome as a true follower and the other she would reject as an apostate.

Though the passions of both men are diametrically opposed, they are equally excessive. That is to say, Falstaff's lust and Hotspur's anger are equally remote from any mean, even though they stand on opposite sides of that mean. It is because of this similarity of excess that the anger of Hotspur is often described in the same terms of self-love and lack of control as Falstaff's lust. Worcester's famous "schooling" of Hotspur is perhaps the best example:

> In faith, my lord, you are too wilful-blame,
> And since your coming hither have done enough
> To put him quite besides his patience.
> You must needs learn, lord, to amend this fault.
> Though sometimes it show greatness, courage, blood—
> And that's the dearest grace it renders you —
> Yet oftentimes it doth present harsh rage,
> Defect of manners, want of government,
> Pride, haughtiness, opinion, and disdain;
> The least of which haunting a nobleman
> Loseth men's hearts, and leaves behind a stain
> Upon the beauty of all parts besides,
> Beguiling them of commendation. 1:III.i.177–89

Falstaff also, as we have seen, is accused of want of government, defect of manners, and stained nobility, and Percy's "pride" is the equivalent of his "vanity." Both stray too far from the moderation of the perfect man. Yet there is a difference between pride and vanity, and that very difference once again points up the opposition between Hotspur and Falstaff. For Hotspur's pride is a haughty disdain of others, where Falstaff's vanity is wholly dependent upon others, whether upon their love and good opinion or upon his ability to dupe them. Falstaff is the least and Hotspur the most self-sufficient man in this play. It is indicative of Hotspur's disdainful pride that his most characteristic grammatical usage should be the ethical dative (1:III.i.98, 256; IV.iii.75, 85), which refers everything back to himself; it is equally indicative of Falstaff's dependent vanity that his most characteristic form of expression is the question, which demands a companion to give the answer. The young man's pride longs for the lonely heights of the moon or the breathless depths of the sea where he will have no "corrival" (1:I.iii.201–8); "out," he exclaims, "upon this half-fac'd fellowship!" But the old man is content to stay in the tavern, surrounded with comrades. One strives for immortality and finds death; the other accepts mortality and preserves life.

The relative ability and inability of the two men to speak — to communicate with others — is a reflection of these characteristics. Falstaff, who has tongues in his belly, is ventriloquent in every sense of the word. He not only speaks from his belly, but his belly, as an object of wit, causes other men to speak. His own wit is in his speech, and it is upon that which he depends for survival. Capable of an infinite variety of speech to meet every occasion, his tongue is his sword and his triumphs are verbal. Hotspur, on the other hand (despite the ironic fact that he is actually the most eloquent person in the play), is always described by himself and by others as being impatient and incapable of speech. He has no use for poetry or song, and he is hopeless at the verbal diplomacy of conference negotiations. He has not well the gift of tongue (1:V.ii.77), and nature has given him the blemish of speaking thick (2:II.iii.24). Unlike Falstaff, he is a man of deeds, not words: he is incapable of speaking with men because his polemic passion urges him to fight with them instead.

The basic difference, of course, is that Falstaff's passions are natural and Hotspur's unnatural — or, more accurately, antinatural. To put it another way, Falstaff's passions are those of life and Hotspur's those of death; for whereas Falstaff is in love with physical things, like sack and capons, and with people, Hotspur is in love with abstract ideals, like honor, and with man-destroying deeds. Those three things which Falstaff loves and upon which his existence is postulated are, according to Lady Percy, the very three that Hotspur's love of war has caused him to lose — "thy stomach, pleasure, and thy golden sleep" (1:II.iii.45). But life means almost nothing to Hotspur, and at the very moment when the old fool abandons all abstract ideals in order to live, Hotspur dies regretting not the loss of life but the loss of honor. "I better brook the loss of life," he says to his vanquisher, "Than those proud titles thou hast won of me" (1:V.iv.78–9). Thus even in death he thinks of abstractions and scorns nature as he always had; he is invariably impatient of what is natural, whether that be love or life or the desire for comfort and ease — or even the natural course of a river, which he would artificially change (1:III.i.96ff).

Insofar as he is opposed to nature and passions are natural, we may look at him another way and see him as a passionless man — the man Stultitia loathed, who was "benummed in all those sensis and understandynges, that naturally other men are ledde by." For, like Stultitia's marble effigy of a man, Hotspur measures everything (like his "moiety") by the rule, forgives no insult, cares for no comrade, dismisses scornfully such gods as Glendower's spirits from the vasty deep, and damns and ridicules as folly all that life holds.[3] Falstaff, on the other hand, is one of those passionate old fools whom Stultitia so obviously loves, an old fellow of Nestor's age, babbling, foolish, and white-haired, madly in love with girls and more inept at love than an adolescent, but exceedingly in love with life and eager to be young.[4]

As the drama of the first part of *Henry IV* unfolds, the antithesis between the young fool and the old fool grows stronger and stronger, and their incompatible ways of life are brought into sharper contrast.

---

[3] ME 52: "qui ad omnes naturae sensus obsurduerit . . . nihil non ad amussim perpendat . . . nihil ignoscat . . . nullum moretur amicum . . . qui Diis quoque ipsis non dubitet mandare laqueum . . . qui quicquid in omni vita geritur, velut insanum damnet rideatque."

[4] ME 54–5: Mei nimirum muneris est, quod passim Nestorea senecta senes videtis, quibus jam ne species quidem hominis superest, balbos, deliros, edentulos, canos, calvos, vel ut magis Aristophanicis eos describam verbis, ῥυπῶντας, κυφοὺς, ἀθλίους, ῥυσοὺς, μαδῶντας, νωδοὺς καὶ ψωλοὺς, usque adeo vita delectari, adeoque νεανίξειν, ut alius tingat canos, alius apposititia coma calvitium dissimulet, alius dentibus utatur mutuo fortassis a sue quopiam sumptis, hic in puellam aliquam misere depereat, et amatoriis ineptiis quemvis etiam superet adolescentulum."

Hotspur and Falstaff do not meet (although they symbolically fight a fictitious battle in Faltsaff's lie), but they know of each other and are aware of the mutual threat they pose. We in the audience are constantly reminded of the polarity of their differences as the scenes shift back and forth between their two worlds. The chivalric world of the castle threatens and pursues the Epicurean world of the tavern, until finally the two worlds meet on the battlefield and fight a long hour by Shrewsbury clock. "In the melee," says Philarète Chasles, "Falstaff, surrounded by cadavers black with powder and red with blood, draws from his pocket a bottle of old and good wine, which he gulps down. Do you see there simply a drunkard's folly? You are wrong. Don't you realize that he is boldly planting on these heaped cadavers the standard of his Epicurean philosophy?" [5]

Though Prince Hal is able, at the Battle of Shrewsbury, to bridge those differences and move at last from the world of the tavern to the world of the palace, the differences themselves are never resolved. It is in the battlefield's moment of reckoning that the teleological goals of Falstaff and Hotspur are brought most clearly to the foreground. Falstaff's goal is, of course, pleasure, those Stultitian pleasures of the tavern world; the goal of Hotspur is honor, the honors of the world of chivalry. The one can be achieved only in life, but the other reaches its fulfillment as fame only in death. Though Hotspur is said to be Fortune's minion (1:I.i.83) and Falstaff claims that he is Fortune's steward (2:V.iii.136), both of them know, as their age reiterated over and over again, that Fortune is fickle. Confronted with the possibility of a sudden revolution of her wheel, they turn to the two accepted ways of dealing with the potential adversity of Fortune — ways which, for simplicty of reference, one may call Boccaccian and Machiavellian. Like those characters of Boccaccio who hide from Fortune's blows in the irresponsible pleasures of the *hortus conclusus*, Falstaff takes refuge in the pleasures of Eastcheap. But Hotspur follows the advice in *Il Principe*, relying upon *virtù* to withstand *fortuna* and hoping for that "never-dying honour" (1:III.ii.106) which is fame to enable him to triumph over Fortune even in death. It is because he is so confident that death will only confirm these honors that he can say to his comrades, "Doomsday is near. Die all, die merrily" (1:IV.i.134).

But Falstaff would live merrily. In his celebrated catechism, he perceives that honor is assured only to the dead. His goal, however, is not the abstract honor of death; and it is precisely upon the basis of the law of nature as opposed to the law of honor, of life as opposed to death, that he rejects such grinning honor as Sir Walter Blunt has. As the day of battle dawns, the old fool wishes that it were instead the night of pleasure; but Prince Hal, evoking the theme of debt and reckoning that runs through these plays, reproves him by saying, "Why, thou owest God a death." As usual, the old Ephesian has an answer:

'Tis not due yet. I would be loath to pay him before his day. What need I be so forward with him that calls not on me? Well, 'tis no matter; honour pricks me on. Yea, but how if honour prick me off when I come on? How then? Can honour set to a leg? No. Or an arm? No. Or take away the grief of a wound? No. What is honour? Air. A trim reckoning! Who hath it? He that died a Wednesday. Doth he feel it? No. Doth he hear it? No. 'Tis insensible then? Yea, to the dead. But will it not live with the living? No. Why? Detraction will not suffer it. Therefore I'll none of it. Honour is a mere scutcheon — and so ends my catechism.

1:V.i.128–44

Honor, he realizes, has no relevance whatsoever to the life of the belly; and, indeed, when he sings his catechism in Verdi's opera, Falstaff appropriately interpolates, "Può l'onore riempirvi la pancia? No!" The point is, of course, that honor does not exist in the law of nature; and Ben Jonson, doubtless remembering Falstaff, has Corvino state this explicity in *Volpone*:

> Honour? tut, a breath;
> There's no such thing, in nature: a meere terme
> Invented to awe fooles. III.vii.38–40

But the real fool, like Stultitia, looks at life and dismisses honor — "as if that had anything to do with it!" [6] For she believes that it is doubly a fault when one pretends to a virtue against one's nature, thus warping one's character.[7] One is reminded of the *locus classicus* of the theme of honor versus nature and the perversion of nature by honor, the chorus in Tasso's *Aminta* — though, to be sure, the *onor* that

---

[6] ME 31: "adeo denique honestam, si quid tamen hoc ad rem pertinet."
[7] ME 28: "Conduplicat enim vitium, quisquis contra naturam virtutis fucum inducit, atque alio deflectit ingenium."

Tasso is speaking of is simply chastity.[8] It has been suggested, however, that Shakespeare may have been indebted to Tasso here by way of Samuel Daniel's translation.[9] Yet wherever Shakespeare got it, Falstaff comes to it from his own observation; for, finding Sir Walter Blunt dead upon the battlefield, he exclaims, "There's honour for you!" And, thinking perhaps of the sin he has been accused of, he wrily observes, "Here's no vanity!" He concludes:

I like not such grinning honour as Sir Walter hath. Give me life; which if I can save, so; if not, honour comes unlook'd for, and there's an end.

1:V.iii.61–4

Hotspur, "the theme of honour's tongue" (1:I.i.81), cannot bear the thought of a life without honor. In the end, of course, he loses both his life and his honor, and Falstaff the fool, who saw the contradiction, bears him away. When Percy is already cold, Falstaff remains "the true and perfect image of life indeed" (1:V.iv.119). The better part of valor is, for him, discretion, and in that better part he saves his life. Nor does Monsieur Remorse feel any shame about his cowardly preference for life over honor. The fool never does. For, as Stultitia put it, "shame, reproche, losse of reputacion, or evill speche, these maie do the as muche hurt as thou felist theim: that and if thou felist theim not, than are they no evils at all." [10] Falstaff's cowardice is as excessive as Hotspur's valor. It is only the prince who, though he might prefer the tavern to the drum, accepts the day of duty when it dawns, achieving in that day the ideal man — an achievement that is visually symbolized when he stands over the bodies of both Hotspur and Falstaff. But the dial's point, though it has come full circle for Hotspur, has yet a while to run for Falstaff who, at the very thought of losing his belly ("Embowell'd?"), rises up again. The man of pleasure has escaped the reckoning that the man of honor would have brought him to, and, in an act of supreme dishonor, he stabs Hotspur's already dead body and carries it off in triumph. It remains for a later time and a man of more ideal honor, Henry V, to call the old fool to an accounting.

It is indeed a world of Carnival, *un monde renversé*, in which the

---

[8] Tasso, *Aminta*, I.ii.325ff.

[9] See G. A. Borghese, "The Dishonor of Honor," *RR*, XXXII (1941), 44–55.

[10] ME 57: "Caeterum pudor, infamia, probrum, maledicta, tantum adferunt noxae, quantum sentiuntur. Si sensus absit, ne mala quidem sunt."

coward bears off the corpse of the valiant hero. But the cowardice of Falstaff, which has troubled so many generations of critics, is quite simply the logical outcome of the philosophy of the fool. All the attempts that have been made to condone or deny Falstaff's cowardice are based upon the assumption that anyone so lovable could not be so base, that we would somehow like him better if he acted more bravely. This is patently false, however. One has only to imagine Falstaff displaying courage and valor at any point in the play to see how ludicrously inconsistent it would be. If he were to show the slightest sign of heroism, he would become incomprehensible as a character and would lose our sympathies. He is what he is, and cowardice is a part of that. For he is the natural man, and, as Plutarch's Gryllus tells Ulysses, "men are not naturally courageous." It is not nature that makes a man practice courage: "one practices courage according to the necessity of law, which is neither voluntary nor willed, but obedient to custom and censure and formed by external beliefs and arguments." [11] In the world of Hotspur cowardice is a vice; but in the world of Falstaff it is a virtue, since it preserves life. It is useless to pretend that Falstaff is not a coward: he is, in Stultitia's phrase, as cowardly in battle as he is clever in speech.[12] Whether one accepts it as praiseworthy or not, one must at least see that it is part of the argument he advances.

Hiram Haydn has pointed out that, in their concepts of honor, Hal, Hotspur, and Falstaff correspond to Plato's tripartite division of man into reason, anger, and desire, as well as to the Aristotelian triad of the mean, excess, and defect.[13] He also makes a suggestive comparison between Shakespeare's three characters and Pantagruel, Frere Jan, and Panurge as they appear in Rabelais' fourth and fifth books.[14] One might indeed claim that Panurge and Falstaff are the two most famous cowards of the sixteenth century, and both are cowards as the result of Stultitian folly. Yet there are important differences between them. By the time that Panurge's cowardice is emphasized, he himself has already been, in some senses, rejected; we lose sympathy with him and, as that sympathy decreases, his cowardice increases. He has, as it were, no philosophical basis for his cowardice: he is simply afraid.

[11] Plutarch, *Gryllus*, 988B.
[12] ME 37: "tam ignavus miles, quam orator sapiens."
[13] Hiram Haydn, *The Counter-Renaissance* (New York, 1950), pp. 600ff.
[14] Haydn, pp. 587ff.

The cowardice of Falstaff, as we have seen, operates in a slightly different way and is more analogous to Stultitia's transvaluation of values. By advancing that vice which corresponds to the basic virtue of chivalry, he does not so much cause us to embrace cowardice as to look with a more critical eye at the tenets of chivalry. His counterpart, Hotspur, displays the inhuman excesses into which the blind acceptance of a quality like valor may lead a man; and, confronted with a choice between the two, one is invariably attracted to Falstaff. Finally, however, such a choice is unnecessary. As with everything else, in Prince Hal we are given the third and most congenial possibility of a mean of honor standing midway between Hotspur's excess and Falstaff's defect.

18

FALSTAFF AND THE LORD CHIEF JUSTICE

As BOTH Stultitia and Panurge knew, the fool's greatest enemy is the law. In whatever form it takes, whether that of the Stoics or the grammarians or the theologians or the jurists, the law conspires to frustrate the fool. By its proscriptions and penalties, it denies him that freedom without which he cannot exist; just as his world must be timeless, so it must be lawless. The only law that the fool can follow and remain a fool is the lawless law of nature. That is why the antics of the Feast of Fools had to be specifically exempt from punishment, and that is why the home that all fools long for is the Abbaye de Thélème, where laws are unknown. In their praises of folly, Erasmus and Rabelais went even further and claimed that the restrictions of the law perverted man's natural inclination to good — thus making of the law the very thing it pretends to oppose and punish, a force of evil. Most fools lack the benefit of such philosophical justification, but they perform the same transmutation nevertheless, attempting, in their upside-down world, to convince us that the law is an evil thing, a handmaiden of vice. Falstaff is no exception, and just as he makes his own fatness a virtue and the thinness of Justice Shallow a vice, so he claims that his lawlessness is the only virtue extant and accuses the law of being the Vice. Indeed, we have barely met him when we hear him refer to "the rusty curb of old father antic the law" (1:I.ii.68–9).

The fool is a law unto himself. But when we say that a man is "a law unto himself," we mean in effect that he is lawless. In the fool's eyes, however, this personal, natural law is still a kind of law, which he obeys with all his heart and which he claims is better than any other. Though his public defenses of it may sound like sophistry, actually they are the expression of a deep commitment. His lawless law is like his timeless time. It is true that Falstaff has no use for clocks that measure the same time for everyone; nevertheless, he does go by a kind of clock, his belly. In the same way, then, that he can claim to keep time, he can also claim to keep the law. To Falstaff, the un-natural rigidity of external law and the strictness of abstract time are both symbolized by the regularity of the sun's motions. His own law and his own time are those of the changing moon. "We that take purses," he claims — that is to say, we that break the law — "go by the moon and the seven stars, and not by Phoebus, he, that wand'ring knight so fair. And I prithee, sweet wag," he continues to Prince Hal,

when thou art king, as, God save thy Grace — Majesty I should say, for grace thou wilt have none . . . when thou art king, let not us that are squires of the night's body be called thieves of the day's beauty. Let us be Diana's Foresters, Gentlemen of the Shade, Minions of the Moon; and let men say we be men of good government, being governed, as the sea is, by our noble and chaste mistress the moon, under whose countenance we steal.   1:I.ii.15–33

The speech is a masterpiece of foolery, with its dubious application of words like gentlemen and government, with its irrelevant literary allusion to a ballad from a Spanish romance, and with its puns on "go by," "grace," "body-beauty-booty-bawdy," "countenance," and "steal." Nevertheless, Falstaff is invoking a kind of law, the natural law of the mutability of the moon and the tide; and that law, he claims, creates a government that is good and noble. Of course, it "counte-nances" stealing, and that is where the joke lies; but in the law of nature stealing is a means to pleasure and thus no crime. It is natural for Falstaff to steal — or, as he puts it, stealing is his vocation — and in the law of nature " 'tis no sin for a man to labour in his vocation" (1:I.ii.117). Like Panurge, Falstaff longs for the day when his per-sonal law will be the law of society, and he tutors the prince to that end: "Do not thou, when thou art king, hang a thief" (1:I.ii.69–70).

When the prince, by his equivocal reply, suggests that on that day Falstaff himself will control the laws of England, the old fool exclaims in ecstatic anticipation, "By the Lord, I'll be a brave judge!" (1:I.ii.72). And his moment of greatest triumph is precisely when he mistakenly thinks the longed-for day has at last come, when, with pathetic irony, he finally gets the horse he has lacked: "Let us take any man's horses; the laws of England are at my commandment. Blessed are they that have been my friends, and woe to my Lord Chief Justice!" (2:V.iii.140–4).

It is of course the Lord Chief Justice, Sir William Gascoigne, who, as a peculiarly English embodiment of the law, personifies those forces that most threaten the fool. If Hotspur, representing the laws of chivalry, stands in contrast to Falstaff in *Part One*, the Lord Chief Justice, representing the laws of society, is the antithesis of Falstaff in *Part Two*. Over Hotspur the fool manages to triumph, but then the clown can always trip up the man who walks on stilts. "De tous tes temps," as Mosca observes in *La Chartreuse de Parme*, "les vils Sancho Pança l'emporteront à la longue sur les sublimes don Quichotte." In his hyperbolic excesses, his overblown pride, and his humorless dedication to an abstract ideal, Hotspur is vulnerable to the common sense of the fool's laughing iconoclasm. Noble though he is, that excess of nobility cannot withstand the withering gaze of Falstaff's excess of humanity; for the irrationality of the heart is always mightier than the rationality of the head. As such, the story of Falstaff and Hotspur is a lesson that was read many times in the sixteenth century — from Ariosto to Cervantes, across the whole of Europe, the knight was, time and again, brought to his knees by the fool. But if Hotspur is the spokesman for noble chivalry, Justice Gascoigne is the representative of the laws of the realm to which, as the original anecdote in Elyot's *Boke Named the Governour* makes explicit, even royalty must submit.[1] That the Justice is a more formidable opponent to Falstaff than Hotspur is the result of the difference between what the Justice and the Knight stand for. Whereas Hotspur stands for war and rebellion, Gascoigne stands for peace and civil order. The one, in his youth and impetuosity, displays all the injustice of excess, while the other, in his age and dignity, upholds the justice of the mean. The

[1] See that portion of the text quoted in Shakespeare, *Henry the Fourth, Part Two,* ed. M. A. Shaaber, New Variorum Edition (Philadelphia, 1940), pp. 552–3.

Lord Chief Justice is as much in opposition to the young fool's war and rebellion as he is to the old fool's rioting and disorder.

As we turn to *Part Two* and the antinomy between Falstaff and the Lord Chief Justice, we are once again conscious of a polarity between youth and age. To be sure, it is no longer the same polarity as that between Falstaff and young Hotspur, for the Chief Justice is as old as Sir John, if not older. He represents all the sagacity and gravity that age and experience should rightly give a man. Thus confronted by a wise old man as an adversary, the old fool, if he is to defend himself, has no recourse but to pretend that the Lord Chief Justice is in his dotage and to insist upon his own youth as an excuse for his folly. Formerly, in the presence of youth, he was not averse to admitting his age, because then he could use it as a kind of advantage. For example, in the mock-trial scene, he describes himself to Prince Hal as "a goodly portly man, i' faith, and a corpulent; of a cheerful look, a pleasing eye, and a most noble carriage; and, as I think, his age some fifty, or, by'r Lady, inclining to threescore" (1:II.iv.464–8). Portraying himself as a Nestor, he asks respect for his age and for the authority of his wisdom. And when the prince, playing his father, proceeds to attack him on the very grounds of his age by claiming that it is sinful to be so old and yet so foolish and by calling him an "old white-bearded Satan," Falstaff only insists the more on how old he is, pulling all the stops on the theme of age as something to be pitied, but also to be loved and respected and counseled by:

That he is old (the more the pity) his white hairs do witness it; but that he is (saving your reverence) a whoremaster, that I utterly deny. If sack and sugar be a fault, God help the wicked! If to be old and merry be a sin, then many an old host I know is damn'd . . . but for sweet Jack Falstaff, kind Jack Falstaff, true Jack Falstaff, valiant Jack Falstaff, and therefore more valiant being, as he is, old Jack Falstaff, banish not him . . .
1:II.iv.514–25

But all this is in the presence of young men. To invoke such arguments before the Justice would be absurd. Here the wind is in another corner, and Falstaff is obliged to try the opposite tack. Though he is almost in his second childhood, he tries to convince the Lord Chief Justice that he is still in his first. Putting on the self-righteousness of youth and adopting the hypocritical solicitude of *si vieillesse savait*, he explains away the Justice's censures by claiming that "You that are

old consider not the capacities of us that are young. You do measure
the heat of our livers with the bitterness of your galls; & we that are
in the vaward of our youth, I must confess, are wags too" (2:I.ii.195–
200). Quite properly outraged by such a contortion of the facts, Gascoigne turns upon him:

Do you set down your name in the scroll of youth, that are written down
old with all the characters of age? Have you not a moist eye, a dry hand,
a yellow cheek, a white beard, a decreasing leg, and increasing belly? Is
not your voice broken, your wind short, your chin double, your wit single,
and every part about you blasted with antiquity? And will you yet call
yourself young? Fie, fie, fie, Sir John!   2:I.ii.201–9

His righteous indignation is understandable, for the description he
gives is, as the audience can see, quite accurate. But Falstaff, wily fool
that he is, knows that the only counter to righteous indignation is more
of the same. Answering what he chooses to consider the doddering
idiocies of the Justice, he replies:

My lord, I was born about three of the clock in the afternoon, with a
white head and something of a round belly. For my voice, I have lost it
with halloaing, and singing of anthems. To approve my youth further, I
will not. The truth is, I am only old in judgment and understanding . . .
                                        2:I.ii.210–16

But it is not the truth, and the holier-than-thou attitude is impertinence, as impertinent as Falstaff's earlier inquiry after the aged Justice's health. Yet it is witty and we forgive it; it is poignant and we
pity it.

For Falstaff is older than he thinks. Or rather, though he may indeed know how old he is, he tries to forget that knowledge. There is
something touching in his self-deceptive claims, especially in the
bravado he adopts in the escapades with his youthful companions,
where he refers to "us youth" and exclaims as he attacks the travelers,
"What, ye knaves, young men must live!" (1:II.ii.89, 95–6). Yet he
knows as well as anyone that desire has outlived performance, and,
holding Doll Tearsheet on his knees, he is obliged to confess, "I am
old, I am old" (2:II.iv.294). When asked by Shallow about the girl
Jane Nightwork with whom they had sported in their youth, he can
only answer, "Old, old, Master Shallow" (2:III.ii.219); and after
listening to the companion of his youth boasting about days long
since past, he sighs, shaking his head, "Lord, Lord, how subject we

old men are to this vice of lying" (2:III.ii.324–5). It is one of the few times he tells the truth; but the moment of self-awareness is heartbreaking, for one remembers Stultitia's warnings about destroying a man's illusions. In *Part One*, Falstaff's adversary was youth — the youth of Hal and the tricks he played on the old fool, the youth of Hotspur and the threat he represented for all foolery. But in *Part Two*, his adversary is age — the growing maturity of Hal, the venerable wisdom of the Lord Chief Justice, and his own aging steps toward death.

When one looks at the second part of *Henry IV* from this point of view, one realizes that there is almost no youth left. In a sense, youth dies with Hotspur on the field at Shrewsbury, and, as the story is resumed in *Part Two*, we are made aware of nothing so much as the inexorable passage of time and the relentless approach of age. Like the *Odyssey* after the *Iliad*, the story is of the same people, but they have all grown older. The prince, on the battlefield, had put away childish things and achieved manhood; the king, his father, returns from the same battle sick and dying. Even Falstaff, old to begin with, seems to have been further aged by the exertions of cowardice, and the presence of the young page he has acquired only accentuates his own advanced years. After the battle, he spends his time not so much with his youthful companion, Prince Hal, as with the companion of his own youth, the aged Shallow. They sit together in the arbor and talk about how many of their old acquaintance are dead (2:III.ii.38); they look with nostalgia upon the days of youth that are gone. The threats of the future, represented by the Chief Justice, and the thoughts of the past, called up by Shallow, are constantly pulling Falstaff out of the timeless present upon which the Epicurean fool depends. As the past recedes, the future draws nearer. "It grows late," admits Falstaff (2:II.iv.299), and, indeed, the shadows do creep up over the world of Henry IV. The night that approaches now, however, is not the night of pleasure, but the night of death and the last of all reckonings. "Pallida mors aequo pulsat pede pauperum tabernas regumque turris" — pale death stalks the tavern as well as the palace.[2] Though he would not be reminded of it, Falstaff too

---

[2] Horace, *Carmina*, I.iv.13–4. Cervantes quotes this celebrated line in the Prologue to Part I (C I.17/I.Prol.), and Sancho tells the Don that "á nuestro Cura he oído decir que con igual pie pisaba las altas torres de los reyes como las humildes chozas de los pobres" (C VI.46/II.xx). But see also the curious and significant application of

knows that finally we die in earnest, not in jest. "Peace, good Doll!" he sighs; "do not speak like a death's-head. Do not bid me remember mine end" (2:II.iv.253–5).

Pervaded as it is with an awareness of old age and the approach of death, this second play is also haunted by the specter of disease and sickness. From the Prologue's description of the crafty sickness of Northumberland, the hero of the overplot, to the Epilogue's anticipation of the sweating sickness of Falstaff, the hero of the underplot, the theme of ill health filters down through the entire play, leaving almost no one but the prince untouched. Caroline Spurgeon counts over three times as many images of bodily sickness in *Part Two* as she does in *Part One*, and only *Hamlet* and *Coriolanus* exceed this number.[3] It is, indeed, hard to know who is well and who is ill in a world so confused that bad news makes one person well (2:I.i.136–45) and good news makes another sick (2:IV.iv.102), but so general is the disease that only the prince seems well enough to be a physician. The king, lying sick at Westminster, is a visible symbol for the sickness of the entire commonwealth (2:I.iii.87), and he himself admits that his kingdom is filled with rank disease (2:III.i.38–40), a disease which, as everyone in the play knows, was inherited from Richard II (2: IV.i.57–8). Even young John of Lancaster is accused by Falstaff of having "a kind of male greensickness" (2.IV.iii.100). On the level of the overplot, the Archbishop claims that his forces intend to purge the body of the state from this illness (2:IV.i.65), but the sham sickness of the rebels' leader at the play's opening foreshadows the real sickness that Mowbray will feel in their moment of surrender (2: IV.ii.80). In the world of the underplot, Mistress Quickly is, if not diseased in body, at least said to be diseased in the mind (2:II.i.113–6); Doll Tearsheet enters "sick of a calm" or a qualm (2:II.iv.40), or, what is more likely, of an even more contagious disease (2:II.iv.49); and even Falstaff's young page is thought to be in danger of "cankers"

the phrase to love as well as to death (C VIII.59/II.lviii): "— Advierte, Sancho — dijo don Quijote —, que el amor ni mira respetos ni guarda términos de razón en sus discursos, y tiene la misma condición que la muerte: que así acomete los altos alcázares de los reyes como las humildes chozas de los pastores . . ."

[3] Caroline Spurgeon, *Shakespeare's Imagery and What It Tells Us* (Cambridge, Eng., 1935), chart 7. According to Miss Spurgeon's count, *2 Henry IV*, *As You Like It*, and *Troilus and Cressida* each have fourteen images of sickness, disease, and medicine, while *Coriolanus* has seventeen and *Hamlet* twenty.

(2:II.ii.101–2). As for Falstaff's conscripts, Mouldy, Feeble, and Shadow, each of them can say with his companion Bullcalf, "O Lord, sir! I am a diseased man!" (2:III.ii.191).

But the sickest of all is the fool himself. He had entered *Part One* asking what time it was, but now he knows it is late. He enters *Part Two* enquiring after his health:

> *Fal.* Sirrah, you giant, what says the doctor to my water?
> *Page.* He said, sir, the water itself was a good healthy water; but, for the party that owed it, he might have moe diseases than he knew for.
> 2:I.ii.1–6

It is not kidney trouble, in any event, but the diagnosis is not very optimistic. Still, the eternal optimism of the fool chooses to regard it as merely another jibe from the hostile world. "Men of all sorts," he says, with an unhappily ambiguous choice of verb, "take a pride to gird at me" (2:I.ii.7). Though he seems thus to dismiss it with his usual facility, the thought obviously haunts him through the rest of the scene, and in his encounter with the Lord Chief Justice he keeps playing with the idea of infirmity and disease. "Tell him I am deaf," he says to his page as the Justice's servant calls to him; but when he is finally forced to acknowledge his adversary's presence, he comes to him asking, with audacious mock solicitude, about the state of his health. To ask about another's health is, in fact, the normal method of greeting in this second play, and Falstaff's initial encounter with the Justice sets the pattern:

My good lord! God give your lordship good time of day! I am glad to see your lordship abroad. I heard say your lordship was sick. I hope your lordship goes abroad by advice, Your lordship, though not clean past your youth, hath yet some smack of age in you, some relish of the saltness of time; and I most humbly beseech your lordship to have a reverend care of your health.   2:I.ii.106–14

To avoid coming to the point, he then enquires about the health of the ailing king, ostentatiously quoting the medical authority of Galen and attributing to the monarch the disease of deafness he had pretended to have. When the Justice points this out, Falstaff quips that his own disease is not deafness but "the disease of not listening, the malady of not marking" (2:I.ii.138–9). And when the Justice offers to become his physician, Falstaff retorts with one of his usual punning answers:

I am as poor as Job, my lord, but not so patient. Your lordship may minister the potion of imprisonment to me in respect of poverty; but how I should be your patient to follow your prescriptions, the wise may make some dram of a scruple, or indeed a scruple itself.   2:I.ii.144–9

In the following act, we are told — what we already know — that Falstaff's sickness is not confined to his body alone. In fact, in comparison with the health of his soul, that of his body seems good.

> *Poins.* And how doth the Martlemas, your master?
> *Bard.* In bodily health, Sir.
> *Poins.* Marry, the immortal part needs a physician. But that moves not him; though that be sick, it dies not.   2:II.ii.110–4

All through these plays, we are aware (and perhaps he is too) that he is in need of the physic of repentance. We are also constantly reminded that he is sick in yet another part, that of his purse. Still obsessed with disease at the end of his first scene in *Part Two*, he complains to his page: "I can get no remedy against this consumption of the purse. Borrowing only lingers and lingers it out, but the disease is incurable" (2:I.ii 264–6). Thus, in each of the three goods which, as Rabelais reminded us, Cicero ascribed to man — those of his soul, his body, and his wealth — Falstaff is badly diseased. His "young limbs" so infirm that he can hardly walk, he waddles off the scene damning his gout and his pox: "A pox of this gout! or, a gout of this pox! for the one or the other plays the rogue with my great toe" (2:I.ii.273–5). But even diseases cannot keep the fool down, and, determined to claim that his venereal disease is a war wound which entitles him to a pension, he exits, vowing to "turn diseases to commodity."

Turning disease to commodity is, of course, what every fool does each time he turns a vice into a virtue — a paradoxically efficacious relationship expounded at some length by Friar Laurence in his pharmaceutical disquisition (*RJ*, II.iii.1–30). Falstaff is no less adept at this kind of transvaluation of values than his predecessors, Stultitia and Panurge. His rhetorical skill in parading his faults as merits is as great as that of Stultitia, and though we may see through the frauds that each of them perpetrates, we may also secretly wish to be taken in by them. When Stultitia says that folly is wisdom, she establishes the mode of argument by which Falstaff will claim that sickness is health; and there are moments when we are tempted to believe both of them.

Similarly, when Falstaff blindly persists in interpreting the future as benevolent, he is deceiving himself as adroitly as Panurge ever did in interpreting the predictions about his marriage. Pantagruel had warned Panurge, even as the Chief Justice and Prince Hal warn Falstaff, that the man who is filled with food and drink will have great difficulty in comprehending spiritual things;[4] but both Panurge and Falstaff reject such counsel, the one for salted beef and wine, the other for capons and sack.

Wine, as we have repeatedly seen, is the solace of all fools: it enables them to forget the working-day world, the horrors of war, the cares of the soul, and the Lord Chief Justices of this world. Panurge says he never saw a fool who didn't gladly drink enormous quantities, and he had seen a lot of fools.[5] To say that Falstaff is no exception is gross understatement; for, given his symbolic relationship to the tavern, wine is not only the solace for his cares, but the source of his being. Without wine he is nothing. Even in his sickness, suspicious as he is of medicines (1:II.i.19–21), he turns not to the aurum potabile which the prince mentions (2:IV.v.163), but to that other "medicine potable" upon which he has relied all along, sugared sack. As an antidote to the ominous warning, *respice finem* ("hearken o' th' end"), he invariably calls for "some sack, Francis!" (2:II.iv.303–5).[6] Most notable of all, of course, is his celebrated praise of sack (2:IV.iii.92–135), which, like Stultitia's praise of herself and Panurge's praise of debts, takes its place in the tradition of the fool's mock encomium. T. W. Baldwin, calling attention to the "dysprayse of wine and drunkenness" as a common literary assignment for Renaissance schoolboys and seeing therein a source of Cassio's dispraise of wine, wonders whence came Falstaff's opinions.[7] But by now it should be obvious that there was a long tradition of what Émile Legouis calls "the Bacchic element" in Renaissance literature,[8] especially in that of the fool;

[4] R V.109/III.xiii: "Bien croy je l'homme replet de viandes et crapule difficillement concepvoir notice des choses spirituelles." As the note in R indicates, Rabelais got not only the idea but the phrasing from Agrippa's *De occulta philosophia*.

[5] R V.318/III.xlv: "Encores ne veids je oncques fol, et si en ay veu pour plus de dix mille francs, qui ne beust voluntiers et à longs traictz."

[6] See T. W. Baldwin, "Respice Finem: Respice Funem," *Joseph Quincy Adams Memorial Studies*, ed. J. G. McManaway, et al. (Washington, 1948), pp. 141-55.

[7] T. W. Baldwin, *William Shakspere's Small Latine and Lesse Greeke* (Urbana, 1944), I, 424.

[8] Émile Legouis, "The Bacchic Element in Shakespeare's Plays," The Annual Shakespeare Lecture of the British Academy, 1926.

and Falstaff is merely following in the footsteps of Stultitia and Panurge when he praises drinking. By the beginning of the next century, the mock encomium of drunkenness, with its inherent transvaluation of values, was common enough to be parodied in John Marston's ship of fools at the end of *The Fawn* (1606), where Hercules, who would seem to be familiar not only with Erasmus' *Encomium* but also with at least two of the *Adagia*,[9] proclaims:

Drunkennes! O tis a most fluent and swelling vertue; sure the most just of all vertues: t'is justice itselfe for, if it chance to oppresse and take too much, it presently restores it againe. It makes the king and the peasant equall; for, if they are both drunke alike, they are both beastes alike. As for that most precious light of heaven — Truth — if time bee the father of her, I am sure drunkennes is oftentimes the mother of her, and bringes her forth. Drunkenness bringes all out, for it bringes all the drinke out of the pot, all the witte out of the pate, and all the money out of the purse.[10]

As folly was for Stultitia and debt for Panurge, sack is for Falstaff the *copula mundi*, but the world he specifically has in mind is "this little kingdom, man." Nevertheless, though wine is his medicine against disease, wine is also the cause of all his diseases. Insofar as it keeps him in the tavern, it threatens his spiritual health; insofar as he consumes an excessive amount, it threatens his bodily health; and insofar as his consumptions run him into debt, it threatens his financial health.

As Panurge demonstrated, money is always a problem for the fool. It would seem that, in compensation for his abundance of natural riches, he is invariably condemned to a shortage of artificial riches. To be sure, one receives no wages for playing holidays, and, since the fool does all he can to avoid the working-day world, he can never have much of an income. What is worse, holidays are expensive, and the pleasures of the tavern upon which the fool depends are never provided free. "You owe money here besides, Sir John," accuses the hostess of the Boar's Head, "for your diet and by-drinkings, and money lent you, four and twenty pound" (1:III.iii.83–6). Faced with this dilemma, the fool has no recourse but to become a parasite, or a thief, or a debtor. Falstaff is all three. The law, however, does not look kindly upon any of these roles, and it is the problem of money that

[9] See LB II.267B–268C (*In vino veritas*) and 527F–528E (*Tempus omnia revelat*) in which the proverbial "veritas filia temporis" is cited.

[10] *The Plays of John Marston*, ed. H. Harvey Wood (London, 1938), II, 216 (*The Fawne*, V.i.170–80).

brings the fool and the justice face to face. Although in the last analysis the objections of the Lord Chief Justice to Falstaff are to his way of life and his corruption of the future king, the legal grounds for his actions against Sir John have to do with money — the robbery at Gadshill and the debt to Hostess Quickly. But even though the robbery is a matter against Falstaff for his life (2:I.ii.151–2) and though he is specifically directed to repay Mistress Quickly (2.II.i.129–30), he manages to elude both reckonings. Not only does he refuse to pay back what he owes, but, presented with his debts, he attempts to borrow more. He persuades his hostess to lend him an additional ten pounds by pawning the little she has left (2:II.i.152–72), and, with supremely ironic audacity, he asks the Lord Chief Justice to lend him a thousand pounds (2:I.ii.250–1). For him to accept his debts would be to end the holiday; therefore, he attempts to increase his debts in order to extend that holiday.

Panurge, echoing Erasmus' Nestor, had claimed that it was lending and borrowing that held the world together, and certainly this is true of the world of holiday, where all fools are, like Falstaff, "as poor as Job." When Pantagruel pays off his friend's debts, Panurge is offended and even terrified; for the cancellation of debt is a threat to his world. Falstaff's reaction to Prince Hal's similar generosity is precisely the same: "Oh," he exclaims, "I do not like that paying back!" (1: III.iii.201). And, that the prince may compensate for his error, Falstaff suggests that he "rob me the Exchequer the first thing thou doest" (1:III.iii.205–6). In the minds of both Panurge and Falstaff, debt is synonymous with love — to lend money is to love and to be in debt is to be loved. Thus, Falstaff regains the love of Hostess Quickly by borrowing more money, not by paying her back. Panurge deliberately confuses the giving of money with the giving of affection when he says to Pantagruel,[11]

the love which you bear me of your own accord and free grace, without any merit of mine, goeth far beyond the reach of any price or value; it transcends all weight, all number, all measure; it is endless and everlast-

---

[11] R V.61/III.v: "car l'amour que de vostre grace me portez est hors le dez d'estimation, il transcende tout poix, tout nombre, toute mesure, il est infiny, sempiternel. Mais le mesurant au qualibre des biensfaictz et contentement des recepvans, ce sera assez laschement. Vous me faictez des biens beaucoup, et trop plus que ne m'appartient, plus que n'ay envers vous deservy, plus que ne requeroient mes merites, force est que le confesse . . ."

ing; therefore should I offer to commensurate and adjust it, either to the size and proportion of your own noble and gracious Deeds, and yet to the Contentment and Delight of the obliged Receivers, I would come off but very faintly and flaggingly. You have verily done me a great deal of good, and multiplied your Favours on me more frequently than was fitting to one of my Condition. You have been more bountiful towards me than I have deserved, and your Courtesies have by far surpassed the extent of my Merits, I must needs confess it.

Falstaff confuses the two in exactly the same way in a scene that echoes the *Tiers Livre:*

> *Prince.* Thou say'st true, hostess, and he slanders thee most grossly.
> *Host.* So he doth you, my lord, and said this other day you ought him a thousand pound.
> *Prince.* Sirrah, do I owe you a thousand pound?
> *Fal.* A thousand pound, Hal? A million! Thy love is worth a million; thou owest me thy love. 1:III.iii.149–57

In the broader sense of love, everyone is in debt to everyone else; but there is also another kind of debt, the reckoning of revenge. Hal owes this other kind of debt to Hotspur, and he vows to his father that he will call the northern youth to strict account or "tear the reckoning from his heart" (1:III.ii.144–52). Just as the theme of disease runs through *Part Two*, the theme of debts and reckoning runs through both parts of *Henry IV*. The king, for example, who "knows at what time to promise, when to pay" (1:IV.iii.53), is indebted to the rebels for his throne, and they are aware of the danger of this debt:

> The King will always think him in our debt,
> And think we think ourselves unsatisfied,
> Till he hath found a time to pay us home. 1:I.iii.286–8

In his truancy, the prince, according to Falstaff, has called the hostess to a reckoning of love many a time and oft (1:I.ii.55–6); but at the same time, he vows that when he throws off his loose behavior he will "pay the debt I never promised" (1:I.ii.233). And when on the battlefield, just before he encounters Hotspur, Prince Hal attacks Douglas, he proudly announces: "It is the Prince of Wales that threatens thee,/ Who never promiseth but he means to pay" (1:V.iv.42–3). In contrast to the prince, Falstaff does not pay. At Shrewsbury, he is afraid that the termagent Scot may pay him, and so he counterfeits; but in a later battle he gets his captive, Coleville of the Dale, for nothing: "I know not how [your betters] sold themselves; but thou, like a kind fellow, gavest thyself away gratis, and I thank thee for thee" (2:IV.iii.74–6).

The aural pun that exists on *debt* and *death* reflects the somber truth that death is the last of all debts — "a trim reckoning," as Falstaff knows. But everyone else in these plays from Prince Hal at the top (1:V.i.127) to poor Feeble at the bottom (2:III.ii.251) knows that it is a debt no man can escape. Even if we do not pay any of our other debts, "the end of life cancels all bands" (1:III.ii.157). Only Falstaff tries to forget this fact: he tries to escape this debt like every other and goes on borrowing. His last victim is Justice Shallow, from whom he obtains the thousand pounds the Lord Chief Justice would not lend him; but then Shallow, who operates on the theory that "a friend i' th' court is better than a penny in purse" (2:V.i.33–5), wants Falstaff to be in his debt. We are, as he says, "beggars all" (2:V.iii.9), and he allows Falstaff to beg from him in order that he may later beg in return, when the day they all hope for comes. When that day finally does arrive, however, it turns out to be the day of judgment, the end of Carnival, the final reckoning. At the new king's command, the Lord Chief Justice and the law call the fool to account at last, and the fool pays the debts he has incurred with his rejection and a heart "fracted and corroborate" (*Henry V*, II.i.130). When the king says, "I know thee not, old man" (2:V.v.51), Falstaff is stripped of all his foolish masks of self-deception and is made aware of the true extent of his vast debts; for he is finally made aware of his folly. The laws of England triumph over the lawless fool, and it is the justice, not the fool, who is now father to the king (2:V.ii.118). Reminding us of the debt of love he had once charged the prince with, Falstaff turns aside from the blinding sun of regal justice to foolish Justice Shallow and bares all his indebtedness and his shattered illusions in the one completely honest thing he ever says: "Master Shallow, I owe you a thousand pound." (2:V.v.77).

Falstaff owes as well a death to God, which he will shortly pay. Like that Greek in the theater whom Stultitia invokes, Falstaff, stripped of his illusions, has been killed, not cured. The fool and his irresponsible holiday world are destroyed by the law, and in the eyes of the world this is justice. In the eyes of the fool, however, the justice of the Lord Chief Justice is as foolish and fallacious as the honor of Hotspur because, as Samuel Daniel's Siren puts it,

> That's out of custome bred
> Which makes vs many other lawes
> Then euer Nature did.[12]

There are two kinds of justice, that which is dictated by nature and that which the law dictates to nature. Each, in this play, receives its personification, the one in Justice Shallow, the other in Justice Gascoigne; and nowhere are their differences made more apparent than in the diptych formed by the first two scenes of the last act.

In the second scene, where Prince Hal and the Lord Chief Justice are brought face to face, we are shown what Gascoigne calls "the majesty and power of law and justice" (2:V.ii.78). The Lord Chief Justice "justifies" his former conduct, explaining to the prince and to the audience why Hal's truancy could not be countenanced by the state. The prince accepts this explanation, as do we, and welcomes the "bold, just, and impartial spirit" (2:V.ii.116) of Gascoigne as a replacement for Falstaff in the role of father to the prince's youth. For that "reformation, glitt'ring o'er [his] fault" (1:I.ii.237) which the prince had promised at the beginning is at last achieved. The throne, we realize, has been saved from the threat of the tavern. In the preceding scene, however, another kind of justice is displayed, which is a parody of the natural justice that would exonerate Falstaff. In its ridiculousness it prepares us, as much as the second scene, for the fool's rejection at the end of the act.

The scene begins with an ominous Sophoclean irony which, in its pun on the word *excuse*, prefigures the last scene:

Shal. By cock and pie, sir, you shall not away tonight. What, Davy, I say!

Fal. You must excuse me, Master Robert Shallow.

Shal. I will not excuse you; you shall not be excus'd; excuses shall not be admitted; there is no excuse shall serve; you shall not be excus'd. Why, Davy!   2:V.i.1–8

The words, of course, are the doddering iteration of the foolish justice, but he anticipates a wiser justice who will also deny Falstaff

---

[12] Samuel Daniel, "Vlisses and the Syren," vv. 50–2, in *Poems and A Defence of Ryme*, ed. A. C. Sprague (Cambridge, Mass., 1930), p. 162.

any excuse. As the scene progresses, however, Master Robert Shallow
displays an excusing justice that is just the opposite of what will be
administered to Falstaff; and we are, I think, expected to interpret the
account of Justice Shallow, Davy, and William Visor of Woncot as
a parody *in parvula* of the scene we shall soon witness between Justice
Gascoigne, Hal, and Falstaff. Davy, the comic personification of the
friend at court, the power behind the throne, pleads for the court's
mercy on behalf of his knavish friend Visor:

> *Davy.* I beseech you, sir, to countenance William Visor of Woncot
> against Clement Perkes o' th' hill.
>   *Shal.* There is many complaints, Davy, against that Visor. That Visor
> is an arrant knave, on my knowledge.
>   *Davy.* I grant your worship that he is a knave, sir; but yet God forbid,
> sir, but a knave should have some countenance at his friend's request! An
> honest man, sir, is able to speak for himself when a knave is not. I have
> serv'd your worship truly, sir, this eight years; and if I cannot once or
> twice in a quarter bear out a knave against an honest man, I have but a
> very little credit with your worship. The knave is mine honest friend, sir.
> Therefore, I beseech you, let him be countenanc'd.
>   *Shal.* Go to. I say he shall have no wrong.   2: V.i.41–58

The corruption of justice is evident, for it countenances, like Falstaff's moon, an errant knave against an honest man. Yet the knave is
an honest friend, even as Falstaff is to Hal, and Stultitia herself had
praised the countenancing of a friend's faults.[13]

Fyrst therfore when you see a man flatter, dissemble, or wynke at his
friendes faults, yea, and sometyme owe favour, or rather wonder at some
great vices of his, takyng theim for vertues, doe you not count hym (I
praie you) next sybbe to a foole?

Loyalty and friendship save William Visor in a way that they will not
save Falstaff. He himself recognizes that Shallow is a "foolish justice"
(2: V.i.73–4), and he goes on to make the moral observation that "It
is certain that either wise bearing or ignorant carriage is caught, as
men take diseases, one of another. Therefore let men take heed of
their company" (2: V.i.83–6). But even he must be aware of the irony
in what he says, just as he must hope that Hal will intercede for him
with justice as Davy does for his friend Visor.

   Forced into the perspective of irony by this scene, we can see the

---

[13] ME 32: "Age, connivere, labi, caecutire, hallucinari in amicorum vitiis, quaedam
etiam insignia vitia pro virtutibus amare mirarique, an non stultitiae videtur affine?"

truth and virtue in both types of justice. Upon that of the Lord Chief Justice, the state and society repose; his justice preserves peace and equality. As such, it must condemn the riotous, unprincipled fool, for he is a corrupting influence and spreads moral disease. If the state is to be well again, it must rely upon the aurum potabile of justice to eradicate this disease. Yet, at the same time, the other justice, that of Shallow, has its own truth and virtue — that of humanity and nature. Corrupt and vain though it is, it would exonerate the fool on the basis of friendship, personal loyalty, and the law of nature. Shallow's application of that justice is, to be sure, ludicrous and absurd, and we laugh at him for it; but then, "what is to prevent laughter from telling the truth?" His justice is as attractive as Gascoigne's is admirable; for, as Dover Wilson has observed, "we find it extraordinarily exhilarating to contemplate a being free of all the conventions, codes, and moral ties that control us as members of human society, a being without shame, without principles, without even a sense of decency, and yet one who manages to win our admiration by his superb wit, his moral effrontery, his intellectual agility, and his boundless physical vitality." [14] When the justice of society condemns Falstaff, we are obliged to concur. Yet in condemning the fool it has banished, if not all the world, at least a very large part of it. It has banished folly, and we do not gladly see it go.

[14] Dover Wilson, *Falstaff*, p. 128.

19

FALSTAFF AND PRINCE HAL

MISTRESS Quickly, in describing Falstaff's death, echoes Plato's account of the death of Socrates, and when Falstaff says that either wise bearing or ignorant carriage is caught by a man from his companions and that, accordingly, men should take heed of their company, he is, though he does not know it, quoting Socrates.[1] At first glance, there would not seem to be the remotest similarity between the wise fool of Athens and the fat fool of Eastcheap; nevertheless, though it is not a comparison one would press very far, there are certain resemblances. Not only are both of them fools because they reject the wisdom of the world, but Falstaff is charged with exactly the same crimes Socrates was accused of — those of "corrupting the minds of young men and not honoring the gods which the state honors, but other, strange gods." [2] Each of them is considered "the tutor and feeder of [youthful] riots" (2:V.v.66); each of them refuses to honor what the state believes in; and, as a result, each of them is brought before the bar of justice by an outraged society. The main difference between them, of course, is that Socrates has a defense and Falstaff does not — the one is a wise old fool and the other a foolish old fool. Yet it remains a part of his paradoxicality that Falstaff can be seen as a kind of Socrates. While it is true that he leads Prince Hal into truancy and vice, we must also realize that he teaches the prince what is perhaps the most valuable lesson he learns.

---

[1] Plato, *Phaedo*, 117e–188a, as cited in J. Dover Wilson's edition of *Henry V* (Cambridge, Eng., 1947), p. 141; and Plato, *Apologia Socratis*, 25d.
[2] Plato, *Apologia Socratis*, 24b.

The theme of the prince and his companion, which lies at the heart of *Henry IV*, was suggested to Shakespeare by such accounts as Elyot's and Holinshed's and is already announced by him at the end of *Richard II*, where the newly crowned Bolingbroke asks:

> Can no man tell me of my unthrifty son?
> 'Tis full three months since I did see him last.
> If any plague hang over us, 'tis he.
> I would to God, my lords, he might be found.
> Inquire at London, 'mongst the taverns there,
> For there, they say, he daily doth frequent,
> With unrestrained loose companions,
> Even such, they say, as stand in narrow lanes
> And beat our watch and rob our passengers,
> Which he, young wanton and effeminate boy,
> Takes on the point of honour to support
> So dissolute a crew.   V.iii.1–12

In this brief speech, most of the themes that characterize the two plays of *Henry IV* are anticipated — the prodigal son, the passage of time, the imagery of disease, the truancy in the tavern, the breaking of the law, the problem of honor, and, especially, the perils of evil companionship. The problem of what companions and advisers the prince or king was to have had become, by the end of the sixteenth century, almost a set theme, and Shakespeare's audience would have seen the two parts of *Henry IV* as another of these didactic lessons. They would also have understood that part of Henry IV's concern about Prince Hal's companions arose from the fact that he himself had just capitalized on the pernicious influence of Richard II's evil companions. But all this — the history and development of the theme of princely companion as evil counselor and the place that *Henry IV* occupies therein — has been so thoroughly examined by others that it need not concern us here.

There is, however, another aspect of the topos of prince and companion that is particularly germane to the concept of folly, and that is the possibility of irony inherent in such a juxtaposition. When we think of it this way, we invariably tend to turn to Don Quixote and Sancho Panza for the *locus classicus*, and certainly the ironic possibilities are most fully developed there. Yet the motif itself goes back at least as far as some of those romances of chivalry which Don Quixote had read. The beauty of the juxtaposition of prince and companion, master and servant, is that it is capable of embodying the paradoxes of truth.[3] Like two opposite mirrors, the two men reflect each other into infinity: together they comprehend a depth that neither alone can achieve. They are able to contain all of the paradoxical contradictions that Stultitia expounded with her irony — that illusion is a part of reality, joy a part of sadness, wisdom a part of folly. Except for *Don Quixote*, where everything is turned upside down, the companion, whether he is Panurge or Falstaff, Tranio, Pandare, Morgante, Pantalone, Sganarelle, or even, in a certain sense, Joe Gargery or Leopold Bloom, is normally older (just as he is invariably fatter and more foolish) than the prince. Yet at the same time he possesses a homespun wisdom of age and a proverbial [4] knowledge from experience which call into question the knowledge and wisdom of the prince. However unlikely it may seem from the nature of their relationship, he always ends by teaching the prince a lesson that he could learn nowhere else, and it is a lesson taught out of folly and love. It is in this sense that the aged companion to the youthful prince acts as a kind of Socrates.

This ironic paradox informs the comradeship of Hal and Falstaff throughout *Henry IV*, but nowhere is it more clearly demonstrated or more fully realized than in the famous mock-trial scene in Act II of *Part One*. "Thou wilt be horribly chid tomorrow when thou comest to thy father," Falstaff warns, and therefore he proposes that the young prince "practice an answer" (1:II.iv.410–2). We realize at once that the fool is longing to play the king; indeed, it is the fool's natural desire to put down the mighty from their seat and to climb into that seat himself. The fool, the epitome of *homo ludens*, also wants simply to play, and his favorite game is to mock by imitation his enemies. Because his most dangerous enemy is the law, his favorite game is the mock trial — a traditional sport of fools that achieves its most terrible form when Lear's fool sits in judgment upon the mad king's filial joint-stool. The game is an illusion, as the etymology of that word implies, but within the illusion lies the reality. That is to say, the game is played in jest, and hence is an illusion; but the same game will soon be played in earnest, and hence is a reality. That

[3] See W. H. Auden, "Balaam and the Ass: The Master-Servant Relationship in Literature," *Thought*, XXIX (Summer 1954), 237–70.

[4] See Auden, "Balaam," p. 264, and Eleanor O'Kane, "The Proverb: Rabelais and Cervantes," *Comparative Literature*, II (1950), 360–9.

reality, however, is as complex as the complexities of the illusory game, where the partners change places. It is, moreover, a game dependent upon words, but the words themselves are undependable, not only because they keep changing their meanings but also because they are uttered in mock seriousness, whether mock majesty or mock humility, mock praise or mock censure. When Falstaff the companion plays first the king and then the son in order to praise himself (whom both king and son would censure), when Hal the prince plays first himself and then the king in order to censure Falstaff (rather than be censured himself — which was the original point of the game), and when that playing is also serious, we are presented with a dramatic, dynamic equivalent of Stultitia's perplexing technique of *spoudogeloion*. It is a play within a play, and there are games within games, mirrors reflecting mirrors. The reality of it all is not any fixed position or isolated moment, but the totality of the performance's endless variations.

The lusory character of the incident is emphasized at the outset, when Falstaff provides himself with props, declaring that the tavern chair shall be his throne, the dagger of lath his scepter, and a cushion his crown — a substitution, incidentally, that ironically anticipates the crown on Henry's pillow and his regal insomnia, compared with Falstaff's ability to fall asleep anywhere at any time. Similarly, the mock seriousness of the scene is also prepared by Falstaff when he calls for "a cup of sack to make my eyes look red, that it may be thought I have wept; for I must speak in passion, and I will do it in King Cambyses' vein" (1:II.iv.423–6). The point to be made is that they all enter into the game not only aware that it is a game, but underscoring that very fact — a fact which, visually, the audience is never allowed to forget. Having firmly established this, the actors are then free to play their roles as though it were not true. Falstaff gets into his part at once, and, when the laughter of the hostess at the spectacle brings tears to her eyes (or perhaps it is that she too is acting the playlet), he pretends that she is his queen and that her tears are real. With sententious gravity he comforts his tristful queen: "Weep not, sweet queen, for trickling tears are vain."

As the mock king confronts his mock son, he daringly introduces the one subject Falstaff might have been expected to avoid: "Harry, I do not only marvel where thou spendest thy time," he charges, "but also how thou art accompanied" (1:II.iv.439–41). It is, paradoxically, the subject of the prince and his companion with which the companion taxes the prince. But the old fool, as usual, turns the theme to his purposes, condemning the prince's comrades so that he can single out for commendation the one virtuous man among them — himself. The Vice, always inclined to righteous indignation, is traditionally given to pretending that he is the one who has been misled. "You have misled the youthful prince," the law accuses the companion; "the young prince hath misled me!" retorts the companion (2:I.ii.164–5). And so, with euphuistic eloquence, Falstaff the Vice not only makes himself out to be the Virtue, but does so at the expense of the innocent he has corrupted:

For though the camomile, the more it is trodden on, the faster it grows, yet youth, the more it is wasted, the sooner it wears. That thou art my son I have partly thy mother's word, partly my own opinion, but chiefly a villanous trick of thine eye and a foolish hanging of thy nether lip that doth warrant me. If then thou be a son to me, here lies the point: why, being son to me, art thou so pointed at? Shall the blessed son of heaven prove a micher and eat blackberries? A question not to be ask'd. Shall the son of England prove a thief and take purses? A question to be ask'd. There is a thing, Harry, which thou hast often heard of, and it is known to many in our land by the name of pitch. This pitch, as ancient writers do report, doth defile; so doth the company thou keepest. For, Harry, now I do not speak to thee in drink, but in tears; not in pleasure, but in passion; not in words only, but in woes also: and yet there is a virtuous man whom I have often noted in thy company, but I know not his name.

1:II.iv.441–61

When the mock king suggests that the prince has one companion who is virtuous, the mock prince, with mock ignorance, asks whom he might mean. Thus given the opportunity, Sir John describes himself:

If that man should be lewdly given, he deceiveth me; for, Harry, I see virtue in his looks. If then the tree may be known by the fruit, as the fruit by the tree, then, peremptorily I speak it, there is virtue in that Falstaff. Him keep with, the rest banish. And tell me now, thou naughty varlet, tell me where thou hast been this month?   1:II.iv.468–75

But at the phrase "naughty varlet" the illusion is momentarily destroyed, for the accent of Falstaff has crept into the voice of the mock king. Seizing this opportunity, Hal points out the incongruity and "deposes" Falstaff. Given the chance to play the king and condemn the prince's companion, Hal makes the most of it; but the mock Hal denies his accusations. Thus Falstaff, the mock prince, is able to agree with Falstaff, the mock king, while Hal, the mock king, is contradicted, and the prince is forced to condemn the mock prince. In this elaborate game, Falstaff always has the advantage because there is no mock companion present and, whichever role he takes, he can praise himself. But the mock prince is always present, and Hal is forced either to hear himself censured or to censure himself. He permits himself to be criticized in order that he may have the opportunity to condemn Falstaff, and, though he does have one triumphant moment, the victory is Pyrrhic. "I do, I will," the prince sternly replies to Falstaff's urging that the companion not be banished. Yet, at the same time, the game itself has compelled us to see the validity of Falstaff's point of view. In one sense, we agree that banishment of the companion would be banishment of all the world, and therefore the prince has lost as well: he is left without a world to rule. This is not to claim that we do not recognize the justice of the censure of Falstaff or the bogus nature of his self-praise. Nevertheless, the game makes it possible for us to see that there may be a kind of virtue in the old fool. Just as the irony of Stultitia's mock encomium makes it possible for us to accept a vice as a virtue, so the dramatic, lusory irony of this mock-trial scene makes it possible for us to accept Falstaff the Vice as Falstaff the Virtue.

It is a combination of the fool's sophistry, which attempts to prove everyone a fool but himself, and the Vice's self-righteousness, which claims that he is the one who has been tempted into sin, that makes possible Falstaff's frequent statements of pious repentance. That he can so suddenly and unexpectedly turn from Sir John Sack and Sugar into Monsieur Remorse is, psychologically speaking, an inevitable consequence of his manic-depressive personality; but the depressive moments, like everything else, he manages to use to his own purposes, turning the disease of remorse to commodity. No matter how optimistic he may be about it, when the fool thinks of the future it inevitably depresses him; not only does the thought remove him momentarily from his congenial state of timelessness, but secretly he may fear that the future will not be quite as rosy as he likes to imagine. All this is beautifully illustrated in the first scene in which we see him where, after covetously fingering the imagined preferment he will have after Hal ascends the throne, Falstaff suddenly sighs, " 'Sblood, I am as melancholy as a gib-cat or a lugg'd bear" (1:I.ii.82–3). His depression after the talk of thievery leads him close to a true moment of repentance, exemplifying Montaigne's perception that vice leaves repentance in the soul like an ulcer in the flesh, which is always scratching itself and causing itself to bleed.[5] "But, Hal," he says, "I prithee trouble me no more with vanity. I would to God thou and I knew where a commodity of good names were to be bought" (1: I.ii.91–4). Yet Montaigne also says that he knows of no quality so easy to counterfeit as piety,[6] and the arch-counterfeiter Falstaff proceeds to turn his remorse into an accusation against the prince:

An old lord of the Council rated me the other day in the street about you, sir, but I mark'd him not; and yet he talk'd very wisely, but I regarded him not; and yet he talk'd wisely, and in the street too . . . Thou hast done much harm upon me Hal — God forgive thee for it! Before I knew thee, Hal, I knew nothing; and now am I, if a man should speak truly, little better than one of the wicked. I must give over this life, and I will give it over! By the Lord, an I do not, I am a villain! I'll be damn'd for never a king's son in Christendom.   I:I.ii.94–109

The tempter-companion thus manages to make his prince change places with him, enabling him to have his cake and eat it too; for he enjoys the respect of the repentant sinner, yet assigns his sin to another.

The next time he is sad, he does exactly the same thing. "I am accurs'd to rob in that thief's company!" he fulminates against Hal after his horse has been stolen, and he proceeds to describe how he has tried to follow the way of virtue but has always been lead astray: "I have forsworn his company hourly any time this two-and-twenty years, and yet I am bewitch'd with the rogue's company. If the rascal have not given me medicines to make me love him, I'll be hang'd" (1: II.ii.16–21). Once again he makes the prince the rogue and the companion the virtuous man, attributing his surrender to temptation, to medicines and love, and not to his own weakness — or inclination. Shortly after the robbery, upon his return to the tavern, the discovery of lime in his sack occasions another outburst of pious indignation:

---

[5] M III.23/III.ii: "le vice laisse comme vn vlcere en la chair, vne repentence en l'ame, qui tousiours s'esgratigne & s'ensanglante elle mesme."

[6] M III.32/III.ii.

There is nothing but roguery to be found in villanous man. Yet a coward is worse than a cup of sack with lime in it — a villanous coward! Go thy ways, old Jack, die when thou wilt; if manhood, good manhood, be not forgot upon the face of the earth, then am I a shotten herring. There lives not three good men unhang'd in England; and one of them is fat, and grows old. God help the while! A bad world, I say. I would I were a weaver; I could sing psalms or anything. A plague of all cowards I say still!   1:II.iv.138–47

With this threnody on the loss of virtue and manhood and the self-pity of his own wronged innocence, he perpetrates the lie about his valorous action on Gadshill and manages to criticize the comrades who deserted him. Even when his falsehoods are exposed, he maintains his self-righteousness, crying, "Is not the truth the truth?" (1.II.iv.255). Until the end he claims that villainous company has been the spoil of him, and his last comment on Gadshill is, like all the others, pious, repentant, and outraged:

Bardolph, am I not fall'n away vilely since this last action? . . . I am withered like an old apple John. Well, I'll repent, and that suddenly, while I am in some liking. I shall be out of heart shortly, and then I shall have no strength to repent. An I have not forgotten what the inside of a church is made of, I am a peppercorn, a brewer's horse. The inside of a church! Company, villanous company, hath been the spoil of me.
                                                                    1:III.iii.1–12

But all this pious repentance is only words. Like Lusty Juventus, Falstaff is "a great gospeller in the mouth," but we cannot seriously believe that he will ever leave fighting and foining and begin to patch up his old body for heaven (2:II.iv.251–3). To enter the church he would have to leave the tavern, and that would be worse than lime in sack. Indeed, he cannot really conceive what true repentance would mean; in his sincerest statement about it — when he is alone on the stage and has no one with him to deceive — he implies that he sees it as a kind of bargain with God. "If I do grow great," he offers, "I'll grow less, for I'll purge and leave sack, and live cleanly as a nobleman should do" (1:V.iv.167–70). But the condition of the bargain is impossible, and, what is more, we know that even if he did grow great he would not repent. Sinner that he is, he has what Pascal called a "nonchalance du salut," which he makes perfectly evident in his letter to the prince. "Repent at idle times as thou mayst," he counsels casually (2:II.ii.140–1); but as for himself we know that he cannot spare the time from sack and capons to do so.

In this respect, he takes as his prototype not Socrates, the wisest fool of antiquity, but the most foolish fool of the ancient world, Herodotus' Hippocleides, whose undoing was also wine. A suitor for the hand of Cleisthenes' daughter, Agarista, Hippocleides had almost won the competition for the maiden, when, at the banquet before the results were to be announced, he got stupidly drunk and danced on the tables, standing on his head and waving his legs in the air.[7] Cleisthenes, shocked by the spectacle, announced angrily that the young man had just danced away his wife, to which the drunken fool gave his immortal answer, "Hippocleides couldn't care less" (*ou phrontis Hippokleidêi*). *Ou phrontis*, as T. E. Lawrence knew when he put it over the door of his house, is not simply the punchline of a good story; it is a way of life. It is the philosophy of the carefree fool who cannot think on the morrow while the moment lasts. To admit the possibility of repentance is to admit that the Carnival will not last forever, and this the fool cannot do. The Lord Chief Justice says to Falstaff that he may pay part of the debt he owes with repentance (2:II.i.132), but the fool cannot afford (in any sense) to pay his debts; if repentance is likely to do so, as it is, he must forego that repentance. Not only couldn't he care less, but he must not care more if he is to preserve the holiday.

But repentance is also, as Montaigne knew, contrary to nature. If one accepts one's nature, one cannot repent what that nature causes one to do. As he explains in his essay on repenting, Montaigne could not often accept to feel remorse: "Excuse wee here what I often say, that I seldome repent my selfe, and that my conscience is contented with it selfe; not of an Angels or a horses conscience, but as of a mans conscience." [8] It was to describe precisely such attitudes on Montaigne's part that Pascal coined the phrase "nonchalance du salut." With equal carelessness of salvation, Falstaff pleads his humanity — his excess of humanity — as an excuse for his sins: he is incapable of repenting because he knows that he is only human, and that is to err.

---

[7] Herodotus, VI.127ff.

[8] M III.22–3/III.ii: "Excusons icy ce que ie dy souuent, que ie me repens rarement et que ma consciance se contante de soi: non come de la conscience [d'] un ange ou d'un cheual, mais come de la consciance [d'] un home."

Dost thou hear, Hal? Thou knowest in the state of innocency Adam fell; and what should poor Jack Falstaff do in the days of villany? Thou seest I have more flesh than another man, and therefore more frailty.

1:III.iii.185–9

Between the angel and the horse there is simply man. Though in a certain sense Falstaff may be "a brewer's horse" (1:III.iii.10), he is at best, spiritually or monetarily, an "ill angel" (2:I.ii.186). First and foremost, he is a man — a whoreson round man at that (1:II.iv.155). He cannot repent that he is not an angel because he pretends to no higher position on the Neoplatonic ladder than that of this foolish-compounded clay, man.

"Repent at idle times as thou mayst," says the companion to the prince, but it is in the perfectness of time that the prince does repent and cast off his companions (2:IV.iv.74–5). Nothing more clearly distinguishes the prince from his companion than their different attitudes toward time. For Falstaff, as we have seen, time is an intrusion on his timeless world. When he thinks of the future, he generally manages to deceive himself into thinking that it will be but an extension of the present, but he is always slightly hesitant about it and secretly afraid of it. "Dans la vie des dissipateurs," observes Balzac, commenting on a later "enfant prodigue de la Bible" and his companion, "*Aujourd'hui* est un bien grand fat, mais *Demain* est un grand lâche qui s'effraye du courage de son prédécesseur; Aujourd'hui, c'est le Capitan de l'ancienne comédie, et Demain, c'est le Pierrot de nos pantomimes." [9] Though he plays the fool with the time (2:II.ii.153) in the present, deep within himself Falstaff also knows that in the future time will shape, and there an end (2:III.ii.358–9). It is that end, of course, that he tries to forestall by forgetting about time. When time finally does catch up with him, it comes ironically garbed as "golden times" (2:V.iii.100), causing him to believe with Pistol that they have indeed managed to outwit time and prolong the present into the future:

> "Where is the life that late I led?" say they.
> Why, here it is! Welcome these pleasant days! 2:V.iii.146–7

But the costermonger's times (2:I.ii.91) are actually over and, just

---

as life is time's fool (1:V.iv.81), so Falstaff the fool is time's subject — and time bids him be gone (2:I.iii.110).

The prince, however, is the representative of history in these plays, and history is inextricably involved with time. If time is Falstaff's greatest enemy, it is Hal's greatest friend and, where the companion would forget it, the prince always remembers it. As we know from his first soliloquy, it is the prince who will obey St. Paul's injunction to such old Ephesians as Falstaff and redeem time (1:I.ii.241). There is a history in all men's lives (2:III.i.80), but Prince Hal is more conscious of his than anyone else, with the possible exception of Hotspur, who wants the hours to be short (1:I.iii.301) so that his honor may fill up chronicles in time to come (1:I.iii.171). The prince's father, who opens the play seeking a time for frighted peace to pant, believes that the hope and expectation of Hal's time is ruined (1:III.ii.36–7), just as his mock father marvels that he spends his time with evil companions. But the prince is perfectly aware of when it is a time to jest and dally (1:V.iii.57) and when it is not. "By heaven, Poins," he laments, with a true remorse Falstaff could never approach, "I feel me much to blame/So idly to profane the precious time" (2:II.iv.390–1).

If he temporizes, it is in anticipation of the ripeness of time in which he will redeem the injuries of a wanton time (1:V.i.50), and he promises that in the closing of some glorious day he will pay his debt. That day's end comes on the battlefield at Shrewsbury, where he keeps his promise, redeeming the time that Hotspur had stolen. In the closing of a later day, he redeems the time that Falstaff has stolen, and as he leaves the tavern world for the last time his parting words are, "Falstaff, good night" (2:II.iv.395). When we next see him, the night is over and he despises its dream; the sun stands at midday and dissolves the dream like foul and ugly mist. Truth, as Rabelais reminded us, is the daughter of time. Hotspur, like young Dendin, would reach that truth without waiting for time, and Falstaff would avoid it by neglecting time; but Prince Hal, like Bridoye, bides his time until the truth is ripened by it.

"Well," the Lord Chief Justice had sighed in despair, "God send the prince a better companion!" But Falstaff had snapped back, "God send the companion a better prince! I cannot rid my hands of him!"

(2.I.ii.223–6). Unhappily for the fool, when Hal becomes a better prince, he does rid his hands of the companion. Yet we must not fail to realize, as many have, that it is partly by means of such a companion that he becomes a better prince. The companion, who is vanity personified, paradoxically teaches the prince the great lessons of humility and fraternity. It is precisely by mingling his royalty with capering fools (1:III.ii.63) that Hal sounds the bass-string of humility. Warwick understands this, as almost no one else in the play does, and properly applies the verbs of learning in his description of Hal's conduct:

> The Prince but studies his companions
> Like a strange tongue, wherein, to gain the language,
> 'Tis needful that the most immodest word
> Be look'd upon and learnt.   2:IV.iv.68–71

To be sure, the prince does not deliberately associate with Falstaff merely in order to learn fraternity. He enters the tavern out of his own vain desires, and he confesses to the Lord Chief Justice after he becomes king that "the tide of blood in me/Hath proudly flow'd in vanity till now" (2:V.ii.129–30). Nevertheless, when he is in the tavern he is aware that he is learning something he could not learn elsewhere.

Shakespeare is careful to point this out to his audience in two parallel scenes, one from each of the plays, between Hal and Poins. The first is in the second act of *Part One*, where Hal describes to Poins what he has been doing at the Boar's Head:

I have sounded the very bass-string of humility. Sirrah, I am sworn brother to a leash of drawers and can call them all by their christen names, as Tom, Dick, and Francis. They take it already upon their salvation that, though I be but Prince of Wales, yet I am the king of courtesy; and tell me flatly I am no proud Jack like Falstaff, but a Corinthian, a lad of mettle, a good boy (by the Lord, so they call me!), and when I am King of England I shall command all the good lads in Eastcheap. They call drinking deep, dying scarlet; and when you breathe in your watering, they cry 'hem!' and bid you play it off. To conclude, I am so good a proficient in one quarter of an hour that I can drink with any tinker in his own language during my life. I tell thee, Ned, thou hast lost much honour that thou wert not with me in this action.   1:II.iv.5–24

Like Warwick, the Prince describes his tavern education as learning a new language, the language of the common people; and it is a language that, as *Henry V* will demonstrate, will last him all his life. When he is King of England he will indeed command all the good lads in Eastcheap, but in a different kind of "action" on the fields of France. Having learned how to be the king of courtesy among the drawers and having become sworn brother to them, he is later able, on the night before his greatest battle, to visit all his host, call them brothers, and provide them with "a little touch of Harry in the night." Hal's allusion to his drinking as a military exploit and his use of the word *honor* are said, of course, in jest. But in this play where all the changes are rung on the word *honor,* we can also see another kind of honor being defined — that of being an honest, humble friend to all men, whatever their station.

In the analogous scene in the second act of *Part Two,* as he comes nearer to the kingship and that rejection of his tavern comrades which he knows he must perform, the prince is less lighthearted about his exploits in the tavern. Now, after achieving his manhood at Shrewsbury, he is "exceeding weary" (2:II.ii.1), filled with remorse for the tavern life he has led, and yet still attracted to the fools' world. He knows, of course, that once he forsakes Falstaff and the rest he will never again know the carefree life of pleasure, and he has seen, in his father's example, the care-laden responsibilities of the life of duty he must assume. When he tries with his father's crown, it is "as with an enemy" (2:IV.v.167). In the tavern world, one sported at night and slept on benches in the afternoon, but in the world of the palace one fights during the day and is deprived of sleep at night. "Who would not prefer to be a fool rather than a king?" Stultitia had wondered; and she had gone on to anticipate almost verbatim the sleepless meditations of Henry IV, who realizes that the "happy low" may sleep, but "uneasy lies the head that wears a crown" (2:III.i.4–31).[10]

Wheras if thei ["kynges and princes"] considred well what belongeth to theyr estates, now I see not what life might be more carefull than theyrs, nor lesse to be desyred. For suche shall never thinke that a kyngdome shoulde either by usurpacion, or any other wrongfull title be sought for, as dooe waie with theim selves, what a charge he susteigneth on his shoulders, that rightly will execute the office of a prince . . . In as muche

---

[10] ME 141–2: "Qui quidem si vel semunciam sani cordis haberent, quid esset horum vita tristius aut aeque fugiendum? Neque enim existimabit vel perjurio parricidioque parandum imperium, quisquis secum perpenderit, quam ingens onus sustineat humeris, qui vere principem agere velit . . . Aliorum vitia neque perinde sentiri, neque tam

as meaner mennes vices be not so muche marked, nor so largely divulged. But a prince is set in that place, where as if he wrie him selfe never so little from that becometh hym, straight waies the infection of the exemple crepeth contagiously to many men . . . And lastly (omittyng treasons, hatredes, and other perilles or dreades, wherwith a prince is infested) if he remembre how the dome also of the heighest, and most rightful kyng of all, hangeth over his head, who soone after will call hym to accoumpte for the least faulte he hath doen, yea and that the narowlier, the greater state he had committed to hym: These thyngs, (I saie) and many like hereto, if a prince do perpende wel, (and perpende theim he must nedes if he hath wisedome) I beleve surely he should take his slepe and fode, with less gladdness, than a farre meaner person dooeth.

Hal knows that he has no choice but to leave the tavern and accept his regal cares. And before the dawn at Agincourt, as he wanders sleepless among the sleeping soldiers, he too, in his speech on ceremony, will have cause to repeat what Stultitia and his father had said. Anticipating all this, he is loath to leave the holiday world of fools; but, at the same time, aware of the responsibilities he must accept, he is ashamed of the life he leads in the tavern. "Doth it not show vilely in me to desire small beer?" he asks Poins; and Poins, echoing the verb of study that had described Hal's tavern activities in *Part One*, replies:

Why, a prince should not be so loosely studied as to remember so weak a composition.
Prince. Belike then my appetite was not princely got; for, by my troth, I do now remember the poor creature, small beer. But indeed these humble considerations make me out of love with my greatness. What a disgrace is it for me to remember thy name! or to know thy face tomorrow!
                                                                2:II.ii.7–17

He may mean that these humble considerations make him forget his greatness, but what he literally says is that he prefers them to his greatness. Poins accuses Hal of not being princely, but Hal claims that he is being human; for nature has given him the same appetite it gives to all men. "I think the King is but a man, as I am," he will say to his

---

late manare. Principem eo loco esse, ut, si quid vel leviter ab honesto deflexerit, gravis protinus ad quam plurimos homines vitae pestis serpat . . . Postremo, ut insidias, odia, caeteraque vel pericula, vel metus omittam, capiti imminere verum illum regem, qui paulo post ab eo sit etiam de minimo quoque commisso rationem exacturus, idque tanto severius, quanto praestantius gessit imperium. Haec, inquam, atque hujusmodi plurima, si princeps secum perpenderet, perpenderet autem si saperet, is nec somnum, nec cibum opinor jucunde capere posset."

soldiers later, and, almost echoing Montaigne, he explains: "The violet smells to him as it doth to me; the element shows to him as it doth to me; all his senses have but human conditions. His ceremonies laid by, in his nakedness he appears but a man" (*Henry V*, IV.i.105–10). It is in the tavern that he learns this lesson, and it is Falstaff the fool who shows him that, as Montaigne epigrammatically puts it, "sit we upon the highest throne of the world, yet sit we upon our owne taile." [11] Stultitia had claimed that if you took away the trappings of ceremony and illusion you would find that he who a little while ago was a king is suddenly a man of low birth,[12] and it is precisely by means of Hal's low transformation from a prince to an apprentice (2:II.ii.193–4) that he becomes aware of this truth. From such experiences in the tavern, he gains that tear for pity and that hand open as day for charity (2:IV.iv.31–2) which he takes with him when he finally ascends the throne.

Hal knows that the world would call him a hypocrite if he were to weep in the tavern for his dying father, but he does weep nonetheless, inwardly if not outwardly: "my heart," he confesses, "bleeds inwardly" (2:II.ii.51). The world has also called him a hypocrite for rejecting his companions when he became king. Yet both the tears and the rejection are sincere. As opposed to the fool, who would not be reminded of his end, Hal would have "the end try the man" (2:II.ii.50–1). And he has warned his companions all along that he will one day leave them. Falstaff had argued the impossibility of Hal's ever banishing him, but Hal had replied: "I do. I will." Conscious of time, he knows the role history has reserved for him to play; yet the fools of the tavern world, Sir John above all, cannot believe that he will ever fulfill that role.

---

[11] M III.480/III.xiii: "au plus esleué trhone [*sic*] du monde si ne somes assis que sur nostre cul."

[12] ME 48: "qui paulo ante Rex, subito Dama."

20

FALSTAFF THE FOOL

"But Falstaff, unimitated, unimitable Falstaff, how shall I describe thee?" The frustration of Samuel Johnson's question has been shared by all who have ever tried to encompass the fat old fool. Embodying nothing less than nature itself, he is so enormous that, as Empson has said, "it is hard to get one's mind all round him." [1] Because he actually is, in a certain sense, "all the world," he contains within himself so much that one can never take account of it all, and most attempts to map out this globe of sinful continents have tended to display the partial and falsified perspective of medieval cartography. Yet the very nature of the fool is such that it could hardly be otherwise. Even Stultitia, who knew more about fools than anyone, could not describe herself, because her influence was so vast and her nature so comprehensive (ME 5–6). Falstaff contains all the contradictions of folly, and just as nature includes both summer and winter, good and bad, Falstaff the Martlemas cannot be said to be either wholly good or wholly bad. If, as Empson claims, one's feelings of distaste for all the false sentiment about Falstaff "should not send one in headlong flight to the opposite extreme," at the same time one must confess that "it is hard to defend this strange figure without doing it too much." [2] In compensation for the affinity he felt with the fat old man, Johnson himself was, in the end, probably too morally censorious of him. But he came perhaps as close as one can to describing Sir John when he addressed him as "thou compound of sense and vice; of

---

[1] Empson, "Falstaff and Mr. Dover Wilson," p. 221.
[2] Empson, "Falstaff," pp. 221, 256.

sense which may be admired but not esteemed, of vice which may be despised, but hardly detested." [3]

In calling Falstaff a compound of sense and vice, Johnson points directly at the oxymoronic nature of the wise fool. As an isolated figure, Falstaff is as filled with contradictions as Stultitia: he acts like a young man though he is old, he talks like a Puritan though he is an Epicurean, he teaches by misleading, he pays by borrowing, he counterfeits in order not to counterfeit, he claims that vices are virtues. One could pile up such self-contradictions endlessly, but these are simple in comparison with the complexities he engenders whenever he is in the presence of someone else; for then our point of perspective is not merely dual, but multiple. The dramatic form in which Falstaff is presented multiplies the complexities even more than the mock-encomiastic form in which Stultitia was presented. And while it is easy for Falstaff to pretend he is resolving all the confusion by mendaciously asking "Is not the truth the truth?" the rest of us come to despair of ever knowing what the truth is.

As perhaps only Prince Hal is meant to see, the truth somehow comprehends all the different points of view that the drama presents. But Falstaff, in his own way, comes close to an understanding of this also. At least, he is the only other person in the drama who is able to understand a point of view opposite to his own; it is because he understands it so well that he realizes he must oppose it so strongly. Another way of looking at this capacity of his is to perceive that he could not operate so successfully as a liar if he did not know what the truth is. He demonstrates this clearly when he boasts that he is not only witty in himself, but the cause that wit is in other men. Boast though it is, it is also the truth, and it is a truth of greater dimensions than either of those facts alone. That he can say he is the butt of wit as well as the source of wit reveals that he is able to see himself as others see him. Despite all the bombastic, conceited, stultiloquent smokescreens that he puts out to conceal it (smokescreens which, at times, confuse even him), he knows very well that he is a fool — that, as Dryden put it, he is "a liar, and a coward, a glutton, and a buffoon." [4]

The ability to see the same fact from his and from the opposite point of view is the capacity of the ironic man, and in this Falstaff

---

[3] *Johnson on Shakespeare*, ed. Raleigh, p. 125.

[4] John Dryden, "Preface to *Troilus and Cressida: or, Truth Found Too Late, A Tragedy*," in *The Works of John Dryden*, ed. Sir Walter Scott and George Saintsbury, VI (Edinburgh, 1883), 269.

represents one of the great flowerings of that Socratic irony which Stultitia replanted in the soil of European lierature. But if he is what Cicero called Socrates, an *eirôn*,[5] he is also what Aristophanes called Socrates, an *alazôn*.[6] When Falstaff admits that he is the butt of other men's wit, he is wearing the mask of the eirôn; when he boasts that he is the source of wit in himself, he is wearing the mask of the alazôn. The distinction between the two is most clearly set forth in the *Nicomachean Ethics* in the course of Aristotle's discussion of the mean to which I have already referred in connection with honor. The passage in which he discusses the characteristics of the eirôn and the alazôn is, however, even more illuminating for the character of Falstaff and must be quoted:

There are also other means, which, though similar to each other, yet are different one from another. They are all connected with intercourse in words and deeds, but they differ in that one is concerned with truth in this intercourse and the others with its pleasure. Of these latter two, one is concerned with giving pleasure in all circumstances of life . . . With regard to truth, the moderate man is a truthful person (*alêthes*) and the mean is truthfulness: pretense, which exaggerates, is boastfulness and he who has pretenses is a boaster (*alazôn*); understatement is false modesty and he who understates is falsely modest (*eirôn*). With regard to pleasure in amusement, the moderate man is witty (*eutrapelos*) and the condition wit: excess is buffoonery and he who exceeds a buffoon (*bômolochos*); he who is defective is a boor (*agroikos*) and the condition boorishness. With regard to the other pleasure, that in the affairs of life, he who is properly pleasant is a friend (*philos*) and the moderation is friendship: he who exceeds is (if he has no ulterior motive) obsequious (*areskos*) or (if he is looking for gain) a flatterer (*kolax*); he who is defective and unpleasant in every circumstance is contentious (*dyseris*) and surly (*dyskolos*).[7]

Reduced to a paradigm, Aristotle's statement looks like this:

	DEFECT	MEAN	EXCESS
TRUTH	*eirôn* (modest)	*alêthes* (truthful)	*alazôn* (boaster)
PLEASURE (amusement)	*agroikos* (boor)	*eutrapelos* (witty)	*bômolochos* (buffoon)
PLEASURE (life)	*dyseris* (contentious) & *dyskolos* (surly)	*philos* (friend)	*areskos* (obsequious) & *kolax* (flatterer)

[5] Cicero, *De officiis*, I.xxx.109.
[6] Aristophanes, *Nubes*, 102.
[7] Aristotle, *Ethica Nicomachea*, 1108a.

No play, of course, can be reduced to a simple paradigm, and any of Shakespeare's characters is always more than whatever abstract quality we may try to assign him. Nonetheless, the application of this Aristotelian schematization to Falstaff can help us to understand some of his paradoxical complexity and may indeed even help us to make his defeat more comprehensible. For once we perceive that Falstaff plays the alazôn as well as the eirôn, we can better understand, it seems to me, not only his personality but also the role he plays in this cycle of history plays. Whatever the old fool is, he is never the man of mean. That role is reserved for Hal to play when he becomes Henry V; and one way of looking at the story of the reign of Henry IV is to see it as a kind of *Bildungsspiel* — an account of a prince's education. Hal's ultimate role, like that of Spenser's Prince Arthur, is to personify Aristotle's magnanimous man, and that goal is reached by way of the middle road upon which he is able to set out only after he has defeated Hotspur in *Part One* and Falstaff in *Part Two*.

While Hotspur himself may be seen as a kind of alazôn, it is really the old lad of the castle who usurps this role. When Falstaff gives his speech on honor, when he admits to being old and white-bearded, when he concedes that he is the butt of other men's jokes, he is the eirôn. At most other times, however, he is the alazôn; for generally we hear him boasting of his prowess in love and war, his friendship with the prince, his courage and virtue. We think of him more often as the buffoon than as the boor. The point is that he incorporates within himself both extremes, and the complexity of his character arises from just this fact. What is more, he confuses things even further because, in a certain sense, he plays his roles in the wrong places. From one point of view at least, the alazôn, the man who claims to be more than he is, may be thought properly to belong to the heroics of the battlefield; the eirôn, the man who claims to be less than he is, would belong to the antics of the tavern world. Yet Falstaff reverses this. It is in the tavern world that he plays the alazôn, "the man of war" (2:V.i.31), boasting that he is more than he actually is. It is in the world of battle that he plays the eirôn, pretending that he is less than he is, even to the extent of pretending that he is dead.

The way of excess is the winding mountain path to the battlefield of tragedy; the way of defect is the crooked back-alley to the tavern of comedy; the middle road is the Camino Real of history. Although history may lead to either comedy or tragedy, the moment of comedy and the moment of tragedy are essentially timeless and outside history. Since time, as we have seen, is the fool's mortal enemy, he can play a role in either of those timeless moments, that of comedy (like Feste) or that of tragedy (like Lear's fool), but he cannot survive in the time of history. Time and history destroyed the comic moment of Yorick's gibes and gambols, but when the moment of tragedy comes he has a role to play once more. Thus Falstaff can be the eirôn and mock at honor and death on the battlefield of tragedy, and he can also be the alazôn and boast of courage and youth in the tavern of comedy. The prince, on the other hand, though he is challenged onto the battlefield by Hotspur and misled into the tavern by Falstaff, has his destiny on the broad King's Highway that leads between them, and, when he finally passes down this highway, the fool must stand rejected at the side.

That highway is, as Aristotle says, the place of truth. Since eirôn and alazôn stand on either side, and since Falstaff plays both, in him we look on truth from both sides. And this is where the greatest complexity of his character lies. By spanning the distance between defect and excess, he also manages to take in the mean. Were he simply on one side or the other, the mean would be external to him; but since he is constantly moving from one extreme to the other, the implication is that he is constantly passing through the condition of the mean, the location of truth. To be sure, he does not stop there (for to stay would be suicide), but he does pass through. In an inexplicable, paradoxical sense that such imagery may or may not help to understand, he comprehends the truth of the mean within his advocacy of the two extremes. And just as he may be looked upon as the most faithful friend (philos) and the wittiest man (eutrapelos) in the play, so he may also be said to be in possession of truth (alêthes) — perhaps even of the greatest truth. Not only does he possess the truth that he is a fool, but also, with his synoptic, comprehensive view of all three conditions of defect, mean, and excess, he possesses the Stultitian truth that folly is truth.

Yet history — the middle road, the moderate position, Henry V — defeats him in the end, rejecting the Stultitian truth he stands for. It was preordained that it should, for otherwise Falstaff would have defeated history. He is, as a recent critic has said, "the fool of the history plays. He steps out of the way of English history, an intruder who announces himself in the face of the commonwealth; and in Falstaff the idea of order meets its most dangerous fact." [8] He had warned that to banish him would be to banish all the world. That is not strictly true, for the world of Henry V goes on. Yet it is true that in order to banish him the world has had to narrow its scope; it has had to shrink, as it were, to fill up the large void the corpulent fool leaves behind. It has had to forego that breadth which can include the opposite extremes of excess and defect and that expansiveness which gives *Lebensraum* to the laughter of irony. As the fool goes off, he takes part, if not all, of the world with him; and Falstaff is entitled to say with Donne, "since you would have none of mee, I bury some of you." [9]

Though we understand why he must be banished, rare is the man who has not been bothered by the rejection of Falstaff. It is easy to dismiss the distress of Bradley and others as maudlin sentimentality; yet it is, I think, much harder to accept the moral justification of the expulsion provided by Johnson. Moreover, that Johnson felt obliged to give a justification and that so many others have indulged in sentimentality betray the more important fact that somehow the rejection does fail to come off properly. Tragic though it is, no one "objects" to the death of Hamlet, and even the shock of Cordelia's death, which Johnson found hardest to bear, has not occasioned nearly so much discontent as this rejection of the fool. Explain it though we may, if we are really honest with ourselves, I think we must admit that we never feel quite right about it. Falstaff has presented his case too strongly to be put down quite so simply. The fool, as he always will if given half a chance, has run away with us.

C. L. Barber has given a valuable explanation of why, though the rejection is morally justified, it is not dramatically cogent, and his comments on this are as valuable as anything that has been written about the end of *Henry IV*. His examination of the problem begins with an analysis of the historical situation that is particularly germane to this study:

[8] Geoffrey Bush, *Shakespeare and the Natural Condition* (Cambridge, Mass., 1956), p. 31.
[9] John Donne, "The Funerall."

But Falstaff proves extremely difficult to bring to book — more difficult than an ordinary mummery king — because his burlesque and mockery are developed to a point where the mood of a moment crystallizes as a settled attitude of scepticism. As we have observed before, in a static, monolithic society, a Lord of Misrule can be put back in his place after the revel with relative ease. The festive burlesque of solemn sanctities does not seriously threaten social values in a monolithic culture, because the license depends utterly upon what it mocks: liberty is unable to envisage any alternative to the accepted order except the standing of it on its head. But Shakespeare's culture was not monolithic: though its moralists assumed a single order, scepticism was beginning to have ground to stand on and look about — especially in and around London. So a Lord of Misrule figure, brought up, so to speak, from the country to the city, or from the traditional past into the changing present, could become on the Bankside the mouthpiece not merely for the dependent holiday scepticism which is endemic in a traditional sociey, but also for a dangerously self-sufficient everyday scepticism. When such a figure is set in an environment of sober-blooded great men behaving as opportunistically as he, the effect is to raise radical questions about social sanctities. At the end of *Part Two*, the expulsion of Falstaff is presented by the dramatist as getting rid of this threat; Shakespeare has recourse to a primitive procedure to meet a modern challenge. We shall find reason to question whether this use of ritual entirely succeeds.[10]

Surely this is the case. An increasingly skeptical century must have found a voice in Falstaff as it had in the two earlier fools; in such remarks as his speech on honor he must have given formulation to the doubts of many who had lived through a century of war. And yet the final appeal of Falstaff involves more than his articulation of doubt. What Barber calls his settled attitude of skepticism does not actually end there. Like the skepticism of Stultitia and Pantagruel, his does not come to rest in the despair of pyrrhonism, but rather it manages to lead beyond that doubt to optimism, which is, as Empson puts it, "a greater trust in the natural man [and] pleasure in contemplating him." [11] Hamlet will be left holding the empty skull of Yorick to symbolize all his disillusionment, but Falstaff goes off displaying his great belly as a symbol of the virtues of the little kingdom of natural man. That is *his* answer to doubt.

If he left us in doubt, we could accept his rejection; it is because

[10] Barber, *Shakespeare's Festive Comedy*, pp. 213–4.
[11] Empson, "Falstaff," p. 245.

he expresses such a positive answer that we find it so intolerable. Unquestionably, Shakespeare invented him in order to create doubt, and the answer to that doubt was to be Henry V; but Falstaff got out of control, so to speak, and answered his own doubt. Fools, if we are not careful, always do. By their very nature, their tendency is to exceed the roles we assign to them, and because we suffer fools gladly we let them take us where we are not supposed to go. The problem can perhaps be seen most clearly as a technical one, and in this Stultitia once again helps to explain Falstaff. Both Erasmus and Shakespeare start out with the intention of attacking the accepted values of society — what Erasmus calls *sapientia mundana*. In order to depose these idols, they ironically praise the accepted vices of society — *stultitia*. The two are expected to destroy each other, leaving (as we know from the *Enchiridion* and the portrait of Henry V) the field free for the triumph of the reasonable man — *homo rationalis*. Now when you have folly challenge worldly wisdom, the advantages, to begin with, are all on the side of worldly wisdom; for that is what the world accepts as its values. Therefore, in order to make the combat equal (and it must be exactly equal, so that the two opponents will destroy each other), you must give folly all the ammunition you can. Since, that is, the spectators start out having all their sympathies with worldly wisdom, the author must do everything possible to transfer some of those sympathies to folly.

The problem, of course, is that the fool enlists too much of our sympathy. His gaiety and license are so appealing that we cannot keep ourselves from falling in with him completely. In terms of the sympathies of the spectators, it is as easy for the author to kill off the wordly wise as it is for him to kill off Hotspur; but the fool has a frustrating habit of staying alive, even when you think he has died. At the end of *Part One* the rational man stands triumphant over Hotspur and Falstaff, and everything has worked out as it should: reason has triumphed over both folly and the false wisdom of the world. But then the fool gets up and takes over again. Erasmus wanted to leave us with a picture of a man reasonable in worldly things and a Fool in Christ. In order to exalt the reasonable man, he had to destroy the man "wise" in earthly things, and he created the fool to destroy him. But the arguments he gives to the foolish man are so compelling that we forget about the reasonable man. Once we are made to see things from the perspective of the fool, the reasonable man bears much too close a resemblance to the wise man. Shakespeare is able to force the triumph of the reasonable man, in a way that Erasmus without the drama at his disposal could not, by having him visually crowned at the end. The audience follows his progress to the palace, but too many of its sympathies stay behind with the rejected fool. Only Rabelais seems to have managed to control the situation as he wanted to. His fool, Panurge, creates exactly the proper doubt to knock down the idols of the "wise." Yet Panurge is as much the victim of the wise as they are his: the result is the defeat of both parties. For though Panurge is made powerful enough to demonstrate that the answers of the wise are wrong, he is not powerful enough to get an answer himself. At this point, the rational man, who is also the Fool in Christ, triumphs over both fool and wise in the character of Pantagruel.

We accept Pantagruel's triumph over Panurge in a way that we never do Hal's over Falstaff. We know that Falstaff must go, for he is far in the devil's book. We also know that "the King is a good king." And yet we are obliged to add, with Nym, "but it must be as it may; he passes some humours and careers" (*Henry V*, II.i.125–6). It is Falstaff who has won our hearts, and we wish, with Queen Elizabeth, to have the old fool back again.

EPILOGUE: THE LAST FOOL

As he goes to Arthur's bosom with the chimes at midnight ringing for the last time, Falstaff does, in a specific chronological sense, make good his threat and take with him, if not all the world, at least his sixteenth-century world. For he parts not only at the turning of the tide, but at the turn of the century as well. Yet centuries are only rough equivalents of ages, and the age of both the Renaissance and the fool was to last beyond the sixteenth century and have in the first decades of the seventeenth the glory of its setting sun. Lear's fool and Hamlet's jester and Cleopatra's clown, more somber and more closely associated with death than any who had preceded them, belong to the melancholy years of the new century, and the bitter fools of Ben Jonson rage in the Renaissance's dying light. The fool that was Falstaff, ever a hard man to put down, even manages unexpectedly to have a final kind of reincarnation in the tragic figure of Antony. Despite all their differences, Antony remains a kind of Falstaffian fool: he is given to wine and lust; he prefers the night of pleasure to the day of duty; he lives out of all order, out of all compass; he lacks the appropriate gravity of his years and is accused of dotage; he is a truant to honor and an enemy to the world and its wisdom. He too, according to Cleopatra, seems lard the lean earth as he bestrides it; and if, like Falstaff, he is finally defeated by his enemy, the state, in another sense he is also, like Falstaff, triumphant over that state even in death.

In the close of the Renaissance, the fool's laughing face takes on an aspect of tragedy and sadness, and the last of the great Renaissance fools is known to the world for his mournful countenance. At the very moment that we watch Shakespeare's fat old fool and all his company leave the tavern world of Eastcheap for the Fleet, in another country and from another prison Don Quixote de la Mancha is preparing to come onstage and enter another inn, which he will call a castle. Older now even than Falstaff and, unlike his younger forebears, gaunt and frail and abstemious in his dotage, Don Quixote rides forth as Daumier painted him, proud and erect on his jaded nag, accompanied by his earthy squire, into the sunset over the barren Spanish meseta. He is the last of the gentle knights to prick upon a plain, and he is a fool. As he rides past it is just slightly more than one hundred years since that spring morning when Stultitia first mounted her pulpit.

Cervantes himself, who was born the year after the appearance of the *Tiers Livre* and who died in the year of Shakespeare's death, is heir to the long tradition we have been following. The pupil of López de Hoyos, he is in fact one of the last direct spiritual descendants of Erasmus, and as a youth he had known at first hand that Italian world which was Stultitia's spiritual home. The extent and nature of his Erasmian humanism have been made plain only in the present century by such scholars as Américo Castro, Marcel Bataillon, and August Ruëgg,[1] but there is now no question about the enormous formative influence that Erasmus had upon the greatest of Spanish writers — and we may recall that a year or so before the publication of the first part of *Don Quixote*, Cervantes wrote an Erasmian colloquy between two dogs. It is not my purpose here to recapitulate what has been expounded elsewhere about Cervantes and his debt to Erasmus and to Spanish Erasmianism. Nor, for reasons already given, do I wish to dwell at any length upon his fools. At the same time, no account of the Renaissance fool would be complete without at least pointing to the Knight of the Mournful Countenance and his jovial squire and indicating the way in which they bring the tradition begun by Stultitia to completion. In many ways, as I have tried to suggest, Stultitia's influence has extended to our own day. Yet in another sense Don Quixote ended the tradition of the fool, as he is said to have ended that of chivalry, by pushing it to its farthest limits. And if he is not the last fool chronologically, he is at least the last fool to enjoy the role of *personnage régnant*.

[1] See Américo Castro, *El pensamiento de Cervantes* (Madrid, 1926), "Erasmo en tiempo de Cervantes," *Revista de filología española*, XVIII (1931), 329–90, and *Lo Hispánico y el erasmismo. Los Prólogos al "Quijote"* (Buenos Aires, 1942); Marcel Bataillon, *Érasme et l'Espagne* (Paris, 1937), and "Cervantès penseur d'après le livre d'Américo Castro," *Revue de la littérature comparée* VIII (1928), 318–38; August Ruëgg, *Miguel de Cervantes und sein Don Quijote* (Bern, 1949), and "Lo Erásmico en el Don Quijote de Cervantes," *Anales Cervantinos*, IV (1954), 1–40.

In *Don Quixote*, Cervantes shares most of the positions occupied by the praisers of folly we have already considered. His position on war, for example, is that of Rabelais; his position on honor is that of Falstaff.[2] Stylistically, he also shares their inclination to irony as a mode of expression and is in fact a greater ironist than any one since Stultitia. We may say of Cervantes' novel what was said of the *Encomium*, that irony does more than affect the meaning: the irony becomes the meaning. Whether directly or indirectly, Cervantes got his irony from Erasmus, and, though he was not by any means the last author to use it, he may be said to have given Erasmian irony its ultimate and most extensive employment. No one since him has used it in quite so pervasive a way or realized quite so fully its infinite potentialities. For the story of Don Quixote the *alazón* and Sancho Panza the *eirón* is quite possibly the most ironic story ever told, and no reader has ever come away from it quite sure what was said in earnest and what in jest. Though the ingenious hidalgo says himself that he acts not in jest but in earnest,[3] and, though Sancho claims to know the difference between the two,[4] the fact is that both the knight and his squire regularly and ironically confuse the two, until the reader is left in the bewilderment of Sancho's gubernatorial major-domo, who can only observe that "every day we see novelties in the world, jests turn'd to earnest, and those that mocke, are mocked at."[5]

Somewhere between jest and earnest lies the truth, but even the protagonists of the tale are not sure where in the ironic labyrinth it resides. "Sancho, Sancho," exclaims his mad master in despair when the squire reveals that he has never seen that *ignis fatuus* who is Dulcinea del Toboso, "ther's a time to laugh and a time to mourne. Not because I say, I have neither seene, nor spoken to the Mistris of my soule, shouldst thou say, thou hast neither seene, nor spoken to her, it being quite otherwise (as thou knowest)."[6] In a certain sense, Dul-

---

[2] See J. E. G. de Montmorency, "Cervantes and War," *The Contemporary Review*, CVI (1914), 689–95; and George T. Northup, "Cervantes' Attitude toward Honor," *MP*, XXI (1924), 397–421.

[3] C II.299–300/I.xxv: "todas estas cosas que hago no son de burlas, sino muy de veras."

[4] C II.171/I.xxi: "pero yo sé de qué calidad fueron las veras y las burlas."

[5] C VII.230/II.xlix: "Cada día se veen cosas nuevas en el mundo: las burlas se vuelven en veras y los burladores se hallan burlados."

[6] C V.169/II.ix: "tiempos hay de burlar, y tiempos donde caen y parecen mal las burlas. No porque yo diga que ni he visto ni hablado á la señora de mi alma has tú de decir también que ni la has hablado ni visto, siendo tan al revés como sabes."

cinea is, as Penelope was for medieval allegorists, the truth personified, but we are never sure just who she is or even if she really exists. She may be the peasant girl seen walking along the dusty road; she may be the maiden encountered on the enameled pastures in the Cave of Montesinos; she may be neither. Truth, which is Cervantes' real subject, is elusive and difficult, uncertain and paradoxical. When Sancho, in his confusion, sighs, "Dios sabe la verdad de todo" (V.280/II.xvi), he is giving voice to more than a puzzled ejaculation. On a more serious level he reflects Cervantes' Erasmian, Pantagrueline trust in God's omniscience and will — a faith which Don Quixote himself articulates when, with words that might have come from the *Tiers Livre*, he observes that the man who is at once wise and a Christian ought not to trifle with the will of Heaven.[7] And if it is God who knows the truth, it is truth's father who will reveal it.[8]

Law ye there (quoth Sancho) did not I tell you that I could not beleeve that all you said of Montesinos Cave could hold currant? The successe heereafter will determine that (quoth Don Quixote) for time, the discoverer of al things, brings every thing to the Sunnes light, though it be hidden in the bosome of the earth.

The wisdom and resignation of the hidalgo are the wisdom and resignation of Bridoye. Both Bridoye and Don Quixote are fools, but both possess the faith of the Fool in God; and if Socrates is, as Byron said, Wisdom's Quixote, Quixote is Folly's Socrates.[9]

When Don Quixote observes to the bachelor that his story must have pleased very few readers, Sansón, quoting a now-familiar phrase from Ecclesiastes, replies: "Rather contrarie . . . for as *Stultorum infinitus est numerus*, an infinite number have been delighted with this History." [10] The comparison is doubtless meant to be complimentary, but it is invidiously ironic. It implies that anyone who enjoys the book is a fool — and we may recall Erasmus' saying that the world was

[7] C VIII.54–5/II.lviii: "El discreto y cristiano no ha de andar en puntillos con lo que quiere hacer el cielo."

[8] C VI.152–3/II.xxv: " — ¿No lo decía yo — dijo Sancho — , que no se me podía asentar que todo lo que vuesa merced, señor mío, ha dicho de los acontecimientos de la cueva era verdad, ni aun la mitad?

" — Los sucesos lo dirán, Sancho — respondió don Quijote — ; que el tiempo, descubridor de todas las cosas, no se deja ninguna que no la saque á la luz del sol, aunque esté escondida en los senos de la tierra."

[9] Byron, *Don Juan*, XIII.x.

[10] C V.81/II.iii: "Antes es al revés; que como *stultorum infinitus est numerus*, infinitos son los que han gustado de la tal historia."

going to the dogs because Erasmus was writing colloquies. As in the case of the *Encomium*, so in *Don Quixote*, the irony is so comprehensive as to include even the author of the book; and indeed there is the same deliberate confusion about who the author actually was. Are we to attribute Stultitia's remarks to her persona or to Erasmus? Is Cervantes responsible for what Don Quixote says or is Cid Hamete Benengeli? The irony in the *Encomium*, which reaches its most intricate complexity almost immediately, gets simpler toward the end of Stultitia's speech, and, when she is describing her followers and then eulogizing the Fool in Christ, there is no confusion about what she means. In *Don Quixote*, however, the reverse occurs, and the irony increases in complexity as the story progresses: contrasted to the straightforward parodistic irony of the Don's first sally, the later episodes of the first part and, even more, the intricacies of the second part are much more confusing. The irony goes on and on, doubling back on itself, until in the last parts of *Don Quixote*, as in the first parts of the *Encomium*, both any given statement and its opposite seem to be simultaneously true. All that we can say with certainty is that the jesting is also seriousness. For Cervantes, like the other praisers of folly, knew that laughter could tell the truth. The ingenious hidalgo himself confirms his author's intentions.[11]

I doe not denie, quoth Don-Quixote, but that which befell us, is worthy of laughter: yet ought it not to be recounted, for as much as all persons are not so discreete, as to know how to discerne one thing from another, and set every thing in his right point.

But it is to Cervantes' two fools that I wish to turn, and we may begin with Sancho Panza. Waldo Frank, in a brief remark, links him with Panurge and Falstaff,[12] and he is indeed their spiritual brother, not only because he is a foolish companion to a noble master, but because he is also one of nature's fools. He is both a natural fool and the foolish embodiment of nature, just as Panurge and Falstaff are, and his earthy common sense is used, like theirs, to prick the bubbles of hypocrisy and false wisdom. Like Richard II's antic, he sits beside his master, "scoffing his state, and grinning at his pomp" (III.ii.163).

[11] C II.154/I.xx: "—No niego yo—respondió don Quijote—que lo que nos ha sucedido no sea cosa digna de risa; pero no es digna de contarse; que no son todas las personas tan discretas, que sepan poner en su punto las cosas."
[12] Waldo Frank, "The Career of the Hero," in *Cervantes Across the Centuries*, ed. Angel Flores and M. J. Benardete (New York, 1947), p. 193.

There is something of the rogue in him, as there is in the companions of Pantagruel and Hal, but he is essentially characterized by his natural folly — and his natural wisdom: "True it is that I am somewhat malicious, and have certaine knavish glimpses: but all is covered and hid under the large cloake of my simplicitie, always naturall to me, but never artificiall." [13] Such a remark reveals that he possesses that astonishing capacity of the fool to see himself as others see him. Panurge, of course, has it least of all, but both Stultitia and Falstaff possess to a high degree this wisdom of self-knowledge. Sancho shares it, or perhaps it is more accurate to say that he acquires it; and he demonstrates what he has learned most poignantly, perhaps, when he leaves his island. Though he has done pretty well as governor after all, he admits that "I was not borne to be a Governour, nor to defend Ilands nor Cities from enemies that would assault them: I can tell better how to plow, to digge, to prune, and plant Vineyards, then to give Lawes, or defend Provinces and Kingdomes." [14] Like all fools, he is not made for the law or for courage, but for the things of nature, and he has come to realize it. He also shares the Falstaffian vision of himself as jester, and he seems to be echoing the old rogue of Eastcheap when he boasts to Don Alvaro,[15]

It is I that am the right Sancho Pansa, that can tell many fine tales; yea more then there are drops of water when it raineth. If so you please, my Lord, you may make experience of it, and follow me at least one yeere, and you shall then see, that at every step I shall speake so many [such things], that very often without knowing what I utter, I make all them to laugh that listen unto me.

The greatest resemblance between Sancho and Panurge and Falstaff is, as befits these children of nature, the natural, physical one. Like Falstaff, Sancho is fat and bearded, and not only a toper but

---

[13] C V.151/II.viii: "bien es verdad que soy algo malicioso, y que tengo mis ciertos asomos de bellaco; pero todo lo cubre y tapa la gran capa de la simpleza mía, siempre natural y nunca artificiosa."

[14] C VII.315/II.liii: "Yo no nací para ser gobernador, ni para defender ínsulas ni ciudades de los enemigos que quisieren acometerlas. Mejor se me entiende á mí de arar y cavar, podar y ensarmentar las viñas, que de dar leyes ni de defender provincias ni reinos."

[15] C VIII.298/II.lxxii: "el verdadero Sancho Panza soy yo, que tengo más gracias que llovidas; y si no, haga vuesa merced la experiencia, y ándese tras de mí, por los menos un año, y verá que se me caen á cada paso, y tales y tantas, que sin saber yo las más veces lo que me digo, hago reír á cuantos me escuchan."

something of an authority on wines as well (V.244–5/II.xiii). When his Baratarian doctor puts him on a diet, he is as wretched and re-fractory as Panurge was when Pantagruel advised him to fast. Writing to Don Quixote, he complains of the outrages of such a regimen in terms that remind us of Panurge's incredulous exclamation, "Ne soupper poinct!"; and he inveighs against the vice of thinness with a pas-sion that recalls Falstaff's criticism of Justice Shallow:[16]

the Medicines [this doctor] useth, are dyet upon dyet, till he makes a man nothing but bare bones; as if leanenesse were not a greater sicknesse then a Calenture. Finally, he hath even starved mee, and I am ready to dye for anger: for when I thought to have comen to this Iland to eate good warme things, and to drinke coole, and to recreate my body in Holland sheetes, and Feather-beds; I am forced to doe penance, as if I were an Hermite: and because I doe it unwillingly, I beleeve at the upshot the Divell will have me.

If Sancho's mention of sheets of Holland reminds us of the shirts of dubious Holland that Mistress Quickly bought for Falstaff, it also reminds us that, like Falstaff, Sancho seems to have been born to sleep (*naciste para dormir* [II.135/I.xx]). Moreover, the sight of his squire asleep calls forth from Don Quixote a soliloquy which must be placed beside the remarks of Stultitia and Henry IV about the insomnia of the great, not to mention the thoughts of Henry V when he too watches his base-born subjects sleep before the battle of Agincourt.[17]

Oh happy thou above all that live upon the face of the earth, that without envy, or being envied, sleepest with a quiet brest, neyther persecuted by Enchanters, nor frighted by Enchantments. Sleepe, I say, once againe, nay an hundred times, sleepe: let not thy Masters jealousie keepe thee con-tinually awake, nor let care to pay thy debts make thee watchfull, or how another day thou and thy small, but streightned family may live, whom

[16] C VII.285/II.li: "y las medecinas que usa [tal doctor] son dieta y más dieta, hasta poner la persona en los huesos mondos, como si no fuese mayor mal la flaqueza que la calentura. Finalmente, él me va matando de hambre, y yo me voy muriendo de despecho, pues cuando pensé venir á este gobierno á comer caliente y á beber frío, y á recrear el cuerpo entre sábanas de hollanda, sobre colchones de pluma, he venido á hacer penitencia, como si fuera ermitaño; y como no la hago de mi voluntad, pienso que al cabo al cabo me ha de llevar el diablo."

[17] C VI.27–8/II.xx: "— ¡ Oh tú, bienaventurado sobre cuantos viven sobre la haz de la tierra, pues sin tener invidia ni ser invidiado, duermes con sosegado espíritu, ni te persiguen encantadores, ni sobresaltan encantamentos! Duerme, digo otra vez, y lo diré otras ciento, sin que te tengan en contina vigilia celos de tu dama, ni te desvelen pensamientos de pagar deudas que debas, ni de lo que has de hacer para comer otro día tú y tu pequeña y angustiada familia. Ni la ambición te inquieta, ni la pompa

neither ambition troubles, nor the worlds vaine pompe doth weary, since the bounds of thy desires extend no further then to thinking of thine Asse; for, for thine owne person, that thou hast committed to my charge, a counterpoise and burden that Nature and Custome hath layd upon the Masters. The servant sleepes, and the Master wakes, thinking how he may maintaine, good him, and doe him kindnesses: the griefe that is, to see heaven obdurate in releeving the earth with seasonable moysture, troubles not the servant, but it doth the Master, that must keepe in sterility and hunger, him that served him in abundance and plenty.

Like the prodigal son whose tale Falstaff was so fond of, Sancho is reminded that he had once herded pigs in his own country (VII.100/II.xlii); yet despite this humble background, when, like Panurge, he gets his governorship, he administers a profound and enlightened justice — a justice based upon his natural wisdom. The main difference, of course, is that Sancho is a far better governor than Panurge. To be sure, his goal in getting an island is the same as Panurge's. He looks forward to being a governor because it will enable him to indulge himself in those Epicurean pleasures and that domination of the law which the fool longs for, and, indeed, the name of his island significantly seems to derive from a root meaning "sharp practice." With considerable justification, Don Quixote fears that Sancho in the governorship will do what all fools do — turn the world upside down (*toda la ínsula patas arriba* [VII.121/II.xliii]). That he does not is because he is a wiser fool than Panurge. His natural wisdom and humanity enable him to settle with justice the most thorny legal problems, such as that of the man who crosses the bridge to be hanged and thereby creates a legal difficulty as paradoxical as that of Epimenides the Cretan. In this respect Sancho resembles Bridoye more than Panurge, and he too is guided in his judgments by God (VII.161/II.xlv). Unlike Panurge, he takes the advice proffered him by his master, and he learns also that positions of authority involve responsibility as well as freedom. So intelligently does he administer his island (in the tradition of the medieval fool Marcolf, who is wiser

---

vana del mundo te fatiga, pues los límites de tus deseas no se extienden á más que á pensar tu jumento; que el de tu persona sobre mis hombros le tiendes puesto; contrapeso y carga que puso la naturaleza y la costumbre á los señores. Duerme el criado, y está velando el señor, pensando cómo le ha de sustentar, mejorar y hacer mercedes. La congoja de ver que el cielo se hace de bronce sin acudir á la tierra con el conveniente rocío no aflige al criado, sino al señor, que ha de sustentar en la esterilidad y hambre al que le sirvió en la fertilidad y abundancia."

than Solomon) that his subjects cannot determine whether they should take their new governor for the fool they had been told he was or for the wise man he appears to be.[18]

Philarète Chasles has admirably summed up the similarities between what he terms this "trinité bouffonne" of Panurge, Falstaff, and Sancho when he says that they

resemble each other in one respect. Born in the sixteenth century, when the Middle Ages were dying, these are types of material sensuality and voluptuous egoism, opposed to serious matters and ideal beliefs. All three have for their bodies a heartfelt and lasting tenderness: good living and well-being, that is their philosophy. They form a mocking chorus, a complete critique of all that carries man beyond the limits of material life — platonic love, the need for conquests, ambition, melancholy, mysticism. It is the pleasures of the senses making fun of the needs of the spirit, the body making fun of the soul.[19]

Surely Sancho does belong in the company of Panurge and Falstaff for precisely these reasons. All three of them are natural fools, critics, iconoclasts, and advocates of the law of nature; all three have as their goal an Epicurean *voluptas;* all three are wise in the same foolish way, the way of nature. One of the traditional interpretations of Cervantes' book sees Sancho as matter itself, as opposed to Don Quixote as spirit. In much the same way both Panurge and Falstaff represent a material, natural wisdom as opposed to the spiritual wisdom of Pantagruel and Henry V. Yet finally, for all their similarity, Sancho Panza stands apart from Panurge and Falstaff: Sancho is not rejected but accepted by the world. The world is on the fool's side for the first time, and the fool acts as spokesman for that world against his master. And the fool triumphs in the end. The entire theme of folly is thus turned inside out, and the silly fool becomes the reality principle of the working-day world rather than the truant from that world. The reason, of course, is that the master he serves is an even greater fool than he. Don Quixote is crazy.

It is true that both Pantagruel and Prince Hal were fools as well. Pantagruel, in the *Tiers Livre*, constantly personifies the wise folly of the Fool in Christ. Prince Hal, as we have seen, is somewhat differ-

[18] C VII.162/II.xlv: "y el que escribía las palabras, hechos y movimientos de Sancho no acababa de determinarse si le tendría y pondría por tonto, ó por discreto."

[19] Philarète Chasles, *Études sur W. Shakespeare, Marie Stuart, et l'Arétin. Le Drame, les moeurs, et la religion au XVIe siècle* (Paris, n.d. [1852]), p. 297.

ent, but still a fool. In the course of the *Henry IV* plays, he progresses from a foolish to a wise folly, even though, in his secular world, he never really becomes the Fool in Christ. Yet there is never the slightest suggestion that either of them is mad. The wisdom of Pantagruel's folly is unquestioned, and, though there are those who do question the wisdom of Hal's folly, nevertheless one of the effects his first soliloquy has upon the spectator is to give all his foolish action an aspect of wisdom, to demonstrate that however foolish he may seem he is always growing toward wisdom. Thus we may say that the two princes are fools in an almost exclusively eulogistic sense. It is their companions, on the other hand, who waver between the eulogistic and dyslogistic senses of the word — between foolish and wise folly. In contrast to Panurge and Falstaff, Pantagruel and even Hal in his way represent a kind of fixed point against which the folly of their companions is measured. The foolishness of Panurge's folly is always exposed by the wisdom of Pantagruel's folly, and, though at times he becomes almost as wise in his folly as Pantagruel, he never becomes wiser. With Prince Hal and Falstaff the situation is different insofar as Hal is less of a static figure, yet at any given moment we know just how foolish or just how wise he is. With Falstaff and (for the same reason) to a lesser extent with Panurge, we are never really sure just what is their wisdom and what is their folly.

Galileo once pointed out that, if you were in a ship moving along a coast and passed a tree on the shore, you would not be able to tell whether it was your ship or the tree which was moving unless you had a third point of reference. It is such a third point that Pantagruel and Prince Hal provide for the reader confronted with the folly of Panurge and Falstaff: the wisdom or foolishness of the companion's folly, like the motion or motionlessness of the tree, is determined by reference to a third, fixed point, the prince. Were the reader deprived of such a third reference he would be in the confusing position of Montaigne when he wondered, playing with his cat, if perhaps his cat were not playing with him instead.[20] Now Sancho, like Panurge and Falstaff, also wavers between foolish folly and wise folly, but the problem is that his master does not provide the expected point of reference. Don Quixote wavers between the two as much as Sancho.

[20] I am indebted to Professor Charles S. Singleton for having suggested to me the juxtaposition of the passage from Galileo and that from Montaigne.

The reader is denied a fixed point of truth from which to judge either the master or his squire; and, like the other characters in the novel, he is hard put to determine whether the Don is mad or sane (*haciéndoles dudar si le podían tener por loco, ó por cuerdo* [VIII.71/II.lviii]). The foolishness (*sandezes*) of Sancho when juxtaposed to the madness (*locuras*) of Don Quixote engenders nothing but confusion. The intensity and complexity of the irony which characterizes *Don Quixote* results from just this lack of a fixed point, from the fact that while the squire is foolish, the master is mad. In this respect, *Don Quixote* is closer to the *Encomium* than either the *Tiers Livre* or *Henry IV;* for in the *Encomium* the same problem was created when Folly mock-encomiastically praised folly.

Cervantes' novel thus carries us back to the relativistic uncertainty of the relationship between wisdom and folly which had distinguished the *Moriae encomium.* Sancho Panza, on the one hand, "hath such sharpe simplicities, that to thinke whether he be Foole or Knave, causeth no small content."[21] Don Quixote, on the other hand, is what his niece says he is:[22]

you . . . know so much Unckle, as were it in case of necessity, you might step into a pulpit, and preach in the streets, and for all that you goe on so blindely, and fall into so eminent a madnesse, that you would have us thinke you valiant, now you are old, that you are strong, being so sickly, that you are able to make crooked things straight, being crooked with yeeres, and that you are a Knight when you are none.

And when the fool Panza comments upon the fool Quixote, he is obliged to say: "This Master of mine, by a thousand signes that I have seene, is a Bedlam, fit to be bound, and I come not a whit short of him, and am the greater Cox-combe of the two, to serve him."[23]

As the two of them move through their world wavering between wisdom and folly, they confuse everything. If they are fools them-

[21] C VI. 279/II.xxxii: "tiene á veces unas simplicidades tan agudas, que el pensar si es simple á agudo causa no pequeño contento."

[22] C V.119/II.vi: "sepa vuesa merced tanto, señor tío, que si fuese menester un una necesidad, podría subir en un púlpito é irse á predicar por esas calles, y que, con todo esto, dé en una ceguera tan grande y en una sandez tan conocida, que se dé á entender que es valiente, siendo viejo, que tiene fuerzas, estando enfermo, y que endereza tuertos, estando por la edad agobiado, y, sobre todo, que es caballero, no lo siendo . . ."

[23] C V.183/II.x: "Este mi amo por mil señales he visito que es un loco de atar, y aun también yo no le quedo en zaga, pues soy más mentecato que él, pues le sigo y le sirvo . . ."

selves, others seem, in comparison, even more foolish; because they do indeed have the faculty of turning into madmen and fools all that have anything to do with them (*pero tienes propiedad de volver locos y mentecatos á cuantos te tratan y comunican* [VIII.142/II.lxii]). And Cid Hamete will give it as his personal opinion that "the mockers were as foolish as the mocked: and that there wanted not two inches of the Dukes and Duchesses utter privation of common understanding, since they took so much paines to mock two fooles." [24]

In these respects, then, *Don Quixote* resembles the *Moriae encomium* more than the *Tiers Livre* or *Henry IV*. In other respects, however, it is essentially different from all three of these books, and it is these differences that I wish to stress. Now the fool, as we have seen, is always a fool about nature. Whether he is a foolish or a wise fool, he is invariably a fool because he takes the side of nature in the dialectic between *nomos* and *physis*. In this Sancho is exactly like Panurge and Falstaff. When he is foolish it is because he is unable to rise above his natural inclinations and appetites. When he is wise it is because he accepts and champions the truth of the law of nature. The revolutionary thing about Don Quixote is that he is a fool about nomos; because of this he turns the entire tradition of folly inside out. Stultitia was originally a fool because she alone refused to accept what was universally accepted by the world. Don Quixote is a fool because he is the only person left who still accepts those things.

He is mad not because he follows the law of nature, which is why all the others were fools, but because he rejects the law of nature for an artificial law, that of chivalry. He is the first fool who could conceivably say that "there is no disputing, or drawing of conclusions against the customes of the time." [25] The medieval fools, as well as Stultitia, Panurge, and Falstaff, were fools because they rejected custom and disobeyed the law, because they were irreverent and, in certain senses, irreligious. They acted according to their natures, not according to law or custom. But Don Quixote acts entirely according to the law and religion of chivalry, and nothing else matters. [26]

---

[24] C VIII.268/II.lxx: "para sí ser tan locos los burladores como los burlados, y que no estaban los Duques dos dedos de parecer tontos, pues tanto ahinco ponían en burlarse de dos tontos."

[25] C IV.257/I.xlix: "contra el uso de los tiempos no hay que argüir."

[26] III.105–6/I.xxx: " — Majadero — dijo á esta sazón don Quijote — , á los caballeros

You bottlehead, replyed Don Quixote, hearing him speake, it concerneth not Knights Errant to examine whether the afflicted, inchained, and oppressed, which they encounter by the way, be carried in that fashion, or are plunged in that distresse, through their owne default or disgrace; but onely are obliged to assist them as needie and oppressed, setting their eyes upon their paines, and not on their crimes. I met with a Rosarie or beades of inserted people, sorrowfull and unfortunate, and I did for them that which my religion exacts, as for the rest, let them verifie it elsewhere: and to whosoever else the holy dignitie and honourable person of Master Licenciat excepted, it shall seeme evill: I say hee knowes but slightly what belongs to Chivalrie; and hee lies like a whoreson and a villaine borne: and this will I make him know with the broad side of my sword.

For Stultitia, Panurge, and Falstaff — each in his own way — love was the result of nature, of natural desires and affections. But for Don Quixote, love is the result of custom. "I am enamoured," he says in an astonishing sentence, "onely because there is a necessity Knights Errant should bee so." And even then, his love is not "natural" but subjected to the astringent restrictions of platonic love.[27] By the same token, he does not sleep, he is not given to wine, nor does he eat very much. Whereas the other fools were exempt from civil law because they obeyed the higher law of nature, he is exempt from it because he obeys the higher law of custom: "Who was he that knowes not how Knights errant are exempted from all Tribunals? and how that their sword is the law, their valour the Bench, and their wils the statutes of their Courts?"[28]

Thus, unlike all other fools, his will is not free but bound to custom and to all those restrictions which the rule of Thélème condemned.

---

andantes no les toca ni atañe averiguar si los afligidos, encadenados y opresos que encuentran por los caminos van de aquella manera, ó están en aquella augustia, por sus culpas, ó por sus gracias; sólo le toca ayudarles como á menesterosos, poniendo los ojos en sus penas, y no en sus bellaquerías. Yo topé un rosario y sarta de gente mohina y desdichada, y hice con ellos lo que mi religión me pide, y lo demás allá se avenga; y á quien mal le ha parecido, salvo la santa dignidad del señor Licenciado y su honrada persona, digo que sabe poco de achaque de caballería, y que miente como un hideputa y mal nacido; y esto le haré conocer con mi espada, donde más largamente se contiene."

[27] C VI.259/II.xxxii: "yo soy enamorado, no más de porque es forzoso que los caballeros andantes lo sean; y siéndolo, no soy de los enamorados viciosos, sino de los platónicos continentes."

[28] C IV.187/I.xlv: "¿Quién el que ignoró que son esentos de todo judicial fuero los caballeros andantes, y que su ley es su espada, sus fueros sus bríos, sus premáticas su voluntad?"

His goal is not pleasure, but fame, which he pursues by way of hardships. He fights where the others ran away, and if he hears the chimes at midnight it is not because he is carousing, but because he is keeping his lonely, knightly vigil. Where the others were jovial and laughing, he is the Cabellero de la Triste Figura. He is thin and abstemious, where the others were fat and gluttonous; he is old where the others (including, in his special way, Falstaff) were young. Whereas Falstaff tried to turn the world of the palace into the world of the tavern, by bringing the young prince to Eastcheap and hoping to follow the future king to Westminister, Don Quixote turns the inn into an enchanted castle. And whereas Panurge and Falstaff and Sancho are all cowards, Don Quixote is valorous: "if thou beest frighted, thou doest onely like thy selfe; and if I bee devoid of terrour, I also doe that which I ought," the knight explains to Sancho.[29] Even Philautia, accepted by all fools since Stultitia, is rejected by Don Quixote, who (though he is not without amour-propre) says what no fool had ever said, that self-praise is degrading (V.285/II.xvi), and who apologetically praises himself only when there is no one else to speak on his behalf.

Yet this significant reversal of the fool's role from allegiance to nature to allegiance to custom is, in turn, once more inverted to provide the final and most pathetic irony. For the fact remains that the custom which Don Quixote follows is one that is dead. One of the most important aspects of that custom or law which fools had traditionally opposed was that it was very much alive and universally accepted: it was this that made the fool a pariah and his philosophy a truancy or holiday from the everyday world. But now, at the beginning of the seventeenth century, it would seem that a century of fools had indeed turned the world upside down; now the fool follows custom rather than rebelling against it, but he finds that the world itself has changed its allegiance. He remains the pariah and the truant, but for just the opposite reasons. Formerly, to the optimistic, idealistic view of man which the quattrocento world had accepted, the fool had opposed a skeptical, realistic view. But it would seem that the fool's view has come to be accepted by the world, which now finds

<hr>

[29] C IV.197/I.xlvi: " — Di lo que quisieres — replicó don Quijote — , como tus palabras no se encaminen á ponerme miedo; que si tú le tienes, haces como quien eres; y si yo no le tengo, hago como quien soy."

its spokesman in the fool Sancho Panza; and Don Quixote is a fool because he is the only man left who holds this idealism.

All of this is symbolically depicted by Cervantes in a variety of ways. Thus, for example, one of the characteristics of the sixteenth-century fool was that he was horseless, and the lack of a horse had indicated a lower order of being: Falstaff, the natural man, is unhorsed; Hotspur, the man of custom, is superbly horsed. Now Don Quixote is the first fool to get a horse, and this indicates his shift from nature to custom. But, at the same time, the custom is dead, and the horse is almost so; Rocinante is a feeble, bony, jaded nag. When Prince Hal appears at Shewsbury, "all furnish'd, all in arms," his donning of armor represents his rejection of the world of the fool for the world of the palace. Don Quixote is also the first fool to wear armor, and he is, in the world's eyes, a fool precisely because he does wear it. Yet Ariosto's celebrated *elmo di Mambrino* has become, for the Don, only a barber's basin. Panurge and Falstaff had been cowards and run from battle; Don Quixote rides directly into the fray, but it is upon his broken hack and in his dented basin, and his opponents are only windmills.

By first pretending and then believing that he is a knight errant, Don Quixote follows a custom that is dead, and this is the source of his folly. Deluded into believing that chivalry continues to exist in his person, he confuses, like all fools, the categories of illusion and reality. Other fools, however, had insisted that nature was the reality and custom the illusion. But for the Don the illusion of custom is the reality, the reality of nature an illusory enchantment. For him, in his madness, Dulcinea is a princess because knights errant always fought for princesses. When he is confronted with the true Dulcinea, he insists that it is an illusion:[30]

as I went heeretofore to have kissed her hands, and receive her benediction, leave and licence, for this my third sally, I found another manner of one then I looked for, I found her enchanted, and turned from a Princesse to a Countrey-wench, from faire to foule, from an Angell to a Devill, from sweet to contagious, from well-spoken to rusticke, from modest to skit-

[30] C VI.270/II.xxxii: "yendo los días pasados á besarle las manos, y á recebir su bendición, beneplácito y licencia para esta tercera salida, hallé otra de la que buscaba: halléla encantada y convertida de princesa en labradora, de hermosa en fea, de ángel en diablo, de olorosa en pestífera, de bien hablada en rústica, de reposada en brincadora, de luz en tinieblas, y, finalmente, de Dulcinea del Toboso en una villana de Sayago."

tish, from light to darknesse, and finally from Dulcinea del Toboso, to a Pesantesse of Sayago.

The fact is, however, as the Duchess goes on to suggest, that there may be no Dulcinea at all, neither the illusory nor the real one. The Duchess thus pushes the paradox of reality and illusion to its extreme point, until the entire structure teeters on the edge of sanity, as it had also in the Cave of Montesinos. Yet the Don is nothing daunted by this, for he has an answer of which both Stultitia and Pantagruel would have approved. Such final questions, he concludes, border on mystery, and the answers are the property of God alone: man cannot prove it one way or another, but must act according to his own wisdom (or folly) and leave the ultimate truth to God. It would appear to Don Quixote that she exists, and if she exists then it must be in the ideal form that is fitting for her (*como conviene*).[31]

God knowes, if there be a Dulcinea or no in the world, whether she be fantasticall, or not: and these be matters, whose justifying must not be so far searcht into. Neither have I ingendred or brought foorth my Lady, though I contemplate on her, as is fitting, she being a Lady that hath all the parts that may make her famous thorow the whole world: as these; faire, without blemish; grave, without pride; amorous, but honest; thankfull, as courteous; courteous, as well-bred: And finally, of high descent; by reason that beauty shines and marcheth upon her noble bloud, in more degrees of perfection, then in meane-borne beauties.

She is, as Herman Melville saw,[32] almost a surrogate for God in Don Quixote's mind, and this passage could serve as an argument for the existence of God as well.

In some ways, Don Quixote is like Panurge and Falstaff when he does this. Panurge, confronted with the natural reality of woman and the sure prediction that he would be a cuckold, insisted that it was not so. Falstaff, confronted with his natural cowardice, insisted that it was only an illusion. For the most part, however, Panurge and Falstaff transvaluate the values of custom, such as worldly wisdom and

---

[31] C VI.272/II.xxxii: "Dios sabe si hay Dulcinea, ó no, en el mundo, ó si es fantástica, ó no es fantastica y éstas no son de las cosas cuya averiguación se ha de llevar hasta el cabo. Ni yo engendré ni parí á mi señora, puesto que la contemplo como conviene que sea una dama que contenga en sí las partes que puedan hacerla famosa en todas las del mundo, como son: hermosa sin tacha, grave sin soberbia, amorosa con honestidad, agradecida por cortés, cortés por bien criada, y, finalmente, alta por linaje, á causa que sobre la buena sangre resplandece y campea la hermosura con más grandos de perfeción que en las hermosas humildemente nacidas."

[32] See Harry Levin, *Contexts of Criticism* (Cambridge, Mass., 1957), p. 102.

honor, by establishing the values of nature. It is Don Quixote's primary role to *re-evaluate* the values they have transvaluated — to claim that custom, which they had proved an illusion, is actually the reality and that nature, which they had shown to be the reality, is actually an illusion. Thus a custom like knighthood, which Falstaff had demonstrated to be folly, only has, according to Don Quixote, the appearance of folly. Actually, knighthood is not comprised of "Chimeras, follies and desperate things"; it only appears to be so because in knighthood things are done by contraries — and we may signalize the recurrence once again of a phrase that runs like a leitmotif through *Don Quixote*, "al revés": "Is it possible, that in all the time thou hast gone with me, thou couldest not perceive, that all the adventures of Knights Errant doe appear Chimeras, follies and desperate things, being quite contrary?" [33] Everything being done by contraries was the significance of the Silenus image invoked by Erasmus and Rabelais; but they claimed that the reality was the god who resided within the grotesque figurine. Don Quixote is claiming that the reality is the figurine itself.

Other fools had claimed that what was accepted as reality by the world was actually an illusion. It would appear that they even managed to convince the world. For when Don Quixote rides forth to insist the opposite, the world no longer agrees. The fools of the sixteenth-century were skeptics; but the Cabellero de la Triste Figura, saddened perhaps by just that skepticism, is an idealist. He would take up again a theme of Stultitia's which Panurge and Falstaff had tended to neglect and agree with her that happiness resides in opinion, not in things as they are.[34]

But *Philosophers* saie "it is a miserable thyng to be begyled, and erre so." Naie, most miserable is it (I saie) not to erre, and not to be deceived. For too too are thei deceived, who wene that mans felicitee consisteth in thinges selfe, and not rather in the opinion how the same are taken.

Stultitia had claimed that the wise of this world were fools, and both Panurge and Falstaff had gone on to prove her point, demonstrating

---

[33] C II.294/I.xxv: "¿Que es posible que en cuanto ha que andas conmigo no has echado de ver que todas las cosas de los caballeros andantes parecen quimeras, necedades y desatinos, y que son todas hechas al revés?"

[34] ME 89: "Sed falli, inquiunt, miserum est, imo non falli, miserrimum. Nimium enim desipiunt, qui in rebus ipsis felicitatem hominis sitam esse existimant. Ex opinionibus ea pendet . . ."

that worldly wisdom was an illusion. But Stultitia had also said that to be a fool was to be happy and that one must beware of depriving man of his foolish illusions.

Don Quixote admits, appropriately enough, that "since I was a boy, I have loved Maske-shewes, and in my youth, I have beene ravished with Stage-playes." [35] The stage, as Stultitia knew, provides the perfect symbol for man's illusions and self-delusions; and Don Quixote carries the story of the Greek in the theater one step further when he climbs up on the stage to fight in the puppet show. It is all an illusion, but he takes it for reality; we see that he is quite mad. Yet, as he himself explains to Sancho after they have encountered the wagon of *The Parliament of Death*, perhaps life itself is also an illusion — and we take that seriously enough. Echoing Stultitia, he explains,[36]

there is no comparison, that doth more truely present to us, what we are, or what we should be, then the Comedy and Comedians: If not, tell mee, hast not thou seene a Play acted where Kings, Emperours, Bishops, Knights, Dames, and other personages are introduced? One playes a Ruffian, another the Cheater, this a Merchant, t'other a Souldier, one a crafty Foole, another a foolish Lover: And the Comedy ended, and the apparrell taken away, all the rehearsers are the same they were.

By introducing himself and his squire into this description with the terms "crafty Foole" and "foolish Lover," he makes us see that, in Stultitia's words, to be a fool is to act the play of life. Panurge had exposed the illusion of wisdom, and Falstaff had exposed the illusions of honor and valor; but Don Quixote would take us back into Plato's (or Montesinos') cave, to gaze on shadows as though they were realities and to be happy.

It is only at the end of his story that we realize quite how dependent we, as well as all the characters therein, have become upon the Don's illusions. His argument, however foolish, is so compelling that

[35] C V.207/II.xi: "desde mochacho fuí aficionado á la carátula, y en mi mocedad se me iban los ojos tras la farándula."

[36] C V.216-7/II.xii: "y ninguna comparación hay que más al vivo nos represente lo que somos y lo que habemos de ser como la comedia y los comediates. Si no, dime: ¿no has visto tú representar alguna comedia adonde se introducen reyes, emperadores y pontífices, caballeros, damas y otros diversos personajes? Uno hace el rufián, otro el embustero, éste el mercader, aquél el soldado, otro el simple discreto, otro el enamorado simple; y, acadada la comedia y desnudándose de los vestidos della, quedan todos los recitantes iguales."

we have come to share his vision of the illusion as reality. Even Sancho, who began as the reality principle par excellence, comes around to his point of view; for, as the Duchess realizes, he believes "for an infallible truth, that Dulcinea was enchanted, hee himselfe having beene the Enchanter, and the Imposter of that businesse."[37] When his master is finally defeated, Sancho, who had long tried to get him to forget his fancies, is overcome with grief: "Sancho all sad and sorrowfull knew not what to doe or say, and all that had hapned, to him seemed but a dreame: and all that Machine, a matter of Enchantment."[38]

When his friends had pulled him back to reality out of the illusions of the Cave of Montesinos, Don Quixote had said to them,[39]

God forgive you, Friends, for you have raised mee from one of the delicatest and pleasingest lives and sights that ever was seene by humane eye: Now at length I perceive, that all the delights of this world doe passe like a shadow or dreame, or wither like a flower of the field.

It is the "pol me occidistis, amici" of Horace's Greek in the theater, and the final disillusionment of Don Quixote actually does kill him. But the world realizes finally what it has done. "O señor," says Don Antonio to Sansón,[40]

God forgive you the wrong you doe the whole world, in seeking to recover the pleasantest mad man in the world. Perceive you not, that this recovery cannot bee so much worth, as the delight that his fopperies cause?

The last irony of all comes in what Proust, with specific reference to Don Quixote, called "that late moment of lucidity which even the most chimerically enchanted lives can have."[41] For after Don Quixote

---

[37] C VI.306/II.xxxiv: "que hubiese venido á creer ser verdad infalible que Dulcinea del Toboso estuviese encantada, habiendo sido él mesmo el encantador y el embustero de aquel negocio."

[38] C VIII.192/II.lxiv: "Sancho, todo triste, todo apesarado, no sabía qué decirse ne qué hacerse: parecíale que todo aquel suceso pasaba en sueños, y que todo aquella máquina era cosa de encantamento."

[39] C VI.86/II.xxii: "Dios os lo perdone, amigos; que me habéis quitado de la más sabrosa y agradable vida y vista que ningún humano ha visto ni pasado. En efecto, ahora acabo de conocer que todos los contentos desta vida pasan como sombra y sueño, ó se marchitan como la flor del campo."

[40] C VIII.195-6/II.lxv: "¡Dios os perdone el agravio que habéis hecho á todo el mundo en querer volver cuerdo al más gracioso loco que hay en él! ¿No veis, señor, que no podrá llegar el provecho que cause la cordura de don Quijote á lo que llega el gusto que da con sus desvaríos?"

[41] Marcel Proust, Sentiments filiaux d'un parracide, in Pastiches et Mélanges (Paris, 1919), pp. 223-4.

has come to his senses on his deathbed, the world prays him to become a fool again and assures him that his illusions were indeed realities.

Thus the last fool triumphs as the others had. He has died, but his foolish life has caused the world to see the wisdom of folly. The tradition of the fool, which turned things upside down, has been turned upside down itself; but the fool has persisted, as he always will so long as man contemplates the mystery and tragedy of life, because the laughter of the fool makes it possible for man to accept life by enabling him to accept himself. It was Stultitia who first brought the fool into predominance, and it is Ben Jonson's versified translation of Stultitia's words that provides the fool with his epitaph — an epitaph whose reiterated closing word appropriately supplies a final chorus of laughter.

> Fooles, they are the onely nation
> Worth mens enuy, or admiration;
> Free from care, or sorrow-taking,
> Selues, and others merry-making:
> All they speake, or doe, is sterling.
> Your Foole, he is your great mans dearling,
> And your ladies sport, and pleasure;
> Tongue, and bable are his treasure.
> Eene his face begetteth laughter,
> And he speakes truth, free from slaughter;
> He's the grace of euery feast,
> And, sometimes, the chiefest guest;
> Hath his trencher, and his stoole,
> When wit waites vpon the foole.
> O, who would not bee
> Hee, hee, hee?

BIBLIOGRAPHY

INDEX

BIBLIOGRAPHY

❦ ❦ ❦ ❦ ❦ ❦ ❦ ❦ ❦ ❦ ❦ ❦ ❦ ❦ ❦ ❦ ❦

The bibliography for such a study as this could easily run to several thousand items. In trying to make it manageable, I have listed only a handful of the many general studies on Renaissance thought and, of the countless articles and monographs on specific subjects, only those most strictly pertinent to the themes discussed in this book; occasionally I have strayed from this policy to admit a work which, though of limited interest, is little known and may be of use to the specialist. I have also tried to minimize unnecessary duplication between the notes and the bibliography, with the result that a number of items appear in one place but not in the other. The primary sources listed have been restricted to a selection of texts and translations for Cervantes, Erasmus, Montaigne, Rabelais, and Shakespeare. The abbreviations used in the notes to refer to works by these five authors are also registered.

CERVANTES

Don Quijote de la Mancha, ed. Francisco Rodríguez Marín. 8 vols. Clásicos Castellanos. Madrid, 1952–57. [In text: C]
Obras completas de Miguel de Cervantes Saavedra, Don Quixote de la Mancha, ed. Rodolfo Schevill and Adolfo Bonilla. 4 vols. Madrid, 1928–41.
The History of Don Quixote of the Mancha, tr. Thomas Shelton, introd. James Fitzmaurice-Kelly. 4 vols. The Tudor Translations, ed. W. E. Henley. London, 1896.

ERASMUS

Des. Erasmi Roterodami Opera Omnia, ed. J. LeClerc. 10 vols. Leiden, 1703–6. [In text: LB (Lugduni Batavorum)]
Erasmi Opuscula, ed. W. K. Ferguson. The Hague, 1933.
Desiderius Erasmus Roterodamus ausgewählte Werke, ed. Hajo and Annemarie Holborn. Munich, 1933. [In text: E (used for text of the *Enchiridion militis christiani*)]
The Colloquies of Erasmus, tr. N. Bailey, ed. E. Johnson. 2 vols. London, 1878.
Inquisitio de Fide, ed. C. R. Thompson. New Haven, 1950.
Dulce bellum inexpertis tr. and ed. Y. Rémy and R. Dunil-Marquebreucq. Brussels, 1953.
The Education of a Christian Prince, tr. and ed. Lester K. Born. New York, 1936.
Handbook of the Militant Christian, tr. and ed. John P. Dolan. Notre Dame, 1962.

Opus epistolarum Des. Erasmi Roterodami denuo recognitum et auctum, ed. P. S. Allen and H. M. Allen and later H. W. Garrod. 11 vols., with 1 vol. of indices compiled by B. Flower and E. Rosenbaum. Oxford, 1906–58. [In text: EE]

The Epistles of Erasmus from His Earliest Letters to His Fifty-first Year Arranged in Order of Time, tr. F. M. Nichols. New York, 1904.

Essai sur le libre arbitre, tr. and ed. Pierre Mesnard. Alger, 1945.

The Free Will, in Erasmus-Luther, *Discourses on Free Will*, tr. and ed. Ernst F. Winter. New York, 1961.

ΜΩΡΙΑΣ ΕΓΚΩΜΙΟΝ *Stultitiae Laus, Des. Erasmi Rot. Declamatio*, ed. J. B. Kan. The Hague, 1898. [In text: ME]

"Sir Thomas Chaloner's Translation of *The Praise of Folie*," ed. Clarence H. Miller. Diss., Harvard University. 2 vols. Cambridge, Mass., 1955.

The Praise of Folly, tr. and ed. Hoyt Hopewell Hudson. Princeton, 1941.

The Poems of Desiderius Erasmus, ed. Cornelius Reedijk. Leiden, 1956.

Woodward, W. H. *Desiderius Erasmus Concerning the Aims and Method of Education*. Cambridge, Eng., 1904.

MONTAIGNE

Les Essais de Michel de Montaigne, publiés d'après l'exemplaire de Bordeaux . . . , ed. Fortunat Strowski and François Gebelin. 3 vols., with 1 vol. by Pierre Villey, *Les Sources des Essais. Annotations et éclaircissements*. Bordeaux, 1919–20. [In text: M]

The Essayes of Montaigne, tr. John Florio, ed. J. I. M. Stewart. 2 vols. The Nonesuch Press, London, 1931.

RABELAIS

Oeuvres de François Rabelais, édition critique publiée sous la direction de Abel Lefranc. 5 vols. and part of vol. VI. Paris, 1913—. [In text: R]

Oeuvres complètes de Rabelais, ed. Jean Plattard. 5 vols. Paris, 1938–48.

Le Quart Livre, ed. Robert Marichal. Lille and Geneva, 1947.

Gargantua and Pantagruel, tr. Sir Thomas Urquhart and Peter Motteux, introd. Charles Whibley. 3 vols. The Tudor Translations, ed. W. E. Henley. London, 1900.

SHAKESPEARE

The Complete Works of William Shakespeare, ed. G. L. Kittredge. Boston, 1936.

SECONDARY SOURCES

Adams, H. H. "Falstaff's Instinct," *Shakespeare Quarterly*, V (1954), 208–9.

Adams, R. P. "Designs by More and Erasmus for a New Social Order," *SP*, XLII (1945), 131–45.

Alexander, W. H. "The Sieur de Montaigne and Cicero," *University of Toronto Quarterly*, IX (1940), 222–30.

Allen, Don Cameron. "The Rehabilitation of Epicurus and his Theory of Pleasure in the Early Renaissance," *SP*, XLI (1944), 1–15.

Allen, P. S. *The Age of Erasmus*. Oxford, 1914.

———— *Erasmus; Lectures and Wayfaring Sketches*. Oxford, 1934.

Auden, W. H. "Balaam and the Ass: The Master-Servant Relationship in Literature," *Thought*, XXIX (Summer 1954), 237–70.

———— "The Fallen City: Some Reflections on Shakespeare's 'Henry IV'," *Encounter*, XIII (November 1959), 21–31.

Auer, Alfons. *Die vollkommene Frömmigkeit des Christen nach dem Enchiridion militis christiani des Erasmus von Rotterdam.* Düsseldorf, 1954.

Baker, Herschel. *The Dignity of Man: Studies in the Persistence of an Idea.* Cambridge, Mass., 1947.

Baldwin, T. W. *William Shakspere's Small Latine and Lesse Greeke.* Urbana, 1944.

Barber, C. L. *Shakespeare's Festive Comedy: A Study of Dramatic Form and its Relation to Social Custom.* Princeton, 1959.

Baron, Hans. "Erasmus-Probleme im Spiegel des Colloquiums 'Inquisitio de fide,' " *Archiv für Reformations-Geschichte*, XLIII (1952), 254–63.

———— "Secularization, Wisdom and Political Humanism in the Renaissance," *JHI*, XXI (1960), 131–50.

Bart, B. "Aspects of the comic in Pulci and Rabelais," *Modern Language Quarterly*, XI (1950), 56–63.

Bataillon, Marcel. "Cervantès penseur d'après le livre d'Américo Castro," *Revue de la littérature comparée*, VIII (1928), 318–38.

———— *Érasme et l'Espagne.* Paris, 1937.

Benardete, M. J. and Angel Flores, ed. *The Anatomy of Don Quixote. A Symposium.* Ithaca, 1932.

Bethell, S. L. "The Comic Element in Shakespeare's Histories," *Anglia*, LXXI (1952), 82–101.

———— *Shakespeare and the Popular Dramatic Tradition.* London, 1944.

Bezzola, Reto R. "Rabelais im Lichte der neueren Forschungen," *Zeitschrift für französische Sprache und Literatur*, LIV (1930), 257–80.

Bing, G. "Nugae circa Veritatem," *Journal of the Warburg Institute*, I (1937), 304–12.

Borghese, G. A. "The Dishonor of Honor," *RR*, XXXII (1941), 44–55.

Borghi, Lamberto. *Umanesimo e concezione religiosa in Erasmo da Rotterdam.* Florence, 1935.

Bouyer, L. *Autour d'Érasme. Études sur le christianisme des humanistes catholiques.* Paris, 1955.

Bredvoid, Louis I. "The Naturalism of Donne in Relation to some Renaissance Traditions," *JEGP*, XXII (1923), 471–502.

Bruns, I. "Erasmus als Satiriker," *Deutsche Rundschau*, CIII (1900), 192–205.

Buck, August. "Aus der Vorgeschichte der querelles des anciens et des modernes in Mittelalter und Renaissance," *BHR*, XX (1958), 527–41.

Burgess, T. C. "Epideictic Literature," *University of Chicago Studies in Classical Philology*, III (1902), 89–261.

Burnet, Étienne. *Don Quichotte, Cervantès, et le XVIe siècle.* Tunis, 1954.

Busby, Olive M. *The Development of the Fool in Elizabethan Drama.* Oxford, 1923.

Bush, Douglas. *Classical Influences in Renaissance Literature.* Martin Classical Lectures, XIII. Cambridge, Mass., 1952.

———— *The Renaissance and English Humanism.* The Alexander Lectures. Toronto, 1939.

302   BIBLIOGRAPHY

Bush, Douglas. *Science and English Poetry, A Historical Sketch, 1590–1950.* New York, 1950.
Bush, Geoffrey. *Shakespeare and the Natural Condition.* Cambridge, Mass., 1956.
Busson, Henri. "Rabelaiseana: 'Science sans conscience,'" *BHR,* VII (1940), 238–40.
———— *Les Sources et le développement du rationalisme dans la littérature française de la Renaissance (1533–1601).* Paris, 1922.
Campbell, W. E. *Erasmus, Tyndale, and More.* London, 1949.
Cantimori, D. "Note su Erasmo e l'Italia," *Studi Germanici,* II (1937), 145–70.
Caspari, Fritz. "Erasmus on the Social Functions of Christian Humanism," *JHI,* VIII (1947), 78–106.
Cassirer, Ernst. *Das Erkenntnisproblem in der Philosophie und Wissenschaft der neueren Zeit.* Berlin, 1911.
———— *Individuum und Kosmos in der Philosophie der Renaissance.* Leipzig, 1927.
Castro, Américo. *Cervantès.* Paris, 1931.
———— "Erasmo en tiempo de Cervantes," *Revista de filologia española,* XVIII (1931), 329–90.
———— *Lo Hispánico y el Erasmismo. Los Prólogos al "Quijote."* Buenos Aires, 1942.
———— *El pensamiento de Cervantes.* Madrid, 1926.
Chambers, E. K. *The Medieval Stage.* 2 vols. Oxford, 1903.
Chappell, Arthur F. "Rabelais and the Authority of the Ancients," *Modern Language Review,* XVIII (1923), 29–36.
Charlton, H. B. "Falstaff," *John Rylands Library Bulletin,* January 1935.
Cohen, Gustave. *Le Théâtre en France au Moyen Age.* 2 vols. Paris, 1928.
Courants religieux et humanisme à la fin du XVe et au début du XVIe siècle. Colloque de Strasbourg, 9–11 mai 1957. Paris, 1959.
Danby, J. F. *Shakespeare's Doctrine of Nature.* London, 1949.
Deckers, Thilde. *Erasmus De Veelomstredene.* Diest, 1943.
Delaruelle, L. "Ce que Rabelais doit à Érasme et à Budé," *Revue d'histoire littéraire,* XI (1904), 220–262.
Dolfen, Christian. *Die Stellung des Erasmus von Roterdam zur scholastichen Methode.* Osnabrück, 1936.
Dominguez y Roldán, Guillermo. *Estudio comparativo de Cervantes en relación con los literatos de su época, así de españa como de la demás naciones de Europa.* Havana, 1905.
Draper, J. W. "Falstaff, 'A Foole and Jester,'" *Modern Language Quarterly,* VII (1946), 453–62.
———— "Falstaff and the Plautine Parasite," *Classical Journal,* XXXII (1938), 390–401.
———— "Sir John Falstaff," *Review of English Studies,* VIII (1932), 414–24.
Dréano, Mathurin. *La Pensée religieuse de Montaigne.* Paris, 1936.
Empson, William. "Falstaff and Mr. Dover Wilson," *Kenyon Review,* XV (1953), 213–62.
Étienne, Jacques. *Spiritualisme érasmien et théologiens louvanistes. Un changement de problématique au début du XVIe siècle.* Louvain and Gembloux, 1956.

Études rabelaisiennes. Travaux d'Humanisme et Renaissance, XXIV. Geneva, 1956.

Evans, G. Blakemore. "Supplement to *Henry IV, Part 1.* A New Variorum Edition of Shakespeare," *Shakespeare Quarterly,* VIII (Summer 1956), 1–121.

Eyot, Yves. "Panurges et Jean des Entommeures," *BHR,* XI (1949), 64–5.

Farnham, Willard. "The Medieval Comic Spirit in the English Renaissance," *Joseph Quincy Adams Memorial Studies,* ed. J. G. McManaway et al. Washington, 1948. Pages 429–38.

Febvre, Lucien. *Le Problème de l'incroyance au XVIe siècle. La Religion de Rabelais.* Paris, 1942.

Ferguson, Wallace K. "Renaissance Tendencies in the Religious Thought of Erasmus," *JHI,* XV (1954), 499–508.

Flittner, A. *Erasmus im Urteil seiner Nachwelt.* Tübingen, 1952.

Flores, Angel and M. J. Benardete, ed. *Cervantes Across the Centuries.* New York, 1947.

Ford, J. D. M. "Plot, Tale, and Episode in *Don Quixote,*" in *Mélanges de linguistique et de littérature offerts à M. Alfred Jeanroy par ses élèves et ses amis.* Paris, 1928. Pages 311–323.

———— and Ruth Lansing. *Cervantes. A Tentative Bibliography of his Works and of the Bibliographical and Critical Material Concerning Him.* Cambridge, Mass., 1931.

Frame, Donald M. "A Detail in Montaigne's Thought: The Source of our Ignorance is the Source of our Happiness," *Word,* V (1949), 159–65.

———— "Did Montaigne Betray Sebond?", *RR,* XXXVIII (1947), 297–329.

———— *Montaigne's Discovery of Man: The Humanization of a Humanist.* New York, 1955.

Francke, Kuno. "Erasmus als Denker und Künstler," *Internationale Monatsschrift für Wissenschaft, Kunst, und Technik,* VI (1912), 269–92.

François Rabelais. Ouvrage publié pour le quatrième centenaire de sa mort, 1553–1953. Travaux d'Humanisme et Renaissance, VII. Geneva and Lille, 1953.

Friedrich, Hugo. *Montaigne.* Bern, 1949.

Frohock, W. M. "Panurge as Comic Character," *Yale French Studies,* XXIII (1959), 71–6.

Froude, R. W. *Life and Letters of Erasmus.* New York, 1894.

Fusil, C.-A. "Montaigne et Lucrèce," *Revue du seizième siècle,* XIII (1926), 265–81.

———— "Rabelais et Lucrèce," *Revue du seizième siècle,* XII (1925), 157–61.

———— "La Renaissance de Lucrèce au XVIe siècle en France," *Revue du seizième siècle,* XV (1928), 134–50.

Gabotto, F. "L'epicureismo di M. Ficino," *Rivista di filosofia scientifica,* X (1891), 428ff.

———— "L'epicureismo italiano negli ultimi secoli del Medio Evo," *Rivista di filosofia scientifica.* VIII (1889), 552ff.

Gaedik, Walter. *Der Weise Narr in der englischen Literatur von Erasmus bis Shakespeare.* Weimar and Leipzig, 1928.

Gaeta, F. *Lorenzo Valla. Filologia e storia nell' umanesimo italiano.* Naples, 1955.

Garin, Eugenio, *La Cultura filosofica del Rinascimento italiano*. Florence, 1961.
———— *Medioevo e Rinascimento. Studi e ricerche*. Bari, 1954.
———— *L'Umanesimo italiano. Filosofia e vita civile nel Rinascimento*. Bari, 1952.
Garrone, M. A. "L'Orlando Furioso considerato come fonte del 'Quijote,'" *Rivista d'Italia*, XIV (1911), 1-124.
Gebhart, Émile. *Rabelais, la Renaissance et la Réforme*. Paris, 1877.
Gedenkschrift zum 400. Todestage des Erasmus von Rotterdam. Publication of the Historischen und Antiquarischen Gesellschaft zu Basel. Basle, 1936.
Gentile, G. *Il pensiero italiano del Rinascimento*. Florence, 1940.
Gewerstock, O. *Lucian und Hutten. Zur Geschichte des Dialogs im 16. Jahrhunderts*. Berlin, 1924.
Gilmore, Myron. *The World of Humanism, 1453-1517*. New York, 1952.
Gilson, Étienne. *Les Idées et les lettres*. Paris, 1932.
———— "Notes médiévales au 'Tiers Livre' de Pantagruel," *Revue d'histoire franciscaine*, II (1925), 72–88.
Gohin, F. *De Lud. Charondae (1534–1613) vita et versibus*. Paris, 1902.
Goldsmith, R. H. *Wise Fools in Shakespeare*. East Lansing, 1955.
Greenwood, Thomas. "L'Éclosion de scepticisme pendant la Renaissance et les premiers apologists," *Revue de l'Université d'Ottawa*, XVII (1947), 69ff.
Grismer, Raymond L. *Cervantes: A Bibliography*. New York, 1947.
Hadzsits, George D. *Lucretius and His Influence*. London, 1935.
Hanckel, Hadumoth. *Narrendarstellungen im Spätmittelalter*. Freiburg, 1952.
Harbage, Alfred. "Shakespeare's Ideal Man," *Joseph Quincy Adams Memorial Studies*, ed. J. G. McManaway et al. Washington, 1948. Pages 65–80.
Hartman, H. "Prince Hal's 'Shew of Zeale,'" *PMLA*, XLVI (1931), 720–3.
Haslam, A. "The Religion of Rabelais," *Contemporary Review*, CLXVII (1945), 38–41.
Hauffen, Adolf. *Johann Fischart. Ein Literaturbild aus der Zeit der Gegenreformation*. Berlin and Leipzig, 1921.
———— "Zur Literatur der ironischen Enkomien," *Vierteljahresschrift für Literaturgeschichte*, VI (1893), 161–85.
Hauser, Henri and Augustin Renaudet. *Les Débuts de l'âge moderne*. Paris, 1946.
Hazard, Paul. *Don Quichotte de Cervantès, étude et analyse*. Paris [1931].
Headstrom, B. R. "The Philosophy of Montaigne's Skepticism," *Personalist*, XII (1931), 259–66.
Heep, M. "Die Colloquia Familiaria des Erasmus und Lucian," *Hermaea*, XVIII. Halle, 1927.
Heeroma, K. "Droom en Satire in de Renaissance," in *Humanisme en Renaissance*, ed. H. A. Enno van Gelder, et al. The Hague, 1948. Pages 129–48.
Hendrix, W. X. "Sancho Panza and the Comic Types of the Sixteenth Century," in *Homenaje ofrecido a Menéndez Pidal. Miscelánea de Estudios lingüísticos, literarios y históricos*. 3 vols. Madrid, 1925. Vol. II, pp. 485–94.
Hicks, R. D. *Stoic and Epicurean*. New York, 1910.
Hollis, Christopher. *Erasmus*. London, 1933.
Hoopes, Robert. *Right Reason in the English Renaissance*. Cambridge, Mass., 1962.

Hudson, Hoyt H. "Current English Translations of *The Praise of Folly*," in *Renaissance Studies in Honor of Hardin Craig*, ed. W. D. Briggs et al. Stanford, 1941. Pages 58–73.

Huizinga, Johan. "Erasmus' Maatstaf der Dwaasheid," *BVGO*, VII (1936), 247–63.

———— *Erasmus of Rotterdam*. New York, 1952.

———— *Homo Ludens: A Study of the Play-Element in Culture*. Boston, 1950.

Hyma, A. *The Christian Renaissance. A History of the Devotio moderna*. New York and London, 1924.

———— "Erasmus and the Reform in Germany," *Medievalia et Humanistica*, VIII (1954), 99–103.

———— "Erasmus and the Oxford Reformers (1493–1503)," *Nederlandsch Archief voor Kerkgeschiedenis*, N.S. XXV (1932), 69–129. (Also printed in *BVGO*, VII [1936], 132–54.)

———— *The Youth of Erasmus*. Ann Arbor, 1930.

Indestege, Luc. *Rondom Erasmus' Lof der Zotheid*. Antwerp, 1942.

Kan, J. B. *Erasmiana*. Rotterdam, 1891.

Keller, Abraham C. "Anti-War Writing in France, 1500–60," *PMLA*, LXVII (1952), 240–50.

———— "The Idea of Progress in Rabelais," *PMLA*, LXVI (1951), 235–41.

Knowlton, E. C. "Falstaff Redux," *JEGP*, XXV (1926), 193–215.

Knox, Norman. *The Word Irony and Its Context, 1500–1755*. Durham, N.C., 1961.

Koch, J., ed. *Humanismus, Mystik und Kunst*. Leiden, 1953.

Kristeller, Paul Oskar. *The Classics and Renaissance Thought*. The Martin Classical Lectures, XV. Cambridge, Mass., 1955.

———— "Petrarch's 'Averroists': A Note on the History of Aristotelianism in Venice, Padua, and Bologna," in *Mélanges Augustin Renaudet, BHR*, XIV (1952), 59–65.

———— *Il Pensiero filosofico di Marsilio Ficino*. Florence, 1953.

———— *Studies in Renaissance Thought and Letters*. Rome, 1956.

Langer, Leo. *Zur Narrenliteratur*. Villach, 1902.

Lanson, Gustave. *Les Essais de Montaigne. Étude et analyse*. Paris, 1930.

Law, R. A. "Structural Unity in the Two Parts of 'Henry the Fourth,'" *SP*, XXIV (1927), 223–242.

Lea, K. M. "Never Call a True Piece of Gold a Counterfeit: What Falstaff Means," *Review of English Studies*, XXIV (1948), 236–40.

Lebègue, Raymond. "Où en sont nos connaissances sur Rabelais?", *Information littéraire*, I (1949–50), 85–9.

———— *Rabelais*. Tübingen, 1952.

———— "Rabelais et la parodie," *BHR*, XIV (1952), 193–204.

———— "Rabelais, the Last of the Erasmians," *Journal of the Warburg Institute*, XII (1949), 91–100.

Lefebvre, Henri. *Rabelais*. Paris, 1955.

Leech, Clifford, "The Unity of 2 Henry IV," *Shakespeare Survey*, VI (1953), 16–24.

Legouis, Émile. "The Bacchic Element in Shakespeare," *The Annual Shakespeare Lecture of the British Academy*. 1926.

Lenoir, Paulette. *Quelques aspects de la pensée de Rabelais.* Paris, 1954.

Lever, Katherine. "Proverbs and *Sententiae* in the Plays of Shakespeare," *SAB*, XIII (1938), 173–83, 224–39.

Levin, Harry. *Contexts of Criticism.* Cambridge, Mass., 1957.

———— "Falstaff Uncolted," *Modern Language Notes,* LXI (1946), 305–10.

———— "Jonson's Metempsychosis," *PQ,* XII (1943), 231–9.

———— *The Question of Hamlet.* New York, 1959.

Lievsay, John L. "Some Renaissance Views of Diogenes the Cynic," in *Joseph Quincy Adams Memorial Studies,* ed. J. G. McManaway et al. Washington, 1948. Pages 447–56.

Lindeboom, J. *Erasmus, onderzoek naar zijne theologie en zijn godsdienstig gemoedsbestaan.* Leiden, 1909.

Lote, Georges. *La Vie et l'oeuvre de F. Rabelais.* Paris, 1938.

Malloch, A. E. "The Techniques and Functions of the Renaissance Paradox," *SP,* LIII (1956), 191–203.

Man, Paul de. "Montaigne et la transcendance," *Critique,* LXXIX (December 1953), 1011–22.

Mangan, J. J. *Life, Character, and Influence of Desiderius Erasmus of Rotterdam.* 2 vols. New York, 1927.

Mann, Margaret (see also under Phillips). *Érasme et les débuts de la Réforme française (1517–1536).* Paris, 1933.

Marcel, Raymond. "Les 'découvertes' d'Érasme en Angleterre," in *Mélanges Augustin Renaudet, BHR,* XIV (1952), 117–23.

———— *Marcel Ficin.* Paris, 1958.

———— " 'Saint Socrate' Patron de l'Humanisme," in *Umanesimo e scienza politica* (Atti del Congresso Internazionale di Studi Umanistici, ed. Enrico Castelli). Milan, 1951. Pages 521–8.

Marchand, E. "Montaigne and the Cult of Ignorance," *RR,* XXXVI (1945), 275–82.

Mason, H. A. *Humanism and Poetry in the Early Tudor Period.* London, 1959.

Mayer, André. *Étude critique sur les relations d'Érasme et de Luther.* Paris, 1909.

Mayer, C. A. "Rabelais' Satyrical Eulogy: The Praise of Borrowing," in *François Rabelais* (q.v.), pp. 147–55.

———— "The Genesis of a Rabelaisian Character: Menippus and Frère Jean," *French Studies,* VI (1952), 219–29.

Menut, A. D. "Montaigne and the Nicomachean Ethics," *MP,* XXXI (1934), 225–42.

Mesnard, Pierre. "Chronique érasmienne," *BHR,* XVII (1955), 312–19.

———— "La Tradition érasmienne," *BHR,* XV (1953), 359–66.

Mestwerdt, P. *Die Anfänge des Erasmus. Humanismus und "Devotio Moderna."* Leipzig, 1917.

Miller, Henry K. "The Paradoxical Encomium with Special Reference to Its Vogue in England, 1600–1800," *MP,* LIII (1956), 145–78.

Moench, W. *Die italienische Platonrenaissance und ihre Bedeutung für Frankreichs Literatur- und Geistesgeschichte, 1450–1540.* Berlin, 1936.

Mönkemöller, Otto. *Narren und Toren in Satire: Sprichwort und Humor.* Halle, 1912.

Montano, Rocco. *Follia e saggezza nel Furioso e nell' Elogio di Erasmo*. Naples, 1942.

Morphos, Panos P., ed. *The Dialogues of Guy de Brués, A Critical Edition with a Study in Renaissance Scepticism and Relativism*. Baltimore, 1953.

Nauert, C. G., Jr. "Magic and Skepticism in Agrippa's Thought," *JHI*, XVIII (1957), 161–82.

Nelson, E. W. "Recent Literature Concerning Erasmus," *Journal of Modern History*, I (1929), 99–102.

Newald, Richard. *Erasmus Roterodamus*. Freiburg-im-Breisgau, 1947.

Nolhac, Pierre de. *Erasme en Italie: Étude sur un épisode de la Renaissance avec douze lettres inédites d'Érasme*. Paris, 1888.

Nouvelles littéraires, 9 April 1953 (Rabelais Anniversary Number).

Nulli, Siro Attilio. *Erasmo e il Rinascimento*. N.p., 1955.

O'Kane, Eleanor. "The Proverb: Rabelais and Cervantes," *Comparative Literature*, II (1950), 360–9.

Ong, Walter J. *Ramus, Method and the Decay of Dialogue*. Cambridge, Mass., 1958.

Ortega y Gasset, José. *Meditaciones del Quijote*. Madrid, 1914.

Panofsky, Erwin. *Hercules am Scheidewege und andere antike Bildstoffe in der neueren Kunst*. Leipzig and Berlin, 1930.

———— *Idea. Contributo alla storia dell' estetica*, tr. Edmondo Cione. Florence, 1952.

———— *Renaissance and Renascences in Western Art*. The Gottesman Lectures. Stockholm, 1960.

Pease, A. S. "Things Without Honor," *Classical Philology*, XXI (1926), 27–42.

Pfeiffer, R. *Humanitas Erasmiana*. Berlin and Leipzig, 1931.

Phillips, Margaret Mann. "Erasmus and Propaganda. A Study of the Translations of Erasmus in English and French," *Modern Language Review*, XXXVII (1942) 1–17.

———— *Erasmus and the Northern Renaissance*. London, 1949.

———— "La 'Philosophia Christi' reflétée dans les 'Adages' d'Érasme," in *Courants religieux* (q.v.), pp. 53–71.

Picot, Émile. "Les Monologues dramatiques," *Romania*, XV (1886), 358–422, XVI (1887), 438–532, XVII (1888), 207–75.

Pineau, Jean Baptiste, *Érasme, sa pensée religieuse*. Paris, 1924.

Pinvert, Lucien. "Louis Le Caron, dit Charondas," *Revue de la Renaissance*, II (1902), 1–9, 69–76, 181–8.

Plattard, Jean. *L'Oeuvre de Rabelais*. Paris, 1910.

———— *État présent des études rabelaisiennes*. Paris, 1927.

———— *Montaigne et son temps*. Paris, 1933.

———— *Vie de François Rabelais*. Paris and Brussels, 1928.

Pollet, J. V. M. "Erasmiana. Quelques aspects du problème érasmien d'après les publications récentes," *Revue des sciences religieuses*, XXVI (October 1952), 387–404.

Popkin, Richard H. *The History of Scepticism from Erasmus to Descartes*. Assen, 1960.

Prost, A. *Les Sciences et les arts occultes au XVIe siècle: Cornelius Agrippa, sa vie et ses oeuvres*. 2 vols. Paris, 1881–82.

Renaudet, Augustin. *Érasme et l'Italie*. Geneva, 1954.

Renaudet, Augustin. *Érasme, sa pensée religieuse et son action d'après sa correspondence (1518–1521)*. Paris, 1926.
———— "Érasme, sa vie et son oeuvre jusqu'en 1517, d'après sa correspondance," *Revue historique*, CXI (1912) and CXII (1913).
———— *Études érasmiennes, 1521–1529*. Paris, 1939.
————"La Critique érasmienne et l'humanisme français," *BVGO*, VII (1936), 247–63.
———— "Le Message humaniste et chrétien d'Érasme," in *Atti del Congresso della Sodalitas Erasmiana*. Rome, 20–23 September 1929. Pages 44–53.
———— "L'Héritage d'Érasme," *Rivista di letterature moderne*, N.S. I (1950), 5–31.
———— *Préréforme et humanisme à Paris pendant les premières guerres d'Italie*. 2nd ed. Paris, 1953.
Ribner, Irving. *The English History Play in the Age of Shakespeare*. Princeton, 1957.
Rice, Eugene F., Jr. "Erasmus and the Religious Tradition, 1495–1499," *JHI*, XI (1950), 387–411.
———— "Nicolas of Cusa's Idea of Wisdom," *Traditio*, XIII (1957), 345–68.
———— *The Renaissance Idea of Wisdom*. Cambridge, Mass., 1958.
Rossi, G. *Agrippa di Nettesheym e la direzione scettica della filosofia nel Rinascimento*. Turin, 1906.
Ruëgg, August. "Des. Erasmus 'Lob de Torheit' und Thomas Mores 'Utopie,'" in *Gedenkschrift* (q.v.), pp. 69–88.
———— "Lo Erásmico en el *Don Quijote* de Cervantes," tr. Guevara, *Anales Cervantinos*, IV. Madrid, 1954.
———— *Miguel de Cervantes und sein Don Quijote*. Bern, 1949.
Ruëgg, W. *Cicero und der Humanismus. Formale Untersuchungen über Petrarca und Erasmus*. Zurich, 1946.
Sackton, Alexander H. "The Paradoxical Encomium in Elizabethan Drama," *University of Texas Studies in English*, XXVIII (1949), 83–104.
Sainéan, L. *La Langue de Rabelais*. 2 vols. Paris, 1922.
———— *L'Influence et la réputation de Rabelais*. Paris, 1930.
Saitta, Giuseppe. *Filosofia italiana e Umanesimo*. Venice, 1923.
———— *Il Pensiero italiano nell' Umanesimo e nel Rinascimento*. Bologna, 1949.
Santini, G. "Cosma Raimondi umanista ed epicureo," *Studi Storici*, VIII (1899), 153–68.
Sardou, Victorien. "Érasme et ses colloques," *Revue des deux mondes*, XCIV (1924), 481ff.
Saulnier, Verdun L. "Dix années d'études sur Rabelais," *BHR*, XI (1949), 105–28.
———— "Le Départ de l'escadre, ou Pantagruel à la recherche du grand passage," *Les Amis de Rabelais et de la Devinière*, IV (1955), 13–15.
———— *Le Dessein de Rabelais*. Paris, 1957.
———— "L'Énigme de Pantagruélion, ou Du *Tiers* au *Quart Livre*," in *Études rabelaisiennes* (q.v.), pp. 48–72.
———— "Le Festin devant Chaneph, ou La Confiance dernière de Rabelais," *Mercure de France*, 1 April 1954, pp. 649ff.
———— "Pantagruel au large de Ganabin, ou La Peur de Panurge," *BHR*, XVI (1954), 58–81.

Saulnier, Verdun L. "Rabelais et le Populaire," *Lettres d'humanité*, VIII (1949), 149–79.

Saxl, F. "Holbein's Illustrations to *The Praise of Folly* by Erasmus," *The Burlington Magazine*, LXXXIII (1943), 275–9.

———— "Veritas Filia Temporis," in *Philosophy and History, Essays Presented to Ernst Cassirer*. Oxford, 1936, pp. 197–222.

Schenk, V. W. D. "The Erasmian Idea," *Hibbert Journal*, XLVIII (1950), 257–65.

———— *Tussen Duvielgeloof en Beeldenstorm. Een studie over Jeroen Bosch en Erasmus van Rotterdam.* Amsterdam, 1946.

Schevill, Rudolph. *Cervantes*. New York, 1919.

Schiaffino, Rafael. *Cervantes y el Rinascimento.* Conferencia pronunciada en la Sociedad Dante Alighieri en Roma, el 20 de julio de 1949. *Revista Nacional*, No. 134, Montevideo, 1950.

Schoell, Franck L. *Études sur l'humanisme continental en Angleterre à la fin de la Renaissance.* Paris, 1926.

Schönfeld, Herman. "Die kirchliche Satire und religiöse Weltanschauung in Brants Narrenschiff und Erasmus Narrenlob, esp. in den Colloquia," *Modern Language Notes*, VII (1892), 78–92, 138–50, 346–8.

Screech, M. A. "De Billon and Erasmus: A Reexamination of Rabelais' Attitude to Women," *BHR*, XIII (1951), 241–65.

———— *The Rabelaisian Marriage. Aspects of Rabelais' Religion, Ethics and Comic Philosophy.* London, 1958.

———— "Some Stoic Elements in Rabelais' Religious Thought," in *Études rabelaisiennes* (q.v.), pp. 73–97.

Sedgewick, G. G. *Of Irony Especially in Drama.* Toronto, 1948.

Seebohm, Frederic. *The Oxford Reformers.* London and Toronto, 1914.

Seiver, G. O. "Cicero's *De Oratore* and Rabelais," *PMLA*, LIX (1944), 655–71.

Shaaber, M. A. "The Unity of *Henry IV*," in *Joseph Quincy Adams Memorial Studies*, ed. J. G. McManaway et al. Washington, 1948. Pages 217–28.

Shirley, J. W. "Falstaff, An Elizabethan Glutton," *PQ*, XVII (1938), 271–87.

Sigwart, C. *Kleine Schriften.* Freiburg-im-Breisgau, 1889.

Small, S. A. "Hotspur and Falstaff," *SAB*, XVI (1941), 243–8.

———— "The Structure of Falstaff's Humor," *SAB*, VII (1932), 114–22.

Smith, Preserved. *Erasmus, A Study of His Life, Ideals, and Place in History.* New York and London, 1923.

———— "Erasmus, Enemy of Pedantry," *American Scholar*, VI (1937), 85–92.

———— *A Key to the Colloquies of Erasmus.* Harvard Theological Studies, XIII. Cambridge, Mass., 1927.

Smith, W. F. "Rabelais et Érasme," *RER*, VI (1908), 215–64, 375–8.

Smulders, P. "De oorsprong van de theorie der zuivere natuur. Vergeten meesters der leuvense school," *Bijdragen uitgegeven door de Nederlandse Jezuiten*, X (1949), 105–27.

Spargo, John W. "An Interpretation of Falstaff," *Washington University Studies*, IX (1921–2), 119–33.

Spens, Janet. *An Essay on Shakespeare's Relation to Tradition.* Oxford, 1916.

Spivack, Bernard. *Shakespeare and the Allegory of Evil.* New York, 1958.

Stadelmann, R. *Vom Geist des ausgehenden Mittelalters. Studien zur Geschichte des Weltanschauung von Nicolaus Cusanus bis Sebastian Brant.* Halle, 1929.

Stapfer, Paul. *Rabelais, sa personne, son génie, son oeuvre.* Paris, 1889.
———— *Shakespeare et l'antiquité.* Paris, 1879.
Stoll, E. E. "A Falstaff for the 'Bright,' " *MP,* LI (1954), 145–59.
———— *Shakespeare Studies.* New York, 1942.
Strowski, Fortunat. *Montaigne.* Paris, 1931.
———— "Montaigne, sa vie publique et privée," *Nouvelle revue critique,* 1938.
Surtz, E. L. "The Defence of Pleasure in More's Utopia," *SP,* XLVI (1949), 99–112.
———— "Epicurus in Utopia," *English Literary History,* XVI (1949), 89–103.
———— *The Praise of Pleasure.* Cambridge, Mass., 1947.
———— *The Praise of Wisdom.* Cambridge, Mass., 1957.
Swain, Barbara. *Fools and Folly during the Middle Ages and the Renaissance.* New York, 1932.
Taylor, G. C. *Shakespeare's Debt to Montaigne.* Cambridge, Mass., 1925.
Telle, E. V. *Érasme de Rotterdam et le septième sacrament.* Geneva, 1954.
Tenenti, Alberto. *Il Senso della morte e l'amore della vita nel Rinascimento.* Turin, 1957.
Thompson, A. R. *The Dry Mock: A Study of Irony in Drama.* Berkeley and Los Angeles, 1948.
Thompson, C. R. *The Translations of Lucien by Erasmus and St. Thomas More.* Ithaca, 1940.
Thomson, J. A. K. "Erasmus in England," in *England und die Antike,* ed. F. Saxl, *Vorträge der Bibliothek Warburg,* 1930–31. Pages 64–82.
———— "Desiderius Erasmus," in *Social and Political Ideas of Some Great Thinkers of the Renaissance and Reformation,* ed. E. J. Hearnshaw. London, 1925.
Thuasne, Louis. *Études sur Rabelais.* Paris, 1904.
———— *Rabelais et Villon.* Paris, 1907.
Timmermans, B. J. H. M. "Valle et Érasme, défenseurs d'Épicure," *Neophilologus,* XXIII (1937), 414–19.
Toffanin, Giuseppe. *La Fine dell' Umanesimo.* Turin, 1920.
———— *Storia dell' Umanesimo.* 3 vols. Bologna, 1952.
Traversi, Derek. *Shakespeare from "Richard II" to "Henry V."* Stanford, 1957.
Treinen, Hans. *Studien zur Idee der Gemeinschaft bei Erasmus von Rotterdam und zu ihrer Stellung in der Entwicklung des humanistischen Universalismus.* Saarlouis, 1955.
Trinkaus, C. E. *Adversity's Noblemen. The Italian Humanists on Happiness.* New York, 1940.
———— "The Problem of Free Will in the Renaissance and the Reformation," *JHI,* X (1949), 51–62.
Uebinger, Johannes. 'Die angeblichen Dialogue Petrarcas über die Wahre Weisheit," *Vierteljahrsschrift für Kultur und Litteratur der Renaissance,* II (1887), 57–70.
Unamuno, Miguel de. *La Vida de Don Quijote y Sancho.* Madrid, 1914.
Vansteenberghe, E. *Autour de la docte ignorance. Une Controverse sur la théologie mystique au XVe siècle.* Münster, 1914.
Villey, Pierre. *Les Essais de Montaigne.* Paris, 1946.
———— *Rabelais et Marot.* Paris, 1923.

Villey, Pierre. *Les Sources et l'évolution des Essais de Montaigne.* 2 vols. Paris, 1908.

Vocht, H. de. *De Invloed van Erasmus op de Engelsche Tooneelliteratuur der XVIe en XVIIe Eeuwen.* Ghent, 1908.

———— *Monumenta Humanistica Lovaniensia. Texts and Studies about Louvain Humanists in the First Half of the XVIth Century.* Louvain and London, 1934.

Warde, F. *The Fools of Shakespeare.* New York, 1913.

Welsford, Enid. *The Fool: His Social and Literary History.* London, 1935.

Whitaker, Virgil. *Shakespeare's Use of Learning. An Inquiry into the Growth of His Mind and Art.* San Marino, Calif., 1953.

Wilson, John Dover. *The Fortunes of Falstaff.* Cambridge, Eng., 1943.

———— "The Origins and Development of Shakespeare's *Henry IV*," *The Library*, XXVI (1945), 2-16.

———— "Shakespeare's 'Small Latin' — How Much?", *Shakespeare Survey*, X (1957), 12-26.

Wind, Edgar. *Pagan Mysteries in the Renaissance.* New Haven, 1958.

Wyss, Heinz. *Der Narr im schweizerischen Drama des 16. Jahrhunderts.* Bern, 1959.

Zumbini, Bonaventura. *Studi di letteratura italiana.* Florence, 1906.

———— *Studi di letterature straniere.* Florence, 1907.

INDEX

❦ ❦ ❦